Inside the Left: Platform, Press, Prison, Parliament
was first published in 1942 by George Allen & Unwin,
then by the Independent Labour Party (*New Leader*)
in 1942 and 1947. In 1975, the ILP became
Independent Labour Publications.

For further information about the ILP,
please email info@independentlabour.org.uk,
or visit www.independentlabour.org.uk,
or write to ILP, PO Box 222, Leeds LS11 1DF.
We would be happy to supply a copy of Fenner
Brockway's Preface to the post-War edition.
In 2013, the ILP celebrates its 120th anniversary.

INSIDE
THE LEFT

Thirty Years of Platform, Press,
Prison and Parliament

by

FENNER
BROCKWAY

SPOKESMAN

To my daughter

MARGARET

1917—1941

First published in 1942.
This edition published in 2010 by agreement.

Spokesman
Russell House
Bulwell Lane, Nottingham NG6 OBT
Phone 0115 9708318
Fax 0115 9420433
e-mail elfeuro@compuserve.com
www.spokesmanbooks.com

ISBN 978 85124 774 8

A CIP catalogue record is available from the British Library

Printed by the Russell Press Ltd. (phone 0115 9784505)
www.russellpress.com

FOREWORD TO
2010 EDITION

Ken Coates

Fenner Brockway lived a long life and it was certainly packed with colourful action. Here we are reproducing the first volume of his autobiography, which was written on the eve of the Second World War. Never afraid to court controversy, this book celebrated the Socialist movement's opposition to the First World War, and the activities of an anti-war movement which continued after that conflict.

A pupil of Keir Hardie and Bernard Shaw, the young Brockway found his natural home in the Independent Labour Party, which developed his talents as an editor and public agitator. He became acquainted with many of the key personalities of international socialism, and with all the leading figures on the British Left, including H. G. Wells, Bertrand Russell and the political spokesmen of the growing Labour movement.

This book contains Brockway's detailed account of the efforts of the British Left to find some kind of political unity during the years of the Labour Party's split, when Ramsay MacDonald formed a National Government. The ILP left the Labour Party, and entered into a variety of negotiations with the Communists and others to attempt to crystallise a Socialist opposition.

A second edition of *Inside the Left* appeared in 1942, and was reprinted in 1947 with the addition of a 'Preface to Post-War Edition', which is appended at the end of this reissue.

After Fenner rejoined the Labour Party and was elected to Parliament for the second time, he published a second volume to his autobiography called *Outside the Right*. Two subsequent volumes of memoirs were to follow this second instalment, culminating in *98 Not Out*, which recorded his days in the House of Lords as a campaigner for nuclear disarmament.

Unfortunately, all these books are out of print, and can be very difficult to find. That is why we decided to restore the first volume to the bookshops. It is still far more relevant than it ought to be, because opposition to war is still a major problem for Socialist movements around the world.

FOREWORD

(I took twenty months to complete this book, giving what time I could during a specially busy period of political activity. Since then publication has been delayed owing to war circumstances. I leave the Foreword as it was written originally, though the days of Munich seem far distant now).

I begin to write this story at the end of a month which has been described as the most critical in the history of man. Perhaps September-October, 1938, has been that *up to this point*; certainly we seem to be on the edge of a war which would outdo 1914-18. Yet I hesitate to adopt the description because the signs are that before this book is published we may be over the edge. . . . .

Those of us who are now in our fifties have been players in three of the five Acts of the era of Capitalist-Imperialism.

Act I. We did not see the first Act—the early years of industrialisation, the cruel exploitation of children in mines and factories, the bestial poverty of the workers, illiterate, without the relief of newspapers and books or of cinemas and organised sport, breaking into revolt in the Chartist Movement, beginning to form their Trade Unions.

Act II. But we are old enough to remember a little of the Second Act—the later Victorian period, the expansion of the capitalist system in triumphant imperialism, the coming of the popular press with universal elementary education, and the heroic beginnings of the Socialist Movement.

Act III. The Third Act introduced us to the stage, and the play was exciting; rival imperialisms clashing in their greed to eat up the world, the Boer War, the confident advance of the Socialist Movement and the winning of concessions from a nervous Capitalism—and then the crash of the World War of 1914.

Act IV. The World War was an Act in itself, separate from what came before and after, not only because of the untellable suffering it caused, but because of the collapse of one of the greatest hopes of the Socialist Movement—the hope of inter-

5

national solidarity. The Act closed with a failure equally disappointing, the failure to seize the opportunity to end the system of Capitalist-Imperialism. The historic Soviet Revolution of October, 1917, was the one great light in four dark years. *Act V.* We are still playing our part in the Fifth Act, but it moves to its conclusion. Capitalist-Imperialism, recovering strength after the anæmia which followed the blood-letting of the last war, drives on towards the blood-bath of a still more terrible war. Its antagonisms grow powerful again. The signs are that our destiny is to be buried under the ruins of the Old World rather than to bury it beneath the foundations of the New.

But we do not yet accept this fate . . . and we are confident, even if the present Act must end like this, that in the next a new generation will arise to realise our hopes.

. . . .

I have had the fortune to live on the "inside" of much of these third, fourth and fifth Acts. I was swept into the Socialist Movement during the first decade of this century and took a rank and file part in its romantic advance. I came in close contact with its leaders, both in this and other countries. I saw some of them, like Keir Hardie and Jean Jaurès, die brokenhearted yet loyal to their faith, and saw others like Ramsay MacDonald and Philip Snowden break the hearts of their fellows before they died separated from the Movement. I went through the years of the War in the centre of the struggle against it, until I was removed to spend thirty months in prison. Since the war I have taken some part in every phase of Socialist development, both national and international, on its platform, at its conferences, in its executive committees, in Parliament, week-ending in the homes of workers, travelling over a great part of Europe, to India and America and to war-ridden Spain.

If I can tell this story rightly it will be more than my personal record. It will be the record, in part at least, of the rise and fall and the rise again of the Movement destined to ring down the curtain on the Final Act of the Capitalist era and to lift it at last for the Prologue of Socialism.

10, Nevill's Court, E.C.4.
October, 1938.

6

CONTENTS

Book One

BEFORE THE WAR

Book Two

DURING THE WAR

Book Three

AFTER THE WAR

Book Four

BEFORE THE WAR

BOOK ONE

Chapter One
GETTING INTERESTED

When I joined the Socialist Movement thirty-four years ago we used to train our speakers by asking recruits to tell us impromptu how and why they became Socialists. I can answer why but not how.

Family associations were against it. My parents were Nonconformist missionaries and my mother's family, with whom I stayed as a child, were Conservative and Church people. I went to Blackheath school (now Eltham College) which discouraged any interest in public affairs—except when it was trying to stimulate patriotism during the Boer War. The only thing I learned to do well there was to play Rugby football.

Yet, despite this environment, I seem to have been a rebel from early years. As a child in India I insisted on playing with native children rather than with European; that I do not remember but so I have been told. I do remember at the age of eight refusing to go to Church and in consequence being put to bed, where I sang "Dare to be a Daniel" at the top of my voice. The Boer War first interested me in political affairs; at its beginning I was a patriot, with my coat covered with badges bearing the portraits of the British Generals, but before the end I was a pro-Boer.

By fourteen I was a keen Radical politician, a subscriber to the red-backed "Reformer's Year Book."

By sixteen I was spending the hours of "prep" writing political pamphlets, doubling over sheets from exercise books, covering them with clear, small text, designing covers, and so producing quite creditable little brochures. My subjects were the Education Acts, "Chinese Slavery," Free Trade and other lively questions of the time. There was only one other boy who ever read them, but I got a lot of satisfaction out of them myself.

The school debating society was a more difficult problem. There was a rule prohibiting the discussion of politics and

9

religion, but after much effort I obtained permission for a debate on tariff reform.

That was the first difficulty. The second was much more formidable. As a boy I stammered badly, and when it was known that I intended to deliver a speech everyone looked forward to it with amusement. I learned my speech by heart and recited it during lonely walks on Blackheath, choosing a deserted gorse-hidden pit to shout it aloud. When the debate came I half sang it in a monotone to avoid stammering; at the beginning some of the boys sniggered, but at the end they applauded generously.

During my later years at school there was an election for the London County Council and my political enthusiasm made me eager to take part. But how? I contrived a way. Although I attended "prep" in what was known as School House I resided at another House and, being over fifteen, I was allowed to stay up two hours later for study if I wished. That made a "get-away" easy. I left School House with the early boys, slipped down to the Progressive Candidate's Committee Rooms, spent two hours delivering leaflets, and got back in time to enter my residential House with the later boys. The L.C.C. election was followed by a Parliamentary by-election in Dulwich, with Mr. David Williamson as Liberal candidate. It was some distance, but I got there on a few afternoons when we had no Rugby games. I can still remember how excited I was when sent out canvassing: in later years I found the task much less attractive and knocked on doors with much more trepidation. Mr. Williamson was not elected, but my personal contact with him was to be of some value.

These early illegal political activities did not go undiscovered. I got back late to the Residential House one night, manoeuvred a window, crept upstairs past the Headmaster's lighted room— and then knocked over a basin in the dormitory. The noise reverberated through the building and the Head appeared; political leaflets were in a pile on my bed and there was no hiding what I had been doing. The Head told me gravely that he would be compelled to remember this serious breach of rules when he wrote my final school record for use when applying for jobs. I regarded myself as a martyr in the cause of progress, victimised for my political activities.

There was one legitimate political experience about this time which lives in my memory. I had joined the League of Young Liberals and obtained permission to attend a demonstration in the Queen's Hall addressed by John Morley. His measured, finely-phrased oratory awed me, but I felt more enthusiasm for the audacious speech of a young recruit to Liberalism—Mr. Winston Churchill.

I did not leave school as soon as I expected. I sat for matriculation at the end of the summer term of 1905 and intended to leave. The Head asked me what I planned to do. "Take classes in shorthand at Pitman's so that I can become a journalist," I said. "If you will stay on here, we'll regard the Pitman classes as part of our curriculum," he replied. "We want you for the Rugby team." So I stayed on for the winter term, travelling up to town each day to Pitman's College in Southampton Row. At the end of the Christmas term I left school, with my Rugby football colours and the Pascoe-Williams prize for essay-writing as my only honours.

My father, still in India, had placed me under the care of an uncle who lived at Muswell Hill, but his guardianship was not very definite, and when he heard that I intended to be a journalist rather than a minister of religion, he declined to take any further responsibility for me, declaring that I was not "clever enough to be a journalist" and would "sponge on him" for the rest of my life. I thereupon borrowed eighteen shillings from his little boy's nurse, packed my bag, and left. I have never been back, because my uncle, a good old-fashioned Tory, was so shocked by my later political activities that he did not wish to meet me.

This incident, however, does not remove the debt of gratitude which I owe to my relatives, who provided me with a home during the school holidays. My parents returned to England every five years or so on furlough. My mother died when I was fourteen. I have a memory of her so beautiful that I cannot write of it. Her life has been told in "Frances E. Brockway," by James H. Brown. My father died in 1929. He did not share my views, but he was generous and open-minded and I had a great respect and affection for him.

But I had no home ties, and after my dispute with my uncle, I was free to go my own way.

Chapter Two
BECOMING A SOCIALIST

I had no private friends in London to whom I could go, and so I turned to my public heroes. I don't think I had ever met the Rev. Silvester Horne, the minister of Whitefield's Mission in Tottenham Court Road, but he combined an aggressive Radicalism with his Christianity and at seventeen that represented my outlook. To Silvester Horne I went.

I am not sure that I told him my whole story—probably I was afraid he would send me back to my uncle—but he gave me a bed, and the next morning I set out to ask for a job from Mr. David Williamson, the Dulwich Liberal candidate for whom I had worked clandestinely when at school. He was editor of the "Quiver," a monthly combining fiction and religion, and his office was in La Belle Sauvage, which I never pass without remembering the adventurous fear I felt when I first entered it.* Mr. Williamson offered me a job for three weeks at 15s. a week, as a kind of superior office boy. I did not stay more than the three weeks. I don't know whether it was the Editor's intention to keep me for that period only or whether I was unsatisfactory.

The day after I became jobless a letter arrived from my father in India urging reconciliation with my Muswell Hill uncle. Instead I went to another "uncle." Mr. Wontner was not really a relative; he was distantly attached to our family by marriage; but I had often stayed at his house on Rusthall Common during my holidays, and had a great respect for him. He was a Quaker and a Radical, a shaggy-headed little man, his eyes hidden by opaque glasses. He had influenced my ideas considerably. He reverenced the poems of Russell Lowell and used to publish a little monthly sheet, distributed from house to house in Rusthall village, consisting largely of Lowell's verses, with a political introduction identifying the Liberal Party with God. "Once to every man and nation comes the moment to decide," he would recite—and to him the general election of 1906 was the moment and Campbell Bannerman the divinely-appointed leader.

I called on the editor of the local Liberal paper and asked for a job. He did not take me on the staff, but encouraged me

*La Belle Sauvage was completely destroyed by "enemy action" in May 1941.

to contribute items. When the General Election came I volunteered as a worker for the Liberal Party and was delighted to find myself, though not yet eighteen, appointed sub-agent at Rusthall. I had few workers and practically no canvassing was done, but we distributed hundreds of leaflets, organised a meeting successfully, and fetched voters to the poll in Mr. Wontner's dog-cart.

The Liberal won the election. I was one of hundreds who dragged the new member in a carriage four miles from Tunbridge Wells to Tonbridge, climbing the hill through Southborough, and descending into Tonbridge, where thousands welcomed us with torches.

There was one figure in this election who remains vivid in my memory. He was the driver of a traction engine, a giant of a man—thick black hair, deep voice, red tie—a member of the Social Democratic Federation. When I called on him to get his vote he poured scorn on Liberals as no better than Tories; both were the Capitalist enemy. He was indifferent about the Tariff and Education issues, and, as for the Chinese slaves, "What are we, comrade, but wage-slaves?" I enjoyed the rough debate with him and when his huge hand covered mine to say good-bye, he exclaimed, "Comrade, go on thinking and reading and you'll be a Socialist within twelve months." I laughed denial, but he turned out to be right.

When the election was over, the problem of a job remained. I was determined to get a start in London and by a fortunate chance I succeeded. The previous year I had attended a Public Schools' Camp. Climbing out of the river one day after bathing, I saw the pathetic figure of the Chaplain, naked, without even a towel, shivering in a cold wind; he was without his glasses and could not look for his clothes. I flung my towel to him and went in search of the clothes which some of the boys had hidden. The Chaplain was the Rev. W. B. Selbie, Principal of Mansfield College, Oxford. Looking through Mr. Wontner's papers, I found a copy of the "Examiner," a religious-literary weekly, and on the front page the name of Mr. Selbie was given as editor. I wrote to him, reminding him delicately of the bathing incident; he gave me an interview, there was a vacancy, and I started at 18s. a week, combining the duties of office-boy, junior sub-editor and junior reporter.

I returned to Whitefield's and took lodgings with the wife of a member of the club. A school friend, Harold Hills, joined me, and there were four other men lodgers. Soon we became dissatisfied. The food was scanty and poor and we were overcharged. The idea came to me of co-operative lodging. Why shouldn't the five of us take rooms together, purchase our food in common and pay a landlady a small sum for cooking it? The others were enthusiastic; we found rooms in Camden Town and all of us gave notice together—a kind of lodgers' strike which was a great shock to our skinflint hostess.

The communal living was a great experience to me. It knocked off rough edges, tore away the veil which my boarding-school and middle class seclusion had thrown over reality, shattered old beliefs and turned my mind in new directions. We used to have cocoa and biscuits at nine o'clock, and then away would go our books (Hills, who was a medical student, sometimes protesting), and we would fiercely discuss every problem on earth.

We were a good mixture. Hills was an incurable sceptic —accepting nothing until it was proved, rejecting idealisms. Olsen, a fair-haired young Norwegian, a watchmaker's assistant, was a spiritualist and an ethical Socialist, a generous, clean comrade. Smith, older, was a woodworker, a typical Trade Unionist, without much interest in Socialism, but with a cynical disbelief in all persons in authority—the Royal family, statesmen, bishops, bosses and Labour leaders alike. Westwood was a young electrician, often out of work, decent and honest but rather weak, the most revolutionary of us all. Charlie Samuel was a little Welshman, a teacher at a Church of England school, but an atheist and Socialist.

By degrees I began to learn some of the realities of life, including the experience of trying to make ends meet. My eighteen shillings a week allowed me sixpence for lunch one day and twopence the next. On the one I would go to the third floor of a vegetarian restaurant in St. Bride Street, where sixpenny meals of dry bread and yesterday's dishes were provided. On the twopenny day I would buy bananas or apples from a barrow, eating them walking by the Thames or listening to the bands in the Embankment gardens. Our household arrangement was that each of us should buy in turn the food for a week from a pool to which we contributed five shillings. Woe to anyone who spent more than the pool! I forget what we ordinarily had for breakfast, but on Sundays we had a special meal of gammon and tomatoes after remaining in bed till mid-day. From the way that that has stuck in my memory I fancy that the other breakfasts were meagre enough. Another memorable meal was Sunday tea. We learned that at White-field's an *ad lib.* high tea was available for sixpence after the Men's Meeting in the afternoon. That meal used to be the biggest of the week!

The Whitefield's Men's Meeting developed my ideas. Silvester Horne presided and he was challengingly political. He nearly always succeeded in securing as a speaker any left-wing politician who had been in the public eye during the week. A by-election took place and the Labour candidate won: the following Sunday he would be speaking at Whitefield's. A member of Parliament was in the news with an intervention in the House of Commons: the next Sunday Silvester Horne was proudly introducing him to the thousand men who crowded his church. This was the period of the first popularity of Socialism and it was surprising how often the address was on some aspect of Socialism. I soon began to grow out of my Radicalism. The Men's Meeting was also valuable to me as journalistic material. I was supplement-ing the 18s. a week paid by the "Examiner" by a good deal of free-lance work for the dailies, and the speeches at the Men's Meeting frequently provided me with paragraphs for the "Daily News."

After about a year on the "Examiner," I transferred to the "Christian Commonwealth," the organ of the Rev. R. J. Campbell's New Theology movement. Most readers of to-day will find it difficult to imagine the religious and social turmoil which this theological heresy caused. The Rev. R. J. Campbell was minister at the City Temple. He was a picturesque figure, a slim body crowned with waving white hair; his features were strangely delicate and his eyes had unusual magnetism. Sud-denly the newspapers discovered that Mr. Campbell was unorthodox. "Jesus was divine—but so am I," they reported him as saying. "Blasphemy!" the orthodox shrieked. In fact Mr. Campbell had added, "So are you," because the essence of his teaching was that all men are divine; but the sensation had been started and for six months R. J. Campbell's "New Theology" caused as much public discussion as any controversy about politics or sport.

The "New Theology" attracted me from the first. My cruder religious beliefs had collapsed before the ruthless criticisms of my fellow lodgers at our after-cocoa discussions; I eagerly embraced Mr. Campbell's more rational interpretation of Christianity. But it was not only his "New Theology" which attracted me. He added to it an ethical Socialism, and this combination exactly reflected the stage of development I had reached. He joined the I.L.P. and toured the country with Mr. Keir Hardie, addressing crowded audiences in the largest halls of all the great cities. His speeches were thin politically and made little impression on convinced Socialists, but upon the outside public, particularly those with a religious background, they had an extraordinary effect. For a time the Rev. R. J. Campbell, New Theologian and Socialist, was the most popular orator in the land.

Whilst I supported Mr. Campbell's views I never became enthusiastic about him personally. I find it difficult to say what estranged me from him; perhaps it was because I saw his circle at close quarters and was repulsed by the hero-worship—and his love of it. Despite this, I owe Mr. Campbell gratitude because his rational interpretation of religion had a steadying effect on me when my reliance on supernaturalism was collapsing.

One of the daily newspapers for which I did occasional work sent me to interview Mr. Keir Hardie on some immediate issue of politics which I have forgotten. I had some difficulty in finding his lodgings. Hardie was living in a little rabbit-warren at the back of Fleet Street. It was a white-washed alley so narrow that if one stretched out one's hands they touched both walls. Here in the very centre of the city was a group of Queen Anne buildings which might have been transplanted from a country village. There were little village shops and cottages with gardens bright with hardy annuals, and standing by their side a splendid old four-storeyed mansion with evergreen bushes, a wide-spaced garden, thick creepers climbing the neighbouring walls, and an impressive porch. On the first floor of this house Hardie had his rooms.

Hardie had a healthy suspicion of journalists and he received me uneasily. His clothes were of tweed, with a belt round his waist, and a white open-necked shirt. A briar pipe was in his hand. His head was magnificent—domed and framed with white hair brushed back in a curve. My first impression was of a gruff old sheep-dog. I sat down, took out note-book and pencil and put my questions. Hardie stood at some distance, looking at me doubtfully. He chose his words slowly and carefully. Before I got to the last question he was impatient. Then he changed completely. "Put away that book and pencil, young man," he said, "and I'll begin to talk."

He talked for an hour and I was entranced. How he started I don't know, but soon he was walking the length of the little room, pipe passing from hand to mouth, telling me the story of the Labour Movement, his beginnings in it, his work as a lad in the pit, how he taught himself shorthand with chalk on the coal face, his start as a local journalist, his early efforts to organise the miners, the refusal of the Liberal Executive to endorse his nomination for Parliament, his realisation that the working class must stand on its own and be independent, his development from Liberalism to Socialism, the formation of the Scottish Labour Party, his election to Parliament as the first Socialist M.P., and in 1893 the establishment of the I.L.P.—and so on and so on. Why Hardie troubled to say all this to me I never understood, but as I left he shook me by the hand and said, "Young man, if you want to serve your day and generation, you'll join the Socialist Movement."

I did not join the Socialist Movement at once, but from that moment Keir Hardie was my hero.

By a strange coincidence I am writing these words in Keir Hardie's old rooms. I now occupy the first floor at 10 Nevill's Court. I was interested to see in William Stewart's biography of Keir Hardie that he used to pay 6s. a week for these rooms. The rent is now 35s. a week!*

The next time I saw Keir Hardie was at a lecture on Socialism which he gave at the City Temple. I can see him now, sturdy and straight and strong like a block of hewn granite. He was like a statue of an emancipated worker, head thrown back, body erect, expressing completely in himself the triumphant self-reliance and the sense of equality, freedom, and

*10 Nevill's Court was destroyed by "enemy action" in May, 1941.

power which he sought to give to the working-class. At the end of his speech Mr. Campbell called on me to move a vote of thanks. It must have been one of my first speeches before a large audience, but the words came easily. I recollect that I made a reference to the "contumely, calumny and contempt" which Hardie had had to face, and was proud of the alliteration. At the end of this speech, Mr. Campbell turned to Hardie and said, "You see what my young men are like." I resented it. I was already more the follower of Hardie than of Campbell.

Chapter Three
JOINING THE I.L.P.

Despite the hold that Keir Hardie had upon me, the Socialist organisation which I joined was not the I.L.P. It was the Social Democratic Federation. One Sunday our Camden Town family was roaming in Regent's Park. We stood on the outside of various crowds, listening to different speakers, and one speaker so gripped us that we remained. He was Herbert Burrows, a veteran of the S.D.F. Unlike many spokesmen of the S.D.F., which was in those days Marxist and materialist in the most extreme form, Burrows spoke with a broad human sympathy which exactly appealed to me. With two of my companions I joined the St. Pancras Branch of the S.D.F. I had no knowledge of the ideological or political differences between the S.D.F. and the I.L.P.; had I listened that Sunday morning to an I.L.P. speaker it is probable that I would have joined just as readily.

The St. Pancras S.D.F. met in a room above a baker's shop in Prince of Wales Road. I remember the subject of discussion at the first meeting; it was the necessity to secure the strongest possible delegation to the Copenhagen Conference of the Socialist International in order to defeat the proposal that the Labour Party should be allowed to affiliate. We took a collection to send a delegate, and under the influence of the urgency of the issue I gave what amounted to the cost of more than one meal.

But I stayed in the S.D.F. for three months only. The hard, sectarian dogmatism of the comrades and their bitterness towards other sections of the Movement, particularly the I.L.P., so disappointed me that I think I would have resigned at the second meeting had not news been brought, just as we were breaking up, that the shop assistants at C. A. Daniels, a large drapers in Kentish Town Road, had decided to strike. Immediately the bickering was forgotten. We volunteered for picket duty, arranged meetings each night, and planned collection-taking. Most evenings I went on picket duty, promenading in front of the shop, handing leaflets to the customers and trying to dissuade them from buying. Sometimes the police would intervene, driving us from door to door. It was my first lesson on the way in which the forces of the State are used to protect the interests of the possessing class.

The excitement of the strike, the keenness of our members, their good fellowship with Labour Party and I.L.P. members on picket duty, renewed my enthusiasm, but as soon as the strike was over we went back to our bickering, denouncing Henderson, MacDonald and even Hardie (despite his leadership at the Copenhagen Conference for the policy of an international general strike against war) far more bitterly than any Capitalist. I returned to our lodgings each Friday night vowing I would resign, but I stuck it until a public demonstration at which Mr. Harry Quelch, the S.D.F. leader, spoke. The contrast between him and my recollection of Hardie decided me. The speech was probably not as scurrilous as I took it to be, but it was a shock to my youthful idealism and, disillusioned, I handed in my membership card.

My reaction was to withdraw for a time from the Socialist Movement altogether. Some of the S.D.F. criticism of the I.L.P. stuck in my memory, and I did not transfer to that Party. Instead, I gave expression to what I will call my "social service" instinct by deciding to live at Claremont Institute in Pentonville. The institute was in the middle of a slum district, and ran clubs, provided cheap baths (there were none in the tenements) and had a staff of welfare and nursing sisters. The head of it was the Rev. F. W. Newland, a distant, dignified, saintly-looking man, and his assistant, an able little hunchback, Mr. Kelly, a bright-eyed, broad-minded man with a rich sense of humour, for whom I quickly developed a friendship. Harold Hills moved to Claremont also, and with Mr. Kelly we occupied rooms at the top of four flights of stone stairs.

But the fact is that I never took to social service. I tried the boys' club but failed; I could not make contact with the boys. I became much more interested in making rounds with one of the welfare sisters. What I saw shocked me horribly. Pentonville was then a centre of sweated "home" industries—cardboard boxmaking, artificial flowermaking, some tailoring, and toothbrush making. The last horrified me most; when I saw dirty hands in dirty bug-infested rooms inserting and gumming the hairs into the bone heads of toothbrushes, I wondered whether brushing one's teeth was the hygienic habit one was led to believe.

It was a common experience to go into a two-roomed tenement, up dark broken-down stairs, the whole place smelling, and find quite late at night one or two women and three or four children at work, in a carpetless room, sometimes with boxes instead of chairs, and a plain table in the middle of the room on which the work was done. It was rare to find men of working age on the job (they earned what little they got as casual labourers), but often older men were helping. The rates of pay were scandalous. A woman working twelve hours a day would earn from twelve to fifteen shillings a week. It was the practice to keep the children away from school when things were specially hard, so that they could make a few extra pennies; sometimes one saw children helping who were even too young to go to school.

There was one incident which I could not get out of my mind for weeks. A girl of twelve was carried into the dispensary of the institute one evening; she had fainted in the street outside. I arrived at the door just as she was being taken in; her clothes were ill-kempt, her face like marble. After she had been revived an ambulance took her to hospital. The next day I asked the welfare sister what illness the girl was suffering from.

"Starvation," was the reply.

"*What?*"

"Starvation. The doctor who examined her found that her stomach was absolutely empty. She had had no food for three days except for some tomatoes which she had picked up under a barrow in Chapel Street."

These experiences drove me back to the I.L.P., which I joined in November, 1907, just after my nineteenth birthday. I immediately felt myself at home among its members. The Finsbury Branch consisted of two sections, industrial and clerical. We co-operated well, but there was a good-humoured rivalry. The industrial section included members who have since achieved prominence: Harry Adams, of the Building Trades Workers, and Colman and King, of the Compositors, who have since become Mayors of Islington and Finsbury respectively. The clerical section were mostly young people attached to the City Temple, and on their nomination the Rev. R. J. Campbell was elected president. We took a shop in Goswell Road, and the industrial section made it attractive, painting the walls a bright green. They built a platform, the branch hired eighty chairs and a piano and we were very proud of our home.

Activities were mostly controlled by the clerical section. On Sunday nights a meeting was conducted rather on the lines of the Labour Church Movement in the North of England—we had a small voluntary orchestra, sang Labour songs, and the speeches were mostly Socialist evangelism, emotional in denunciation of injustice, visionary in their anticipation of a new society. This was balanced by lectures delivered on a week-night by the young intellectuals of the Fabian Nursery—G. D. H. Cole, Harry Slesser (now Lord Justice Slesser), Clifford Sharp (first Editor of the "New Statesman") and others. This was before any of them had made reputations.

One evening Bernard Shaw came. I was a Shaw worshipper, and was thrilled by this opportunity of meeting him at close quarters. His theme was an appeal for economic equality on the ground that only when class divisions are abolished will natural selection take place in the mating of human beings, and until that happens the superman and the super-race will not be developed. I can still see Shaw as he stood on the shallow platform at the end of our shop-hall — crowded to suffocation, of course—tall, slight, straight-backed, arms folded across his chest, throwing out his stream of challenging sentences with the confidence of a god, taking a delight in uttering ideas which shocked. There was still a little red in his beard and hair then, and he spoke with extraordinary vigour, on and on for an hour and a half, the crisp sharp sentences, so definite, so ruthless in their destruction of old idols, so clear and bold in the creation of new gods, poured out with a rapidity that held us all spell-bound. Even the industrial section, rather contemptuous of the Fabian Nursery intellectuals, were conquered. The rest of us were entranced.

At the end we asked Shaw questions. I must still have been a rather subjective youth, for the question I put was this: "Mr. Shaw, we are young and we want to make the best use of our lives. What is your advice?" His answer came in a flash: "Find out what the Life-Force is making for and make for it, too." How many times since have I used that answer in perorations to Socialist speeches!

No sooner had I joined the I.L.P. than I began public speaking. Socialism had become the passion of my life, and I wanted to win others. My first indoor lecture was on the subject of India. My conclusions were moderate; I proposed joint British-Indian Councils! My first open-air speech was on unemployment, and there was no moderation about that. We were passing through a trade depression and I was bitter about the conditions of hunger in the homes of Pentonville. Keir Hardie had introduced a "Right to Work" Bill, 'and the Party was forming "Right to Work" committees throughout the country. Night after night we held large and stormy demonstrations outside Finsbury Town Hall. I was selected to lead a deputation to the Holborn Board of Guardians. I was still not twenty and those comfortable, grey-haired men and women evidently felt that the red-tied youngster who addressed them was a harbinger of revolution. The unemployed crowded the gallery and cheered me uproariously despite commands of silence from the chairman and clerk. I was asked to withdraw whilst the Board considered our demands — extra monetary relief, milk for the children, coal during the winter and so on. I joined the unemployed in the gallery to listen to the Board's deliberations.

The first speaker was a Catholic priest who denounced me as an impostor. I didn't live in Pentonville at all, he said; I visited it only for political agitation. I was so angry that I jumped to my feet and protested from the gallery, the unemployed gathering round me as a bodyguard. I can still see the startled faces of those "guardians of the poor" as they looked up; the chairman did not attempt to stop me, and I must acknowledge that the priest apologised handsomely. We did not get any increase in monetary allowances, but we did get free supplies of milk and coal.

This was a period of great progress and optimism in the Socialist movement. The Liberal Government returned in the General Election of 1906 had at first resisted the demands of the Labour Party for old age pensions, the maintenance of the unemployed, the feeding of necessitous school children, and so on. The consequence was a series of sensational Labour victories over both Conservative and Liberal candidates in by-elections. The working-class vote which had been Radical was transferring itself to the Labour Party and, more important, Socialism was a subject of general discussion and recruits were being won by the hundred every week. The young membership of the I.L.P. in those days had no doubt that victory was only a little way ahead.

Most sensational of all the victories was Victor Grayson's in the Colne Valley of Yorkshire. Grayson was a student at a Unitarian theological college at Manchester, and as soon as he became a Socialist he applied his exceptional gifts of speech to the Movement. He spoke all over Lancashire and Yorkshire, and there were stories of how, returning late at night from distant meetings, he used to climb the college wall and scramble through his bedroom window. His campaign in the Colne Valley was like a religious revival. How many times I have heard stories of it from the old comrades in the Valley—"Eh, lad, those were gradely times!" Grayson's oratory, supported by the Rev. W. B. Graham (described by Robert Blatchford as "six feet Socialist and three inches parson"), Bruce Glasier (himself a poet, prophet and idealist), his wife Katharine, and others, swept through the mill towns like a fire. There was no talk of current political problems. Socialism was preached as a new hope of deliverance to the poor, and the poor responded.

Grayson immediately became a hero to the Movement. He spoke ceaselessly from one end of the country to the other and no hall was big enough to hold the crowds which came to hear him. Someone said that he had the eyes of a poet and the mouth of a clown, and that described his character as well as his features. His speeches combined a fervent passion for social justice with a humour which tended to become gross. When he reached the House of Commons he electrified us all by getting suspended when demanding justice for the unemployed. That night we were holding an unemployed meeting at the back of Finsbury Town Hall. The newspaper boys came shouting "Socialist M.P. suspended." I rushed to get a copy and the comrades gathered excitely round. I pushed the speaker from the platform, jumped up and read the description to the crowd. It unanimously decided to send Grayson a telegram of congratulation.

This first protest had the dignity of sincerity and made a deep impression, but the day following there came a second suspension, and even in reading the press reports one sensed that it was theatrical. Later I was told that Grayson was drunk and that the second suspension destroyed all the effect of his first.. Keir Hardie assured me that a group of Members of Parliament had deliberately set about encouraging Grayson to drink in order that he should make an exhibition of himself. I trust Hardie's word so much that I accept this as true.

Grayson eventually lost his seat in Parliament and sank into miserable destitution.

My last contact with him was shortly before the war, when he and his actress wife literally had no money and no food and nothing to pawn to get food. A few comrades collected enough to send them to New Zealand. Then came the report that he had enlisted in the army on the outbreak of war—and after that silence. Rumours have spread from time to time that he is alive—for he is still a legend in Yorkshire—and Ernest Hunter, of the "Daily Herald," once ran a feature for days collecting this and that story of his whereabouts. But the veil has not been lifted.

My socialist activity in Finsbury made me well known in the district. At last I found a congenial activity at Claremont. I started the Islington and Finsbury Parliament, and all the leading politicians of the two constituencies joined. The Rev. F. W. Newland was the Speaker and never has the House of Commons had a more dignified figure to preside over its proceedings. We treated the debates with great seriousness, and on one occasion the Socialist Party, which I led, withdrew in protest against some grievance as heatedly as though those on the Government benches really had issues of life and death in their hands! I remember that we gathered in a room below and sang the Red Flag. I also remember something else. As we stood there singing, members of the Boys' Brigade entered to pack their rifles away in a cupboard. I saw the sneers on the faces of some of my socialist colleagues and felt ashamed to be connected with an institution which in the name of Christianity taught boys to kill. The incident had a deep effect on me and I seriously considered leaving Claremont, but the decision was taken out of my hands. The I.L.P. decided to nominate me and my friend among the welfare sisters (who had also joined the Party) as candidates for the Finsbury Borough

Council in the Pentonville ward. This gave Mr. Newland a shock. Another welfare sister served on the Borough Council, but she was an Independent—for two residents of the institute to stand as *Socialists* was unthinkable! I was indignant, threw out remarks about the rich Capitalists who subscribed to Claremont as a salve to their conscience, and decided to leave.

I then joined a remarkable household, of which Alfred Harvey-Smith, the young I.L.P. Branch Secretary, was the head. I find it difficult to remember how many of us lived there. Alfred had six sisters, two adopted sisters and two brothers, and from time to time all appeared to be in the house. Four of the girls belonged to the permanent household, while Lilla, a student at Eltham Training College, spent her holidays with us, and the rest of the family descended upon us whenever they got an opportunity to come to London. This was the first time I had lived in the same household with girls, and at the beginning their number made the experience rather overwhelming, but they were all so natural and free from sex-consciousness that I soon lost my embarrassment.

In addition to the family we had three boarders: Jack Ames (afterwards regarded as a deserter because he became secretary of the National Alliance of Employers and Employed), his lovely but frail wife (she died while she was with us), and, when Parliament was sitting, Mr. J. R. Clynes, M.P. Mr. Clynes was often wise in his advice to us adventurous youngsters, but, nevertheless, disappointing to me because of his caution and moderation.

But our fraternity did not end there. Clem Bundock, then a young newspaper colleague of mine, now secretary of the National Union of Journalists, was one of our frequent visitors. Four of the men attached to our domestic club afterwards became Labour M.P.s. Reg. Sorensen, now Member for West Leyton, was then one of the Rev. R. J. Campbell's "pioneer preachers." Ernest Thurtle, M.P. for Shoreditch, made contact with our clerical section through the National Union of Clerks. Fred Montague, afterwards Under-Secretary for Air in the Government of 1929-31, was down on his luck in those days, selling a healing ointment in various London markets; previously he had been a very able full-time propagandist on one of the vans run by the "Clarion." Jim Thorne, now a Labour

Member in the New Zealand Parliament, was also a "Clarion" vanner; he was a tall, fair-haired young man, a breezy, laughing colonial, very popular with the girls. Dolly Lansbury, one of G.L.'s daughters, was in the crowd and many others, too many to mention. One of the Harvey-Smith sisters, Violet, looked after us; how she did it single-handed I do not know.

We were a happy crowd, happy in our activity for Socialism, happy in the fun which followed. A group of us did some study together—classes in Marx and psychology. Earlier I had entered as an evening student at the London School of Economics and, though I didn't keep it up, becoming overwhelmed by I.L.P. work, I read economics heavily. We ate together, the visitors paying their whack in a collection box. We went to theatres together, and for rambles over Hampstead Heath and beyond, sometimes by day, sometimes by night. Of course most of us ended by marrying one another. I married Lilla, the student at the Training College (but this was later). Sorensen married Muriel, a younger sister; a cousin of mine married Violet; Ernest Thurtle married Dolly Lansbury. When we began to pair off like this our community broke up, but it was a great and happy experience while it lasted.

The election in Pentonville was the first concerted political effort of our Myddleton Square fraternity. At that time there was only one Labour member on the Finsbury Borough Council and none for the Pentonville Ward. We contested all three seats; Harry Adams, of the Building Trades' Workers, was one of my colleagues. I was twenty-one years of age on the election day and have not decided to this time whether my nomination was legal. We did not win, but were only thirty votes behind the three Conservatives and the Liberals were well at the bottom of the poll. Later in the year I stood for the Holborn Board of Guardians and was defeated by one vote only. To-day there is a Labour majority on the Borough Council; thirty years ago we were pioneers.

Our large vote encouraged us to think in terms of a Parliamentary candidate, and it was not mere youthful optimism because Finsbury was already represented by a Liberal-Labour Member, W. C. Steadman, secretary of the T.U.C. He was a dry old stick, not alive to any socialist ideas, but his Trade Union connection gave us some little right to claim the succes-

B

sion of the seat from which he was proposing to retire. We invited W. C. Anderson, who was then the national chairman of the I.L.P., to be our candidate. Most Socialists of the post-war period have no knowledge of W. C. Anderson, but if he had lived he would certainly have become a big figure in Labour politics. He was not heroic, but he had a firm grasp of socialist principles, a clear mind, common-sense, a great capacity for getting on with people, a powerful personality and brilliant gifts as an orator. He had remarkable, friendly brown eyes and a rich warming voice. W. C. Steadman did not resign his seat, however, and W. C. Anderson would not consider standing against him.

The "suffragette" agitation was at its height in these days and I was an enthusiast. I was flung out of a Lloyd George meeting at the Queen's Hall for shouting "Votes for Women," and on one occasion I was part of a masculine body-guard for women seeking to enter the House of Commons with a petition. There were thousands of people in Parliament Square, mostly attracted by the prospect of seeing women grappling with police-men, their hats pulled off, their hair falling down, their clothes in disarray, and perhaps trodden under the feet of the horses of the mounted police. It was a horrible and humiliating experience. The laughter of the crowd angered me more than the lost tempers of the policemen.

I had one humiliating experience with the suffragettes. After attending an enthusiastic meeting—I remember only Mrs. Zangwill's brilliantly witty speech — I wrote to Christabel Pankhurst offering my voluntary services to the cause as a journalist. Days passed and I was disappointed to get no reply. Then came a telegram asking me to attend at the offices in Lincoln's Inn. I went with all the zeal of a young crusader. I was shown into a room and asked to wait. The door opened and Christabel and Mrs. Pankhurst came in. They entered with all the dignity they knew so well how to command, Christabel in flowing white, her head held haughtily in the air, Mrs. Pankhurst bearing herself like a queen. Then they saw me—a boy of twenty! Their pose collapsed, they gasped, and Mrs. Pankhurst slipped out of the room.

"I am afraid there is a mistake," said Christabel, distantly. "We were expecting a journalist."

"I *am* a journalist," I said, unable to hide a smile, "but I am prepared to do anything—from addressing envelopes to writing an article."

Christabel withdrew, and a junior member of the staff was sent in. She brought me envelopes to address.

At Easter, 1910, I attended my first I.L.P. Conference. It was held in the Memorial Hall, London, and I went as a reporter. I must acknowledge that I do not remember a single speech, but after the Conference I interviewed W. C. Anderson for a "Progressive Figure of the Week" feature, and when he had seen my work he asked me whether I would go to Manchester to become sub-editor of the "Labour Leader," the organ of the Party. I agreed. A month later I packed my bag and went north.

Chapter Four
STARTING AS EDITOR

The Party had a printing press on the Salford bank of the Irwell, and the office of the "Labour Leader" was there. I had never seen a river so dirty and it seemed to me to typify Manchester. Everything was black. In London I had lived in a slum, but nearby were squares and gardens and Hampstead Heath was not far away. Manchester and Salford gave an impression of unrelieved drabness. My lodgings, however, were in a garden village in Levenshulme, and I made the most of the morning walk to the tram, regarding each tree on the roadside as a friend, noting every change in tint and form.

The Editor of the "Labour Leader" was Mr. J. Mills, a tall, thin, gloomy man, who kept his hands deep in the pockets of a long coat and always seemed cold. After the warm comradeship of the Finsbury I.L.P. I felt that Manchester was an iceberg. There were two girls on the staff of the Press who were friendly; one of them, Muriel Wallhead, daughter of Dick Wallhead, afterwards M.P. for Merthyr, and then the most popular propagandist of the Party. The Wallheads lived in the garden village and I was often in their home. Dick is now known only to the older generation of Socialists, but his oratory did much to build the Labour Movement in the years before the war. In appearance he was the double of Disraeli. In repose his features were like a statue of a Red Indian chief, but they were so mobile in action that they might have been made of rubber. He was a melodramatic speaker, with the husky voice of a stage tragedian. He tramped the full length of the platform, acting every thought and feeling, laughing at his own stories so that the audience could not help laughing, too. I was with him at Blackburn market place once when he was foretelling a depression. Suddenly he stopped, bent forward, put his hand over his eyes, and looked intently into the distance. Then out went an arm excitedly, his fingers pointing to the horizon.

"There," he exclaimed. "I see it coming." The audience turned like one man to see the approaching depression.

My "Labour Leader" work brought me into close touch with another famous propagandist — "Casey" and his fiddle. "Casey"—Walter Hampson was his never-used name—had been first violinist in the Hallé Orchestra, but he was a vagabond by nature and took to the road, earning his livelihood by giving recitals, accompanied by Socialist comments rich in their humour, to crowded audiences in all parts of the country. "Casey" wrote a weekly humorous article for the "Labour Leader," and one of my duties was to sub-edit it. His spelling, punctuation and grammar were atrocious, and sometimes his humour was beyond repetition. Whenever I cut it he was indignant. "Boy, you should be on 'The Old Maids' Soother'," he used to say.

I began to go about speaking. My first meeting in the north was at Blackburn. where the Branch held meetings which drew crowds of two thousand on the market square every Sunday night. Ernest Townley, then a Blackburn mill-worker, introduced me from the lorry as "the young London Socialist orator," and after that I had to do well.

It was some time later that I had a trying experience associated with Mr. Philip Snowden, who was M.P. for Blackburn. I was still in bed one Sunday morning when a telegram came. It read: "Snowden ill; you must take his place at Empire Theatre to-night." I went apprehensively, and, when the curtain rose and I was seen on the stage instead of Snowden, the "O-oh" of disappointment from the packed audience made me wish to run away. But, as has happened often when I am nervous, I spoke above my form, and Ernest Townley booked me for the following Sunday as well. On the second occasion I was confident—and my speech was a flop. That night I wasn't happy, even at the Townleys.

After I had been with the "Labour Leader" about a year I was summoned before the Board. Its membership included Philip Snowden, W. C. Anderson, Bruce Glasier and Dick Wallhead, with Edgar Whiteley, a keen business man, and later a Co-op director, as secretary and manager. I was still only twenty-three, and their proposal astonished and excited me. They wished me to become acting-editor of the "Labour Leader," with W. C. Anderson as writer of the editorials. Did I know someone who could act as my assistant? I thought of Clement Bundock and telegraphed him. He wired back that he would come. But I was uncomfortable in the presence of Mr. Mills: he had not been told of the decision to dismiss him, and I had been asked to keep it confidential. Afterwards I am afraid he regarded me as a conspirator against him, though in truth no one was more surprised by the proposed change than I was.

Clem joined me in my lodgings. When he came I was still living in the garden village, but, after spending a Sunday tramping in the Derbyshire Hills, we decided to remove to the little village of Mellor, on the Cheshire border. We took rooms with Mrs. Saint in Red Row, which looked down over fields to the ruins of an old mill and beyond to the wooded valley and river and Marple Lake. I was told that Red Row was originally built to house poor-law children of tender age who worked in the mill below. I should think it likely.

The country was beautiful. By the river a road turned past the old mansion of the lord of the manor up a steep bank, rising under arched trees like a Gothic chancel. At the top was a lodge and large iron gates, and then one stepped into the England of the early industrial revolution. There was a courtyard of stones, and on three sides stone cottages and a pump in the middle. I was told that Arkwright, inventor of the spinning-frame, had lived in one of these cottages. As I looked at them, and then through the iron gates down the drive to the mansion of the mill-owner, and then across to the old mill and Red Row, which had housed its child workers, I had a clear picture of the social divisions which inaugurated British Capitalism.

Clem and I soon had a companion. One day there was a knock on the office door and a big-limbed man, with a large artist's portfolio under his arm, burst in. Black hair swept down over his forehead, his face was all smiles, his confidence unbounded. "My name is J. B. Nicholas," he said. "I saw your paper in Wales. I want to draw cartoons for you." In a second his folio was open and his cartoons were spread over my table. They were good. "We only print one a week and can't pay more than ten and six," I said. "That will do. I'll soon get more commissions." He sat down immediately to do a drawing for our coming issue. When he had finished he asked us where he could get lodgings. We took him to Red Row.

Clem, "J.B." and I rapidly made a reputation in the north as the "Labour Leader" trio. We took meetings together. Clem

would speak first. He was a shy boy until he got on the platform—then he was self-assured and audacious. He had a surprising flow of words and he could say witty things. After him
"J.B." took the platform, standing in front of a blackboard
with large sheets of drawing paper attached. In a few seconds
he would sketch contrasts of riches and poverty, military
and educational expenditure and the like, driving home his
points with a few piercing phrases. He would do rapid sketches
of well-known Socialist leaders—Hardie, MacDonald, Snowden
—giving the sketch to the member in the audience who guessed
the portrait first. Finally, I would conclude with a more serious
speech. This friendship between Clem, "J.B." and myself was
one of the best things in my life. We worked together, tramped
the hills together, went to our week-end meetings together, lived
together, studied together. We used to read a good deal in the
evenings—not only Socialist classics, but a wide field of literature. Shaw and Strindberg were favourites of Clem: Keats of
"J.B." I read philosophy, politics and economics.

The women's suffrage movement still had my enthusiasm
hardly less than the Socialist movement. When the National
Union of Women's Suffrage Societies threw in its lot with the
Labour Party, and particularly with the I.L.P., I spoke at their
meetings frequently and took part in a number of their by-
election campaigns. Their Labour organiser was Margaret
Robertson, a woman with dark hair and classical features, with
whom I became very friendly. She was an able speaker and
had an exceptionally good political mind. She joined the I.L.P.
and I expected her to become a leader of the Party. Why she
did not I shall tell later.

These women's suffrage gatherings were the most imposing
meetings I had yet addressed. My I.L.P. meetings were mostly
on market squares or in branch halls, but with Mrs. Fawcett
and Margaret Robertson I spoke at the Newcastle Town Hall,
the Usher Hall, Edinburgh, and at the Royal Albert Hall. The
suffragists staged these occasions impressively. The speakers at
the Albert Hall marched in procession through the vast
audience down the central aisle, Mrs. Fawcett leading, with
myself nervously bringing up the rear. When we reached the
platform a steward signalled me to the press table—she thought
I was a press messenger! I was only twenty-three, and I remem-

ber that one of the reports described me as a "mere stripling."

It was on this question of women's suffrage that I first came into conflict with Ramsay MacDonald. The Government was introducing a Bill to extend the suffrage to more men. The women suffragists demanded that the Bill should be opposed unless it also enfranchised women, and I took this line in the "Labour Leader." Keir Hardie and Philip Snowden supported this view, but MacDonald, whilst prepared to fight for women's suffrage, was not ready to vote against an extension of the franchise to more working men. I am inclined now to think that from a class point of view MacDonald was right, but at that time the equality of women with men was a principle stronger with me than the principle of class. It may be, however, that Hardie and Snowden were correct when they argued that strong opposition to the Bill would have secured both an extension of the male suffrage and the enfranchisement of women.

In 1912 I was made responsible editor of the "Labour Leader." As such I was entitled to attend the meetings of the National Council of the Party, but I rarely did so. Probably this was due to a certain youthful shyness; Hardie, MacDonald, Snowden and the others were still on pedestals in my mind and I was of another generation. Once W. C. Anderson asked me why I did not mix more with the National Council members, and said that they had the impression that as a person of middle-class origins I felt superior. I don't think I have ever been more surprised by any remark. I felt exactly the opposite.

Despite Anderson's invitation I did not attend the National Council meetings regularly until the war years, but I became involved in some of the controversies which divided its members. MacDonald was already showing, as leader of the Parliamentary Labour Party, the moderation which became his dominant characteristic later. He was quarrelling violently with Philip Snowden, Keir Hardie, George Lansbury and F. W. Jowett regarding the insurance schemes for unemployment and health which the Liberal Government, under the influence of Mr. Lloyd George, had introduced. The controversy broke publicly into the columns of the "Labour Leader," where Philip Snowden wrote denouncing MacDonald in his most acid style for supporting measures which imposed a weekly "poll tax" on the workers. He argued for the non-contributory principle, in which the cost would be met by taxation of the rich. Mac-Donald replied more philosophically, arguing that a contribution from the workers was justified in order to remove the taint of "State charity" from the benefits received. Editorially I backed Snowden and he wrote me an appreciative letter. In later years, when I sat in the House of Commons and heard Snowden as Chancellor of the Exchequer say that the rich could stand no more taxation, my mind went back to those letters.

My first meeting with MacDonald had been on the occasion of an interview for the "Christian Commonwealth" in 1909. It was at his flat in Lincoln's Inn Fields. He received me in his study, lined with shelves of blue-bound Hansards, and he impressed me immensely. He was then very handsome, with waving black hair, a heavy moustache, strong features, and a fine figure. He expressed his opinions with the manner of a god and I felt at least that I was in the presence of a great man. Afterwards when I descended into the living-room, where Mrs. MacDonald was hunting out a portrait for me, I was almost startled by the homely domestic scene—MacDonald had seemed above common life in his Olympian heights! Mrs. MacDonald was dressed as a simple housewife and around her played the children—Alastair, Ishbel, and Malcolm. They were as untidy and noisy among their scattered toys as any family, and I would have liked to romp with them—but that, with Alastair at least, was an anticipation. As I crossed the gardens of Lincoln's Inn Fields, where the beautiful child-figure memorial to Margaret MacDonald now stands, I contrasted my impressions of Hardie and MacDonald. I felt then that they were both great men, but it was Hardie who had won my affection.

I often heard MacDonald speak at meetings in these days, and his rich organlike voice and oratory captivated me. I remember a magnificent speech which he delivered at an international demonstration in the Albert Hall, though it is the impression of his voice which remains rather than anything he said. Another speaker at that meeting was Jean Jaurès, the French Socialist leader, who was shot in a Paris café by some mad patriot on the eve of the war of 1914. The speech was delivered in rapid French and I could not follow it.

but the energy of his gestures makes the memory a film rather than a portrait. He was a thick-set man, with huge shoulders and a noble head covered with shaggy hair. At one moment he crouched on the platform so that his hands were only a few inches from the floor. His head was lifted, the words poured forth, his hands moved rapidly about his feet. Steadily he raised himself, his hands rotating about his knees, then about his waist, then they swept up to the level of his shoulders, and finally he was on tip-toe, his arms flung above his head, his fingers stretched and quivering, his uplifted face shining with a vision which set his eyes on fire—and all the time the words rose and rose in a crescendo. It is doubtful whether one man in a hundred who heard him understood his words, but we all understood that he was illustrating the rise of the workers from slavery to freedom, and at his final cry of triumph we were all on our feet cheering with him.

The conflict between MacDonald and Snowden about Parliamentary policy became increasingly keen. Snowden wanted the Labour Party, which often held the balance of power with its forty odd votes, to be aggressively independent. MacDonald directed it rather as an advanced ally of the Liberal Government. Early in the spring of 1914 I had an appointment with Keir Hardie, who shared Snowden's view, at the House of Commons. He was late and I waited for him in the central lobby. When he came down the corridor I saw that he was uneasy about something. He was white and looked worried. He took my arm and led me to a seat.

"Fenner," he said (he had treated me with great personal friendliness ever since the Nevill's Court interview), "something has just happened which I could never have believed. MacDonald has suggested to the Parliamentary Executive that we make an alliance with the Liberal Party at the General Election." He drew his hand across his forehead and was silent for a few moments. Then he turned to me. "Laddie, we must kill this plan at the I.L.P. Conference. Do what you can."

I took this as a command. I wrote a series of articles in the "Labour Leader" attacking the Liberal Party, which were afterwards published in book form with a preface by Hardie—my first book. I prepared material for a speech at the Conference. It was the Coming-of-Age Conference of the Party and was held in Bradford, the birthplace of the I.L.P. Hardie, who had presided over the first Conference, was in the chair. We had a private session for the discussion of internal policy, and there I raised the issue. By now I had become used to speaking, but I was nervous about this effort. I can see now the long, low, crowded hall and its platform on which, grouped around Hardie, sat members of the National Council and the fraternal delegates, including Camille Huysmans, the Belgian Secretary of the International, and Arthur Henderson, secretary of the Labour Party.

My difficulty was that I had no direct evidence that anything in the nature of a Liberal alliance was contemplated and I could not give away Hardie as the source of my information. I had to base my statement on tendencies in the House of Commons and in MacDonald's speeches. I showed how the members of the Parliamentary Group voted in larger numbers when issues critical to the life of the Government came before Parliament than when our own working-class motions were under discussion, and I "read between the lines" of MacDonald's declarations. The speech was well documented and instinctively the delegates seemed to realise that there was something behind what I said.

Robert Smillie, the miners' leader, followed. Smillie came second only to Hardie in the respect felt for him by the Party. He combined in a wonderful way kindness towards all comrades with an uncompromising front towards the enemies of the working class; rarely have I known this combination of gentleness and sternness so complete. He began by justifiably remarking that my speech was suited to a Labour Party Conference rather than to an I.L.P. Conference, but proceeded to declare in the most categorical terms against a Liberal Alliance; he gave a threatening emphasis to his words, which showed that he knew what had been happening. I smiled across the delegates' heads at Hardie, but from the impartiality of the chair he made no sign in response. I was satisfied, however. The plan was killed.

Then came MacDonald. He tore me to shreds. With scathing scorn he referred to my phrase "reading between the lines": that was the habit of his critics—they could not attack what he said or did and so they "read between the lines." He denied emphatically that any motion for a Liberal alliance had ever been made on the. Parliamentary Executive. He challenged us to produce the Minutes. He left the impression that the idea had never occurred to him or to anyone else and that my case was built entirely upon unworthy suspicions. Towards the end of his speech a spasm of pain crossed Mac-Donald's face. He apologised that he was ill, and amidst murmuring sympathy, left the hall. I was happy that the "plan had been killed," but I resented bitterly the impression Mac-Donald had left. I don't think I ever fully trusted him after this—not even during the war years.

But the impression was not to remain. Snowden rose. He regretted that MacDonald had gone—and then he told the whole story. I have never heard a speech which caused a greater sensation. The delegates whistled as he described how again and again the Parliamentary Executive had decided not to press working-class demands, such as the abolition of the tax on tea, because they feared it might lead to the defeat of the Liberal Government, and then he described exactly what had happened about the Liberal alliance plan. "Comrade Mac-Donald says that no motion for a Liberal alliance was ever made and challenges us to produce the minute book," he said, his lips thin and bitter. His finger went out in deadly climax. "Comrade MacDonald did not tell you that when he made the proposal he expressly asked that it should not be minuted so that the movement should be kept in ignorance."

The delegates gasped, and Hardie had to ring the president's bell to silence the cries of indignation. The "plan had been killed" all right!

Snowden's speech nearly put me on the National Council of the Party. I think I was only five votes behind W. C. Anderson for the fourth place. Hardie never mentioned the matter to me except in one brief phrase as he passed me in a corridor. "Well done, laddie," he said.

There was one other event at this Conference which I must mention. A great meeting was held in the St. George's Hall on the Sunday afternoon. Behind the platform sat tier above tier of children. Hardie was speaking. Suddenly he turned to the children and addressed them directly. I was sitting near the children and saw his face; never during all the times I had heard him speak had I seen it like this—the glow of its earnestness was almost unearthly. Never had I heard his voice like this—it rang with a timbre which went to the centre of one's being. He stood there, his arms outstretched, speaking to those children as though he had never had anything so important to say.

He appealed to them to love flowers, to love animals, to love their fellows, to hate injustice and cruelty, never to be mean or treacherous to their fellows, always to be generous in service. He pictured the loveliness of the unspoiled world and the loveliness of the world as it could become. He told them how unnecessary are poverty and war and how he had tried to pass on to them a world where happiness and peace would be theirs. He and those who had worked with him had failed, but they— they, the children—could succeed. "If these were my last words I would say them to you, lads and lasses. Live for that better day." There must have been many who heard that utterance who remember it; many of those children, now grown men and women, will remember it. We did not know then, but we were within four months of the world war, the war which killed Hardie. His words were in fact the last which most of those in the St. George's Hall were ever to hear from him.

Chapter Five
JOURNEYING ABROAD

It was the poverty of Pentonville which drove me passionately into the Socialist Movement, but as I understood what was happening in the wider world, another reason made me devote myself to Socialism even more earnestly—the gathering danger of war. Twice I had been abroad and I had learned that other peoples were the same, that they suffered the same injustices, that many of them were inspired by the same socialist hope.

While still living in London I had gone on a holiday-journalist trip to Hungary with Alfred Harvey-Smith. In Budapest we had met Socialist comrades in the political and Trade Union Movements and had learned of the repression they had to face. Even in the cafés detectives sat at neighbouring tables if our socialist friends were with us; at a meeting in a beer garden a military officer sat near the speaker and a group of soldiers stood at the back. Once the speaker went too far—immediately the officer rose, the soldiers leaped to attention and their hands went to their rifles. The speaker paused, enquired, the officer threatened, men in the crowd growled. The speaker laughed it off and soon had the audience laughing; the officer sat down again and the soldiers stood at ease.

We went from Budapest to the Carpathians. I had never seen peasant poverty before—at least not since my childhood days in India, and then I was too young to understand. It was even uglier and more indecent than slum poverty. That human beings should be hungry, with the fruits of the earth all about them and the grandeur of the mountains above them, was to me an outrage. We drove one day in a carriage and I felt a criminal to be sitting there in lordly comfort while the children of every village literally fought each other with teeth and nails for the smallest coin that we threw them—for we could not resist their begging. We did not see an able-bodied man in those villages. Women did the hard stone work on the roads and old men worked in the fields. Our driver told us that all the younger men had gone to the towns or emigrated: sometimes they saved enough to send for their families; sometimes they were never heard of again.

One of our companions in Budapest was George Lukacz, afterwards to become People's Commissar of Education during the short-lived Soviet dictatorship in Hungary. Lukacz developed into a rigid materialist of the most extreme Marxist school, but in those days he was an artist, a mystic and an idealist, a Socialist because Capitalism was hideous both in material things and in its prostitution of the human spirit. He was a gentle philosopher, already distinguished for his Heidelberg University studies on the effect of the social system on the arts. I remember him pointing from Queen Elizabeth Bridge to the reflection of the moon in the Danube and building dreams from the fairy-like islands glistening white in the middle of the river. He took us to the Houses of Parliament on the banks of the Danube. It was during the recess and we were shown round by a caretaker, who was perplexed to hear me delivering a speech in an unknown language to the empty benches—the first Socialist utterance ever made in the Hungarian Parliament.

Lukacz told him that I was an architect trying out the acoustics of the building.

I met another of the subsequent Red "dictators" during this visit—Eugene Landler, who was then a Social Democrat. Landler was engaged in organising the railwaymen, a difficult task because Trade Unionism among State employees was illegal. He also was an intellectual, and had an amazing grip of detailed economic facts about Hungary. I took them down in my note-book at a café table, whilst a nearby detective endeavoured to listen in. "You had better take care of that note-book," said Landler laughing. "That tec. would give a lot to get hold of it." Later Landler became a leading economic expert of the Communist International.

Back in London, I wrote scathing articles about the poverty of Hungary and the suppression of the workers' movement. The Socialist daily in Budapest, "Nepsava," reproduced the articles, with the result that angry questions were put in the Hungarian Parliament about this abuse of hospitality by a journalist who had been provided with a free railway pass. Fortunately I was able to send "Nepsava" a copy of the letter in which I had accepted this privilege only on the condition of being free to write exactly what I wished.

My second trip was entirely non-political. It was taken with Harold Hills, now a doctor, nine months before war broke out. We went to Cologne and thence by boat up the Rhine to Mayence, across the Swiss Alps by the newly-built Oberland railway, and then climbed over the range between Switzerland and Italy by the Monte Moro pass.

My woman suffrage friend, Margaret Robertson, was staying in a little village on the banks of Lake Orta; by looking at the map we could see that only one range divided us from it. "Damn your women," said Harold, but he finally agreed to go on a promise from me that we would spend one day only at the lake village. Next morning, Harold suggested that we should stay on to rest ourselves thoroughly. We stayed on until the very last moment of our holiday, travelling back to London without a break in fifteen hours. Two months later Margaret and Harold announced their engagement; I gave them a painting of Lake Orta for a wedding present. I congratulated Harold on marrying Margaret, but I have never forgiven him for taking her out of politics. Margaret left the public platform for the domesticity of home and children.

One political memory remains of the little village by Lake Orta. To the trunk of the tree which gave shade to its picturesque square was attached a poster with the heading: *Parti Socialista Italiano.* That Party was afterwards to become particularly close to the I.L.P.—first during the War, when it boldly maintained an international stand, and later by its association with the International Bureau of which I was secretary. When next I visited Italy no Socialist posters were permitted. Instead, on every available tree trunk were stencils of the Duce. *

*This was in 1930, when I paid a visit to some American friends living on Lake Lugano. The Fascists found out who I was, had the house watched by gendarmes who dogged my steps whenever I went for a walk, and finally when I left sent a police boat to accompany me to the frontier on the lake!

BOOK TWO

Chapter Six

FACING THE SHOCK OF BETRAYAL

The war of 1914 came suddenly. Ten days before it started I spoke at Oldham and my audience thought I was an hysterical scaremonger when I said that we were near war. An archduke had been killed in Serbia and Russia was threatening to attack Austria. What had that to do with us? Right up to the last moment it was denied in the House of Commons that Britain had any commitment to France involving us in war. The persistent F. W. Jowett, I.L.P. member for East Bradford, had put his searching questions to the Foreign Secretary, who had repudiated categorically any obligations. Lies? Well, secret diplomacy ceases to be secret if you must tell the truth about it publicly.

When I spoke at Oldham, Irishmen in the crowd shouted "Talk about Ireland, not Serbia." The issue in the public mind was the Constitutional crisis arising from the threat of Ulster to resist Home Rule. In the "Labour Leader" of July 23, Keir Hardie wrote not on the war menace but on "The King's Arrogance," denouncing His Majesty for throwing in his lot with "the reactionary peers and the rebellious Ulsterites." By the following week, however, the bigger crisis was evident. I wrote an article, "The War Must Be Stopped," and displayed it heavily on the front page.

During the last week of July the Bureau of the Socialist International met at Brussels. It declared, of course, against war, but it also declared that Socialist Parties would be justified in participating in national defence. On the Sunday before the war great demonstrations of international solidarity were held in all the capitals of Europe. Hardie and Henderson spoke in Trafalgar Square to a crowd which, despite the pouring rain, spilled over to the side streets. War came within two days, and by the following Sunday, Henderson (with the Hendersons of the Social Democratic Parties on each side) was declaring that the war was one of national defence and must be supported. The Belgian soldiers sang "The Internationale" as they trained their guns on their German brothers. The German soldiers sang "The Internationale" as they trained their guns on their Russian brothers.

My meeting on Sunday, August 2nd, was at Great Harwood, a Lancashire mill-town in Ernest Townley's Federation. The crowd was wondering and silent. When the Church services were over the congregations joined the edge of the meeting, a clergyman amongst them. I was bitterly but accurately prophetic. "Comrades," I said, "Don't be under any delusions. Your Labour leaders will urge you to fight to save democracy. Your Church leaders will urge you to fight in the name of the Prince of Peace." The clergyman protested, but the following Sunday ministers of religion of all denominations were preaching that the war was a holy crusade. Ernest and I returned to Blackburn full of foreboding. Outside the office of the "Northern Telegraph" there was a little silent crowd, reading telegrams posted in the window. They told of the first skirmishes between Russian and German troops. "It's coming," I said to Ernest.

When I got back to the "Labour Leader" office on the Monday my chief concern was about the attitude of the Labour Party and particularly of Ramsay MacDonald, the leader of the Parliamentary Group. The first news which came through was that MacDonald had resigned his leadership of the Party because the non-I.L.P. majority had refused to endorse his line on the War. Then came the big newspaper headlines about his speech in the Commons—"MacDonald says the Government is wrong." I felt ashamed of my distrust. But the next day I read the speech in full and the distrust returned. It is true he criticised the foreign policy of Sir Edward Grey, but he proceeded to declare in favour of war in certain circumstances:—

"I want to say to this House, and to say it without equivocation, that if the right hon. gentleman had come here to-day and told us that our country is in danger, I do not care what Party he appealed to, or to what class he appealed, we would be with him and behind him. If this is so, we will vote him what money he wants. Yes, and we will go further. We will offer him ourselves if the country is in danger."

He declared that he would support the war on a limited scale if Belgium were in danger. These sentences alarmed me. Of course the "country" would be in danger. Of course Belgium would be in danger. If MacDonald made such reservations, how long would he stand out? Nevertheless, I found myself within a few hours championing MacDonald. The fury of the attack upon him by all sections of the capitalist press compelled us to rally to him.

MacDonald's speech was delivered too late for publication in the "Labour Leader" and to the next issue he contributed a special full-page article which made its reproduction unnecessary. The article was an able and strong criticism of Sir Edward Grey's policy. It contained these sentences: —

"It is a diplomatist's war, made by about half-a-dozen men. Up to the moment that the Ambassadors were withdrawn the peoples were at peace. They had no quarrel with each other; they bore each other no ill-will. A dozen men brought Europe to the brink of a precipice and Europe fell over it . . . . And when we sit down and ask ourselves with fullness of knowledge: 'Why has this evil happened?' the only answer we can give is, because Sir Edward Grey has guided our foreign policy during the past eight years. His short-sightedness and his blunders have brought all this upon us."

The Party reproduced this article as a leaflet and it was distributed by the hundred thousand. The membership was reassured. Whatever MacDonald had said in Parliament, this declaration was the best anti-war propaganda we could have.

There had been no meeting of the National Council of the I.L.P. before the outbreak of war, but I had no doubt about the line to take in the "Labour Leader." A copy of the issue of August 6 is before me as I write and even across twenty-five years I can feel something of the passion with which it was prepared. I covered the whole front page with a manifesto in black type. Both at the top and bottom were the slogans "Down with the War!" The contents were a simple working-class appeal: —

"Workers of Great Britain, you have no quarrel with the workers of Europe. They have no quarrel with you. The quarrel is between the RULING classes of Europe. Don't make this quarrel yours . . .

"Workers of Great Britain, unite with the organised workers of France and Russia in saying that, though our Governments declare war, we declare peace.

"Stand true in this hour of crisis. The flag of International Solidarity is greater than the flag of Britain, of Germany, of France, of Austria, of Russia. It waves over all . . .

"Whoever else deserts the ranks, whatever you may have to face, stand firm. The future is dark, but in the solidarity of the workers lies the hope which shall, once again, bring light to the peoples of Europe."

The leading article that week was by Hardie. "At midnight on Tuesday war against Germany began," he wrote. "Already the roar and song of a war-maddened people is filling the streets of London. The I.L.P. at least will stand firm. Keep the Red Flag flying!"

The National Council of the Party met the following Sunday in the sitting-room of a grubby hotel on the other side of the Irwell from our printing press. I can see the grouping round the table now. Hardie, although only fifty-eight, seemed an old, old man, crumpled in body and broken in spirit. The lines on his forehead were deep as his head sank on his hand.

"I can't fight this war like I fought the Boer War," he said. "I must leave that to the younger comrades."

The war struck Hardie like a physical blow and a spiritual blight. He had had such faith that the international forces of the working class would resist it—and now in every country the Socialist leaders were voting war credits and urging their followers to fight. At Basle, in November, 1912, Hardie had been one of the speakers in the great Peace Demonstration in the Cathedral, when the representatives of the Austrian, Russian, German, Belgian, French and British working class had all sworn their unbreakable solidarity. Now they were calling on the workers to murder each other at the behest of their Capitalist Governments. Hardie was utterly crushed by the tragedy of it.

I think there were only two members of the National Council who supported the war; Harry Dubery, the London representative, was one, the other I forget. Hardie produced a draft Manifesto. It was unlike him—a heavy, plodding document, analysing foreign policies in a pedestrian way, giving no clear inspiring call. Bruce Glasier read a second draft, but it, too, was unsatisfactorily vague. Then W. C. Anderson read his draft. He read it well, and we knew at once that it was the document we needed. Some of the phrases were magnificent, and even to-day I can feel the emotion with which I heard them : —

"We are told that international Socialism is dead, that all our hopes and ideals are wrecked by the fire and pestilence and European war. It is not true.

"Out of the darkness and the depth we hail our working class comrades of every land. Across the roar of guns, we send sympathy and greeting to the German Socialists. They have laboured unceasingly to promote good relations with Britain, as we with Germany. They are no enemies of ours, but faithful friends.

"In forcing this appalling crime upon the nations, it is the rulers, the diplomats, the militarists who have sealed their doom. In tears and blood and bitterness, the greater Democracy will be born. With steadfast faith we greet the future; our cause is holy and imperishable, and the labour of our hands has not been in vain.

"Long live Freedom and Equality! Long live International Socialism!"

The Party membership was not so united as the National Council. The I.L.P. had no clear-cut philosophy or policy at this time; its idealism impelled it to oppose war, but socialist sentiment was up against another sentiment, the intense emotion of patriotism, and probably one-fifth of the Party succumbed. Two of the I.L.P. members of Parliament went over to the war side—James Parker, of Halifax, and, though he stayed with the Party for a time, my old companion of Finsbury days, J. R. Clynes.

There was one leader of the Party who was absent and about whom we were anxious. Philip Snowden was on a lecture tour in Canada. A brief cabled report told how he had declined to express h. views on the war; he wished to consult his colleagues first. But there was a hint that he would take the pro-war line and I went to Liverpool to meet him fearful and hopeful in turns. In a hotel sitting-room he gave me an interview. Clear and straight the sentences came—the most uncompromising and direct anti-war utterance that any public man in Britain had yet made. Excitedly I took down his words. He smiled when I told him we had been doubtful about him.

In the first month of the war there was little bitterness against those of us who opposed it, but by the autumn patriotic feeling had mounted and I heard stories of Party members who were suffering boycott, animosity and sometimes physical assault from their neighbours and workmates. I was fortunate in this respect; nearly all my friends and associates were in the I.L.P. But sometimes at meetings one experienced the wrath of crowds. The worst time I had was at Marple, at a meeting held by my branch of the I.L.P. Clem Bundock and I were there together, and we tried in vain to speak to a howling mob for two hours. When we descended from the platform police gathered to protect us from violence, and we walked towards Mellor with a hundred or so angry patriots accompanying us. As we crossed the canal bridge there was a rush to throw us over, but the police closed in. Finally we reached the iron gates leading to the Mellor estate. The lodge-keeper, greatly scared, ran out with the keys: the police pushed us through the gates; the crowd rushed to grab us whilst still in their reach. One of our pursuers got through, only to find the gates locked behind him. I remember how the confident exulting expression on his face turned to fear when he found himself alone with Clem, myself and two policemen. It was the one thing we had to laugh at when we got home.

There was another incident worse than that. Five Marple men waited for me at a lonely place on the canal bank and beat me up. I must have been a pacifist in temperament as well as conviction in those days, for even when the first blow came directly in my face I did not lift a hand in retaliation. Soon I was down in the black mud of the canal bank and they were kicking and dragging me to the edge. Fortunately at that moment someone appeared in the distance and the five fled.

Despite the antagonism shown by the people of Marple, there was a small group there even outside the I.L.P. which took the anti-war view. They were associated with the local Woman's Suffrage Society and sent me as their delegate to the Annual Conference of the National Union of Women's Suffrage Societies at Buxton. The Conference was the scene of a split. A number of its ablest leaders, including Catherine Marshall, its Parliamentary Secretary, Mrs. H. M. Swanwick, and Miss Courtenay, argued that the philosophical basis of the women's movement impelled it to oppose the physical violence of war. The leading spokesman of the opposite view was Eleanor Rathbone, later M.P. for the Northern Universities. I can see her at the conference—fury personified, bushy black eyebrows over flashing eyes, a mass of black-grey hair, her face red with patriotic fervour, her physical energy and her vigorous words denying in themselves the philosophical basis which her opponents urged. I spoke on the pacifist side and Miss Rathbone used this to prove that sex was not the dividing line between patriotism and pacifism. She insisted that if women gave themselves wholly to the nation in its time of peril they would win the right to political freedom.

None of us realised during these earliest months of the war the kind of struggle which was before us. We did not share the patriotic confidence that the Allied troops would be in Berlin before the end of the year, but our assumption was that the war would prove merely an interlude in the normal peace-time advance of the Labour Movement towards Socialism and that it demanded no far-reaching changes of policy. We did not foresee the long dark years of the war or the dark longer years which were to follow—years destined to shatter to bits the easy-going conceptions of pre-war Socialism.

Chapter Seven
MAKING CONTACT WITH GERMAN SOCIALISTS

One of the bitterest blows we had to face in the early months of the war was the fact not merely that so many Socialists in other countries were uniting with their Governments, but that we could make no contact with the minority who were standing out. Again and again at our meetings we were met by the taunt that the German Socialists were supporting the Kaiser. We could tell of the courageous anti-war attitude of Karl Liebknecht, Rosa Luxemburg, Clara Zetkin and others, but they seemed lost and distant voices. I was determined to make contact with them. I spent an afternoon in October writing letters to them, making enough copies to send through the Socialist Parties in the neutral countries—Holland, Denmark, Sweden, Norway, Switzerland, Italy, America, and even Spain. One I hoped would get through. Towards the end of December a bulky envelope arrived through Sweden with their replies. I regard their letters as of historic importance and I wish I could give them in full. These are extracts:—

"I am particularly happy and proud," wrote Liebknecht, "to send my greetings to you, to the British I.L.P., who, with our Russian and Serbian comrades, have saved the honour of Socialism amidst the madness of national slaughter.

"Each Socialist Party has its enemy, the common enemy of the International, in its own country. There it has to fight it. The liberation of each nation must be its own work . . . .

"It is the duty of every Socialist at the present time to be a prophet of international brotherhood, realising that every word he speaks in favour of Socialism and peace, every action he performs for these ideals, enflames similar words and actions in other countries, until the flames of the desire for peace shall flare high over all Europe . . . .

"In this way, even during the war, the International can be revived and can atone for its previous mistakes. Thus it *must* revive, a different International, increased not only in numerical strength but in revolutionary fervour, in clearness of vision and in preparedness to overcome the dangers of capitalist dictatorship, of secret diplomacy, and of capitalist conspiracies against peace."

Rosa Luxemburg was ruthless in facing the realities of the absolute collapse of the International. She did not share the view, common in the I.L.P., that after the war all could be as it had been before, and insisted on our rejecting the theory that during war the workers must inevitably "cut each others' throats at the command of their ruling classes," and then, when the war is over, "again exchange brotherly greetings as if nothing had happened." With characteristic directness she wrote:—

"An International which accepted the terrible downfall of the present time as a normal occurrence for the future, and which nevertheless pretended that it had never existed, would be but a caricature of Socialism, a product of hypocrisy just as much as the diplomacy of the Capitalist States with their alliances and agreements about the 'rights of peoples.'"

But still she had faith that "international Socialism is too firmly and deeply rooted to allow this breakdown to be permanent":

"Upon the horrible ruins of civilisation which Imperialism has created the resurrection of the International, as the only salvation of humanity from the hell of a degenerated and outgrown class rule, shall take place . . . .

"From this war the rank and file will return to our old flag of International Socialism, only with a more vehement determination not to betray it again at the next Imperialist orgy, but to defend it unitedly against the whole Capitalist world, against their criminal intrigues, their infamous lies, and their miserable phrases, and to establish it victoriously on the ruins of their bloody Imperialism."

One of the encouraging features of these letters was the indication they gave of the knowledge among the German workers of the I.L.P. stand. This was particularly expressed in Clara Zetkin's letter. Clara was the leader of the Women's section of the Social Democratic Party and editor of its paper. There was a specially personal note in Clara's message. She wrote of "the very truest feeling of international brotherhood, which unites all who, even amidst deceitful battle cries, have not forgotten that the working classes of all nations have one common country, great and sublime, in Socialism." She continued:—

"And with the consciousness of this brotherhood is mingled a deep and hearty feeling of gratitude for the undaunted strength, courage and fidelity with which the British I.L.P. has . . . remained true in action to the principles of International Socialism. This steadfast attitude, which knows not doubt, compromise or failure, will be a treasure of invaluable worth to the future of Socialist Internationalism and to the emancipation of the working-class of the whole world . . . .

"Moved by the same socialist feelings, thousands upon thousands in Germany, as in other countries, stretch out their hands towards you, dear friends and comrades in Great Britain, saying from the depth of their hearts: 'We thank you, we stand with you, as you stand with us, against Imperialism and for Socialism. You have preserved the honour of the International, your attitude is a lofty example of faith and strength in the present, a hope and warrant for the future.'"

During the winter of 1914 the I.L.P. made the first of several attempts to arrange in some neutral country a meeting between representatives of the anti-war Socialists on the opposite sides of the trenches. At last, in September, 1915, a conference was planned in the mountain village of Zimmerwald in Switzerland, but our delegates were refused passports. It was not until after the war that I appreciated the full significance of this conference. Lenin was present and he challenged not only the "social patriotism" of the Labour and Social Democratic Parties, but also the "peace by negotiation" of many of the anti-war parties, including the I.L.P. He insisted that any treaty negotiated by the Capitalist Governments would only sow seeds of future wars and that the correct Socialist policy was to end the war by social revolution. At the time I was not more than a pacifist Socialist and did not understand the importance of this controversy.

Despite the glowing tributes of Karl Liebknecht, Rosa Luxemburg and Clara Zetkin, the truth is that the I.L.P. had no unifying anti-war philosophy. One section of it was pacifist; another was opposed to a "balance of power war" on the Continent but in favour of national defence; a third, while ready to take part in a class war, was not prepared to support an Imperialist war, though even this section had no thought-out revolutionary tactic. Such differences of basic view led not only to the confusion of MacDonald's utterances, but to many conflicting declarations. I remember an anti-Conscription meeting near Bradford where I took the pacifist line, to be followed by an I.L.P. leader who argued that the front needed not more men, but more and better guns!

It was when I visited Scotland and came in contact with James Maxton, David Kirkwood, John Wheatley, Emanuel Shinwell, Tom Johnston and others that I realised the distinctions of policy most keenly. They were speaking a different language from the English I.L.P'ers. Whilst we were exposing the duplicity of the foreign policy which had led to the war and advocating a peace of no conquests and no indemnities, they were denouncing rent increases and profiteering and the speed-up and long hours of munition workers. We concentrated on peace. They concentrated on the class struggle.

Maxton was then making reputation in Glasgow. I must have met him at I.L.P. conferences before this, but my first personal recollection of him was at an open-air gathering which I addressed at Paisley. He came along at the end of the meeting and stood listening at the edge of the crowd. I remember his big black slouch hat, his black hair curving round from ear to jaw, his Indian-brown skin, his brilliant blue eyes and the glow of his cigarette.

The I.L.P. leaders in Glasgow were a remarkable group; I believe the way in which they took the leadership of the workers in their class struggles at this time is largely responsible for the much greater strength of the I.L.P. in Scotland than in England. They joined with others in forming the Clyde Workers' Committee, which carried on a vigorous campaign for working-class rights, including a forty-hour working week and Workshop Committees and shop stewards chosen by the workers. When Lloyd George took action against the leaders of this Committee, imprisoning John McLean and deporting from Glasgow Kirkwood, McManus, Tom Clark and others, Maxton urged the workers to down tools. "Not a blow should be struck on the Clyde until these men have been returned to their homes," he exclaimed. For this seditious utterance he was sentenced to one year, but even in prison his human qualities proved irrepressible—and irresistible. It was during a prison visit, despite the presence of a warder, that he became engaged to be married.

In England we failed to unite the anti-war struggle with the class-struggle sufficiently, with the result that we became isolated from the mass of the workers and too often tended to become bourgeois pacifist rather than working-class Socialist.

I can illustrate this clearly by contrasting with the remarkable group of Glasgow leaders the equally remarkable group which established the Union of Democratic Control in London. The U.D.C. was not linked organisationally with the I.L.P., but Ramsay MacDonald was its chairman and its pamphlets provided much of the ammunition for our anti-war propaganda. The U.D.C. was not even specifically anti-war. It set out to prepare public opinion for a democratic peace in which secret diplomacy should have no part. If you had entered a room in which the Glasgow group and the U.D.C. group were together, you could have distinguished them at once. The Glasgow group were not all working-class in the strict sense of the word, but all had a ruggedness and directness about them which marked them off from the bourgeoisie. The U.D.C. group, on the other hand, were bourgeois to their finger-tips. They were suave, gracious, cultured. They might have been lifted out of any gathering of the gentlemen of England.

I do not write this disparagingly, because finer men and women have never been associated than those who started the U.D.C. They included Charles P. Trevelyan, who had resigned his post as Under Secretary for Education when war broke out, a man of utter sincerity and almost boyish enthusiasm, frankness and trustfulness; Arthur Ponsonby, an equally fine type, whose character almost made one feel that aristocratic breeding was worth something; E. D. Morel, a tower of moral strength, fearless and undefeatable champion of the most forgotten sufferers from injustice (the freeing of the Congo slaves was his first "cause"); J. A. Hobson, a quiet literary intellectual who placed truth above every consideration; H. N. Brailsford, brilliant journalist, who resigned from the "Daily News" on the suffrage issue before the war; Mrs. H. M. Swanwick, wise, persuasive and cautious, yet holding fast to first principles; Lowes Dickinson, Cambridge Professor, a living proof that one historian could prefer integrity to the prostitution of facts for Government propaganda—these and others gathered round Ramsay MacDonald to stem the tide of war hysteria by reason and by taking the longer view.*

The intellectual honesty, courage and steadfastness of this group and the quality of their personalities were something

* Both J. A. Hobson and Mrs. Swanwick died while I was writing this book.

which perhaps only the isolation and persecution of war-time could have revealed. Many of them, with writers like Vernon Lee, Gilbert Cannan, Bertrand Russell and Edward Garnett (I laugh still when I think of his article on "The Liberals Who Lost Their Trousers") contributed to the "Labour Leader," and it was a great experience for a young man like myself to be associated with them. Nevertheless, they gave a wrong twist to the I.L.P. in England in war-time. We were not Revolutionary Socialists. We were democratic pacifists.

I had two literary heroes before the war—H. G. Wells and Bernard Shaw. Wells attracted me by his philosophical breadth and depth. Shaw was the great destroyer of idols. Gaudy hypocrisies burst and vanished at the touch of his rapier, one saw realities naked and learned not to be ashamed. When war came I was as disappointed by the one as I was pleased by the other. It would be unkind to remind readers to-day of all that Wells wrote during the war, but I had a feeling then that he was not happy about it. He wrote frequently to the "Labour Leader" and I can see his "copy" in my mind's eye now—his thin spidery but clear caligraphy, with after-thoughts inserted in circles and linked to their appropriate places like balloons on string. He wrote so often that I passed on one of his controversies to Clem Bundock to handle, whilst simultaneously I handled another. I don't know whether it was a compliment to me or to Clem when he refused to believe that Clement Bundock was not Fenner Brockway under another name.

Bernard Shaw was silent during the first few weeks of the war. Then it was announced that his view would be published as a supplement to the "New Statesman" under the title "Commonsense About The War." How eagerly we looked forward to it! Clem and I ordered an extra copy that week because neither of us could wait whilst the other read it. In a sentence, Shaw's view was that British policy had been just as infamous as German, but that now we were in the war we must fight it out. Clem, who saw things in black and white, was dissatisfied. I was relieved. I saw that Shaw's ruthless exposure of British Imperialist policy could be used with tremendous effect in our anti-war propaganda. Later Shaw wrote a preface to a pamphlet containing my speech at Manchester University when I debated with Professor Ramsay Muir.

He argued that my frank statement of the truth about British diplomacy was a service to the British cause, because it showed that we were not all liars or idiots; but about that estimate I did not worry. I was satisfied to get a Shaw preface to help secure the circulation of unpopular views.

During the first year of the war our isolation caused us to minimise differences in the I.L.P. As early as September, 1914, however, an incident arose which threatened to destroy our unity. MacDonald wrote a letter to a recruiting meeting at Leicester (he represented one of its divisions), which appeared to line him up with the Labour Party leaders whom we had denounced for going on recruiting platforms. He wrote that he was very sorry that he could not be at the meeting; that the war must be won; that the young men of England must settle the immediate issue; that the serious men of the Trade Union, Brotherhood and similar movements should face their duty—and so on and so on. I was present at the meeting of the National Council of the Party at Bingham Hotel, off Holborn (it was afterwards hit by a bomb)* when MacDonald was questioned about this letter. He simulated astonishment that anyone should misinterpret his words. He had said he was sorry he could not be at the meeting? Of course he could not; his convictions would not allow him. The war must be won and the young men must settle the issue? Well, was not that self-evident? But meantime, while they did their duty on the military front, we must be carrying out our task on the political front, which was to maintain the spirit of internationalism and to popularise the idea of just peace terms. MacDonald looked pained that anyone should have misunderstood the letter. I was mentally stunned. MacDonald's colleagues heard him with sceptical silence. I shall not forget W. C. Anderson's cynical smile.

Nevertheless, MacDonald's attitude during the war must be explained by something more than mere political opportunism. The persecution which he bore was too great for such an interpretation to be satisfactory. I was present with him at a meeting in the Corn Exchange, Leicester, when he was howled at by the very constituents who had previously hero-worshipped him. There were meetings, such as one at Cardiff, where he

*As it was in the last war.

was in physical danger from the angry mob. He was a proud man, accustomed to adulation; the isolation into which he was thrust, the boycott, personal as well as political, which he suffered from old friends, the despicable attacks made on him in the public press, required great moral courage to face. The meanest attack was the publication of his birth-certificate by "John Bull," then edited by Horatio Bottomley, criminal and patriot.· I saw the poster in Market Street, Manchester— "Ramsay MacDonald's Birth Certificate." I bought the paper, expecting to find "John Bull" making out that MacDonald was a German—no, the purpose was to reveal that he was an illegitimate child. One pitied the Editor who did not realise that the shame was his own and that MacDonald was to be honoured for having made good in Puritan Scotland despite this handicap. I heard MacDonald tell a small group of friends of the shock which he received on seeing this revelation. He was travelling to York for a speaking engagement. There was only one fellow-traveller in the carriage and he got out at Northallerton. He left a paper on the seat. MacDonald picked it up; it was the issue of "John Bull."

What is the explanation of MacDonald's attitude and of the public reaction to it? I give my interpretation of his conduct as I saw it at close quarters.

MacDonald was opposed to the policy of secret continental commitments which led Britain into the war. During the week-end prior to the outbreak of hostilities he found that large and influential bodies of opinion shared his view—Lloyd George, Sir John Simon, Lord Morley and John Burns in the Cabinet, a large part of the Liberal Party outside, the Free Church leaders and their considerable followers, organised Labour, powerful papers like the "Daily News and Leader," the "Manchester Guardian" and the "Daily Citizen" (the newly established Labour daily). He decided to place himself at the head of this Movement by his speech on August 3, *and failed to realise that by then the issue of continental commitments had been made irrelevant by the German threat to Belgium.* The issue had become the straight one—"Are you for war or against?"

Parliament and the country were irritated by MacDonald's speech. What he had intended as a rallying call to large sections of the nation became in effect a quibbling and pettifogging criticism. The main feature of the speech was an attack on Sir Edward Grey. That would have been understand-able if MacDonald had gone on to express direct opposition to the war, but instead came niggardly support of the war: "Tell us the country is in danger, and we will vote you all the money you require." One can imagine the reaction of the average patriotic Member: "Good God, man, of course the country is in danger!" The next day MacDonald found that his expected followers—Liberal, Free Church, Labour—had put their criticism of Sir Edward Grey in the background. Most of them came out for the war, and like all war supporters they resented MacDonald's attitude. The march of events had made obsolete the issue which separated them from the Government.

But the viciousness of the attack on MacDonald rallied the anti-war forces to him. He turned to the I.L.P. and its plat-form and press; it was his party. On the I.L.P. platform and in our press, however, he stated only a part of his view. The Party would not have tolerated support of the war; MacDonald therefore limited his speeches and writings to what it would support—denunciation of the foreign policy which had led to the war, a denunciation of the militarist spirit, a plea for the retention of the spirit of internationalism in preparation for the peace. These views he held sincerely.

Then another intention grew. Although the Liberal and Labour forces had deserted him at the beginning of the war, he anticipated that before the end they would regain political poise. They, like himself, would want a just peace without revenge. He had lost leadership at the beginning; he would prepare to recover it at the end. The Union of Democratic Control was formed of the Liberal elements which had stood by him. He developed the theory that while the soldiers were winning the war at the front he and his colleagues must win the peace at home. There were two fronts, military and political, and the fight must proceed on both.

But all the time MacDonald's mind was made uneasy by the storm of abuse which swept over him—and perhaps by his own conscience. If he really believed that the war must be won, was it not his duty to help by strengthening the military side, too? Anyone who reads his letter to the Leicester recruiting meeting can see this conflict in almost every sentence. Was there not some method by which he could break through the public hostility and carry conviction that he wanted the country to win and was prepared to take his part? His ill-fated attempt to join the Ambulance Corps in Belgium, when he was turned back by the military authorities as "unwanted," was an expression of this desire.

And there was a difficulty: every step he took in this direction would lose him the support of the only section of the public which was with him—the I.L.P. and the other anti-war elements. Thus MacDonald wavered indecisively from course to course. Rejected by those whose goodwill he wished to win, supported by those who thought his views other than they were, he never recovered an honest position throughout the war. He dared not disillusion his friends; he could not convince his enemies.

I write this estimate twenty years after the war. During the war itself we were too hotly engaged in the struggle to take part in heresy hunting within our own ranks. Anyone who was prepared to stand with us and bear all the unpopularity that that involved was certainly not against us. MacDonald was hissed and hounded from one end of the country to the other for his "opposition to the war." We rallied to him. In the inner circles of the Party we shook our heads and had our regrets, but the following day we would be on the platform with MacDonald again, going much further than he did, yet able to endorse the limited but necessary and valuable things which he said with such oratorical power.

C

Chapter Eight
EDITING IN DIFFICULTIES

We were, of course, always under the shadow of Government repression during the war years but, looking back, it is surprising how rarely the Defence of the Realm Act and the Sedition Acts were used. There were a few prosecutions, but there was comparatively little interference with our freedom of speech and writing until Conscription came into force in 1916.

So far as I can remember there were only two occasions when the "Labour Leader" was interfered with by the authorities while I was its editor (that is up to August, 1916). On one occasion our office and printing press were raided by the police, every cupboard and drawer searched, and the whole edition seized. The Public Prosecutor brought an action under D.O.R.A. for the destruction of the copies seized; it was the issue of August 5th, 1915, and the prosecution was based chiefly on an imaginative article by Isabel Sloan, which described how a British and German soldier killed each other in battle, but before dying realised that their experiences, their loves and ideals made them one.

I was taken aback when at the beginning of the proceedings the prosecuting counsel asked that the case should be heard *in camera*. Our barrister argued that no official secrets were involved, there was no suggestion that we had reported movements of troops or details of armament construction which might help the enemy; why then should the case be heard in secret? But his plea was in vain. The request of the prosecution was accepted and press and public left the court. The prosecuting counsel was Sir William Cobbett: a curious rôle for the bearer of such a name. I went into the witness-box, and enjoyed myself immensely. Platform experience in wartime, when one had to be careful and reasonable yet confident and unequivocal, was exactly the training required to meet the kind of questioning I had to face. At first the interrogation proceeded smoothly, but when Sir William failed to catch me out in any indiscretion he began to show irritation. He produced a bundle of newspaper cuttings of my speeches, in particular of the Marple meeting which had been broken up, and worked himself up into great patriotic fury. I retorted vigorously, and he then used phrases which seemed to me to overstep the mark. I turned in protest to the magistrate, who remarked that we were both tending to lose our tempers. That was enough—the newspaper cuttings were put aside and I was treated with respect. I think I held my own to the end. Anyhow, to our surprise, we won the case. The Court found that there was nothing in the issue of the "Labour Leader" to justify destruction and ordered that all copies should be returned. I am not sure that the judgment was a political compliment—if we were not dangerous to the Government, we were failing in our duty—but our satisfaction can be imagined, and also our smiles when the police vans arrived with our returned property.

On the second occasion the police appeared just as the paper was going to press. They demanded the page proofs and took them away to Salford Police Station. Clem Bundock and I accompanied the police, Clem with notebook and sharpened pencil so that he could report the interview. They must have been a little perplexed by the weak opposition I put up when they proposed that any item should be cut out. The truth was that, once I realised they did not intend to suppress the issue as a whole, I hoped eagerly they would censor some of it. I knew that if we appeared with blank spaces and a note to the effect that the matter had been censored by the police, we should get valuable publicity. As they passed column after column and page after page, I feared that we were to be denied this advantage. Then they fastened on a letter from Clive Bell. It was not particularly provocative, but they held that it might prejudice recruiting and ordered that it should be taken out. Going over the pages again they found an advertisement of a book by Clive Bell. If his short letter were prejudicial to recruiting, what would be the effect of a whole book? I was ordered to take out the advertisement. We returned well pleased with ourselves, and the next day circularised the daily press. Mr. Scott, of the "Manchester Guardian," sent round for copies of the suppressed items and wrote a strong leading article against police censorship. The matter was raised in Parliament and at every I.L.P. meeting throughout the country, the new threat to liberty was denounced. We certainly got our publicity all right, and had to print a second edition.

The police also raided our Party bookshops both in Manchester and London, taking away lorry loads of anti-war literature. Among the confiscated books was my one-act play, "The Devil's Business," exposing the international armaments ring. In Manchester the police returned all copies of this play as unobjectionable. In London they gave me an opportunity to be represented at the Mansion House to show cause why the copies seized should not be destroyed. Although I was legally represented, I lost the case. My solicitors advised that I should appeal. My difficulty was that I had no money to meet the costs, but when I wrote to a number of friends they contributed generously. One of the refusals was from Mr. Bernard Shaw. He wrote: —

Dear Mr. Fenner Brockway,

I do not like to leave your letter unanswered, though I have no hope of anyone but the solicitors getting anything out of an appeal. I have refused to help Norman* because my experience is that of all useless ways of wasting money the most useless is trying to fight the Government on its own ground in the law courts. (Under the Defence of the Realm Act, the Government can do what it likes.) When Norman procured a decision that the Act gave the magistrate no power to try the case in camera, all the consolation he got was a further judicial decision that the proceedings in camera were not a trial. Even when there is no way out for the Government—as when they shot their first spy and then found that the shooting was *ultra vires*—nothing happened except that they passed an amending Act to put themselves in order next time.

I think it would be wiser to avail yourself of Justice Avory's dictum that there was no trial (in which case there can, I suppose, be no contempt of court in disregarding the decision) and reprint "The Devil's Business" as if nothing had happened. It would not cost more than an appeal, which might produce a decision that would make such a proceeding very dangerous.

I think it would be wisest to drop the business for the present. A decision in your favour would not re-establish liberty: the military authorities might seize the book again next day

---

* With great ingenuity C. H. Norman took the case of his proscribed pamphlet from court to court, but finally without avail.

if they pleased. For that matter, they might shoot you quite privately, without informing your friends or mentioning your name. And at the present pass the publication of the facts can do no good. The British Empire has just been handsomely beaten and driven into the sea by the Ottoman Empire; and at such moments jobbery scandals are not opportune: it is more important to get plenty of munitions than to bother about the shareholders who are making money out of them.

The day of reckoning for the jobbery will come when the fighting is over, and the bill comes in. If I were you I should wait until then. You cannot be too careful to do nothing discouraging in the meantime.

Yours faithfully,

G. BERNARD SHAW.

Mr. Shaw proved right. Although I was well served in the Appeal Court by Mr. Harold Morris, a rising young barrister, my appeal was dismissed.

We thus had the curious position that in Manchester "The Devil's Business" had been O.K'd by the police, while in London it had been condemned to destructon. To have it on your shelves in London was an offence, whilst in Manchester it could be sold publicly, and in fact was sold. Towards the end of the war Philip Snowden quoted this case in a Parliamentary speech as an instance of the stupidity of the censorship. Until then we kept the matter quiet so as not to interfere with the Manchester sale.

There was one personal anxiety which weighed on us during the summer of 1915: the health of our leader, Keir Hardie. I had been with him at the I.L.P. Annual Conference held in Norwich at Easter. At the last moment the letting of the hall was cancelled, but we were provided with accommodation in a large Primitive Methodist Church, the minister of which was a pacifist. On the Sunday evening no hall was available for a public demonstration and we had to hold our meeting in the I.L.P. Club. It was here that I heard Hardie's voice for the last time.

At night Norwich was pitch black; since it was a town near the East Coast not a light was to be seen through the house windows or in the streets.* As I approached the I.L.P. Club I

* This was exceptional: no black-out was applied generally in the last war.

Inside the Left

saw some ghostly white figures grouped together. Suddenly the strains of "O God, our Help in Ages Past" rose from them. The vicar had brought his choir to sing outside the hall in protest against the holding of an anti-war meeting.

Hardie made this incident the opening theme of his speech. The little hall was crowded to suffocation and the lights were dimmed. Hardie's bushy white hair and his white beard shone out in the darkness with almost phosphorescent radiance. His head was held high, defiantly; his voice was strong and deep. His speech was the most uncompromising denunciation of war I had heard from him. Mass murder he called it, and the statesmen and parsons and Labour leaders who appealed for recruits were guilty of incitement to murder. His voice nearly broke when he spoke of the tragedy of Socialists murdering each other, but then he spoke confidently of the rebuilding of the International Socialist movement and of the final triumph of Socialism and the ending of war for all time.

Having heard this speech my dismay can be understood when I read articles in the I.L.P. paper at Merthyr, Hardie's Parliamentary seat, which suggested that even he was wavering. I learned that he was ill. "I cannot fight this war as I fought the Boer war" he had said at the meeting of the National Council of the Party in August, 1914. He was too weak physically to do it, and the disappointment and horror of the war, which he felt intensely, made him still weaker. Trouble left by an attack of appendicitis recurred, and it became aggravated by a chill caught when walking one evening in the garden of his home in Old Cumnock, in Ayrshire. On September 26th, 1915, he died.

I will not attempt to pay a tribute to him. He was the real founder and father of the Socialist movement in Britain and he was worthy of the role. To me he showed a personal kindness which meant much in the choice of the path which I was to tread. To thousands of workers, and particularly to the members of the I.L.P., he was leader in the march towards the new society where the barbarities of poverty and war will be ended. I did not go to the cremation at Glasgow; I was busy trying to produce a memorial issue of the "Labour Leader" which should fit the occasion. I heard that the ceremony was not worthy of him, but the real tribute of the workers, above all of the Glasgow workers, was given in the crowded St. Andrew's Hall the following Sunday evening. Ramsay MacDonald spoke and many of those who heard him say that his oration rose to heights greater than they had ever known in human utterances. If there were doubts about MacDonald before in the minds of Scottish Socialists, this speech removed them.

The extraordinary loyalty of Glasgow to MacDonald, which was responsible for his election to the leadership of the Parliamentary Labour Party in 1921, and was never dispelled until the betrayal of the workers by the second Labour Government, had its roots in this speech more than in anything else.

Chapter Nine
ORGANISING WAR RESISTERS

The Youth Movement is generally considered to date from after the war. Its beginnings are interpreted as a revolt by the younger generation against the civilisation bequeathed to them by their war-making elders. In Britain that revolt began during the war. Until its later stages, the movement of resistance to Conscription was almost entirely organised by young men under twenty-five years of age. Indeed, during 1914 and the earlier part of 1915, the older leaders even in the I.L.P. scouted the idea that Conscription would come. It was in November, 1914, that my wife (we had married a fortnight after the outbreak of war) made the proposal that those who intended to refuse military service should band themselves together, and we issued an invitation to prospective resisters to join a "No-Conscription Fellowship." Lilla acted as the provisional secretary and our cottage in Derbyshire was the headquarters. We had little idea then of how big the organisation would become or of the sort of conflict in which it was destined to take part.

One of the earliest members was Clifford Allen, later Lord Allen of Hurtwood. I first met Allen when travelling to London after the Labour Party Conference in 1913. Four of us had a meal together in the dining car—Henry Slesser, his wife Margaret, Allen and myself. I was a little overwhelmed by them; they were immaculately dressed, their manners perfect, their conversation highbrow and witty. I was fascinated by Allen. In physique he was frail and his charm had an almost feminine quality, but never had I met a man with a keener brain, or more confident decision. He was tall, slight and bent of shoulder; his features were clear-cut and classic, but his skin was delicate like that of a child; his shining brown hair was waved, his large brown eyes had sympathy in them and also a suggestion of suffering. His voice was rich and deep, surprisingly so for such a slight physique. He was dressed like a young barrister, with Gladstone collar and large black tie. He was very different from the members of the I.L.P. among whom I usually moved—textile workers, engineers, miners,—yet I recognised him at once as a potential leader; his personality was so dominating, his mind so clear.

Allen became the chairman of the No-Conscription Fellowship. Three of the members of the first committee served throughout the struggle—Clifford Allen, C. H. Norman, and myself as secretary. Norman was also an unusual man. He had become known by sensational articles exposing hidden scandals behind the war. There was the atmosphere of conspiracy about him; some even suspected that he was a Scotland Yard agent, but that was soon disproved by his own courage. He was a startling and provocative individualist, with ideas and proposals which took away our breath.

Our house in Derbyshire remained the headquarters of the N.C.F. until the beginning of 1915, when the membership had grown so large that it became necessary to open an office in London. In November we held our first national convention in the Memorial Hall. Lord Derby was then conducting his national recruiting campaign; those who "attested" were supplied with khaki armlets, and young women were presenting white feathers to young men in the streets who did not wear them. Our Convention met with a storm of abuse from the press. I suppose the editors thought they would kill us with contempt by printing ghastly pictures of the "platform," with captions referring to us as "cowards," "Hun-lovers," "The save-their-skins-brigade," and "The won't-fight-funks," but the effect was exactly the opposite. Applications for membership overwhelmed us and we had to appoint a full-time secretary and staff. The committee elected by this convention had one veteran—Edward Grubb, the treasurer. He was a lovable Quaker, admired widely for his scholarship and revered by all who knew him for the nobility of his character. We came to regard him as the father of the movement, and his wisdom, strength and calm courage exerted a great influence on us.*

Except for Edward Grubb, we were all youngsters. There was Barratt Brown, now Principal of Ruskin College, Oxford, then on the staff of Woodbrooke College, Birmingham. My chief memory of him is of a boyish mischievousness, which he showed even at the most anxious moments. Another member was Morgan Jones, a Welsh school-teacher, afterwards

* Edward Grubb died early in 1939; few men can have been more loved and respected.

to become a Junior Minister in the Labour Government of 1929-31.* Philip Snowden's Parliamentary Secretary in the 1929-31 Government was also a member—James H. Hudson, at that time a leader of the Lancashire I.L.P., the most pugilistic of pacifists. A different type was Will Chamberlain, a Tolstoyan despite his red Kaiser-like moustache; he is now chief of the Press Department of the Labour Party. For a time James Maxton served as the Scottish member of the Committee, but he was not at home among us. We were too removed from the class fight.

The N.C.F. attracted to itself some devoted and brilliant associates. Among these was Bertrand Russell, the philosopher and mathematician, who was dismissed from his academic post at Cambridge University because of his activities on our behalf. Russell was delightful. He worked with unquenchable enthusiasm, but his humour and simple comradeship are what I most remember. Although an heir to an earldom, he was very hard up during this period and arrived late for committees more than once because he hadn't any coppers to pay for a bus—but perhaps this was due to his forgetfulness of mundane things, or, more likely, because he had emptied his pocket for some down-and-out. He was full of a spirit of fun, like some irrepressible but clever Puck.

Another brilliant collaborator was Catherine Marshall, who had learned all there was to know about political strategy as the Parliamentary Secretary of the National-Union of Women's Suffrage Societies. She became our political secretary. She organised the Record Department, which had such full facts about every resister and what camp or prison he was in, that the War Office made a practice of ringing her up to obtain information for persistent M.P.s—not knowing that it was Catherine Marshall who had inspired the M.P.s to put their questions with the object of bringing out publicly the information which she then proceeded to supply for the War Minister's answers! It was she who organised the influential campaign on behalf of the C.O.'s in prison towards the end of the war, winning the support of Lords, Archbishops and literary men to such a degree that the Government became uneasy about the

* Morgan Jones died in 1939 after serving on a Government Commission to the West Indies.

effect of the agitation upon the popularity of the war itself. All the time Catherine Marshall maintained a contact with individual resisters and their families in a way which made us feel that she was our personal friend.

Although the N.C.F. was based on the principle of the "sacredness of human life" its membership extended beyond absolute pacifists. In its branches, scattered throughout the country, were Socialists, Anarchists, Quakers, and other religious objectors, and it was remarkable how well they pulled together. From the first, however, the movement was much more than an expression of personal objection to military service; it was political. When the Military Service Bill was introduced, the organisation conducted a tremendous campaign of opposition. Over a million leaflets were distributed, hundreds of meetings were held, M.P.s were besieged with communications and deputations, and the Political Committee watched every stage of the Parliamentary proceedings, constantly feeding the opponents of the measure with material for their case.

My time and interest were inevitably concentrated upon this struggle, but at the beginning I continued to edit the "Labour Leader" and to live in Derbyshire. Later, after Conscription was introduced, I secured leave of absence in order to give my full time to the work. The publication of the Regulations of the Military Service Act decided me on this course; they exempted editors from service. After the leadership which I had given to the resisters, I felt that I must go through with it on the same basis as the other members. I moved to London and devoted myself wholly to the resistance movement.

In April, 1916, just as the first arrests were taking place (news of them arrived dramatically during the proceedings), we held the second National Convention of the N.C.F. It met in Devonshire House, then the headquarters of the Society of Friends in Bishopsgate. The old, vast, dim building was crowded. On the way to the convention I saw a "John Bull" poster: "Take him to the Tower!" Someone handed me the paper; there was a full page article demanding my arrest and execution!

The patriotic press was of course furious that the convention should be held at all. Some Jingoes got hold of a group of sailors and incited them to make an attack on the building. The iron gate at the entrance was locked, but two or three of them succeeded in climbing it. Inside, instead of fists, friendly hands were extended to them. They stood perplexed, cut off from their supporters, surrounded by the hated "Pro-Germans," yet finding them the best of good fellows. The sailors stayed to take tea with the stewards, and left with a very different idea about "conchies."

Clifford Allen, who was in the chair, inspired a unique gesture. When the building was being stormed outside he did not wish to incite further attack by the noise of our cheering. He therefore asked that enthusiasm should be expressed silently, and with absolute discipline the crowded audience responded. No one who was present will readily forget the effect of this. When Philip Snowden, Dr. John Clifford and Bertrand Russell rose to speak they were received with thousands of fluttering handkerchiefs, making the low sound of rising and falling wind, but with no other sound whatsoever. At no other meeting have I witnessed such a thing.

The N.C.F. was never actually suppressed, but in readiness we had a duplicate organisation throughout the country, and it proved necessary because of the progressive arrest of those of our members who were of military age. And if our organisation was not itself declared illegal, many of its activities were, chief among them the publication of our weekly newspaper "The Tribunal." One of its series of editors was Bernard Boothroyd, famous later as "Yaffle" of the "New Leader" and "Reynolds Weekly." The police came to the offices one day to find it occupied by a charming young lady. They left without their man, though they got him later. The young lady was "Yaffle."

The National Labour Press, owned by the I.L.P., was dismantled for producing "The Tribunal." Then a sympathetic printer, S. H. Street, took on the job, only to have his press converted into scrap iron. When the detectives found this press they declared triumphantly—"We have done for you this time,"—but three days later the "Tribunal" appeared again. We had made preparations for this situation. A small hand press had been bought and stocks of paper were deposited in various safe quarters. Two skilled comrades gave their whole time to the task, sometimes shutting themselves up in a house for days on end and moving from place to place whenever there was the least suspicion that the whereabouts of the press might have become known. Scotland Yard searched hundreds of houses, but without avail. They arrested Joan Beauchamp, whose imprint appeared on each issue, and she received a sentence of £200 fine or 51 days' imprisonment, but she won her case on appeal because the judge ruled that since the prosecution contended that her name was used to hide the identity of the real printer, she could not be held guilty for another's offence! Joan was sent to prison, however. The judge asked her the name and address of the printer and, when she refused to tell, sentenced her for "contempt of court" to remain in custody at the court's pleasure. For ten days they kept her in the cells, but she would not open her lips and, defeated, the court released her.

As early as September, 1915, the suppression of the N.C.F. was considered. Our comings and goings used to be watched carefully by plain-clothes policemen, and often at the last minute the venue of a committee would be changed because our scouts would find the meeting place under observation. One night, when arrests seemed imminent and six detectives were in the street, we crowded three taxi-cabs to the home of Earl Russell in Gordon Square, Bertrand gleefully wondering what his absent brother would say if we were arrested on his premises.

On one occasion, owing to a terrifying mistake on my part, the entire plans of our "underground" organisation were within a hair's breadth of falling into the hands of the police; indeed, they were actually in their hands, and then returned innocently to us! Our committee was meeting over Saturday and Sunday in London. After the Saturday session, which continued as usual late into the night, Allen and I went by taxi to his flat—and I left my bag, containing the full details of our duplicate organisation, in the cab! Never have I felt more humiliated than when reporting this disaster to the committee the following morning; as they listened, the members sat back stunned into silence. The practice was for taxi-men to hand over lost bags to the nearest police station, to be forwarded to a central depot at Scotland Yard where an inventory of the contents was taken; the chances were a hundred to one that the police, at either the local station or the central depot, would read our incriminating documents.

"Well," said Bertrand Russell, with a fatalistic chuckle, "I move that we adjourn to Scotland Yard—we may as well save the police the trouble of arresting us." But Catherine Marshall was equal to the occasion. Her brother was a high official of Scotland Yard. She telephoned him, describing the plight of a young country friend who had left his bag in a taxi and was returning to his Derbyshire home that night: was there any method by which he could recover it in time for his journey? Well, replied the brother, it was very irregular, but he would give Scotland Yard instructions to 'phone the police stations in London and if the bag had been handed in anywhere her friend could go there and collect it.

At last the telephone bell rang. Scotland Yard speaking: the bag was at Lambeth Police Station; if Miss Marshall would send someone with written authority, it would be handed over. We sighed relief, but were not yet out of the wood. The chances were still great that the police at Lambeth would examine the bag, and it was thought wiser not to send me lest I should be arrested on the spot. Violet Tillard went—about half-an-hour later her voice was heard over the 'phone saying that she had got the bag and the documents were intact!

My first taste of imprisonment was in July, 1916. The Government took proceedings under D.O.R.A. against the members of the National Committee of the N.C.F. for a leaflet issued against the Conscription Act. We were tried at the Mansion House and on appeal at the Guildhall. The only member not charged was Clifford Allen, apparently on the ground that he was to be proceeded against separately under the Military Service Act.* It was agreed to rely on two witnesses—the Rev. Leyton Richards, later well known as minister of Carr's Lane, Birmingham, one of Nonconformity's

---

* During the week when I corrected the typescript of this chapter news came of the death of Allen from tuberculosis in Switzerland. In his later years he followed a political course with which I disagreed, but until the end he showed the same courage. He travelled over Europe trying to find the basis of peace. Before his last journey he was told that the inclement weather might mean his death, but he felt the crisis of war so immediate that he went. The journey did mean his death. The disease was driven from lungs to stomach and he did not recover.

cathedrals, and myself. The Public Prosecutor, Sir Archibald Bodkin, and Mr. R. D. Muir, were the Prosecuting Counsel; Lord Derby gave evidence against us. I found Sir Archibald easy to face. He was of the loud-voiced, blustering, bullying type and by keeping one's head and temper it was not difficult to score off him. Mr. Muir's methods were exactly the opposite. He was quiet and tricky and at every question one had to think, "What is he getting at? What is the next question going to be?"

Bodkin was an erratic fast bowler, Muir a googly bowler. Allen afterwards applied cricket terminology to our appearance in the witness box. He said that I was the careful first-wicket batsman, blocking every straight ball, breaking the heart of the other side by an impenetrable defence, whilst. Leyton Richards went in and hit out at every ball on all sides of the wicket, a short but exhilarating innings. Richards certainly hit out. Sir Archibald was unwise enough to quote Bible texts, which Leyton promptly completed with devastating effect. We were sentenced to fines of £100 each or two months' imprisonment. The Committee decided to pay the fines in the cases of Edward Grubb and Leyton Richards, but on the appointed day in July the rest of us gave ourselves up at the Mansion House to fulfil the two months' sentence at Pentonville Prison.

We were taken to Pentonville in one of the old horse-drawn Black Marias. Tiny little boxes lined its sides, with larger boxes at the far end. We were all locked in, but we could see and hear each other through grilles. In the passage between the boxes a policeman sat. I served only ten days; the N.C.F. Committee had decided that if Allen were arrested my fine should be paid so that I could direct the organisation. I won't describe general prison experiences until I come to my longer sentences, but I had one unforgettable experience which was peculiar to Pentonville. Sir Roger Casement was in the prison under sentence of death for high treason. My Irish readers need not be told that after a distinguished career in the Consular Service, where he had won fame particularly by his exposure of the cruelties practised on natives by a British rubber company in Putamayo, Sir Roger espoused the cause of Irish Independence during the war, went to the length of crossing to Germany with the object of persuading Irish prisoners to fight against Britain, and then attempted to land in Ireland with munitions. The ship was sunk and Sir Roger taken prisoner.

The one topic of conversation among the prisoners in Pentonville was: Will they hang Casement? I say "topic of conversation" though the prison rules did not permit conversation, because I worked in a shop with an easy-going warder who permitted quiet talking on the understanding that we were all silent when a senior officer appeared. The general view was that Casement would not be hanged. "Big bugs" never were. News passed round that certain prisoners had been given the duty of cleaning the gallows, but still there was scepticism. They wouldn't hang a man who had been presented with a gold medal by Queen Victoria and had been knighted by King Edward. I was shocked by the way with which the chances of the execution were discussed as though it were a sporting event, but as the day approached there was a change. Both prisoners and warders showed signs of tension; prisoners became restless and undisciplined, warders became ill-tempered and bullying. One afternoon I was transferred to a cell on the ground floor on the opposite side of the landing. As soon as I had arranged my things and the warder had locked the door on me, I climbed on a stool and looked out of the window. I was delighted. Pentonville is the drabbest of prisons; everything is dusty grey. Yet here I looked out on a charming little garden, with a green lawn and narrow paths between flower-beds rich with yellow, red and blue. Later that evening I heard steps outside. Cautiously I stepped up on my stool. Almost within reach of my arm was a man, his skin sun-browned, a rough black beard hiding his jaws and chin, his features rugged and strong like a gypsy-king's. Over the garden the sun was setting. The sky was golden red and everything was illuminated by it, so that the green of the lawn and the colours of the flowers shone radiantly. The man looked to the setting sun, and he was lost within it; there was more than yearning in his eyes, they had the calmness of eternity in them as though his yearning had been satisfied. For a moment or two I stood watching him, unable to take my eyes from him, yet a little ashamed to continue watching because I felt I was witnessing something

intensely intimate. Then a voice spoke, kindly and reluctantly:
"It is time to go in, Sir Roger." A warder was at the door with
keys in his hand; another warder stood on the path beyond the
man. I got down from the stool and heard the door clang and
the key turned.

That evening I was liberated. Will Chamberlain tells how
the warder who came to take me from my cell was surprised
that I exclaimed "damn!" when he told me I was to go out.
"The first bloke I've known who didn't want to get out of here,"
he said. Will interpreted my disinclination as unwillingness to
leave my four comrades to serve out their sentences whilst I
had freedom. It was partly that; it was also partly annoyance
that the N.C.F. would have to pay the fine of £100 to get me
released, and I did not think anything I could do justified that
payment. But beyond either of these reasons was one which I
have never acknowledged: a desire to remain near Sir Roger
Casement until his end. I realise that this desire had no
rational basis: but during those moments when he had looked
into the sun I had become very close to him. I did not wish to
leave him.

The struggle against conscription was not confined to the law
affecting British citizens. Residents from the allied countries
were given the alternative of joining the British forces or being
deported to their countries of origin, and many of them
resisted. This particularly affected Russian Socialists who were
not prepared to fight for Tsarist Russia, and they formed a
Russian Anti-Conscription League of those "who cannot participate in an Imperialist War, considering it contrary to the
principles of the international solidarity of Labour." The
organisers came to me for help, and I put at their disposal all
the political and organisational resources of the N.C.F. Mr.
Maisky, the present Soviet Ambassador in Britain, and Mr.
Chicherine, afterwards Soviet Commissar for Foreign Affairs,
were among the organisers of this League. Mr. Chicherine
used to write long and almost undecipherable letters to the
"Labour Leader" in purple ink. Clem Bundock and I
despaired when we saw his envelopes. "Another letter from
Glycerine" would be our comment. Both Maisky and
Chicherine were then in desperate circumstances. It never

crossed our minds that they would later become prominent representatives of the Russian Government.

We also gave a hand to the Irish opponents of Conscription. Although Ireland was included in the Conscription scheme passed by the British Parliament in 1916, no attempt was made to impose it until 1918. Then the British Capitalist press began to agitate, and a day was fixed for the inauguration of Irish compulsory service. How should the Irish people resist? They sent representatives to England to consult N.C.F. representatives. I was in prison by this time, but I heard how the meeting took place in the Lake district (at the lovely home of Catherine Marshall on Lake Derwentwater, I suspect) and how the Irish representatives were convinced that a demonstration general strike was the most effective method. On the day when Conscription was imposed in Ireland, no work was done over the greater part of the island. In Dublin and the Southern Counties no work was done at all; I heard afterwards from journalists how they had to get their own meals in the hotels. Even in the North the strike was remarkably extensive, despite the boasted patriotism of Ulster. In face of this united demonstration, the British Government never dared to apply compulsory service to Ireland.

Chapter Ten
RESISTING IN THE ARMY

It was not until the end of November, 1916, that I was arrested under the Military Service Act. By the Local and Appeal Tribunals I had been granted exemption from military service on condition that I would do "work of national importance." My case (though this was rare) was sent on to the Central Tribunal, which referred me to still another committee, generally known as the Pelham Committee, for the purpose of arranging what work I should do as a condition of exemption. Again I refused such exemption, though it was difficult to reject the suggestion of Mr. T. Edmund Harvey, the Quaker M.P., that I should regard my work for peace as work of national importance within the meaning of the Act.

Before coming to the story of my arrest I must tell of the critical days which decided whether "conscientious objectors" should be shot. There were officials at the War Office who thought they could break the C.O. movement in its early stages by executing a batch of resisters as an example, but they were in the difficulty that soldiers could be sentenced to death for refusing military orders only if they were at the Front. Despite promises in Parliament, they decided to rush thirty-seven men from barracks at Harwich, Richmond (Yorks.) and Seaford to France. No doubt they hoped they would get the men away secretly, but the N.C.F. system of communications was too complete to allow that. News came first that our men at Harwich were in irons at Landguard Fort. A Quaker chaplain was hurried down and found that they had left for France. Even before his wire arrived, news was received that they were on the way to Southampton to be shipped; one of the men threw a letter out of the train as it was passing through a London suburb and it reached us. The lives of these men were probably saved by an outbreak of measles in the corps at Southampton. The epidemic caused a brief delay, and the delay gave us time to exert political and press influence.

Catherine Marshall organised an influential deputation to the Prime Minister and somehow got Mr. Asquith to receive it. I went off post-haste to the north to appeal to the Editor of the "Manchester Guardian" (one of the few papers in Britain which retained elements of liberalism) to take up the matter.

I saw Mr. H. Sidebotham (afterwards to become famous as "A Student of War," "A Student of Politics" and "Scrutator"), then its chief leading article writer. He gave us an excellent first leader.* Mr. Asquith expressed consternation that the military authorities should have defied the pledges given in Parliament and immediately sent a telegram to Southampton forbidding the transference of the thirty-seven men to France. The reply came that they had already gone. Despite the epidemic of measles, they had been separated from the rest of the corps and shipped to Le Havre—evidence of the determination of the military to rush through a court-martial at the front.

In France the men were separated. Seventeen were taken to Cinder City and here, alone in the British Expeditionary Force, they carried on their resistance. They were handcuffed to poles, subjected to "crucifixion" (ankles and wrists tied to a cross), put on bread and water diet, and confined in dark and crowded punishment cells. Still they stood out. Then they were taken to the front and court-martialled for maintaining resistance. In due course they were paraded before thousands of soldiers, who were marshalled in serried rows three sides of a square to hear their sentences read out. I quote from the diary of one of them: —

"As I stepped forward I caught a glimpse of my paper as it was handed to the Adjutant. Printed at the top in large red letters, and doubly underlined, was the word 'Death' . . . I can hardly analyse the thoughts that flashed through my mind as I caught sight of the word. They could certainly not be described as an emotion. I had faced the possibility of a death sentence before and now accepted the fact almost without concern, whilst my mind was occupied mechanically and dispassionately with considering the immediate practical effects. It would be a great trial for Mother. My sister would have to leave school. People in England would make a great fuss . . . 'Private ——— No.—— of the 2nd Eastern Company N.C.C., tried by Field Court Martial for disobedience whilst undergoing field punishment. Sentenced to death by being shot'— (Here a pause)—'Confirmed by General Sir Douglas Haig'—(a longer pause)—'and commuted to ten years' penal servitude.' . . . So it was not so after all!"

* Mr. H. Sidebotham died in March, 1940.

Thirty men were sentenced to ten years' penal servitude. They went to the convict prisons and were thus isolated from the rest of us. They served until six months after the Armistice—rather more than three years.

When my turn for joining the actual resisters came, I received the first news of impending arrest from the landlady of my London lodgings. She reported that the police had been for me; I wrote them immediately making an appointment at the N.C.F. Head Office a week later. Then I went into the country to finish a book which I was writing on "Socialism for Pacifists." When the day came the police took me to Bow Street Police Station and I was locked in a cell to await trial next morning. It contained a low broad wooden shelf, to serve as a bed, and a w.c.—nothing else. I stretched myself out on the wooden bed and read a book which my friend, Chris Massie, had written about his experiences in the army. I knew that Chris had gone into the army from exactly the same motives that had led me to refuse—in order to end war—and I was so moved by his book that there and then I wrote him a letter. The cell door opened and a policeman brought in a tray laden with a sumptuous tea; my friends outside had done me well. He also brought in two blankets and early I stretched myself on the bed board to get what sleep I could.* I did not feel like facing a trial next morning, but I was allowed out of the cell for a wash and shave in the passage, and when I was taken into court my spirits rose to the occasion. The court was crowded with my friends; their smiles were a tonic. The magistrate was Mr. Graham Campbell. Inevitably the judgment came that I was to be fined £2 and handed over to the military authorities. I don't know whether the fine was ever paid. It was to be deducted from my military pay—and I never had any!

I was put in charge of a military escort of two—an earnest-minded lance-corporal who had been a clerk, and a private who

---

* Only at this point I remember that I had been arrested under the Military Service Act before this. I recollect it because the "bed" in the Glasgow cell was even harder than at Bow Street. Walter Ayles, J. H. Hudson and I had gone to Glasgow to address a conference. The military and police arrived, arrested us, and took us to the Police Station cells. The beds in those cells consisted of a slab of raised sandstone with a ridge to serve as pillow. I was released, so did not have to spend the night on a stone couch, but I have often wondered if Glasgow Police Stations still have those barbarous beds. How can any prisoner be fit to face trial next morning after spending aching hours stretched on stone?

had been a navvy. They were to take me to the barracks at Scotland Yard, less than a mile away. An idea occurred to me. "Is there any reason why you should not be my guest at lunch before reporting at the barracks?" I asked the lance-corporal. He hesitated. "Well, it's irregular, but I think we could do it." I led my escort to the Strand Corner House and we descended to what was then the Mirror Hall. The walls shone brilliantly with the gold frames of the mirrors. "Gaw-blimey," exclaimed the navvy private, looking round him with amazement. "Wish I 'ad this job every day. It's my birfday. Best birfday party ever I 'ad." He had beefsteak, boiled potatoes, brussels sprouts, carrots, apple pie and a pint of beer. We let him get on with it, whilst I talked in freedom to the N.C.F. staff for the last time. They left me at the corner of Whitehall. At the barracks' entrance I saw two N.C.F. pickets on duty, but I showed no sign of recognition lest they should be arrested as loiterers or on some other convenient charge.

I was put in the Guard Room, large and bare, was taken before an officer and questioned, and then taken under escort to the Tower of London. So was I to be confined in the Tower after all! Perhaps the editor of "John Bull" would get some satisfaction from this, even if I were not shot.

At the gateway there were two more N.C.F. pickets who smiled a careful recognition. A sergeant took me to the guard room. It was a large, dim, white-washed dungeon, with a heavily-barred and opaque window. Along one side was a sloping wooden stage with a ridge its full length by the wall; this I learned was the communal bed. Otherwise there was no furniture. There were about twenty prisoners, half a dozen of them in civilian clothes; the latter were conchies and welcomed me excitedly. I greeted the soldiers also, to be met with sullen looks and the remark "Another bloody coward" from one of them, evidently their spokesman.

The door opened and the sergeant shouted "Fetch in your biscuits." Supper? No, I found that the biscuits were our mattresses. Three made one bed, and they were dotted with holes like giant dog biscuits. The mattresses covered the full length of the platform bed and, following the example of the soldiers we overlapped our blankets so that it became in fact a communal bed, with twenty men lying in a row. We had hardly got to sleep when the sergeant entered and ordered my fellow conchies to get up and dress; their escort had arrived to conduct them to their camp. I wished them "Good luck" and settled down to sleep again. But that was not to be for a long time. The spokesman of the soldiers stood at my feet and cursed me in the vilest language I had yet heard. The other soldiers gathered round. They all began cursing me with rising voices and their attitude became threatening. I wondered what was coming. Then the spy-hole on the door clicked and the sergeant's voice commanded silence and "Get back to your beds." The soldiers went back, but continued to mutter imprecations. It was hours before I slept. Despite all my resolution my nerves were on edge and I could not discipline my brain. The future did not look pleasant.

In the morning the soldiers boycotted me. I ate my three slabs of bread and scrape and drank my mug of strong tea alone. We were allowed to receive letters and the post brought me a copy of the evening paper of the previous day with a report of the trial. I stood by the wall near the window reading it. The door opened and the sergeant and a private entered, accompanied by an officer. The soldiers leaped to attention in a row. I went on reading the paper. "You, there," shouted the officer. "Fall in. You're in the army now." I folded the paper and walked leisurely across the room until I was within arm's reach of the officer. Then I sat down on the bed and crossed my legs. My action was perhaps provocative, but my voice was courteous. "I am sorry, sir," I said. "I mean no discourtesy to you, but I am not prepared to obey any military order." "Then you'll be put in the cells," barked the officer. After asking formally whether there were "any complaints" and receiving a chorus of "No, Sir" from the line of soldiers, the officer and his companions disappeared.

I did not anticipate the scene which followed. The soldiers gathered round me laughing. "Never seen anything like it!" "Told the Colonel off, proper." "'E's not a coward, any'ow." In a moment I had become a hero.

When the sergeant next opened the door to tell me to "pack up" because my escort had come to conduct me to camp, I was standing in the middle of the group of soldiers explaining why I was a conchie and they were listening eagerly. Some of them were hearing the socialist case against war for the first time. One of them asked me for the evening paper I had received because it contained a photograph of me leaving the police court.

My escort (composed of a sergeant and a private) were friendly. When we got out of sight of the Tower Gates, they allowed the N.C.F. picket to speak to me and told me they were taking me to Chester via Euston. "Any reason why my wife and a friend shouldn't join us for lunch at Euston?" I asked the sergeant. "They're welcome," said the sergeant. The picket 'phoned the Head Office of the N.C.F. whilst I bought the escort some cigarettes. At Euston my wife informed me that she was travelling to Chester with us to stay with a friend until my court-martial. Our journey to Chester was good fun all the time and when we reached our destination my guard insisted on escorting my wife to her lodgings before taking me to the barracks at the Castle. I lost all sense of being a prisoner. We were four pals.

We arrived too late for me to be allocated to a dormitory and I spent the night on the picket room floor just inside the Castle gates. I settled down for sleep on three "biscuits" before a gigantic red-glowing fire. Once more there was an interruption; an escort brought in another conchie. He was a frail, pale boy, who did not look the eighteen years required of recruits. He had black silky hair and delicate features. I noticed his long smooth-skinned fingers. His eyes were bewildered and timid. "Welcome, brother," I said, sitting up in my shirt. He looked at me, startled, but said nothing. "You're a conchie, aren't you?" I asked. "They call me that," he said, in soft tones. "Are—are you one, too?" When I assured him I was, his eyes lit up with surprise. "Are there many?—conchies, I mean," he said. "Six thousand, brother." He looked at me with astonishment and then his face shone as though this were a revelation. "Six thousand! I thought I was about the only one!" I helped him to arrange his bed and he lay down at my side. Slowly he told me his story.

He was not a member of the N.C.F.; he had never heard of it. He lived in a small Cheshire village. His people were in favour of the war, but he was horrified by it and he knew he could not bring himself to kill. He hoped to be an artist, and loved beautiful things. He had a sister who was sympathetic; but that was all. He had a name historic in the struggle for freedom—Wolstencroft,—but when I asked him if he were related to Mary Wolstencroft, the pioneer of women's liberty, he had not heard of her. I was moved with compassion for this boy. He had come out of a sheltered life to resist the most remorseless power on earth: the military machine. Only the previous week the newspapers had carried stories of the attempt of the Cheshire regiment (*our* regiment) to break in George Beardsworth and Charles Dukes.* They had been forcibly taken to the drilling ground and kicked, punched, knocked down and thrown over railings until they lay exhausted, bruised and bleeding. I looked at the boy beside me with his delicate limbs and soft skin and shuddered at the thought of what such treatment would mean to him. He must be saved from it, if possible.

I explained to him that next morning we should be taken to the doctor for medical examination. I urged him to accept it; I could not believe that he was fit to be a soldier. He looked at me out of large wondering eyes. "Will you be examined?" he asked. I laughed off my intention to refuse, saying that my resistance was political and that he was not interested in that. "Well, I'll see," said Wolstencroft.

On the way to the doctor's we were joined by three other conchies who had spent the night in the guard room. They were three young anarchists from Stockport whom I knew as N.C.F. members. When we got to the doctor the sergeant made no doubt that we should understand. "I am going to give you a military order," he said. I cursed him for being so definite; it would be more difficult for Wolstencroft to obey now. "Private Brockway, strip for medical examination." "Sorry, sergeant, I must decline." The sergeant signalled to two soldiers and they stepped smartly to attention each side of me; I was under military arrest. My name had been called because it was the first in alphabetical order. The three anarchists followed and joined me between the soldiers. Wolstencroft came last. I watched anxiously. When the order

*Dukes is now the Secretary of the General and Municipal Workers' Union, and Beardsworth a prominent official of the Distributive Workers' Union.

came he didn't speak. He shook his head and stepped over and joined us in the line. He had his eyes on the ground, but half looked up at me as though to excuse himself for disobeying my advice.

We were marched between six soldiers across the parade ground in front of the castle. I chatted to the anarchists as we went. "Stop that talking," shouted the sergeant. "Sorry, sergeant, but these are friends whom I've not seen for quite a time." The sergeant glowered, but gave it up. The soldiers escorting us sternly tried to hide their smiles; the anarchists carried on with their story.

The guard room at Chester Castle was a dungeon and much dingier than at the Tower; it was dark even at ten o'clock in the morning. There was one small dust-covered barred window high in a wall; through a grating low in the wall a gas jet burned, giving a fitful light. The communal bed occupied most of the floor space. The atmosphere smelled of urine. There was a recess in which a pail stood for sanitary purposes; a dark streak of liquid flowed from it under the bed. We lived in this place for ten days awaiting our Court-martial. Soldiers came and went—"drunks," deserters, men with wounds self-inflicted to escape the next draft.

For one blessed hour a day we were allowed to exercise on the ramparts of the Castle. The days were cold but the sun was kind, and as we came blinking out of that dim, smelly dungeon-like guard room the wonder of the clear, bright light of the fresh clean air and of the beauty of the scene were like heaven to us. The ramparts looked across the river to the country and the sky had colour and cloud. We drank in every minute of that precious hour.

Each morning we were taken across the parade ground to face the Colonel of the regiment. It was regarded as a formality and he looked up with surprise when in answer to his routine question "Any complaints?" I replied in the affirmative. "What is your complaint?" "The guard-room is not fit for human habitation. The urine from the pail spreads itself over the floor. The atmosphere is foetid." The sergeant of the guard looked thunder at me. "Does the pail leak?" asked the colonel of the sergeant. "No, sir." "But drunken men in the dark miss the pail," I said, "and the floor slopes down into the room." "I will send an officer to make a report," said the colonel, dismissing us. The sergeant cursed me. "Who the bloody hell d'you think you are? Won't fight and then whine." "I'm concerned about the soldiers who'll be in that guard room after we've left." "You're making a ———— big mistake if you think you're going to a health resort when you leave here."

When we got back to the guard room the sergeant ordered us to get down on our knees and wipe the floor. We refused; we were not going to remove the mess before the officer came. He made three soldiers in the guard room do it and even called on the guard to lend a hand. The officer when he came was not taken in. "Had a busy morning cleaning up, sergeant? Good. I like to see a guard which takes pride in its quarters." To the sergeant's surprise he ordered a soldier to get a pail of water and throw it in the recess. The water flowed quickly over the floor of the guard room. "You'll have to do some more cleaning up," said the officer to the sergeant. This time we helped. The next day two soldiers from the engineering squad appeared and the flow from the recess was stopped.

We spent our time in the guard room in discussion among ourselves and with the soldiers (it provided a grand opportunity for propaganda), reading books by the gas jet or by candle light, playing card games, inscribing slogans with our signatures on the walls, and preparing our statements for the court-martial. Candles were an innovation, but we coaxed the sergeant to allow them on the understanding that they would be invisible when the superior officers came on their daily visits of inspection. Once we had a surprise visit from the officer who had ordered the repair to the recess, but he pretended not to see when the lights round our card party were blown out.

The candles were brought by our visitors. My wife came to see me daily and we were allowed to sit and chat on a form outside the guard room. We were also allowed visits from our court-martial "friend"—a Quaker from Manchester. These visits were formalities, because we had all decided to defend ourselves but the contact with the outside world and the hour of freedom from the dark stuffy guard room were a privilege which we treasured.

One night a curious event took place, the significance of which I do not yet know for certain. We were lying on the bed in a row, packed tightly because we were crowded out by drunks and disorderlies (some of them overflowed on the floor), when the sergeant entered and ordered me to dress. I hesitated whether to obey—and then decided that any adventure would be a relief. I was marched to the officers' quarters and taken to one of their rooms. The occupant greeted me in a friendly way, bade me sit down in an easy chair, and offered me a drink, smoke and food. I was bewildered. "This is quite unofficial," he said. "Forget I'm an officer and you a prisoner. It can't be too pleasant in that guard room. Thought I'd get you over for a chat." "This is certainly better," I said, and waited for him to go on. He assured me that he wanted to hear my views. He disliked war as much as I did and particularly the regimentation in the army which turned men into automata. He could understand my not wanting to kill Germans, who after all might be as decent chaps as ourselves. What could we do about it? I was always glad to put our view forward and seized the opportunity. The officer listened, but when he spoke again it was of my personal position.

"Look here, Brockway, you're an intelligent chap. No one doubts your sincerity. You know what you'll get—one year's hard, probably. What's the use of that? We shan't like doing it, and you won't like doing it. Why make us do it? Why go through it unnecessarily?" "Unnecessarily?" "Yes. We don't want to make you do any shooting if your principles are against it, but you're a clever chap, used to writing and all that, and you could be used in other ways. Lots of press work to be done in Whitehall." I smiled. "You expect me to use my pen for the war when I won't use a gun?" "Well, we can't help ourselves, can we, old chap? Everything we do is helping the war in some way." "Except agitating against it and resisting it."

When the officer saw that I wouldn't listen to the proposal. his thoughts turned to my immediate comfort again. "Like to sleep here, tonight? I can only offer you the floor, but we could get some 'biscuits' in and it would be better than the guard room." I hesitated. I still did not know whether his approach was a gesture of friendship or an attempt to get me as a leader to compromise in order to break the resistance of others. I decided that there would be no harm in staying, and the officer ordered his batman to bring in "biscuits" and blankets. I made up a bed and settled down to sleep. The next morning I breakfasted with the officer without any further reference to the conversation of the night before. He behaved like a pal, and when the time came for me to be marched back to the guard room expressed the hope that I would think less badly of the army in the future.

Was the whole visit a "plant" or was it due to good-heartedness? The mystery remained unsolved, but when I got back to the boys in the guard room they had no doubt that the officer had been speaking for higher authorities.

The three anarchist boys from Stockport were splendid. Two of them were only eighteen and the third could not have been more than twenty. They were all working-class lads accustomed to roughing it and were blessed with a great sense of humour. Bob Seaton was a strong, good-looking boy, with the open, ruddy type of face one usually associates with the country. Williams was quiet and thoughtful, a pale-face. Sam Brookes was a little chap, with the features and fun of Punch. I went through a good deal of my imprisonment with these boys and found them of sterling character.

About Wolstencroft I was worried. The roughness of the guard room evidently hurt him much more than the rest of us; one could see his sensitive personality shrink before vile language and threats. He spoke very little and his one occupation was sketching in a note-book. He took no trouble in preparing a statement for the court martial and finally wrote only two or three simple sentences stating that he would not be a soldier because he would not kill. His sister came to see him once or twice and then he would smile. He had the sweet smile of a girl. I dreaded the effect of long imprisonment on this lad.

A few days before my court martial I got a letter from my friend Miles Malleson, the dramatist and actor. He had joined the army in the early days of the war and had been sent to Malta. Then he had thought his way through to the socialist pacifist position and had refused to obey orders. He was discharged and was now back in London. An amazing incident occurred over my letter in reply, in which I congratulated him on an anti-war play which he had written. Our letters were censored by the sergeant and a few minutes after I had passed mine out, he threw open the door, face red with rage. "Private Brockway, what do you mean by using bad language in your letter? You know it's against the Regulations." "Bad language?" "Yes. What the —— hell will they think of the bloody army if we allow letters with —— swear words to go out from the guard room?" The boys received this utterance with roars of laughter, as well they might. I glanced at the sergeant's face to see if he were serious. There was no doubt about it.

"Where did I use swear words?"

"You bloody well know you did. There were 'hells' all over the letter." The explanation dawned on me. It was the reference to Miles's play, "Black Hell," to which the sergeant objected! I laughed and explained. "You shouldn't have friends what write books with such names. Anyhow, it's crossed out. No —— swear words are going out from this guard room." As the door slammed, we laughed like hysterical schoolgirls. Our nerves had become overwrought by the confinement in this dark, stuffy, crowded dungeon. Our experiences, however, were easy compared with those of the men who had preceded us. We suffered from practically no physical violence and no attempt was made even to force uniform on us. The decision not to force uniforms on objectors was reached just before my period in the army.

The court martial proceedings were as good as a pantomime. The room was small and few could get in except the pressmen and one or two visitors, including my wife, my official "friend," and Bruce Glasier, the I.L.P. veteran, who had come to give evidence on my behalf. We were tried separately and I was taken first. Soldiers stood at attention each side of me and the sergeant a few feet away. My "friend" told me afterwards that their faces were a study as the proceedings went on. They were old army men and did not know whether to be outraged or amused.

The three officers who composed the court were new to their job and did not know a thing about it. They had before them the Military Regulations, but were lost by their complexity. As they pored over them I would say, "Excuse me, I think you will find what you want on page so and so," or "The procedure for giving evidence is defined in paragraph— on page—." After this had happened a third time and I had proved right, the officers accepted my guidance openly. It became a case of a prisoner conducting his own trial.

When the time came to read my statement I am told that I addressed the small court as though it were the Albert Hall. I knew that this would be my last chance of a propaganda speech for many months—perhaps years—and I took full advantage of it. My defence was reported widely in the Press and was reprinted as a leaflet not only in Britain, but in Canada, Australia and New Zealand. Three days later our sentences were announced. We were marched on to the parade ground where the soldiers were lined up three sides of a square. My name came first again and as it was announced the sergeant pushed me forward. Our punishment was six months' imprisonment with hard labour.

From the moment the sentences were announced we were fully prisoners. No more visits or letters were allowed and we were no longer provided with "biscuits" to sleep on; a "hard labour" prisoner had to sleep on boards for a fortnight. In fact we did not do so; there were enough soldiers in the guard room to cover the broad bed with their mattresses and we slept tight.

I want to emphasise, after my account of the bad reception given me in the guard room at the Tower of London, that never again did I find ill-will in the army. The soldiers, particularly those who had been to the front, sympathised and often regarded us as "bloody heroes" for defying the "brass hats." Our guard room sergeant was of the old army school, but even he was kindly underneath his rough tongue. On our side, we never regarded the soldiers as enemies. We recognised them as victims of Conscription and War no less than ourselves—indeed, much more than ourselves.

Chapter Eleven
DOING TIME

We were taken to Wormwood Scrubs under escort, and the sergeant in charge was instructed to put the handcuffs on us if we gave trouble. We formally declined to carry our military kits, but as soon as we were out of sight of the Castle we offered to do so out of consideration for the soldiers who were loaded with them. On the train my wife joined us, and the sergeant allowed her to travel in our carriage. Nevertheless he kept a sharp eye on us. If we went to the lavatory he sent a soldier with us. "I have to take back a receipt for the bodies from the gaol," he laughed.

I took care in the train to sit beside Wolstencroft. I was scared by his white face and nervous manner. I urged him to accept the Home Office Scheme. He listened carefully while I explained it, but all he would say was "I'll see."

At Willesden Station, where we changed, there was a group of about twenty from the London N.C.F. to welcome us. They came on by the same train and, when we marched off to the prison, lined up behind and sang "The Red Flag" and other songs all the way. We passed through the great prison gate with the sound of their cheers in our ears.

The sergeant was given his receipt for our bodies. Immediately the escort had gone there was a new atmosphere. "You're in prison here," thundered the Chief Warder. "No more talking. Pick up those kits and follow me. Remember—its bread and water for anyone who breaks orders here." I hesitated —and picked up my kit. The others did the same. I felt a little ashamed of myself. In the army I had had no hesitation in refusing to obey orders. Here I was obeying—even recognising the kit of army uniform as my property.

Wormwood Scrubs prison was less terrifying in its entrance than Pentonville. We passed through arched cloisters along the edge of a green lawn overlooked by a chapel built in the Gothic style; this gave the appearance of a college rather than of a gaol. But inside the prison halls were of the same pattern —long buildings with five storeys of cells, and spidery gangways and stairways. We were lined up and particulars of name, sentence and religion noted on a card. At Pentonville I had been advised by an old-hand to say I was Church of England.

because one got bread and wine at Communion and sometimes there was a chance of swigging the left-over wine, but I described myself as a Unitarian, which vaguely represented my religious beliefs at the time; that is to say, I did not believe in the supernatural but interpreted the universe spiritually. I was a vegetarian (as I still am) and on the first morning put down my name to see the doctor and ask for a meatless diet. He shook his head. He was allowed to order a change of diet only if a prisoner showed a serious loss of weight. I petitioned the Home Secretary and began a partial hunger strike, declining to eat anything with meat in it. This meant that my diet was restricted to skilly and bread for breakfast, bread and sometimes pudding at dinner (the pudding was often greasy with lard), and bread and cocoa for supper. I was naturally so light in weight, however, that I had little hope that the monthly weighing ceremony would convince the doctor that I required another diet.

It was three months before the vegetarians won the right to diet. When we did it was much more varied than the ordinary diet, and news of this soon got about the prison. The result was that there was a long queue of prisoners at the Governor's office asking to be transferred to the new diet. Hardened criminals, including a man who was serving a year for hitting his wife on the head with a poker, assured the Governor that their consciences would no longer allow them to eat meat. The Government did not in these cases set up tribunals to judge conscience. Indeed, because of the war-time shortage of meat they were probably grateful for the wave of vegetarianism which swept over the prisons.

To re-capture the temper in which I entered prison I have re-read some of the letters I sent out. Except for a postcard formally announcing our arrival, we were not permitted to write for two months. At first I was not in mental revolt against imprisonment or its conditions; I was proud to undergo it as a witness to our anti-war convictions and I accepted punishment gladly as an honour in the cause. I regarded my cell as a kind of monk's retreat in which I could meditate and, so far as was allowed, read. It inspired me to know that I was one of six hundred men who were in the prison for refusal of war service. It was a heartening experience to go out on the

D

exercise yard and see there a hundred fellow-resisters. The abomination of prison exercise—walking round concrete circles, the men five yards apart, never allowed to speak—did not then impress me; it was enough to be there with these other comrades who were resisting war.

Chapel was the greatest experience of all, not because of its religious significance, but because there, row after row, were the whole six hundred massed together. The hypocrisy of the prison service did not yet dominate my mind; it was grand to be with these boys who from one end of the country to the other were standing out. Probably many of us had the feeling that the "resistance" part of our struggle was over; we had done that in the army and now, by willingly accepting the consequences, were witnessing to our faith. This mood changed later on, as I shall describe. The fact that we entered prison with it shows that we went in as pacifists rather than as socialist rebels.

My first experience of the prison technique for overcoming the silence rule was in chapel. We were singing one of the chants. Instead of the words of the Prayer Book, I heard these:—

Welcome, Fenner boy,
When did you get here?
How did you like the skilly this morn?
Lord have mercy upon us!

I looked round and there was A. W. Haycock, a Manchester I.L.P. member, afterwards to become Member of Parliament for one of the Salford Divisions. He continued singing without any sign of recognition. I had made a fatal mistake in turning round. At the end of every five rows was a raised seat occupied by a warder; he sat with his back to the altar and the chaplain —but discipline was more necessary than courtesy either to God or his representative. As soon as I turned, a voice barked: "D—Two-Thirteen, you'll be for the Governor to-morrow." The warder, as was the custom in prison, addressed me by my cell number carried on a yellow disc on my coat.

The warder did not report me, but later on I was reported for an offence which experience subsequently taught me to commit without danger. During our first month in prison we were allowed only the Bible and one "educational" book. I forget what my book was, but it was a trifling one and I had learned everything in it before a week had passed. Coming in from exercise one morning I heard whispered words behind me. I listened without turning my head. "I've done a month and got a novel," the voice said. "I'll slip it into a mail bag and pass it on to you. Let me have it back in one of your mail-bags." I blew my nose and under the protection of the handkerchief said: "Thanks." We were all engaged in sewing mail-bags and each morning mine were exchanged with those of the prisoner in the next cell for some special part of the job which he did.

I got the book all right and had an enjoyable evening reading it. The next morning the cell doors were not opened. Instead, there was a curious periodical sounding of cell bells. I did not understand. My cell door opened and two warders appeared. One of them tested my bell; the other proceeded to run his hands over my clothing, feeling with particular care along the hemmed ridges. Meanwhile, the second warder was searching my cell in detail and in due course found the library book in the mail bag. "Thought so," he said. "It was missing from the next cell. You'll be for report to the Governor in the morning." Both my neighbour and I were reported. We were put on bread and water for a day and lost one day's remission.* This loss was of no importance because there was no freedom for us at the end of the sentence; we were to be taken back to the army, and there the process of refusing orders, guard-room, court-martial and a sentence would re-commence.

The minimum task of mail bag sewing was seventy feet a day. We sewed with large needles which looked like skewers, pressing them through the canvas by a lead knob strapped to the palms of our hands. At first the seventy feet of sewing seemed an impossible task; working hard I could get done only thirty feet in ten hours. But we were given a period for learning, and though the task-warder grumbled at my slowness I had reached the seventy standard in about three weeks. Before the end of my prison experience the seventy feet seemed child's play; I could do it in four hours. This speed was due to a simple knack. which a sympathetic warder taught me, enabling one to do three stitches at one pull of the thread.

*Prisoners were entitled to a remission of one-sixth of their sentences for good conduct and work.

After working for a month in my cell I was placed in the "garden party." This had the advantage of being outdoor work, but there wasn't much gardening about it. Our job was to dig up one of the exercise yards between the concrete tracks so that vegetables could be grown. The yard was stone and bricks and we had to work more with picks than with spades. It was a bitterly cold winter, with frequent snow-storms, and most of the time we worked in canvas capes which protected us to the waist, though our trousers got wet through and our bodies cold.

The time came for us to go before the Central Tribunal. I had had no chance to speak to Wolstencroft again, but, when I found a few days later that he was not transferred to Wandsworth Gaol with the rest of us who had refused the Home Office scheme, I concluded that he had accepted and was relieved. Wandsworth was a dismal prison.

I was entitled to one visit during this sentence and my wife came with our baby. It was under the humiliating "meat safe" arrangement. We stood in cubicles like telephone boxes opposite each other and looked and spoke through thick and dark wire gauze. Behind me stood a warder to censor my conversation; we were not allowed to talk about prison conditions. Audrey was then about eighteen months old. I can still see the wondering eyes with which she looked at her father in a cage. Towards the end of my sentence it was nearing the time for the birth of our second child. My wife had gone to a Manchester Nursing Home run by a friend. Prison was irksome with this anxiety on my mind, but a few days before "release" I received a telegram that Margaret was born and that "both were doing well." My chief concern was to manœuvre a visit to Manchester before I got sentenced again.

I was met at the prison gates by a sergeant and private from the Cheshire regiment, and by some local N.C.F. supporters. My escort willingly agreed to go to their home for breakfast, and the attitude of the sergeant was so friendly that I put to him a proposal on which my mind had been working. It was that we should take train to Manchester instead of Chester, that I should spend the afternoon with my wife and baby, and that we should proceed to Chester by the last train. The sergeant agreed to take the risk and to Manchester we went. I gave the

escort a generous allowance for tea and proceeded to the Nursing
Home. In good time I left for the station to catch the last
train to Chester. My escort was not there; five minutes before
the train was due to leave they were still not there. I smiled
over the irony of the situation; I, the prisoner, was anxious lest
my escort should not turn up in time to conduct me back to the
army, the guard-room and another sentence! With a margin
of two minutes they ran laughing on to the platform. We got
to the Castle all right and I was even in time to sleep in a
dormitory instead of the picket room. The soldiers were
friendly and eager to hear of my prison experiences.

The three anarchist boys had been released from Wandsworth a day earlier because of my loss of a day's remission, and
were already in the guard room again for renewed disobedience
of military orders. That I expected, but my astonishment was
great when I found that Wolstencroft was with them. He had
not accepted the Home Office scheme after all; once more his
"I'll see" had meant "I won't."

It was good to be back with my comrades, to be able to talk
freely to them after the silence rule in prison. My main anxiety
was Wolstencroft. He was more silent than ever, started when
one spoke to him, smiling in a friendly way but timidly resisting every invitation to draw him into conversation or games.
For the first few days during this second guard room experience
he seemed almost to have lost the power of speech and his eyes
were dull and lifeless. I tried to get him to accept medical
examination, but he shook his head. This time we were
sentenced to two years' imprisonment (subsequently commuted
to one year).

I entered Walton Gaol, Liverpool, in a mood quite different
from my mood at Wormwood Scrubs. I had gone through
my period of initiation and no longer had the spiritual exultation
of a novice. I was as determined as ever not to give way, but I was
not in the temper to accept penalties gladly. I would pit my
wits against those of the authorities and defeat them whenever I
could. Prison experience taught us a lot. The supreme dis-
ability which we had to overcome was the rule forbidding
communication between prisoners. To speak was not always
easy, but if we could succeed in getting a supply of leads into
prison there were many opportunities to pass written messages

to each other. The N.C.F. tackled this problem with its usual efficiency. Every C.O. received from his branch a packet containing leads and court plaster, and instructions how to avoid discovery. The procedure on entering prison was to strip, to enter a hot bath (when one's civilian clothes were taken away) and then to put on the prison uniform. This did not seem to give much opportunity for smuggling anything through, but there is one part of the human body where, though standing naked before a warder, one can still hide a packet of leads from his watchful eyes: beneath the arch of the foot. With the use of court plaster it is possible to pack in six leads; we smuggled thousands into gaols during the war.*

But I nearly gave away our technique to the authorities. I undressed and stood naked awaiting my turn, very conscious of the packet under each foot. When I stepped into the bath I found to my horror the water turning purple about my feet; I stirred it, but the more I did so the more purple it became— *some of my hidden leads were copying ink!* The warder stepped to the foot of the bath—and gasped at the sight of the coloured water. I kept my body moving to prevent a darker pool gathering at my feet, but every moment I expected accusation. Instead the warder turned and angrily called for the prisoner on duty as his assistant.

"B-1-13, are you skatty? This isn't a hospital case! What've you put disinfectant in the water for?" The prisoner came up puzzled and was about to claim innocence when he saw my wink. "I'm sorry, sir. Must have dropped some in by mistake. Sorry, sir." "Well, won't do him any harm, but be more careful another time and get the bath clean before the doctor comes." I breathed calmly again. As soon as the warder had passed I got out of the bath, dried my feet on the prison socks to avoid marking the towel, and got into them. It had been a narrow squeak.

The C.O.s, about sixty in number, were accommodated in the basement floor of one of the halls. As soon as I got to my cell I appreciated how useful the leads could be. The warder in charge was assisted by a bright-eyed laughing boy, wearing the grey costume (spattered with broad arrows) reserved for military

---

* I can give away this device now because it was discovered by the authorities towards the end of the war.

prisoners. He was the eighteen-year old son of a Welsh farmer; his name was R. A. Jones and we called him "Raj." He bumped against me in the passage and I felt his hand touch mine; without any sign of communication I took a slip of paper from him and tucked it in my trousers. When my cell door was locked on me, I stood in a corner out of sight of the spy-hole straightened out the little bit of toilet paper and deciphered the contents. To my astonishment it was headed "Telephone Code." There followed the alphabet, with varied dots and lines beside each letter. Below was an explanation: a dot meant a sharp tap, a line meant two taps in rapid succession. The instrument of communication was the hot-water pipe passing from cell to cell; the telephone number of each prisoner was his cell number. I still remember the "repeat" sign if one failed to understand a message: it was two double taps, two single taps and a double tap, that is: — — . . —

As I was studying the "code" I heard a sound of tapping on the pipe. I tried to follow the taps, but they were too rapid—no doubt the bright-eyed boy was telling the other prisoners of our arrival. I spent the evening learning the code by tapping out the letters quietly on the cell table. "Lights out" came and the same sequence of raps was constantly repeated. I was able to spell them out: prisoner after prisoner was saying "Goodnight, comrades" and then a message came which I took longer to work out—"Welcome, Fenner." This was all so different from the first nights in Pentonville, Wormwood Scrubs and Wandsworth that I felt prison to be a new and exciting experience.

To communicate with the prisoner in the next cell it was not necessary to use the pipe: one could tap softly on the wall. I found that my neighbour was a chess expert and he taught me to play. We marked out our cell slates as chess boards and at first drew the men in their positions with our slate pencils, erasing and sketching at each move. Later we improved on this by using a set of men made from the white and brown wax supplied for canvas sewing. My companion was more skilful with his hands than I and presented me with a beautiful set. Alas, they were discovered by a warder (though not until after months of use) and confiscated. Probably they are on view to-day in the Liverpool Prison Museum of curios.

With a pencil in my hand I immediately began to plan a prison newspaper. The "Walton Leader" was produced twice a week and was quite a creditable journal. It consisted of about forty toilet paper pages, and included news items, cartoons, serious articles, humorous stories and correspondence. Our cartoonist was Arthur Hagg, whose work is now often to be seen in the press; the news items were sent in by prisoners who had received letters and visits or who had newly come in, whilst articles, stories and letters were contributed in abundance. "Raj.", who was the cleaner on our landing, acted as postman and very rarely was any communication discovered. We were rapidly becoming experts in breaking the prison rules, and some of the warders, who became increasingly friendly, made this easier by winking their eyes at offences so long as their chiefs did not get to know.

Certain items of news which appeared in the "Walton Leader" stand out in my memory. There was the wonderful news of the Russian Revolution. The Kerensky revolution thrilled us at first, but we were bitterly disappointed when we learned that the new People's Government intended to continue the war in alliance with Capitalist Britain, France, and America —I made the comment that this proved that it was not a genuine socialist revolution. We followed with intense interest the reports of the Bolshevik opposition, its suppression in July, 1917 —and then its triumph in October. Again I remember my comment that the cry "Bread, Land and Peace" showed it was dependable. We were excited, too, by the news that the I.L.P., with others, had taken the initiative in calling the Leeds Congress to establish Workers' and Soldiers' Councils in this country. Our hopes were exaggerated; we saw the revolution coming in Britain and our prison doors being opened by comrade workers and soldiers. A copy of the "Labour Leader" with a report of the Leeds Congress reached us; its pages became yellow and torn, but still they circulated.

Another subject of discussion among us was the announcement of President Wilson's "Fourteen Points" for peace. They were read aloud triumphantly by the Chaplain at the Sunday service; he had been a little uneasy about Christian support for the war, but he felt that President Wilson's Peace Terms proved that the Allies were really concerned to establish a New World of co-operation and justice. I was sceptical. I could not see imperialist Britain and France, or even the really determining forces in America itself, accepting a Peace of no indemnities or annexations.

One other item of news I remember—an exclusive story of the slaughter at Passchendaele brought in by one of our boys who had been in a guard room with a survivor. It told graphically of the ruthless, machine-like way in which the generals sent wave after wave of thousands of men to be massacred—and all with no result. As I read it, existence seemed intolerable: the thought that whilst I sat there in my cell, men were being shattered to bits in their thousands. In recent years I have read Mr. Lloyd George's indictment of the generals who wasted this army of lives, but even his dramatic story did not move me more than the bitter account which we gave in the "Walton Leader" from one of the men who had come back. The press outside was not allowed to publish the story: you had to go to prison to get uncensored news!

I used to spend hours in the production of the prison paper, re-writing in small, neat capital letters every contribution, leaving only the cartoons in the original form. The subscription was a ration of toilet paper from each prisoner's supply; it was collected by "Raj." when we were absent on work (his job was to assist the warder in the hall) and each evening I found my supply made up plentifully. But with the distribution side of the paper I was dissatisfied; to pass a copy from prisoner to prisoner took a week and news and articles became stale. The solution of this difficulty came to me suddenly. We all used the lavatory and in privacy: why not make it the reading room for the paper? I hid it there and tapped out a telephone pipe "Call to all Cells" announcing that it would be there every Tuesday and Thursday morning. I ought to have anticipated the result. On Tuesday and Thursday mornings there were queues; if a prisoner were unlucky enough to get the wrong cubicle, he was back again before long. The prison authorities were puzzled. Why Tuesdays and Thursdays? The Medical Officer was ordered to report on the diet on Mondays and Wednesdays . . . but, alas, before his report was prepared the "Walton Leader" was discovered by an unusually inquisitive or officious warder. I was put on trial before the prison magistrates.

The magistrates turned up in record numbers. Generally two or three would attend; on this occasion there were twelve— intrigued no doubt by the unique item on the Charge Sheet: "Production of a Prison Newspaper." But the Governor's difficulty was that, whilst he had no doubt that I was the editor, he had no proof; no names, either of the editor or of the contributors, were given and the paper had not been found in any-one's possession. This was my eighth trial during the war and by now I was at home in dock or witness box. Moreover a trial, whatever its consequences, was a welcome break in the monotony of prison existence and I deliberately set out to enjoy myself. The first witness was the Chief Warder of my hall. He identi-fied me as editor, saying he recognised my handwriting. "When have you seen my hand-writing?" I asked. "I saw you write your name on the back of photos in your cell." (We were each permitted two photos after serving six months.) "Take the 'Walton Leader' in your hand. Thank you. Look at it care-fully. Is the handwriting easy or difficult to read?" "Easy, sir." (I smiled at this designation of a prisoner.) "Do you remember saying when I signed the photos in my cell that no one would be able to read my signature?" "I don't remember." "You are on oath, Chief Warder. Can you swear that you did not say that?" "I don't remember, sir." "We'll soon settle the matter" I said in the best Patrick Hastings manner.

I asked that the photos should be brought from my cell. A warder was sent for them. When he came I requested that they should be handed to the witness. "Are you prepared to swear on oath that the signature on the photos is similar to the block letters used in the 'Walton Leader'?" The Chief Warder hesitated. "Well, I'm not saying there isn't a difference, sir." "What is the difference?" I asked. "One's in capital letters and easier to read, sir." "The signature is not easy to read?" "Not very, sir." I turned to the magistrate with a satisfied smile. "I have no more questions to put to the witness," I said.

The magistrates were in a quandary. The photos were passed round and it was evident at once that there was no like-ness between the signatures and the block letters. I had an acquaintance amongst the magistrates, Joseph Bibby, wealthy

Theosophist, head of a big Liverpool cattle food firm. Now that he was sitting in judgment upon me, he was as nonplussed as his fellow magistrates. He appealed to me as a friend. "Look here, Brockway, you know you are guilty and we all know you are guilty—can't you help us by acknowledging it?" I smiled my regrets. It wasn't my duty to help the authorities to put me on bread and water. For a moment or two the magistrates sat in uncomfortable silence; they must all have realised how unsatisfactory was the evidence against me and that in any public court I could not possibly have been condemned. Nevertheless, I was pronounced guilty and sentenced to six days on bread and water diet and the loss of so many days of my remission. I didn't worry. The fun of the trial had been worth it, and, as a matter of experience, I was prepared to have a taste of the punishment cells and a period of starvation diet.

I was taken to a dark basement cell. The windows were small, heavily-barred and opaque with dust. The only furniture was a stool, a chamber and a bible. Here I was to spend nine days, six on bread and water and three intervening days on "B" diet (considerably below the normal) to enable me to stand the strain. The warder in charge was brusque and the "cleaner" only dared to wink. The daily ration of 1lb. of bread was given in three instalments; I ate it slowly and wetted my finger tips to collect every crumb. I found the second day on bread and water the worst. I became so weak that I lay down on the cell floor, using the bible as a pillow, and relaxed my limbs and even my mind so that I was in a kind of coma, half-awake, half-asleep. At night I was permitted to lie on a bed board, which was at least warmer than the stone floor.

Smiling faces, whispered greetings and pipe-'phone messages gave me a great welcome when I got back to my fellow C.O.s. I was able to look at them with fresh eyes after my brief absence and I was immediately disturbed by the appearance of Wolstencroft. He was deadly white, his eyes were vacant, and it was a moment or two before he showed any recognition. I slipped a note to him to go and see the medical officer, but the next time I saw him he only shook his head.

Shortly afterwards I myself got into hospital. My teeth were troubling me and I asked for a dentist; I was allowed one at my own expense. I was taken over to hospital for the treatment. He decided that a wisdom tooth, a double tooth and an eye tooth must be extracted, and proceeded to lever out the wisdom tooth whilst I clung to the seat of the chair. I think the severest indictment I can pen of the prison system is this fact: *I definitely looked forward to the dentist's visits as breaks in the monotony of existence.* The extraction of the wisdom tooth caused my throat to swell so that I could not swallow and the extraction of the eye tooth caused the eye above it to close. I was not sorry to be in hospital. I remained in a cell, but there was a bed with mattress, sheets and blankets. Discipline was slacker and I was given new library books whenever I asked.

When I got well again I was kept in hospital for a time as an orderly. The most distressing sights in prison were the obvious idiots. The mental cases were accommodated on a floor which was known by prisoners and warders alike as "Rotten Row." My first contact with them was on exercise, when their antics were sufficient to convince anyone that they had lost their wits. I remember one shaggy-headed wild-eyed man, who, despite the icy-cold weather, would spend the whole exercise hour standing before a wall, moving three paces to the left and three paces to the right, with a seriousness which could not have been greater if the safety of the world had depended on it. Sometimes he would raise his hand for permission to go to the lavatory. He would start off for the latrines on the other side of the yard and then forget what was his purpose. He would stand dazed and lost and then become frightened by the figures circling round him on exercise; a warder would have to go to him and lead him to the latrines. Later I spent a week in "Rotten Row," because my bed was required for an epidemic of influenza which brought a sixth of the inmates of the prison into hospital. Many of the cell doors on this floor were replaced by iron bars through which the inmates looked like animals in a cage. They gibbered like idiots or committed self-abuse with grinning faces.

I was in prison when three murderers were executed. At Liverpool the sentenced men used to be brought every lunch hour through the hall where the C.O.s were accommodated. We heard the steps of the two warders and of the condemned man; even contact with the execution tragedy through cell doors had a bad effect on us. Prisoners and staff alike became jumpy; prisoners became more uncontrollable, the warders lost their nerve more easily and bullied more readily, the Medical Officer became sharp and short in tone, the Governor more than usually fussy and officious.   The effect on the Chaplain was most marked of all.   At Liverpool Gaol he was a sincere, sensitive man and for days before an execution he went about with pain on his face and in his bearing.   On the day of the execution we were kept in our cells after breakfast instead of going on exercise or to work.   The place was deadly silent, each man listening for the opening of the door of the condemned cell, for the sound of the steps to the gallows, and then for the striking of the fatal hour on neighbouring clocks and the sound of the tolling bell which told that it was all over.   It was an unhealthy, degrading experience for us all.

I have written mostly of unusual incidents, and in so doing may have failed to give an impression of the deteriorative effect of prison life.   We C.O.s had the same treatment as all other hard labour prisoners (that is, the harshest treatment meted out in English prisons), but we had the strengthening sense of comradeship and of standing out for our convictions.   Yet even for most of us imprisonment sometimes became unbearable. We were locked in our cells for eighteen out of twenty-four hours each day.   We could not speak to each other without the risk of bread and water punishment.   We received and wrote one censored letter a month and had one half-hour visit, always in the presence of a warder.   We were treated like caged animals, without minds or personality, and were starved of all beauty.   The strain of this month after month was disastrous to self-control, and the long hours of solitary confinement drove one to the verge of mental and nervous breakdown, which could be conquered only by a great effort of discipline.

On one occasion I was in a hall when every prisoner seemed to lose control.   One poor fellow who had not been able to stand the strain smashed everything on which he could lay his hands.   Within a few minutes from cell to cell the nervous storm spread; every prisoner appeared to be thundering at his door in a fury of pent-up emotions which swept reason away.   I had the greatest difficulty in not joining in.   I stood at my door, my fists clenched within an inch of it, my whole body tense, my arms vibrating, my teeth clenched, a bursting pressure in my head. The warders came running along the corridors and dragged off prisoners to the padded cells. That intensified the storm; shrieking protests and shouted imprecations were added to the bangings on the cell doors. To me it brought futile despair. I flung myself on the ground and held my head tight in my arms to overcome the temptation to crush it against the wall.

But that happened only once. The deprivation which I felt most was the absence of beauty. No one could take the glimpse of sky by day and night from us; but colour and loveliness of outline did not otherwise exist. There was a period when my cell window looked out only on crude buildings and walls; I exercised in a stone-paved yard closed in by drab walls. I never saw the green of plants or trees or any colour beneath the sky except the dirty grey that was all about me. Then one day I saw a few blades of grass growing between two slabs of stone in the exercise yard; they were young and of a fresh green and excited me like wine. For three days I feasted my eyes on them, and then on the fourth day they had gone—the "garden party" had cleaned up the yard.

This may seem absurd when you read it in cold print, but tears came to my eyes. Perhaps the drabness of prison existence can be measured by that.

Chapter Twelve
RESISTING IN PRISON

My sentence ended and I was back at Chester Castle. By now the martyr in me had become aggressively a rebel. When my sentence of two years' hard labour for continuing to disobey orders was read out by the colonel before three thousand soldiers, I said defiantly: "I shall be proud to do it." The soldiers were standing to attention, line behind line, but at my words their lines seemed to shiver with shock. My sergeant was furious. He kicked my heels all the way to the guard room, but I laughed with satisfaction. The three thousand soldiers had been marshalled on the parade ground in order that they should be impressed by the severity of the sentence imposed. Instead they must have got an impression of defiance of military power, which, in the third year of the war, they were beginning to resent as much as I did. The propaganda effect had been the opposite of what was intended.

Reports from all the prisons showed that the C.O.s were getting rebellious. This was interpreted by our religious pacifist friends as a sign of breaking morale, and no doubt it was partly a reaction to the long strain. But it was more than that.

A discussion arose as to whether we should do Government work in prison. It was true that we were given only "civilian" work, but this released other prisoners to do war work such as sandbag-making for the front. Was not our work a form of alternative service? Some men began to refuse work. There was another consideration. We had refused to obey orders in the army as a protest against the military regime. Should we not refuse to obey orders in prison as a protest against the penal regime? It, too, was destructive of all that was best in human personality.

The combination of unrest among the C.O.s in prison (expressed in refusal of work, hunger strikes, and general recalcitrance) and political pressure outside brought about certain modifications in our treatment in the early months of 1918. The most important of these were the right to have books sent in and the introduction of "talking exercise" for those who had been in prison a year or more. At "talking exercise" we were permitted to walk round the yard in couples and to converse for a precious forty minutes a day. At the first "talking exercise" I made a point of walking with Wolstencroft. I had been worried by his appearance and manner for a long time, but had had no opportunity of making contact with him. When I stepped to his side on the exercise ring he looked up with a distant wondering air and then turned away. His arms were folded tightly across his chest, as though he were holding his frail body together or trying to give himself warmth. I spoke to him cheerily; he did not reply or even turn. I took his arm; he turned to me but almost without recognition. I was alarmed. I continued to speak, gently and of impersonal things, but still there was no response. He walked on, his head bent down over his folded arms. "What books are you reading?" I asked. At last he spoke, but timidly, "I can't read." Before the exercise was over I got a few more words from him, but very few. I returned to my cell shocked.

The next morning I put my name down to see the doctor. When I told him I wished to draw his attention to the condition of Wolstencroft he pulled me up sharply. Prisoners were permitted to see him about their own condition, not about the condition of others. "But the boy is broken to bits," I protested. "That is my responsibility," he said. During the dinner hour my cell door opened and the doctor entered. "Thank you, Brockway, for drawing my attention to Wolstencroft," he said. "I have transferred him to hospital for observation. I had to speak to you as I did, but I shall be grateful if you will report other cases to me if you think there is need. Don't ask to see me in my office; tell the landing officer that you want to see me in your cell. I'll have a word with him." The doctor had gone. I was surprised and pleased. How much better the prison officials were than the prison regulations!

Ten days later I heard that Wolstencroft had been released. I was told that he had gone to a nursing home, but I cannot say whether this was true. I have never been able to make contact with him since, but I think he was the most courageous boy I have ever known.

My own mind at this time was in conflict. A part of it was becoming terrorised by the prison regime. I don't mean that I went about in fear and trembling, but, if I were discovered breaking a rule, concern about the consequences would fill my mind. A warder found me one night speaking through the window to the man in the next cell. "You'll be for the Governor to-morrow morning," he shouted through the door. I jumped down trembling and had a wakeful and uneasy night, wondering whether the warder would carry out his threat, whether I should be put on bread and water. I had been reported more than once, and I had experienced bread and water and knew that there was nothing to be terrified about. Yet here I was, all jittery about it, allowing fear to make me servile.

But side by side with this surrender of my personality to the prison regime there was an intellectual revolt against it. I saw that what had happened to Wolstencroft in an extreme form was happening in greater or less degree to nearly every prisoner, was happening to myself. The mind and spirit were becoming crushed. This wasn't its effect only on C.O.s; it happened to all prisoners. Indeed, it probably happened less to C.O.s than to others because C.O.s had an unusual sense of fellowship in prison, despite the cellular confinement, and had the inner support of their convictions. I had many opportunities of coming into contact with the ordinary prisoners and observed how those who served long or repeated sentences became robots with no mental characteristics except a crafty cunning in evading discovery when they broke rules, and a grudge against society. They left prison with no idea in their heads except to continue the course of crime which had brought them there.

The more I thought about this the more convinced I became that it was the duty of C.O.s to use their experience of prison to change the system. My decision was finally made one day when a warder caught me talking with "Raj.", the smiling, bright-eyed "cleaner." I stopped talking at the warder's command. Then revolt burned up within me. Was I so spiritless that I would allow anyone to forbid me the elementary right of human speech? That was surely acceptance of the last tyranny! In my cell that evening I wrote an impassioned yet reasoned indictment of the prison system. I decided that I would smuggle it out under the foot of the next prisoner liberated, for publication in the press; it wouldn't get full publication everywhere, but I could count on the "Manchester

Guardian," the "Nation," and the "Labour Leader," and perhaps the general press would quote from it since it began by announcing somewhat dramatic action.

The dramatic action was this: I intended to go to the Governor and tell him that I would disregard henceforth inhuman prison rules like the silence rule; if I wished to speak to another prisoner I would do so. I decided to do this even if I were alone, but I proposed first to approach others whom I hoped might act with me. Four others agreed to do so—the three Stockport anarchists and Percy Bartlett, who subsequently became known as secretary to George Lansbury on his "Embassies of Reconciliation" to the rulers of Europe. The Governor was very upset by our ultimatum and pointed out that our action might be interpreted as mutiny, for which flogging is the punishment. We went back and joined the C.O.s, seated five yards apart on stools silently making mail bags. As soon as I reached my seat I began to talk openly. The four others did the same. We were confined to our cells and the next morning were reported to the Governor. He was very nervous and to our surprise we were not removed to the punishment cells. Instead we were taken to the hall in which prisoners on remand were accommodated. Three of us were placed on one side of the hall and two of us on the other. We did not occupy neighbouring cells, but by standing on stools at our windows those on the same side of the hall could talk to each other easily. We did so freely and continued to do so despite orders to stop. For an hour a day we were taken out into a yard to exercise. We were ordered to walk behind each other ten feet apart, but we walked in a bunch and even played games. We were left like this for a week without anything happening, except one significant thing. Our revolt against discipline spread to the whole hall. The prisoners occupying the other cells were not C.O.s, but when they saw us "getting away with it" they followed suit. Nearly all of us talked to each other through the cell windows and warders' orders were ignored.

One evening I heard the voice of a new prisoner from the cell above mine. He reported that he had just come in and that my action and letter to the press had caused a sensation outside. As a remand prisoner he was allowed newspapers and he proceeded to read me various paragraphs and articles. He read at length an article by Hilaire Belloc in the "Sunday Chronicle." Apparently my plan had worked as I intended; it had created public discussion not only of the position of the C.O.s but of the barbarities of the prison system. It appeared to have been successful beyond anything I had anticipated. When this prisoner had won my confidence, he began to put questions about my intentions. Was the action of my four colleagues and myself a first step? Was I proposing to extend the defiance of prison rules to the other C.O.s in the prison? Was I in touch with C.O.s in other prisons and was I planning to make the resistance general among them? How had I got my letter to the press? Had any warder helped me?

These questions made me suspicious. They made me wonder whether the reports of press stories were genuine, but they rang so true in form and style that I felt they must be. The article by Hilaire Belloc was particularly convincing. I had read a lot of Belloc and the use of simple Saxon words, the frequent explanatory sentence beginning with "that" and even Catholic references were all there. I am now convinced that this prisoner was a C.I.D. man. I ascertained later that there was no press sensation; Hilaire Belloc never wrote the article in the "Sunday Chronicle." My letter appeared in the "Manchester Guardian" and a few other papers, but no notice was taken of it generally in the press. I must congratulate whoever was responsible for the hoax on his skill and acknowledge that I was at first badly taken in. But at least I was sufficiently cautious not to give anything away.

We had been in the Remand Hall four or five days when voices calling our names reached us across the well of space dividing us from the neighbouring hall. I climbed on my stool and saw faces at cell windows and hands waving through the open panes. I recognised the voices and faces as those of C.O.s—and then realised that they were occupying the whole line of punishment cells. From their shouted words I picked up the story. After our removal a mass resistance to prison rules had begun among the C.O.s. Almost without exception they were refusing to take any notice of the silence rule. The following day the five of us in the Remand Hall and the twenty or thirty in the Punishment Cells were all returned to the C.O.s' hall. The prison authorities were frightened that our revolt would spread throughout the gaol—already indiscipline was becoming general—and decided to concentrate it in one hall. They were probably wise in that, but they enabled us to organise our revolt on a firmer basis.

We elected a committee with equal representation of each side of the hall. This committee drew up new prison rules. The reaction against the silence rule had gone too far; all day long prisoners were at their windows shouting to each other and the pipe telephone was tapping incessantly. We had no quiet time for reading and the din was getting on our nerves as much as the previous silence had done. The Committee worked out a time-table, including periods of silence and an hour each evening for lectures and concerts. Two lectures and concerts were given simultaneously—one on each side of the hall. The lecturer or artiste would perform through the open pane of his window and his voice would reach not only all the C.O.s along the landing, but the prisoners on the landings above and on the near side of the next hall; I suppose the audience of prisoners listening at the cell windows would number two hundred. I was delighted by the quality of the concerts. We had a number of Welsh boys and some of them sang beautifully. Lancashire contributed its humorists.

For ten days we continued to run this prisoners' administration of prison conditions. It was a gay and exciting time. Our liberty was of course severely limited: once the doors were locked upon us, we could not get out of our cells. Nevertheless, we all felt that the weight of the repression had been lifted. After months of a regime which had crushed all self-expression, we had become individuals again with opportunities to throw our ideas, talents, personalities into the common pool of our life. It is difficult to describe the sense of mental and spiritual liberation which this experience brought.

Those of us who were leading knew that it could not last; indeed, we were surprised that it continued so long. We knew that a revolt in one prison only could not succeed; the one chance of success would be to get the revolt extended to all the 1,200 absolutist C.O.s who remained in prison. But to plan common action rapidly from inside prison was impossible and the N.C.F. committee outside, whilst prepared to distribute information of what was happening, was not ready to organise a general revolt. My strategy had undoubtedly been faulty. Before beginning the revolt at Liverpool I should have circularised the other prisons; then a very wide revolt would have taken place. Later a "mutiny" took place at Wandsworth Prison, reaching such dimensions that the Home Secretary had to set up a Commission of Enquiry.

This unrest in the prisons synchronised with a powerful agitation outside for the release of the absolutists. Mrs. Henry Hobhouse, whose son, Stephen, was in prison, wrote a book, "I Appeal Unto Cæsar," which made a deep impression. A call for our release was made by influential figures in the Church and in academic and literary circles. If effective pressure from inside had been exerted simultaneously we might well have secured our liberation—and at the same time exposed on a bigger scale than ever before the ugly realities of the prison system. But we had not prepared our action in this way and after ten days the ring-leaders of the Liverpool revolt were transferred to other prisons.

Four of us, including Sammy Brookes, the companion of my Guard Room days, were removed to Lincoln.

We were taken from Lincoln station by taxi to the prison, mounting the hill past the Cathedral. This prison, like many others, had a pleasant entrance (to impress visitors, I presume), with a well-kept garden of hollyhocks and other flowers. Inside, I came into conflict with the authorities immediately. The medical officer, an army man in khaki, ordered me to be weighed. I was interested to know what my weight was and stood facing the indicator. "Turn about the other way," ordered the medical officer. "We are not weighing you for your information but for ours." "I'm not a sack of coals," I protested. "We'll weigh you in a strait-jacket." "All right— but the public shall know about it." The next day the medical officer came to my cell and was visibly impressed when I swanked a bit about being an editor and my friendship with members of Parliament. 1 was weighed and was allowed to face the indicator. We continued our resistance, were separated in distant cells, and were sentenced to three days' bread and water. One of the others suggested a hunger strike and only I opposed it. Partly my opposition was on the principle that we were not justified in forcing our liberation by threatening to take our lives (remember that I was still a pacifist) and partly on the practical ground that by forcible feeding it would be possible to defeat our aim. On the latter point I turned out to be right. My companions were forcibly fed—and they gave up resistance altogether. I was left alone in a hall of about 120 cells, with about half a dozen old lags, mostly vagrants who made a practice of getting a prison sentence in the autumn to cover the winter months. I was placed on punishment diet.

My cell had one advantage. It looked out on a vegetable garden with fruit trees scattered about, and, until the leaves fell, I feasted my eyes on the green and the autumn tints of brown, yellow and red. I also made friends with a robin, which advanced from a nearby tree to the window-sill and then, wonderful day! to the floor of my cell, where I had scattered a few crumbs from my punishment rations. I was becoming weak and lay on the floor for hours, my mind bordering on vacancy. Then came a marvellous relief. One day I heard steps outside my window. I got up on the stool and looked through the open pane. A prisoner was there, a red-band round his arm indicating that he was the privileged handy-man permitted to go about to do odd jobs without a warder. He was a remarkable looking man: tall, broad and straight, with a leonine head of waving grey hair, and a flowing beard.

He looked left and right and stopped under my window. "Who are you?" "Brockway—you won't know me." "What are you in for?" "A conchy." "What are they treating you like this for?" "I refuse to keep their rules." "Be on the look-out for me to-morrow, same time." He turned and walked on. I was trembling with excitement when I got down from the stool. My isolation was broken! I lived for the same time to-morrow.

I had learned to tell the time without a clock by the shadow thrown by the sun on the wall of the cell. The next day I was waiting for the steps when I heard them. "Get down," said the prisoner as soon as he saw my face at the window. I did so, disappointed, thinking there must be a warder about. A little brown packet fell on the floor beside me. I opened it excitedly. It contained a note, a pencil and a sheet of paper on which to reply. The note read:—

"Dear Brockway—Just heard you are here. What can we do for you? De Valera, Milroy and sixteen other Irish rebels are interned. We are Irishmen and can do anything you want—except get you out. Have your reply ready for 'Trusty' when he calls to-morrow. Cheerio! ALASTAR MACABA.*"

I laughed at the typical Sinn Fein confidence and put my demands high. I replied that I wanted my wife and friends outside to be informed that I was all right, and secondly— *news*. It took two days to get the answer. Then Alastar told me that one of the Irish prisoners, not expected to live, was to be liberated; if I would write a letter to my wife they would smuggle it out with him. As for newspapers, if I would send a list of what I wanted they would order them. They were permitted to have any papers—except Irish ones. Meanwhile he enclosed a copy of the "Daily News."

Only those who have been cut off from family, friends and the world can understand what this meant to me. I sat in a corner of my cell outside the line of the spy-hole and read the "Daily News." I wrote a letter to my wife and made out a list of the papers I wanted—the "Manchester Guardian" daily, the "Labour Leader," "New Statesman," "Economist" and "Observer" weekly. Three days later the "M.G." arrived and from this time until the end of my sentence I had all the papers regularly. They formed too bulky a package for "Trusty" to throw through the open pane, so we used the "fishing" method—the package was attached to a line of thread lowered from my window and then pulled up.

I want to pay a tribute to my "Trusty" friend. He was doing a three years' sentence (incidentally his is the only case I know where the maximum hard labour sentence of two years was accompanied by a *consecutive* sentence of hard labour for one year). His offence was criminal assault upon his two daughters. Yet the generosity of his character was shown by what he did for me. He had the best job in the prison; if he had been discovered acting as a go-between he would not only have lost this job but would have been punished severely, besides losing valuable remission marks which reduced his sentence by six months. I could do nothing to repay him for

* Alastar was elected M.P. for Sligo whilst still in prison in 1918.

what he did; it must have been human sympathy alone that actuated him.

After I had had punishment diet for a month the medical officer would not allow more. The cold cell, accentuated no doubt by my habit of lying stretched out on the stone floor, had given me neuritis. It began in my head and passed right down my body, causing me excruciating pain when it reached the stomach. Finally it settled in my left leg, making it practically paralysed. In Liverpool prison I should have been transferred immediately to the hospital had this trouble developed. At Lincoln the medical officer merely moved me to a warmer cell on the first floor of the hall. When taken off punishment, I had bedding in the cell and this enabled me to keep warm and comparatively comfortable—I flung a blanket over my shoulders and sat on the mattress. But even so a prison cell was hardly conducive to an improvement in my condition.

I had one great fear when I was transferred from the ground floor to the first floor: that I would lose contact with "Trusty" and the Sinn Feiners. But it is remarkable how difficulties like this can be overcome in prison. The next day when I went to the lavatory in the exercise yard I saw a piece of folded paper projecting from a crevice between two bricks; it was a note instructing me to lift the cover of a drain pipe. I did so—and the "Manchester Guardian" was inside! It was one of "Trusty's" daily duties to clean out the lavatory—a primitive pail affair—and he timed to do it always just before I came on exercise. I got away with this traffic in contraband more easily because after the medical officer had forbidden further punishment the warders never troubled to search my cell. I was so utterly isolated, shut in my cell for 23 out of 24 hours, cut off from other prisoners by exercising alone and by being the only occupant of the landing, that it must have been inconceivable to the authorities that I could obtain illegal articles.

About this time I had unusual attention from the medical officer and the Governor which I could not understand, and one afternoon, to my astonishment, the secretary of the Prison Commission, Mr. A. J. Wall, entered my cell. He enquired about my health and then pleaded with me to conform to the rules, emphasising the hardship which I was imposing upon my family by following a course which involved a cessation of letters and visits. It was a kindly interview, but did not change my views. Only when I had been liberated from prison did I learn the cause of this official attention. A rumour had spread outside that I had become a victim of tuberculosis. Catherine Marshall and my wife had gone to see Mr. Wall about it; but they had not been satisfied with that. Catherine had got the Bishop of Lincoln to lead a deputation to the Governor of the prison to enquire about me and, more astonishing, the central Shop Stewards' Committee in the Lincoln engineering works, on which I.L.P. influence was strong, had stopped work whilst they visited the prison to make sure that my life was not in danger. This is one of those generous, illogical actions characteristic of British workers. How puzzled the Governor must have been to receive a deputation of munition workers concerned so seriously about the welfare of a "conchy"!

During those months I found the newspapers exciting. The Labour Movement was recovering its independence. Arthur Henderson had been "left on the mat" by his War Cabinet and had resigned. An effort had been made to hold an International Socialist Conference at Stockholm and the British Labour Party would have participated had passports been available. In Germany the anti-war Socialists were threatening revolt. The anti-war Socialists in France and Austria had become majorities in their parties. The whole atmosphere in the working-class movement, both at home and abroad, was changing from one of subservience to the War Governments to one of self-reliance and independence.

November came and the papers carried increasingly stories of the cracking of national unity in Germany. I was particularly excited by the Socialist Revolution in Bavaria, in which Kurt Eisner* and Ernst Toller† were involved.

Then came reports of the cracking of the German military front. Suggestions of an armistice followed and finally the news of British terms. At eleven o'clock on November 11 German acceptance or rejection would be made known. This must have happened while I was still on punishment diet,

---

* By a coincidence, Kurt Eisner's daughter, whom I had never met before, came to see me just after I had written this. She is a refugee in Britain and carries on her father's ideals.

† Toller, with whom I became friendly later, died whilst I was writing this book.

because I remember sitting on the shelf-table in the denuded cell, my feet on the stool, watching the sun creep along the wall towards eleven o'clock. I cannot reproduce the chaos and intensity of my thoughts.

Was the slaughter of four years to end? Was the daily story of casualties to be a thing of the past? Were the men to be liberated from those long lines of trenches, Was all the anxiety to be over? Was our long imprisonment to end? Was I to see my family and children? What work should I do? Was my prison dream of running a daily paper with Clifford Allen to be realised? How could we recreate the International Socialist Movement? Would it be possible to extend our British N.C.F. into a War Resisters' International? Was this strain of solitary confinement and punishment diet to pass? Was I to see the fields and woods and hills and sea?

The line of the sun on the wall approached eleven. I watched it, fascinated. The warder had so far forgotten official reticence as to tell me that the hooters in the town would sound if the armistice were signed. I listened for them, body and mind tense. The sun crept on. It reached the crack in the wall which I estimated would be eleven. Still silence. I lost my head. I leaped across the cell and dug my fingers into the wall and tried to hold the sun back. Then in a great blare came the sound of the hooters. I broke down . . . .

But imprisonment was not over; it was more than five months before we were released. From now on, however, I was light-hearted. Partly because the war was over, partly because one could look forward to the end of imprisonment. Even if I had to finish my sentence there was at least a limit; that was only a year ahead. Previously there had seemed no limit: the war went on and on and no one could tell for how many years it would continue.

Two incidents of those last five months stand out in my memory. One morning I opened the "Labour Leader" and on the third page was a large portrait of W. C. Anderson. Across the page the type announced that he was dead. It was a terrible shock. We heard of the death of comrades at the front and in prison (over seventy C.O.s had died since arrest), but one never thought of the death of comrades outside. Anderson had been a specially good friend to me and a hundred and one little

⸰personal memories flooded my mind. The other incident was happier.

One morning Alastar Mac's note (we wrote to each other every day) advised me in careful language that I might expect something exciting. I spent that day on the tip-toe of expectation, half expecting release, straining my ears to interpret distant sounds. Eight o'clock came and the turning down of my cell light. I got down my board and made my bed. I stood on my stool at the window for a long time and looked at the stars. A feeling of great depression came over me. Alastar's note had tuned me up to thrilled expectation; now I went down to the depth of reaction. How like a tomb this cell was! Perhaps I was already dead; perhaps all this thinking I was alive was sheer delusion; perhaps this was really a coffin. . . . . Then suddenly I was sitting up straight, my heart bumping with excitement. Whistles were blowing, voices shouting, doors banging. I listened intently. More warders were being marched into the prison. They were being paraded at the centre and instructions given to them. I could hear steps in the yard outside. I jumped up, dragged the stool to the window and looked into the night. Lights were flashing here and there, into odd corners. There could be only one explanation. There had been an escape.

I was as excited as though it had been myself. I put my mouth to the open pane and jeered at the warders outside. "You won't find him," I shouted. "You won't find him. We'll all escape and you won't find any of us." A warder lifted his light to my window for a moment and then went on with his task, walking gingerly, throwing his light from side to side. I stood at the window and jeered until the search of the yard had concluded and the lights had gone. Then I listened at the door, trying to appraise the various sounds until they had ceased. I was fairly confident that the escaped prisoners had not been recaptured. The warders would have shouted the news to each other if they had caught them.

It was several days before the details came through from Alastar Mac. De Valera and four of his colleagues had got away. This is the story as I heard it in prison.

The Sinn Feiners were interned in a separate hall. The doors were guarded by armed sentries; in the hall itself a warder was always on duty. But within these limits the Irishmen were allowed considerable freedom; they were not confined to cells and could speak, write, read or join in games as they wished. One day the Catholic priest had left his master-key to all the prison locks lying on a table. Quick as a flash Milroy had placed a sheet of clean paper underneath and run a pencil round its outline. The priest found the key where he had left it apparently untouched.

It was Christmas time and Milroy designed a humorous Christmas card for a friend in Manchester. It was entitled "Locked Out" and "Locked In" and had two illustrations. One showed a Christmas reveller trying in vain to insert the key into his front door latch. The second, "Locked In," showed a warder with a gigantic key at his waist; the key was drawn to the outline of the master-key of the prison. The Manchester friend was amused by the card but did not understand its significance. He sent it on to Dublin where, with the assistance of oblique references in letters, the importance of the Christmas greeting was realised. A key was made to the pattern of the warder's key.

The Sinn Feiners were allowed to have food sent in to the prison and a cake was despatched containing the copy of the master-key. It did not fit. Disappointment was conveyed in the next letter to Dublin and a second copy was sent. It did not fit. The third time the copy of the key was accompanied by a file. It was made to fit. Then by letters the date and time of the escape were fixed, the references being apparently to the most innocent domestic events. It was arranged that a car should be in readiness beyond a field at the back of the prison. At five o'clock a Chief Warder always visited the Sinn Feiners' hall. As soon as he had departed on the chosen date, the Irishmen knocked out the warder in charge of them, flung him into a cell, gagged him and locked the door. Then De Valera, Milroy and three others let themselves out by a door which opened on a yard at the back of the prison. The one missing link in my story is how they contrived to pass the armed sentry.

The thirteen Sinn Feiners who remained carried on normally so as not to arouse suspicion, playing their games and singing their songs with a little more noise than usual in order to make up for their absent comrades. It was not until their time for lights out, at ten o'clock, that they were visited and the escape discovered. By then De Valera and his colleagues had had five hours' start and by separate routes they got safely to Ireland. The next time De Valera returned to England it was to sign the Irish Treaty which recognised him as the head of the Free State.

* * *

It was in April, 1919, nearly six months after the Armistice that we were released. I had been in prison twenty-eight months; the final stretch of solitary confinement had lasted eight months. I caught the earliest train to London, so stunned by my freedom that I could not take in the scenes and persons about me. At King's Cross Station I was met by my wife and we travelled down to Stanford-le-Hope, in Essex, where she and our two girl bairns were living at a pacifist-community centre.

Often I think that our wives had a harder time than those of us who were prisoners; they had to live in the middle of a war-mad world and to undergo the contumely which opposition to the war and relationship to an imprisoned "conchy" involved. Lilla did it with unfailing courage, living for many months in a bare caravan looking after Audrey and Margaret, mere babies, going through the last eight months with only one letter from me.

The *finale* of my war-time experiences came a few weeks later. The postman brought a buff envelope with "On His Majesty's Service" printed bold and black. Inside was a form from the War Office recording that I had been discharged from the Army and stating that my behaviour had been so bad that if I ever attempted to join the Army again I would be subject to a sentence of two years' imprisonment with hard labour. The War Office certainly has no sense of humour.

BOOK THREE

Chapter Thirteen
THE PRISON SYSTEM ENQUIRY

It was nearly six months before I was fit to resume work in the Socialist Movement. Through the kindness of N.C.F. friends I convalesced first at Scarborough and then at a guest house standing on rocks jutting out into the sea on the Devon coast. I lived in the sunshine, and prison and war became almost incredible memories. But not quite. Sometimes the freedom I was enjoying made the thought that men and women were still confined in narrow cells intolerable. As I watched my children on the beach I vowed to do what I could to save them from war.

I did not take a complete holiday during these six months. Indeed, ten days after my release from prison I was at the annual conference of the I.L.P. at Leicester. My memory is of a tremendously vital conference, proud of the international socialist stand of the Party during the war and stimulated by the revolutionary atmosphere which had spread from Europe even to Britain. Some members of the Party, notably Philip Snowden, had been critical of the Russian Revolution of October, 1917, but it was significant that the most applauded speech was a eulogy of Soviet Russia by Arthur Ponsonby. I did not intend to speak, because my nerves were still on edge, but when a young Merseyside delegate moved a resolution condemning the prison system I was impelled to do so. I said that half of myself was still in prison with the men and women, whatever their crimes, undergoing what had been my experience. As the days passed I found that this was my dominant emotion. I did not feel that I should be free from prison until I had done what I could to expose and end the system. Very soon I was to have the opportunity I wanted.

When I was ready to return to activity, there was some difficulty about the work I should do. Mrs. Bruce Glasier had edited the "Labour Leader" during my absence and the Party leaders wanted her to remain while I took on the job of London correspondent. I resented this and had a rather sharp correspondence with Philip Snowden. Somehow news of this dispute reached Fleet Street and "John Bull" had paragraphs about it, championing me and even offering me a job. I laughed. Three years earlier its editor, Mr. Horatio Bottomley, had demanded that I should be taken to the Tower and shot! I took on the London correspondence, but only as a part-time job. In addition, I became joint-secretary of the British Committee of the Indian National Congress and joint-Editor of "India," succeeding Sir Evan Cotton.* My colleague was Mr. Syed Hussein, a brilliant young Indian, exquisite in appearance, manners and speech. We didn't have much work to do. The Indian National Congress, beginning to accept non-co-operation, had become sceptical about the value of propaganda in London and we had to hold our hands. Finally, a decision came to close down the British Committee.

My association with Marguerite Louis, who worked with me for seventeen years, began whilst I was editing "India." I 'phoned the National Union of Clerks for a shorthand-typist and Marguerite, a nervous girl of seventeen, arrived. I have teased her since with the story that she began her trial letter "Deaf Sir" and ended it "Frightfully Yours," but it had no foundation in fact: from the first she was the most competent and reliable helper I ever had. Another but more intermittent association dates from this time. A young University student, with a dark skin showing Indian blood, came to ask my advice whether he should accept an invitation to become the Editor of a new paper in India. He was keen-brained and shrewd beyond his years and when I told him that in my experience these journalistic ventures in India often failed to keep their financial obligations, he decided to turn down the offer. That young student was Mr. Palme Dutt, now the leading theoretician of the British Communist Party.

Meanwhile I had taken on another part-time job. Mrs. Sidney Webb invited me to join her nephew, Mr. Stephen Hobhouse, as secretary of the Prison System Enquiry Committee. "Stephen," she said, "is in danger of being buried under the mountain of material he has piled up. I want you to rescue him from it." In addition to these part-time jobs I was doing a good deal of journalistic work and altogether was

* His death is announced on the very day that I am writing this chapter.

making good money—something like a thousand a year. I got Runham Brown to build me a house at Thorpe Bay at the mouth of the Thames. We called it Keir Cottage after Hardie. When the British Committee closed down, I made Keir Cottage my working headquarters. Stephen Hobhouse came and lived with us and Marguerite Louis took lodgings near at hand. It was here that we reduced our mountain of material into the quarter-of-a-million word Report of the Prison System Enquiry Committee.

I learned to revere Stephen Hobhouse for something that I can only describe as his refinement of personality. He came from a rich and influential family—his father was a member of the Liberal Cabinet in pre-war days,—but he deliberately disinherited himself from both the wealth and the social position he had been born to. Becoming a Socialist, he took the view that to live on unearned income was wrong, and went to live in a workmen's tenement in East London, earning his living with great difficulty. I had visited Stephen there before the war and had been deeply moved by the way in which he and his wife, Rosa, devoted themselves with utter selflessness to the Socialist cause. At Thorpe Bay, Stephen was continually struggling against ill-health; his long war-time imprisonment had seriously undermined his frail physique. But with unfailing courage he stuck at our job, doing it with a conscientiousness which was a lesson to me.

Our Committee, despite its imposing name, was in no sense official. The Prison System Enquiry was started by the Labour Research Department, then closely associated with the Labour Party. Later we became an independent organisation. I was not involved in the controversy which brought about the split, but the issue was apparently whether money should be accepted, directly or indirectly, from Soviet Russia. The L.R.D. proposed to supply information to the Soviet Trade Delegation, for which no doubt it would have been paid handsomely. Mr. Bernard Shaw, a member of our Committee, was the severest critic of this intention. I find this passage in a letter which he wrote to me on October 24, 1921 :—

"I have resigned my membership of the Labour Research Department and its Executive Committee. Matters came to a head last Friday when I moved a resolution that the Department must not sell information to Foreign Governments. The Committee muddled itself into passing an addition to my resolution, and then defeated both on their being moved as a substantive resolution. As it is evident that money will be taken from the Russian Trade Delegation, and the Communists on the Committee are too inexperienced and ignorant to avoid compromising themselves, I cleared out. I could have carried a general meeting against them, but not carried on the Department without them; so I fled from the wrath to come."

Although unofficial, our Committee had great standing because of its influential members. Lord Olivier, who had been Governor of Jamaica (the wisest Governor that unfortunate island ever had) was Chairman, and, in addition to Mr. Bernard Shaw, Mr. and Mrs. Sidney Webb, and Miss Margery Fry (then Secretary of the Penal Reform Committee, later Principal of Somerville College, Oxford, and a Director of the B.B.C.) were active members. This was the first time I had come into close contact with the Webbs. Mrs. Webb had joined the I.L.P. in 1912 or 1913 and, unlike her husband, took our view of the war. This was one of the rare occasions when these wonderful Socialist partners differed on a political issue and they solved the difficulty by refraining from expressing their opinions publicly, concentrating instead upon the social issues raised in Britain itself in wartime. I used to go to the Webbs' home in Grosvenor Road, overlooking the Thames on the Westminster side, and, after a meal, we had cosy discussions in their very homely sitting room. Mrs. Webb did most of the talking, with Sidney intervening now and again with a perky little comment accompanied by a little treble chuckle.

Mr. Bernard Shaw was not only a regular and valuable attender of committee meetings; he read every line of what Stephen Hobhouse and I wrote and was active in suggestions. Before this association with Mr. Shaw I knew only his public reputation for dogmatism, egotism and intolerance. I found him exactly the opposite. He was considerate almost to the point of humility on matters where he felt others had greater knowledge.

E

I have been looking at the letters and postcards which Mr. Shaw sent me. Mostly they were postcards written in his neat, thin hand, the address cramped in the top left-hand corner, the card crowded with microscopic writing above the initials "G.B.S." The evidence of a prison chaplain who advocated sterner discipline made him angry; the proof came back annotated: "The scoundrel!" Although G.B.S. was generally appreciative, I have one proof on which he criticised us scathingly. The offending paragraph suggested that if the principle of "indeterminate sentence," were accepted, warders should be selected who could exert "the influence of a wise and warm-hearted friend" because they "naturally have far the best opportunities of judging of a man's true disposition." Shaw's note on the edge of the proof was:—

"This is monstrous. How can wisdom be expected from a warder? His pay does not run to it. What warm-hearted man would choose such an occupation? And how can a man feel friendly to a promiscuous scoundrel whom he has not selected as a friend, and who may be naturally antipathetic to him? The book has not so far sinned in this sentimentally thoughtless way; but this is more than any sane reader can stand. A warder is not a god; and it is idle to say that he 'should naturally' be one."

Our Committee took evidence from over 400 witnesses, three hundred of whom were ex-prisoners and one hundred prison officials. We had the collaboration of many experts, including Mr. Alec Patterson (now a member of the Prison Commission) who wrote the section dealing with Borstal. The Home Office refused us facilities, but I don't think we could have obtained much more first-hand information even if it had opened the prison doors to us. We obtained detailed evidence, not only from conscientious objectors, but from many ex-prisoners who had served sentences for criminal offences, as well as from warders, chaplains, medical officers, governors, prison magistrates, and officials of the Discharged Prisoners' Aid Societies. When our Report, entitled "English Prisons Today," was published, it caused a considerable sensation and the demand for changes in the prison regime became so strong that many reforms were introduced. It became recognised as the standard work on the English Prison system.

There were two features of our Report which mystified the press and the Home Office. We published a series of censored extracts from letters of convicts and we reproduced photographs taken in prison. How had we secured these? We declined to reveal the secret to enquiring journalists, but I think it is safe to do so now. Certain prisons during the war, as I have explained, accommodated "conchies" under the Home Office scheme. They were allowed a good deal of freedom, and the men at Dartmoor found a store-room containing uniforms both of convicts and of the various grades of prison officials. They donned these uniforms and, from their own knowledge of imprisonment, proceeded to act every phase of the routine, whilst one of their number, a press photographer, took the excellent series of pictures which came into our hands.

About the ethical aspect of our method of getting quotations from convicts' letters, there may be differences of opinion. One of the "conchies" at Dartmoor was put on the job of repairing the roof of the office. Instead of repairing the hole he enlarged it and let himself in. There he found a large manuscript volume containing copies of all the extracts from convicts' letters which had been censored by the Governors over a period of years. He climbed back on to the roof with the volume, made a thorough job of repairing the hole, and when he had his next week-end leave (men on the Home Office scheme had this privilege periodically), took his find home. These extracts reflected the reaction to imprisonment of hundreds of convicts more vividly and spontaneously than any other evidence. I was surprised by their literary power; it is evident these men had suffered so deeply that even their illiteracy became eloquent. I quote a few of the extracts here:

During eleventh year of first sentence: "My bitterest enemy I would not send to prison. Never. This place makes curses and sots of men. Some say it is the men, not the place. Partly; but let them do a lagging and find out how quickly all bad qualities come to the surface."

During first sentence: "This life reduces one to the level of a wild beast, and every bit of one's better self is literally torn out. If you come to meet me in August, look out for something between a man and a beast."

During third sentence: "I should like to see anyone make me tender. Why, this life has taken all the feeling out of me. Shall have neither compassion or pity on anyone for the future if they get in my way."

During first sentence: "I won't be sent here any more for being on a roof; I will get inside next time."

During fourth year of third sentence: "Twelve months in this place and a man is eligible for a situation in a deaf and dumb asylum; two years will make him eligible for a padded cell in Colney Hatch; three years for the dogs' home and annihilation. I am eligible for all these."

During second sentence: "This is worse than death. It is a wonder one can suffer so much and yet live. It is a living death."

During first sentence: "Can't sleep, can't read, can't rest; oh, Christ!"

During second sentence: "For God's sake and your own, and for the sake of us all, stretch out a brotherly hand and pluck me from this brand of hell (for it is hell)."

The Committee asked Mr. Bernard Shaw to write the preface of our Report; I was excited when he agreed, for G.B.S. was still my hero among literary men. Within a little more than two months he had completed his 30,000 words. The preface was brilliant and penetrating and I read it with great delight. This was the letter which announced that it was finished.

6th January, 1922.   Ayot St. Lawrence,
                                     Welwyn, Herts.
Dear Fenner Brockway,

At last the terrible preface is finished: thirty-thousand words. You will not get it for a day or two, as I have sent it to my secretary to copy my corrections into her carbon duplicate, so that we may have a second edition to fall back on in case of fire or loss. She will send it on to you by registered letter post . . . .

It is of course possible that the Committee may find that it has got more than it bargained for. My conclusion that there are people who have to be tenderly chloroformed out of existence, and my citation of Queen Victoria as an example of the criminal type produced in domestic life by the imposition of prison conditions on children, may shock them. In that case the sooner you get another preface on the stocks the better . . .

I hope I shall not trip over Hobhouse's confounded conscience or your curious objection to killing, which suggests that you have never lived in the country, where the rabbits and things will kill you if you don't kill them, and that you have never been attacked by a flea. I am a vegetarian purely on humanitarian and mystical grounds; and I have never killed a flea or a mouse vindictively or without remorse; but what ARE you to do with a chap like Landru or a woman like— well, you can supply half a dozen names—if you cannot find some morbid person to lead them about on a leash?

Faithfully,
G. Bernard Shaw.

I suppose I must have replied to Mr. Shaw suggesting that M. Landru and the unnamed woman should be put in special asylums, because I find a postcard, dated four days later, which reads as follows:—

"The difficulty is that the special asylum must be an autocratic one; otherwise you are sacrificing useful and comparatively innocent human lives to maintain noxious ones; and unless you can get volunteers for this *dis*service, who is to man the special asylums? Even now you get warders only because the alternatives are so poor. That wouldn't be so under a higher social development. If under Socialism there were still volunteers, I should regard their task as so morbid that I would kill them too.

G.B.S.

I retorted that I should not expect to find Landru or the unnamed woman under Socialism; but this argument was only incidental—I welcomed the preface and looked forward eagerly to its appearance with our Report. But not so Stephen. He announced that if Shaw's preface were accepted by the Committee he would withdraw his name as one of the Editors. I was bitterly distressed. After all the work Stephen had put in it was impossible not to have his name with mine as an Editor.

But the thought of losing Shaw's preface nearly broke my heart. Then Mr. Shaw made a great gesture of conciliation. He offered to re-write all the paragraphs in the preface which contained the Lethal Chamber proposal so as to include an alternative—the care of the incurable criminals by volunteers who had a sense of vocation for the task. Mr. Shaw reported this to me on a postcard which indicated his inability to attend a special meeting of the Committee to discuss the "crisis." He wrote :—

"However, I want to add to the preface an explanation that the Class A lethal treatment is not an essential part of it, and that it is possible to make an absolute condition that life is not to be taken *all at once* under any circumstances from idiot or criminal or anyone else, and that this condition can be carried out if custodians can be found for the Impossibilists. Also, of course, that many people and some nations take this view.

"But the lethal chamber must be dealt with and faced frankly if we are to affect the very vigorous and influential people who are not opposed to State powers of life and death. I will do what I can to make the preface acceptable; but the foreword plan will not do.* It is silly to adopt a preface and then cry stinking fish. I don't mind a minority report on a point or two, but *I won't be disclaimed*. Unless the Committee is prepared to back up my general principle for all it is worth, it must be honest and drop me altogether."

Stephen Hobhouse, however, would not accept the compromise, and I had the humiliation of hearing the decision to transfer the Preface from our Report to the book on "Prisons Under Local Government," which the Webbs had written. The only consolation I had was that the Preface remained a "boost" of our Report. I wrote to Mr. Shaw expressing my disappointment, but paying a tribute to Stephen's loyalty to principle. This is the final (undated) letter which I had from Mr. Shaw on the matter :—

"I quite understand your side of the affair. In fact, I made the alterations to satisfy you, knowing quite well that they

---

* A suggestion that there should be a foreword making Mr. Shaw alone responsible for his Preface.

would only intensify Stephen's real objection to my intrusion. I have written him to say that he must now provide a preface himself: he can't leave the book incomplete, and throw away a chance that will never recur in our lives, after turning down my completion. If he will not (which will mean that he can't) something might be done by having the last chapter elaborated by Lowes Dickinson or Olivier; in fact, there is a great deal to be said for the preface coming at the end instead of at the beginning. But the moral must be drawn. I think Stephen can do it if he sets about it: he writes well; and this affair shows that he is an artist at heart, with all the artistic horror of having his work meddled with by anyone else, and a considerable touch of the artist's infernal egotism; so he must pay the price of his privilege as an artist by giving out all that he has to give, no matter how exhausting the labour involved may be.

Faithfully,

G. BERNARD SHAW.

The Report went out with a final chapter largely written by Mr. Lowes Dickinson on the need to revise penal theory and a note by the Chairman, Lord Olivier. I was not satisfied. We had exposed the prison system, but we had not made proposals for any comprehensive alternative and the wish to do so persisted in the background of my mind. Seven years went by, however, before I had an opportunity to write " A New Way With Crime."

The supreme lesson which I learned from my study of criminology and penal methods was that the problem is inseparable from the problem of the social and economic system. The vast majority of those in prison are the victims of economic conditions, and when they leave they have little chance to obtain the security which would encourage them to turn their backs on the petty thefts and similar offences which take them to prison again and again. Most startling of all was the realisation that, intolerable as are the conditions in prison, many actually find them preferable to the hunger and the slum life which are their lot outside.

My work on the Prison System Enquiry Committee finished, I was ready to return to the struggle for Socialism and Peace.

Chapter Fourteen
THE FIRST YEARS OF PEACE

During the years when I was engaged on the Prison System Enquiry, my mind made no progress politically. I was interested, but I was a spectator on the bank of the stream and did not move with it. They were disastrous years for the working-class, witnessing a retreat from the revolutionary mood which followed the Armistice to the "class collaboration" mood of the threatened depression of 1921. I did not realise at the time the real significance of what was happening. I was sufficiently a Socialist to be disgusted by the huge posters adorned by portraits of Trade Union leaders carrying appeals to the workers to produce more, but I continued to put confidence in the mere Parliamentary advance of Labour, pinning all my hopes to a Labour Government. I had not yet become disillusioned either about Labour Party post-war policy or about constitutional possibilities. My main political interest was in the Peace Movement rather than the class struggle. I became Chairman of the British No More War Movement and of the War Resisters' International and devoted to their activities most of what time the Prison System Enquiry left me.

The story of the War Resisters' International is an epic. Those of us who resisted in Britain during the war had little knowledge of other resisters, but we felt confident that our convictions must be held by similar groups in other countries. When we were released from prison we learned of strong movements of resisters in America and New Zealand, but we were disappointed to find that in Europe resisters were limited to groups of religious objectors and to a few isolated individuals; we had not recognised that conscription was so much a part of the Continental system, taking young men into the army as a matter of course, that the idea of resistance could hardly take root.

Nevertheless, my fellow C.O. friend, Runham Brown, had faith enough to set about establishing the War Resisters' International and, after endless seeking through isolated contacts in one country after another, similar movements began to reveal themselves. The beginning of the movement in Germany was of particular interest; it was initiated by two Germans who were interned in this country during the war and who were so impressed by the No Conscription Fellowship that they started a parallel movement as soon as they got back to Berlin and succeeded in forming a quite strong organisation during the reaction against war in the early twenties. At its headquarters in Berlin the organisation installed a plaque in memory of the seventy British resisters who died after arrest; it depicted a cell scene, with rays of light from the window carrying the message "No More War" in nine different languages, and beneath were inscribed the seventy names of the men who died during our struggle. A photograph of this plaque hangs on my office wall; sometimes I wonder what has happened to the original.*

Those of us who founded the War Resisters' International insisted from the first that it must be anti-capitalist as well as pacifist. We repudiated "bourgeois" pacifism, wished to extend individual resistance to a general strike against war, and stood for "revolution by non-violence." The membership was both anarchist and socialist and, while assistance was given to religious objectors to war, the influence of the organisation was always exerted to emphasise the identity of the struggle against war and the struggle against the economic system which is its cause.

My work in the W.R.I. brought me into contact with many interesting personalities from other countries. There was Dr. Helene Stöcker, leader of the feminist movement in Germany, medical initiator of Birth Control Clinics, Socialist and friend of Soviet Russia, an enormous woman, as large mentally as physically, generous in spirit and comradeship. There was Bart de Ligt, the Dutch author, whose book, "The Conquest of Violence" has outlined the technique of non-violent revolution in elaborate detail, only ignoring the fact that Capitalism has created a psychology which will not allow its mass application. I was distressed to hear of the death of de Ligt in 1938; he was a fine and brave comrade of great dynamic power. Another magnetic personality, gentle and persuasive, was Rajendra Prasad, a friend of Gandhi, and later the Chairman of the Indian National Congress. He addressed one of our international conferences held in a mountain village in Austria.

* Alas! my copy has also been destroyed by the Nazis. The I.L.P. Head Office and all it contained were destroyed in a blitz in May, 1941.

One W.R.I. visit abroad of which I have a clear memory was to Bilthoven, in Holland, where, amidst the sand-dunes and pines, Kaas Böcker and his English wife—a daughter of the Birmingham Cadburys—ran a small community on equalitarian lines. Mrs. Böcker had transferred her considerable income to the Works' Council at Cadbury Brothers and she lived with the other members of the Bilthoven community in extreme, and sometimes anxious, simplicity. After our committee meeting at Bilthoven we held a big demonstration at Amsterdam, attended by thousands. The result of my speech, advocating a general strike against war, was an order to leave the country at once, together with instructions prohibiting my return. As, however, visas to Holland were abolished shortly afterwards, this prohibition never inconvenienced me.

The most memorable event during these years was the decision of the entire British Labour movement in 1920 to declare a general strike if the Government took any hostile step against Soviet Russia. Under Winston Churchill's influence, the British Government had financed the White Russian forces of Deniken and Kolchak to the extent of one hundred million pounds, but Trotsky's Red Army had defeated the Whites despite the British assistance. Then another opportunity arose for Churchill and his friends. Poland and Russia were at loggerheads; British support for Poland might bring about the downfall of the Leninist regime. At the height of the crisis, workers at the London docks were ordered to load munitions on a ship called the "Jolly George" bound for Poland. The dockers refused to touch the munitions and immediately the whole working-class movement of Britain flamed into action. I have never known any action so spontaneous; in every town in the country, at a day's notice, the workers poured in their thousands into the central squares or meeting places and everywhere Councils of Action were formed and the demand raised for a general strike.

I was one of the I.L.P. delegates at the National Labour Conference which was called; it represented the united political and industrial strength of the movement. The fact that Mr. J. H. Thomas presided indicates that it was by no means a conference of the Left, and the Right was in favour of the most drastic action no less than the Left. With absolute unanimity a resolution was adopted authorising the calling of strike action should the Government take any step against Russia; the transport workers, the engineers and the miners would be called out at once and the rest of the movement would be levied to support them, each section pledging itself to join the strike if required. Nor was there any hiding of the implications of the decision. I remember Mr. Thomas saying from the chair, "with a full sense of responsibility" (how that phrase pleased his pride!), that the decision was "revolutionary" and challenged not only the Government but the Constitution. The temper of the workers was such that they were ready for this; if the choice were between defiance of the Constitution and war against Russia, they would defy the Constitution.

The Government announced the next day that it was all a misunderstanding; it had never intended any action hostile to Russia. But, if I may anticipate, when the Trades Disputes Act was introduced in 1927, following the failure of the General Strike on behalf of the miners the preceding year, it included a clause making strike action against war illegal, and Mr. Churchill justified it by saying that Labour's threat of unconstitutional action in 1920 was aimed at compelling the lawfully elected government of that time to modify a policy which in its considered opinion was best for Britain, Europe and the world!

In 1922 the No More War Movement initiated a world-wide campaign of demonstrations which had great spectacular success. The demonstrations were held on the first Sunday of August, the anniversary of the outbreak of war in 1914, and took place simultaneously all over the world—in France, Germany, Poland, Austria and most of the countries of Europe, America, the Dominions and India. The most remarkable one I attended was in Max Reinhardt's vast theatre in Berlin. It was organised by the People's Theatre Movement, and it was carried through with impressive drama and colour. The vast open stage was carpeted and curtained in red; in the centre stood a lonely lecture desk. Those of us who were to speak were grouped in a box level with the stage and as our turns came the Chairman led us each to the desk and then returned to the box, leaving us alone in the wide red space to face the crowd of many thousands which crowded the auditorium and galleries. This was sufficiently nerve-racking, but the lighting technique was still more disturbing. As soon as one faced the audience, all the lights went out except a terrifically powerful spot light thrown on to the speaker alone. I have never spoken under more weird conditions, dazzled by light, yet facing an audience in utter darkness.

The speakers were German, English and French—the German, Crispien; the French, Jean Longuet. Later I came to know both Crispien and Longuet well as members of the Executive of the Second International. Both of them courageously opposed the war of 1914-18, but, like myself, as pacifist Socialists rather than revolutionary Socialists; indeed, that was their temperament. Crispien was tall, sandy-haired and bearded, blue-eyed and of a gentle demeanour; on the International Executive we used to call him "Jesus Christ." Jean Longuet, although the son-in-law of Karl Marx, looked like a kindly sentimental business man. He was a generous soul, a great peacemaker between quarrelling sections in the French Socialist Party or the International, but, like many peace-makers, a compromiser rather than a leader.*

But if our speeches at the Berlin demonstration were not revolutionary, the stage immediately afterwards became a messenger of the Revolution. A speaking choir composed of hundreds of men, women and children enacted the hopes of the pre-war years, the horror of the war years, the misery of the post-war years—and finally the overthrow of Capitalism and war. It was the first time I had heard a speaking choir and I was tremendously impressed. The voices of the men, women, boys and girls approached the harmony of base, tenor, soprano and contralto singing voices. We heard the moaning of misery, the ferocity of anger, the earnestness of exhortation, the cry of triumph. I shall not forget the last scene, when the hundreds of actors massed on the platform with red banners to sing "The Internationale," the audience joining in with sweeping emotion. When will Berlin witness such a scene again?

I acted as Publicity Secretary for these demonstrations and did the work thoroughly, not only making the movement front page news in the dailies, but syndicating news and articles to all the provincial press and running a press service in French,

*Longuet died early in 1939.

German and Spanish for newspapers abroad. Among those whom I invited to write and to speak was Mr. Bernard Shaw. In my collection of his letters I find this reply:—

Tenby, 26th July, 1922.

MY DEAR BROCKWAY,

I grieve to say that I don't believe in these demonstrations. People who get emotionally excited about peace are precisely the people who get emotionally excited about war. In this matter, action and reaction are equal. Lloyd George will do all that is necessary to make the nation send Christmas cards to all the other nations until he wants to send them to the trenches again. Ten minutes after that he will have them telling stories of enemy sergeants (probably French this time) with their pouches full of gouged English eyes and throwing bricks at you as you are dragged back to prison.

It is a mistake to suppose that every evil in the world can be eradicated by an article of a thousand words by me. I write so well that it is a pleasure to read what I have to say on any subject for the few people who read anything at all: but the world goes on just as it did before.

I shall not be within reach of Hyde Park when your big demonstration comes off. I don't know yet where I shall be; but if there is a demonstration on that favoured spot, I shall no doubt tell the inhabitants what I think of war and what I think of them if they ask me to . . . .

Faithfully,

G. BERNARD SHAW.

Writing in this year of war crises, 1939, one realises how superficial was the effect of the imposing No More War demonstrations which we organised from 1922 to 1924 and how justifiable was Mr. Shaw's cynicism.

My concentration in the Peace Movement did not prevent me from accepting an invitation to become the Parliamentary candidate for the Lancaster division. This was my first effort to get into Parliament and I took it very seriously, arranging an impressive platform campaign which included Ramsay Mac-Donald, Lord Haldane, Bernard Shaw, Robert Smillie, Maude Royden, J. R. Clynes, C. R. Attlee, and Philip Snowden as speakers. Lord Haldane's participation came about in a curious way. Mrs. Webb had arranged a drawing room meeting in the West End of London to raise funds for the Prison System Enquiry and Lord Haldane presided. Both Stephen Hobhouse and I spoke and Mrs. Webb introduced me to the chairman as the candidate for Lancaster.

"You certainly ought to be in the House," said Lord Haldane. "May I come and speak for you?" I was embarrassed. Lord Haldane had been a Liberal Imperialist and was one of the three men in the Cabinet who kept secret the British commitments to France. I was very disturbed when after the war the Labour Party accepted him as a member.

"I have been one of the most vigorous critics of your part in the diplomacy which led to the war," I said to him. "Does that matter?" Lord Haldane replied smilingly. "Neither of us wants another war. Besides, I will avoid controversy. I will speak on education." So Lord Haldane came and delivered one of the most remarkable speeches I have heard. There was no rhetoric and his theme was confined to a plea that every growing citizen should have the opportunity to learn to think by correct processes so as to enable the community to attain to Truth. But there was a quality about this speech which made rhetoric irrelevant—it lifted one to mountain altitudes of icy whiteness in which the heat of passion and the colour of emotion ceased to exist.

When Ramsay MacDonald came to Lancaster, he travelled with me from London. It was one of the most uncomfortable journeys I have had. We hardly spoke half-a-dozen sentences all the way, although we had the carriage to ourselves for the five hours. I cannot explain this antipathy; I was never easy in MacDonald's presence and, judging from the last words which I heard him utter, I think he must also have been conscious of a strain. On that occasion I was crossing the lobby at the House of Commons with James Maxton when MacDonald approached. It was about two months before he died and, despite the honours and adulation which had been his, he looked a lonely, disappointed man. He laid a hand on Maxton's arm. "Oh, Jimmy," he said, "I was staying with Sir James Barrie last week-end and he was enquiring most kindly after you." He hesitated and then added rather wistfully: "It's good to think that we can have mutual friends even if fate has separated us from each other." "Och, Mac," said Jimmy, characteristically, "I shall always have a warm place in my heart for you for old times' sake." MacDonald looked wonderingly at me. "I'm not so sure about Fenner," he said. "I'm not sure that he was my friend even in the old times." He and Jimmy laughed, and I laughed, too, rather uneasily. MacDonald passed on without another word.

Bernard Shaw's visit to Lancaster was memorable in an unusual way. His speech was a failure—a hopeless failure. For an hour and a half he rambled on, with none of the vivacity or audacity with which I had known him to fascinate other audiences. Then came the concluding sentence, and it so saved the speech that there were some who believed that Shaw had deliberately bored us all for those disappointing ninety minutes in order to stage his climax. Shaw paused, drew himself up to his straightest height, crossed his arms over his chest, and his worried features turned into a smile. "Ladies and gentlemen," he said. "You will at least be able to inform your incredulous grandchildren that you heard Bernard Shaw when he was dull." He turned, walked sharply to his chair, sat down and glared at the audience, which broke into laughter for the first time.

But if those who thought the dullness deliberate had accompanied Shaw back to the hotel they would have been surprised: he was humiliated by his failure. He could not have apologised more feelingly if he had been the most ingenuous novice.

When the election came we polled the record vote of 9,000 against 18,000 for the Conservative. My opponent was Mr. Singleton, a leading Lancashire barrister and now a Judge.*

I still made a point of attending the I.L.P. Annual Conferences. The keenest controversy raged round the new Communist International. The Second International had failed tragically in the war. Did the Third International offer a new hope for the workers? A strong section of the Party, led by Saklatvala, the fiery Indian orator, Ellen Wilkinson, a sharp-tongued little fury just out of college, and Walton Newbold, a convert from Quakerism to Communism, favoured

---

* I contested Lancaster again under war conditions in November, 1941, polling 5,418.

affiliation to the Third. At the other extreme, Ramsay MacDonald wanted to return to the Second. The main body of the Party was uncertain. The I.L.P. was associated with the Vienna Union (sometimes described contemptously as the "Two-and-a-Half" International), consisting of Parties which had dis-avowed the wartime "social patriotism" of the Second, but which were unwilling to go into the Third. The Vienna Union did not aim at being an International, however, and left the main issue unsettled.

In 1920 the National Council of the Party sent R. C. Wallhead and Clifford Allen to Russia to investigate the conditions of affiliation to the Third International. They published a report against affiliation, together with a vigorous reply from Moscow to the questions they submitted, written (I afterwards learned from Harry Pollitt) by Lenin himself. I agreed with their advice, first because as a pacifist I rejected the view that Socialism could be established only by civil war, and second because I felt Russian psychology and methods could not be applied successfully to Britain. At the same time I was opposed to reunion with the war-supporting parties of the Second International, because they showed no sign of having fundamentally changed their view. I favoured the "reconstructionists" of the Vienna Union, who advocated an International of the anti-war Parties and such sections as had "repented" of their treachery to international Socialism during the war. This plan, however, was destroyed when the Italian Socialist Party decided (temporarily) to join the Third International and when the German Independent Socialists split, some going to the Communist Party and some back to the Social Democrats. The I.L.P. then advocated a reunion of all international forces—Second, Third, and Vienna Union.

These issues were fought out violently at the Party conference held in Glasgow in 1920 and in Southport in 1921. My recollections are scrappy. At Glasgow Clifford Allen first made his mark as a national figure in the I.L.P. Before the war he had had only a local reputation at Cambridge; during the war his activities had been concentrated in the No Conscription Fellowship. At Glasgow, having recovered from the serious illness which had resulted from his imprisonment, he came out as leader of the line which got the majority—no affiliation with the Second and non-committal enquiry about the Third. In three years Allen was to become chairman of the I.L.P. This Glasgow success was his baptism in Party controversy.

The Communists split from the I.L.P. after the Southport conference a year later, but among the leaders neither Ellen Wilkinson nor Walton Newbold (although he became Communist M.P. for Motherwell) remained in the Party long. Saklatvala won a Battersea seat and continued with the Communists until he died, though there were rumours of differences with the Party in his later years.

The second big political issue inside the I.L.P. during these years was its relationship with the Labour Party. After the reconstruction of the Labour Party in 1918, the I.L.P. had begun to recede in influence within the Labour Movement. The disappearance of MacDonald, Snowden and its best known leaders from Parliament in 1918 meant that it also had less standing among the general public. This coincided with a great leap forward by the Labour Party, which ousted the Liberal Party from its historical role as the governmental alternative to the Conservatives by becoming the second Party in the State. For a time I myself began to doubt whether it was necessary to maintain the I.L.P. This was due partly to the marking-time phase in my views which I have described, but also to the fact that in the sphere of international politics which then interested me most, the Labour Party had moved far towards the I.L.P. position, denouncing the Versailles Treaty as strongly as we did.

Then another development took place which added to the doubt whether the retention of a separate I.L.P. was necessary. At the General Election of 1922 the I.L.P had a "come-back" which appeared to place the control of the Labour Party in our hands. Over one hundred I.L.P. members were elected to Parliament, including the lively Scottish contingent of Wheatley, Maxton, Johnston, Kirkwood and others, and the triumphant return of MacDonald and Snowden ended their period in the political wilderness. Thanks to the vote of the I.L.P. M.P.s, MacDonald was elected leader of the Parliamentary Party in place of J. R. Clynes.

These political considerations were complicated by an organisational difficulty. Before 1918 no individual could join the Labour Party except through an affiliated organisation; in practice, this meant that Socialists joined through membership of either the Fabian Society or the I.L.P. But in 1918 the Individual Sections of the Labour Party were established and in many parts of the country they entered into competition with the I.L.P. Many in the I.L.P. wished to challenge the effort of the Labour Party to build up an individual membership; this view was held vigorously in areas like Scotland, Bradford and Norwich, where the I.L.P. was strong and where for all practical purposes it served as the individual membership of the Labour Party. We discussed this question at a series of conferences, where I argued against an organisational conflict between the two parties and urged that the function of the I.L.P. within the Labour Party was educational, leading it towards a more challengingly Socialist position.

Temporarily the controversies within the I.L.P. were to settle themselves by a dramatic development of its policy and organisation. Clifford Allen led this Party revolution.

Chapter Fifteen
CLIFFORD ALLEN PUTS THE I.L.P. ON THE MAP

I returned to activity at the Head Office of the I.L.P. at the moment which marked this historical change in its policy. It was the beginning of the Clifford Allen period. Allen's influence on the Party, first as Treasurer and then as Chairman, was so great that I must try to interpret his personality and explain his political plan more fully than I have yet done.

Allen was an exceptional man. He had great personal charm, which ensured the co-operation of almost anyone whom he selected for his purposes. He had a magnetic personality which enabled him, more by the poignant appeal of his voice than by use of rhetoric, to hold an audience in rapt attention. He was the best chairman I have known, either in committee or conference, and the most efficient administrator, seeing everything through to the last detail. He was a wizard with money. His plans were breath-taking in their scope, but he could always produce the finance required, whether a hundred pounds, or a thousand, so he got his way. It was this which finally gave him his power.

When Allen became treasurer of the Party in 1922 it had reached a critical stage. I have described how the I.L.P. appeared to be down and out in the years immediately after the war. A come-back was staged at the Woolwich by-election in 1920, when Ramsay MacDonald was nominated. We put our all into it (I spent night after night canvassing), but we lost: the Party was still in the wilderness. In addition, it was rent in twain by the internal conflict about the Communist International. There were many who doubted whether there was any future for the I.L.P.

This was the situation when Allen deliberately set out to put the I.L.P. on the map again. He discussed the problem one memorable evening when he invited me to his flat in Battersea shortly after his return from Russia in 1920. He was enthusiastic about the big things which Lenin and his colleagues were doing, but he shrank from repeating their methods in Britain. "Our task," he said, "is to make the fundamental change to

Socialism as speedily and thoroughly as it has been done in Russia, but by the method of persuasion rather than force. We must state the case for Socialism so convincingly that all people of intelligence and goodwill will turn to it. Persuasion and courage—these are the two things we need. Persuasion in advocacy; courage in action. If the I.L.P. can become the instrument of such a policy, it will sweep all before it."

I was greatly attracted by this approach and joined Allen and a few friends in a kind of unofficial group within the Party. We set out to re-state its policy, to re-organise and re-invigorate its activities, and to win key positions which would enable us to apply our plans. Clem Attlee, now Labour's Parliamentary Leader, was one of us. Attlee joined the army during the 1914-1918 war and had become a Major, but he reacted from his experiences, as so many other soldiers did, to an extreme anti-militarist and socialist position.

The first activity of the Allen group was to draft a new Constitution for consideration by the 1922 conference. I think Allen, Attlee, and I must have been a sub-committee on this because I have memories of prolonged lunch-hour discussions. There was a fourth member of our committee who escapes my memory. Was he H. N. Brailsford, G. D. H. Cole, Creech Jones or Allen Skinner? All of them co-operated with us. The main controversial points were insistence upon workers' control within socialised industry and the policy of total disarmament for the International. At the Nottingham Conference we succeeded in getting considerable portions of our draft accepted and as in addition Clifford Allen was elected treasurer, we considered the proceedings a great triumph. Allen immediately used his control of the purse to put into operation his plans for re-organising the Party and re-orientating its policy. He became in effect the directing head of the Party.

I was drawn into this development by the publicity work which I began to do for the Party at Allen's request. Then in December, 1922, he invited me to join the Head Office staff as Organising Secretary. I went to see him in his delightful new home in the pine woods above Friday Street in Surrey; here he had settled down with his wife Joan, a lovely girl whom he had met during a holiday trip to Rome, where she was an art student. That week-end Allen outlined his whole plan, and.

although I was a little disappointed not to be asked back to
the editorship of the "Labour Leader," I was enthused by its
scope and gladly agreed to become one of his lieutenants.
I.L.P. salaries during the Allen régime were high compared with
the present maximum of £250, but even so the acceptance of
this post meant a drop in my income from £800 to £450 a year.
I was so much under the glamour of Allen's personality and
plans, however, that I returned home more excited about future
prospects than I had been since the war.

The renaissance of the I.L.P. in the years which followed
was not all due, of course, to the leadership of Allen; the march
of events was on his side. But the expansion of the Party
which followed was phenomenal. In the four months between
December, 1922, when I became Organising Secretary, and
Easter, 1923, when the Annual Conference was held, 116 new
branches were formed. During the following two years the
number of branches rose from 637 to 1,028. In paragraphs of
the Annual Report for which Allen was responsible I was praised
for this, but in fact the advance was due to favourable political
circumstances exploited to the utmost by his skill and imagination. In more recent years I have been responsible for Party
organisation when political circumstances have been unfavour-
able, and have learned how much greater is the test of adversity
than of success.

Before I describe the changes which Allen carried through,
I must sketch broadly his conception of policy because this
dominated all that he did and had a big influence on the
development of the Party and, indeed, on Socialist theory and
practice in wider spheres. The key to his central purpose was
in that scrap of conversation I had with him on his return from
Russia. He set out to elaborate a policy which would make the
fundamental change from Capitalism to Socialism rapidly but
without violent revolution, and to state it in such persuasive
terms that the intellectual sections of the community, as well
as the working masses, would be won for its support. Often I
heard Allen say that the socialist task must be approached as
scientifically as medical specialists approach any case of disease.
The body politic is suffering from ills: what is their cause, what
is the remedy, how is the remedy to be applied? Both the
diagnosis and the treatment must be made with exactness.

But Allen went further than this, challenging the accepted outlook of democracy. Circumstances might give Socialists an opportunity to apply their remedy before public opinion had been converted; Social Democrats argued that in such a position they could not go faster than public opinion. To Allen this was apostasy. If a doctor were called in to deal with a critical case, would he apply less than the remedy required because those who summoned him to the patient's bedside were ignorant of medical science? If he did he would be unworthy of his calling and a traitor to truth. The same with the Socialist. Given an opportunity to remove the ills of society he must seize it boldly, winning public opinion by the success of his operation. At the moment when Allen argued thus his theory was not merely academic. The Labour Party was on the eve of its first period of office, and Allen was using the considerable influence of the I.L.P. to secure the adoption of his tactic by those who would control the Government.

Starting out with these objects, Allen gathered round him a group of intellectuals to work out a Socialist Plan scientifically. Just as during the war the I.L.P. was invaded by middle-class pacifists, so now it was invaded by middle-class "experts." The committee set up to elaborate the Socialist Plan consisted of H. N. Brailsford, J. A. Hobson, Creech Jones, and Frank Wise. Wise was an ex-civil servant of distinction; he had been economic adviser to Lloyd George at international conferences, and had since become London head of the Russian Co-operative organisation. Creech Jones was head of the Research department of the Transport Workers' Union. Hobson was, of course, the distinguished economist, and Brailsford at that time was at the height of his reputation as a socialist thinker and author. Round this central committee hummed and buzzed sub-committees on different aspects of policy, manned by civil servants, professors, economists and authors.

Allen saw that his first step to win the intellectuals must be the production of a Party paper which would compel their respect. The "Labour Leader" had slumped badly both in circulation and content; under his inspiration a clean break was made. The title of the paper was changed to the "New Leader," Brailsford was appointed Editor with a salary of £1,000 a year, a Fleet Street manager was brought in at £750, and an editorial and business staff of considerable proportions was appointed. Brailsford produced a paper of great literary and artistic merit, loved by school teachers for its Nature Notes, adored by artists for its woodcuts, and revered by intellectuals for its theoretical features.

Allen was elected chairman of the Party at the Easter Conference, 1923, and I became secretary of the Party during the same year. One of Allen's first actions was to transfer the Head Office to impressive premises in Great George Street, Westminster, within a stone's throw of the House of Commons. With the exception of the Board Room (which had a wonderful Adam fireplace) my room was the most impressive of all; there was an arched doorway in peacock blue, and an oak mantelpiece with grey-green tiles. The I.L.P. was very respectable in these days. The Labour Party was rising to the crest of its strength and wealthy careerists buzzed around us, anxious to be adopted as candidates, proffering contributions in the hope of securing rewards after the manner of the old parties. I remember one young man who explained that he had a sufficient competence in the advertising world and wished "to take up politics." For three weeks he had considered which Party he should join and had decided that prospects were most promising in the Labour Party. "I've come to you, old fellow," he explained patronisingly, "because I'm informed that the I.L.P. is the boiler-house of the Labour Party. Can you find me a seat?" I sent the young man sorrowfully away. On another occasion a disagreeable-mannered gentleman offered me £25,000 on the understanding that a Liberal Nonconformist business man in the north of England, for whom he was acting, should be given a peerage when Labour came to power! I played with him a little because I was then preparing a pamphlet on "The Honours System" and wanted juicy evidence, but he became suspicious and disappeared.

A visitor of another kind was introduced by my friend Arthur Ponsonby. He explained that the son of John St. Loe Strachey, the editor of the "Spectator," had become converted to Socialism while at Oxford, and wanted to find a niche of service in the movement; could I find him an opening? John Strachey made the impression of a vast over-grown boy, sincere in his desire to help the Socialist Movement, but knowing very little about it. I roped him in to help in the Information Department and, finding that he had a clear, persuasive style of writing, to write for the "New Leader." He contributed a series of articles for our paper which caused a fierce controversy: the subject was "What Youth Is Thinking," and he described with considerable freedom the new views on the sex relationship. The articles outraged the Nonconformist-minded Labour M.P.s, of whom there were many. One hotly remarked that they would lose the general election for the Labour Party because they would be interpreted as a defence of free love! A more useful service which Strachey rendered later on was to edit the paper which we started to help the miners during their long lock-out in 1926. "The Miner" reached a circulation of 90,000 a week and carried the fiery message of Arthur Cook even more widely than the speeches which he delivered so tirelessly to crowds of thousands from one end of the country to the other. Strachey had one characteristic that astonished me in an Oxford graduate. His handwriting was so bad that one typist had to be trained specially to read it. His spelling would have disgraced a child of ten at an elementary school. He spelled "which" as "wich" and "people" as "peeple," not because he believed in phonetics but because he could not spell any better. Since those days he has become a distinguished author. I wonder whether he still writes and spells as badly?

An elaborate I.L.P. organisation developed during the Allen régime was the Information Department. Its Secretary was Ernest Hunter, now the political expert of the "Daily Herald,"* who had the great gift of reducing any subject to popular and propaganda terms. The Information Department maintained a status semi-independent from the Party and was controlled by a committee of which Ramsay MacDonald was Chairman. It was known as his "pet" and Ernest Hunter as his Good Man Friday. Later, when the Party and MacDonald came into conflict, the Department was a useful "nest" for him inside headquarters. One of its most enthusiastic collaborators was Mary Agnes Hamilton, afterwards Labour M.P. for Blackburn, biographer of MacDonald ("The Man of To-morrow") and later MacDonald's selection as a Director of the B.B.C.

*Hunter afterwards became Chairman of the Journalists' Union.

The I.L.P. Summer Schools were revolutionised in character by Clifford Allen. In his day they were very high-brow affairs with lectures delivered exclusively by the "intellectuals," and with the students drawn almost as exclusively from the middle-class. Allen himself presided all through the month, setting the mood of an almost religious "search for Truth." For a time the schools were held in various parts of the country, but they settled down for several years at Easton Lodge, the stately seat of the Countess of Warwick, where the students used laughingly to boast that they had slept in the bed of Edward VII, whose portrait seemed to adorn every room.

A frequent visitor to the school at Easton Lodge was H. G. Wells. Sometimes he would join in the discussions, but he evidently enjoyed more the social parties which we ran in the evenings. I shall never forget his part in the game of "The Grand Old Duke of York." Every time a girl danced down between the two opposing rows of men and women he was not satisfied with clapping his hands. He jumped up and down as excited as a child exclaiming "Pretty, pretty, pretty" in his piping voice. Sometimes we adjourned to Wells' house for the parties, playing in a barn a vigorous and exciting ball game which he had invented and at which Oswald Mosley became an adept. Despite our different conceptions of Socialism, I had a very great respect for the mind of H. G. Wells. I remember how angry I was with Mosley at one of the later Summer School discussions, when he answered a contribution from H. G. Wells by a demagogic playing-to-the-gallery class war speech composed of sheer thoughtless invective. This must have been in 1925 just after Mosley joined us, and I was appalled at the indecency of this bumptious utterance from a rich young recruit who took it upon himself to act as spokesman of the poor and condemn a man who, whatever his faults as a theoretician, had contributed much to the Socialist thought of our time. It is a little ironical to remember the incident now. The best that can be said for Mosley's Fascism is that it is an adaptation of the view which Wells then expressed that the new ordered world must come through the dictatorship of brains rather than of the proletariat —but the Fascists have substituted "brutality" for "brains."

Another reflection of Allen's influence on the Party was the creation of the "Masses Stage and Film Guild," of which I was

Chairman; it produced plays and showed films on a scale never before attempted by the Socialist Movement in this country. Miles.Malleson was appointed Director and gave most of his efforts to the establishment of amateur dramatic companies, which produced, and quite creditably, plays like Toller's "Masses and Men." The Guild also had the help of leading professional actors and actresses, including Sybil Thorndike, Lewis Casson, Milton Rosmer, Elsa Lanchester, and Harold Scott. Arthur Bourchier and Kyrle Bellew loaned us the Strand Theatre, and every Sunday night it was packed. Reginald Stamp, who now controls the amusements of London as Chairman of the L.C.C. Licensing and Entertainments Committee, was the organiser of a remarkable series of shows, half drama, half music. Bernard Shaw, John Galsworthy, Laurence Housman gave their support, allowing us to use their one-act plays. Once a month we had a film show, crowding the Regal Cinema at Marble Arch with members of the Guild and their friends; the star film was usually Russian, but we also ran shorts by John Grierson and others.

But while all these developments, organisational and educational, were proceeding, Allen's main interest was in the political application of his new socialist theories. During 1924 the Socialist Plan Committee published its Report. It elaborated a programme which aimed at two things: the establishment of a minimum standard of life for all and the nationalisation of the pivots of Capitalism. The Plan was simple in design. It laid down a minimum living income and required all industries to pay that minimum within a specified period. To facilitate this, the banking system, land, mining, electrical generation and distribution, and transport would be nationalised. Any industry which did not pay the minimum within the required period would, if essential to the community, either be taken over by the State or be provided with a subsidy in return for proportionate public control.

This programme was described alternatively as "Socialism in Our Time" and "The Living Income Policy." It was bitterly attacked by Ramsay MacDonald and marked one of the early stages of his rift with the I.L.P. In his first references to it, MacDonald didn't even pretend to have read it; it was enough for him to catch sight of headlines in the newspaper of a fellow-strap-hanger in a London tube to ridicule it. I have never quite understood why MacDonald rushed in to condemn the report in this way. Perhaps it was the phrase "Socialism in Our Time" which irritated his gradualist evolutionary mind. Whatever the explanation, MacDonald could not find gibes too scathing to apply to the Report. MacDonald's reaction was a cruel disappointment to Allen. Allen always held MacDonald in high esteem and I believe he really hoped that Britain's first Labour Prime Minister could be won to acceptance of his socialist philosophy and programme. Brailsford and MacDonald got into bitter conflict over the report, but never Allen and MacDonald.

Chapter Sixteen
JAMES MAXTON REPLACES ALLEN

An incident at the 1923 conference of the I.L.P., held impressively in the Queen's Hall, London, stands out in my memory. James Maxton rose from among the Scottish delegates. In appearance he embodied the revolt against the bourgeoisie. His dark skin made him look dirty, his hair fell untidily over his face, his clothes hung loosely on him, his eyes flashed fire and his language and gestures were fierce. From the platform Allen replied—Allen looking the typical bourgeois, exquisitely groomed, hair waved, a perfect gentleman in speech and manners, a little consciously superior. This incident occurred on the eve of Allen's chairmanship, but it was prophetic of the end. Here we had personified the two forces in the Party which came into conflict and led finally to the replacement of Allen by Maxton.

On the issue which Allen and Maxton were debating my convictions were with Allen—Maxton had criticised the view that the Ruhr should be returned to Germany (John Wheatley, David Kirkwood and he had visited the Ruhr and returned with the proposal that it should be "internationalised"), but as time passed my sympathies went to Maxton emotionally. I felt that the Socialism of Hardie, based on the struggles and aspirations of common men and women, was becoming stifled by Allen and his friends. The clash which led to Allen's downfall had its roots in three things. First the I.L.P. became increasingly dissatisfied with the MacDonald leadership of the Labour Party, particularly after the first Labour Government of 1924. Second, the rank and file membership outside London, which remained proletarian, became impatient with the middle-class domination of Head Office and the grand scale of its upkeep. Third, the membership, having accepted the "Socialism in Our Time" Plan seriously, were in the mood to challenge aggressively the gradualism of the Labour Party.

The Clydeside Group in Parliament, particularly John Wheatley and James Maxton, assumed the leadership of the revolt in the Party. Alllen was held back by the social environment in which he lived, and when the issue arose sharply between MacDonald and the "intellectuals," on the one side, and the working-class membership of the Party and the revolutionary implications of his own policy on the other, he chose the former. As I have indicated, Allen had unbounded admiration for MacDonald. During the period of the first Labour Government, he lunched with the Prime Minister at Downing Street once a week, together with Ernest Hunter, Mrs. Hamilton and other admirers. When Allen told me of these luncheons he was excitedly hopeful of influencing the Premier, but I realised that it was Allen who was being influenced. He began to demur at the vigour with which Brailsford and Wise advocated the "Socialism in Our Time" policy in the "New Leader" and the sharpness with which they criticised the Labour Government's policy. He began to reflect the annoyance with which MacDonald soon regarded the uncompromising attitude of John Wheatley and F. W. Jowett within the Cabinet and the recalcitrance of James Maxton and the Clydesiders outside the Cabinet. He tried to persuade me to use my influence within the Party to encourage an attitude of patience towards the policy of the Government and the Prime Minister, and it was my own impatience which started the political estrangement between Allen and myself.

Wheatley and Jowett began their careers as Cabinet Ministers with a gesture which shocked MacDonald as much as it pleased the general body of I.L.P. members; they refused to put on the officially-required Morning dress when they went to Buckingham Palace to receive from the King their appointments as Minister of Health and First Commissioner of Works. The same refreshing democracy was reflected in the departmental reception which Jowett gave; I was delighted to find that Fred had invited the junior members of his staff as well as the senior and he paid as much attention to a messenger as to a First Secretary. The atmosphere suggested that the working-class had really taken command of Whitehall. Wheatley and Jowett were not content with gestures. Wheatley's Housing Act was one of the few successes of the Labour administration; he insisted on a subsidy to enable houses to be built at rents within the reach of working-class incomes and compelled the monopolists who controlled building materials to reduce their prices by threatening to commandeer their supplies. Jowett had smaller opportunities, but in minor matters he did courageous things—for example, to the inscription on Nurse Cavell's statue outside the National Portrait Gallery he added her dying words, "Patriotism is not enough. I must have no hatred or bitterness for anyone." Both Wheatley and Jowett openly declared their support of the "Socialism in Our Time" programme, despite the opposition of MacDonald.

The Clydesiders rapidly took over the leadership of the I.L.P. Group in Parliament and its conflict with MacDonald grew. At first Ernest Hunter acted as secretary of the Group, but he was known to be in MacDonald's inner circle and some of the M.P.s did not trust him. This led to my becoming the Group Secretary, and more and more I found myself associated in action as well as in sympathy with the "rebels." It was one of my duties to convey the views of the M.P.s to the Prime Minister. It was not a pleasant duty. I remember the occasion when the Group carried a resolution protesting against the retention of reparations from Germany in the Dawes Plan. I asked for an appointment with MacDonald and was summoned to the Prime Minister's room at the House of Commons. He stood with his back to the fireplace, superbly attired in evening dress. He looked a grand figure, Olympian and contemptuous. "Well, Brockway," he said with savage irony, "what commands have you brought me today?" "Not commands, Mr. MacDonald, but considerations," I replied as courteously as I could. "I suppose the I.L.P. want to damn me for the Dawes Plan when everyone else recognises it as a great achievement of international reconciliation." He paused. Then his anger got the better of him. "You can tell them that in damning me they damn themselves." "In the view of the Group," I began quietly . . . . "I have no time to listen to the view of the Group," shouted MacDonald. "I have an engagement." At that moment Arthur Henderson entered, also in evening dress. With a goodnight to William Leach, M.P., who was also present, and completely ignoring me, the Prime Minister strode with his Foreign Secretary from the room. Leach, who idolised MacDonald, was at pains to excuse his chief's conduct on the ground that he was tired out by his heavy responsibilities. That I understood, but I think it was from this moment that I realised that a breach between MacDonald and the I.L.P. was inevitable.

For a time the gathering conflict between the Party and MacDonald was smoothed over by a by-election in the Abbey

Division of Westminster in 1924, when I was the I.L.P. candidate. This contest probably attracted a greater public interest than any by-election in modern times. This was due in great part to the intervention of Mr. Winston Churchill, no longer a Liberal, not yet a Conservative, who stood as Independent anti-Socialist. The I.L.P. accepted Mr. Churchill's challenge with alacrity. My election address was entirely devoted to a persuasive but bold statement of the socialist case; it was in fact written by Allen,—I was so completely in agreement with it that I had no hesitation in adopting it without the alteration of a word. Churchill of course occupied the limelight, the popular Conservative press supporting him against the official candidate, a Mr. Nicholson, better known for his gin than his politics. Next to Mr. Churchill I attracted public attention as the champion of the sinister Socialism which was the issue of the fight; it was obviously the game of the powerful press to emphasise the menace which I represented. Mr. Churchill fought the contest with great vigour and much sensational glamour, combining the alarmist oratory of which he is a master with the melodrama of a circus (including a tour round the constituency in a coach and four, complete with a trumpeter). The organiser of these spectacular stunts was a young man with flaming red hair and sparkling eyes named Brendan Bracken, who treated his chief as a god.* I replied with activities which also caught the eye of Fleet Street, including a canvassing mission to St. James' Palace, where I addressed the domestic staff in the kitchen, and similar visits to the staffs of other mansions of royalty and aristocracy. The election had an additional personal interest because the Liberal candidate was Mr. Scott Duckers, who had been associated with me as a "conchy" during the war.

As the campaign proceeded I was excited by the support forthcoming. In the working-class district round Horseferry Road my photo-card was in every other window. More surprising was the support which came from well-known people. Every professor, author, artist, actor and actress of note seemed to live in the Abbey division and they all seemed to have

* To become during the war Mr. Churchill's Parliamentary Private Secretary and later Minister of Information.

decided to vote for me. "Here, I can't get this election straight," said my agent, Mr. Windle, to me one night. "You're not the Conservative candidate, are you? Who do you think have been canvassing for you tonight? The two sons of Lord Swaythling, the banker!" One of those sons—Mr. Ivor Montagu—has since become well known as a specialist in film propaganda for Communism. I was deluged with messages from electors famous in the world of letters and art: I select Bernard Shaw's because at this distance of time it still retains its provocative interest:—

My dear Fenner Brockway,—I hope you are not contesting Westminster under the impression that the whole electorate is as intelligent as I and my neighbour, Sir James Barrie. Westminster once elected John Stuart Mill; but it has never recovered from the shock of finding that it had elected a really great man. Needless to add, it turned him out at the next election, and has been very careful not to let it occur again. If you are elected it will be quite unintentional.

I should like to vote for Mr. Churchill, because I am the only man alive who dares now confess that he thought Gallipoli a good idea, and still thinks it would have justified itself had it been carried out as it was conceived. But Mr. Churchill's program is simply war with Russia, on grounds that would eventually mean war with modern civilisation. He wants the Tsardom back; the Tsardom that imprisoned women for twenty years for teaching children to read, and forced Europe into war after luring us and France into an unholy alliance against which the leaders of Labor protested in vain. Even after we had paid the terrible penalty of this crime against civilisation, Mr. Churchill spent £100,000,000 of our money in trying to put the clock back in Russia to his own feudal date, which is about the middle of the fourteenth century. As my own date is a little later, a vote cast for Mr. Churchill by me would be a mockery.

Mr. Nicholson also appeals to me because I see no good reason why the hereditary principle should not apply to Westminster as well as to Windsor Castle. The peasant who asked Wordsworth's son whether he was going to carry on the old man's business shewed a great deal of horse sense. Unfortunately, Mr. Nicholson sends me an election address in which he declares quite gratuitously (for I never said a word to him about it) that he is out to defeat Socialism. I think this is ungrateful. In 1915 Socialism saved the country when private enterprise had brought us within two inches of defeat. Throughout a frightful war it fed and clothed our people better than most of them had ever been fed and clothed before; and it would do the same today if Mr. Nicholson's friends would let it. Imagine Westminster without Socialism: no streets, no bridges, no public lighting, no police, no schools, no water supply, no courts, no posts and telegraphs and telephones, no army, no navy, no Returning Officer, no election, no Big Ben, and no Parliament! That is what Mr. Nicholson stands for. A regular Anarchist, I call him. I wish him well because I think he means well. But as I think so because I feel sure that he does not understand what he is talking about I should feel like an idiot if I voted for him.

Mr. Scott Duckers' program is to keep out Mr. Churchill, which is short and simple. If he contrives to combine that operation with letting you in, he will not have lived in vain.

There seems nothing for it but to vote for you; but please do not tell anyone, as nothing would terrify the average Westminster voter more than the prospect of voting with—Yours faithfully,

G. BERNARD SHAW.

Polling day came. We had obviously done well. The count in Caxton Hall was exciting, the voting papers of the leading three stretching along the tables in almost identical length, with poor Scott Duckers an insignificant fourth. Then my papers lagged. Suddenly Mr. Churchill's agent dashed across the floor to where his chief was standing with his wife and friends. "You're in, Mr. Churchill—in by forty-three votes." Churchill's face shone. His wife took both his hands in glad congratulation. Someone else dashed across the floor. "No, no," he cried, "He's *out* by forty-three." Mr. Churchill's hands dropped. He had set his heart on winning this election; it was to be his great come-back to politics. His friends surrounded him to commiserate. He shook them off and began to tramp the length of the hall, head down, body lurching, like a despairing animal. In later years, when I sat in the House of Commons with Mr. Churchill, I often thought what a great cinema actor he would have made. I know no man who more fully expresses in changing features and gestures the moods he feels; on this occasion he was the embodiment of disappointment and frustration. He stopped at my side. "You know, Brockway," he said, "you and I have had no chance. We represent ideas—Nicholson represents the machine. In ten days the machine has defeated ideas. Three days longer, and ideas would have defeated the machine. You or I would have been elected." I think this was probably true. The Returning Officer read the figures—Nicholson and Churchill with eight

F

thousand odd, myself with six thousand, and my Liberal friend, Scott Duckers with 291. Our large socialist vote in the "home of Conservatism" caused a political sensation.*

For a time the Westminster election turned I.L.P. enthusiasm into a positive channel, but quickly criticism of the MacDonald Government burst into flame again. The Government sanctioned the building of four cruisers and this was regarded bitterly as a surrender of our international principles to the jingo demands of the Tory Opposition. Then came the dingy story of the defeat of the Labour Government and the still more discreditable circumstances of MacDonald's handling of the Zinovieff letter during the subsequent general election. When it was announced that the Communist, J. R. Campbell, had been arrested for seditious writings, the protests which poured in to Downing Street were so heavy that within eight days the charge was withdrawn. The Liberal Party, upon whose votes the Government depended, immediately challenged this right-about-turn as a case of political interference with the course of justice and, when MacDonald refused to give way, joined the Tories in defeating his Government. I was one of the crowd which received the news in the central lobby of the House of Commons by singing the "Red Flag," but all of us recognised, despite the enthusiasm with which we set out on the election campaign, that the Government had blundered badly by ever beginning the prosecution and that it had been forced on to the defensive.

The bad beginning of the election was nothing compared with its end. The "Daily Mail" published the famous Zinovieff letter, alleging that whilst the Soviet Government was pretending to be friendly, it was plotting against Britain through the medium of the Communist International. Labour spokesmen from one end of the country to the other immediately denounced the "Daily Mail" production as a fraud, but Foreign Office officials would not repudiate its *bona fides* categorically, and MacDonald himself, speaking in some distant part of Wales, was equivocal. The consequence was that all fight went out of the Labour campaign, the Party suffered the inevitable defeat and MacDonald's stock fell to zero.

---

*The figures were: Nicholson, 8,187; Churchill, 8,144; Brockway, 6,156; Duckers, 291.

It was at the meeting of our National Council during the Labour Party conference at Liverpool in October, 1925, that the crisis was reached between the Allen and Maxton sections in the I.L.P. The final issue was MacDonald's editorship of the "Socialist Review," the monthly discussion organ of the Party, but it was another matter which aroused to breaking point Allen's anger against Maxton and his fellow-rebels. Maxton had represented the Party at the Standing Orders Committee of the Conference when a resolution on the subject of land nationalisation was discussed. The Party policy, under the influence of experts, was against confiscation; instead it proposed that the owners should be "compensated" out of revenue raised by the taxation of the rich. Maxton, however, was in principle for confiscation and he had apparently agreed to the incorporation of the I.L.P. amendment in a composite amendment which was against compensation. Maxton argued, I believe, that he had to compromise part of the I.L.P. case in order to get agreement; but Allen interpreted the whole thing as a "slick" dodge and developed a moral indignation about it.

It was in this thundery atmosphere that the National Council met. Allen sat at the head of the hotel-room table, a bottle of thick pink medicine before him. His critics said unkindly that he became faint and stretched out his thin hand to this bottle whenever a crisis which required sympathy arose; but this night the clash had gone too far to allow personal feelings to determine the issue. It was fought out round a motion from the Maxton Group that MacDonald should no longer be editor of the "Socialist Review" since he differed so seriously from Party policy. Allen met this by a plea for tolerance, liberty of thought, and a tribute to MacDonald's intellectual pre-eminence. He was defeated, dramatically resigned his chairmanship, and, with white face and lips tight shut, walked out. I followed him to his room and he was a broken man. Because of our long association I had personal sympathy with him; but politically I was on the other side. His attitude towards me was *"et tu, Brute!"* For the six months before the I.L.P. Conference at Easter, F. W. Jowett served as interim chairman. At the 1926 conference Maxton was elected Chairman. Clifford Allen did not even attend.

Chapter Seventeen
ON THE EXECUTIVE OF THE
SECOND INTERNATIONAL

It was just before the end of the Clifford Allen period that I was appointed as the I.L.P. representative on the Executive of the Labour and Socialist International. I was thus brought into personal contact with the best-known Socialist leaders of all countries.

It was only a last-minute decision which kept me from the inaugural conference of the reconstituted International at Hamburg in 1923. I was to have been secretary to the I.L.P. delegation, but a crisis sprang up between Britain and Russia and I stayed in London to help mobilise working-class resistance to any rupture. When Frank Wise telephoned me advance news of the crisis, I rang up Jim Middleton, Assistant Secretary of the Labour Party, and we got busy. I drafted a letter to be sent to working-class organisations throughout Britain, whilst Middleton put through a telephone call to Arthur Henderson, the Chairman of the Hamburg Conference, telling him what was afoot. This rapid action meant that resolutions couched in the strongest terms poured in upon Downing Street before the Government had prepared public opinion for its move. We influenced the "Daily Herald" to write sternly and the rest of the press carried our statements as well as reports of our activities. The memory of Labour Action in 1920, when a general strike was threatened, was in the mind of the Government and for a time, but for a time only, the crisis passed.

The main achievement of the strong I.L.P. delegation at Hamburg (it included Allen, Brailsford, Roden Buxton and Wallhead) was to leave the door open for the full unification of the international working-class movement by the coming in of the Communist International. For a time the secretariat of the International was in London, and Friedrich Adler, its secretary, together with his assistants, Dr. Pollak (who had been editor of the Vienna Socialist daily, the "Arbeiter Zeitung") and Mrs. Pollak, associated themselves closely with our Party. This was due partly to political sympathy (the Austrian party had been attached to the Vienna Union), but also to appreciation of the comradeship which has always been a feature of

I.L.P. life in contrast with the colder machine-like organisation of the Labour Party.

I had of course heard of Adler as the man who had opened the way for the end of the war in Austria by assassinating the Prime Minister, Count Stürgk. I had pictured a grim-looking revolutionary. He was the exact opposite—a big, kindly, bespectacled man, with untidy brown hair crowning the head of a professor rather than of a pugilist, and with a professional disregard of appearance which allowed his baggy clothes to flop about his body like sacks. His wife was the sweetest little woman, the last mate one would expect for a political "terrorist." The truth is that Friedrich Adler was opposed both in theory and temperament to "terrorism" as a general political method. It must have cost his nature a lot to fire the fatal shot which killed Count Stürgk.

The headquarters of the International were moved in 1925 to Zurich, and I went there three or four times a year to attend its Executive meetings. In these days of "prosperity" journeys abroad for the Party were enjoyable trips as well as politically interesting. We travelled second class and stayed at good hotels, not so luxurious as those honoured by the Labour Party, but palaces compared with the cheap proletarian hotels or, whenever available, the homes of kindly working-class comrades to which we now go after travelling over-night third-class! My membership of the Executive led to invitations to visit many European countries. The fact that I belonged to the Left at first encouraged rather than discouraged invitations: this was partly a result of pressure from the Left within the Parties and partly a deliberate manœuvre by the Right to make use of me in order to hold their Left in check. I addressed big meetings in Berlin, Vienna, Paris, Zurich, and other cities.

My visit to Berlin must have been during the early stages of the Nazi threat, when Hitler's private army of Storm Troopers was met on more than equal terms by the Reichsbanner formed by the "democratic" parties. I was astounded by the thoroughness of the protection afforded me. From the hotel door to the waiting car two lines of men, wearing black, gold and red uniforms, cut the pavement; a Reichsbanner officer sat by the driver; a similar avenue of uniformed men lined the pavement when I reached the hall in a Berlin suburb; and the entrances to the hall were guarded by strong detachments. In those days our German comrades were confident that their Reichsbanner would prove more than a match for the Storm Troopers. My speech at this meeting was an appeal for working-class unity in Germany to meet the Fascist menace. The chairman did not like it, but the audience rose to it.

The Social Democratic headquarters surprised me. We thought our I.L.P. offices in Great George Street quite impressive; the Labour Party offices in Eccleston Square, occupying a whole house, seemed to us imposing. But these were mere sideshows compared with the German headquarters. The Berlin building was like a Whitehall State Department, with endless corridors and rooms, hundreds on its staff, each section— Organisation, Propaganda, Finance, Literature, "Vorwaerts," Parliamentary, Youth—larger than all the combined sections we had in London. I was staggered by the size of the printing press housed in the extensive basement of the building; there was no newspaper house in London which had larger or more up-to-date machines. But I was disillusioned as well as impressed. In this vast establishment I found little of the spirit of Socialism or, indeed, of any *movement;* it was a machine, its directors keen to defend it from the threatened Nazi attack, but with no urge to use it for positive and transforming ends. To my astonishment I learned that on election all the Executive members of the Party were made full-time officials, well-paid and practically irremovable: each was put in charge of a separate department at a managerial salary. I met several of them; they were heavy, self-satisfied bureaucrats, the last men on earth to lead the German working-class in the critical stage it was approaching.

Let me describe an inspiring gathering in contrast. In 1929 the Second International organised an international demonstration on the German-French Frontier by the shores of Lake Constance. The Executive went in charabancs to the frontier and had lunch at an old chalet in the woods at Schloss-Wyden, where German and French veterans uttered speeches of fraternity—Bernstein was the German, the Frenchman I have forgotten. Then we separated, half crossing to the German side, half to the French side, and took up positions at the head of two vast processions, brilliant with red flags, which marched towards each other, met in the middle of a frontier bridge, stood at attention, sang the Internationale in the two languages, and proceeded side by side to a huge square, where the best-known leaders spoke to a crowd estimated to be a hundred thousand strong. Was it all superficial romanticism, this demonstration of solidarity between the German and French workers? I think not: the day of realisation will still come.

The Labour Party representatives on the Executive were Arthur Henderson, Charlie Cramp, secretary of the National Union of Railwaymen, and Willie Gillies, permanent head of the International Department of the Labour Party. Henderson persisted in obstinate insularity. Gillies had to be at his hand day and night, buying his tickets, ordering his meals, summoning his taxis, arranging his hotel accommodation. I don't believe "Uncle Arthur," as we all called him, ever attempted to utter a word in another language. Later he became Foreign Secretary and, within the limits of his policy, a successful Foreign Secretary, but his personal helplessness in a foreign country always remained.*

Henderson made one diplomatic mistake when Home Secretary of which no explanation has been given. At the moment when Ramsay MacDonald was carefully courting better relations with France, the new Home Secretary, making good the loss of his Parliamentary seat at the General Election, was contesting a by-election at Burnley. Suddenly the world was startled to read that he had made a vigorous attack on the Versailles Treaty; the French were outraged and all MacDonald's diplomacy was required to recreate good feeling.

The explanation of this strange occurrence, as told to me, was amusing. Henderson left for Burnley with a good stock of speeches (it was his custom to read from a manuscript). A week before polling day, however, he had got through them, and telegraphed to London for more. His office sent him a bundle of old speeches outlining Labour policy on major issues, Among them was the fatal speech on the Versailles Treaty, and Henderson proceeded to read it at his next meeting without grasping its immediate significance. Probably no one was

*An associate of Henderson tells me that when he became Chairman of the Disarmament Conference he made dogged efforts to learn French.

more surprised than he when he read next morning about the sensation he had started.

There had been a decision that the parties associated with the Vienna Union should act together in the wider Executive, but experience showed that the distinction between the anti-war parties of 1914-18 and the "social patriotic" parties was unreal under peace conditions.   I remember our collaborating once only, and that was to invite the Swiss Socialist Party to join the International.   I made frequent attempts to organise a Left group, but never really succeeded.   My one unfailing supporter was the Polish I.L.P., a small Party represented by Dr. Josef Kruk, with whom I became very friendly.*   When the Swiss Party came in I hoped for collaboration because it had a great Left reputation, but, after a few promising discussions, it fell away.   Its Secretary, Robert Grimm, with his close-cropped grey head, round as a bullet, and tidy clothes and precise manners, looked like a German business man and had a business man's caution.   Reinhardt, the chairman, had much more the appearance of a revolutionary—a powerful man with waving black hair and big-boned face, but he did not often attend the Executive.   In later years I had the same experience with the Polish Bund, which hesitated to enter the International because of the moderation of the dominating parties, but which, after a preliminary show of boldness, became equally subdued.   Its two representatives were Alter and Ehrlich, the former dark, flashing-eyed, sharp thinking and speaking; the latter a quiet man, with a little grey-pointed beard and grey clothes.†

Most disappointing of all were the Austrian and French parties.   Otto Bauer, the Austrian leader, once called the I.L.P. the conscience of the International.   My speeches certainly seemed to disturb him.   He would walk up and down the room with his hands behind his back, thinking hard, his forehead puckered, and when later he took part in the discussion I would at first be hopeful.   He would accept our analysis completely . . . then began the buts.   We must carry the big parties—the

---

* Kruk joined the Paole Zion (Labour Zionists) after the suppression of the I.L.P. in Poland.   When Germany and Russia invaded Poland in September, 1939, he escaped to Lithuania after hair-breadth escapes in both the German and Russian territories.   He is now in Palestine.

†Alter and Ehrlich were taken prisoners by the Soviet authorities when Russia invaded Poland in the autumn of 1939, and were subsequently executed by them.

German Social Democrats and the British Labour Party—with us. We must understand their difficulties. We must not split the International. My resolution would go to a drafting commission and Bauer's draft, embodying enough of our socialist principles to make it read well, but never going in action beyond what could be accepted by the Right, would be adopted. Despite my disappointment, I had a profound respect for Bauer. He was the intellectual giant of the Executive. In his appearance there was nothing of the Socialist agitator. His shining black hair was brushed close to his head; his features were rounded and sleek; his clothes were well-tailored and might have been worn by any diplomat or orthodox politician. But there was an atmosphere of distinction about him, a dignity of bearing and the calm of a philosopher and thinker, which marked him out in any group of men.

The French delegates were Longuet, Bracke and Blum. Longuet, the perfect compromiser, I have already described. Bracke was a distinguished French litterateur, but he looked like a rugged grey workman and behaved in moments of excitement like a bad-tempered dog. He never came down decisively on the Left. Blum did not often attend the Executive, but when he did there was always a glamour about him. He obviously felt himself to be an important person, his exaggerated gestures and smiles suggesting that he thought a camera was always directed on him. He gave an impression of superficiality compared with such a man as Bauer, but he had a genuis for popular leadership, which combined a hail-fellow-well-met attitude towards his supporters with an unmistakable indication that he was the great man among them. At night one would see him at a café table, French comrades about him, paying for their drinks, laughing at their stories, but always commanding silence when he had anything to say and saying it with the authority of the Pope.

The Belgian Party had two exceptionally able leaders— Emile Vandervelde and de Brouckère—both on the Right Wing of the movement. Vandervelde had been chairman of the old Second International and, when Henderson became a Cabinet Minister in 1929, became chairman again. He was a fascinating orator. Broad shouldered, with a massive head, waving black hair and pointed, jet-black beard, he spoke not only with his voice, but with the whole of his body. His voice more nearly justified comparison with the notes of an organ than any I have heard. Both in deep bass and high tenor it had a rich fulness, and it could tremble like a sensitive instrument. The climax of his oratory was accompanied by outstretched arms, his fingers fluttering in reflection of his voice, his features and his limbs throbbing in rhythm. I have witnessed the vibration of his voice and body pass right through an audience, caught and shaken by his emotion.

De Brouckère was a great bear of a man—his head and face covered with grisly black hair, his huge arms threatening to crush an opponent. In debate he gave the impression of a bully, but socially he was a kindly companion. He had a clear, shrewd mind and later made a considerable reputation both as a Belgian Minister and as Belgium's delegate to the League. If reforms were able to solve the world's problems, de Brouckère would be the man to see them through.

By the Germans I was not impressed. In contrast with the Jesus-like Crispien, Otto Wels, their leader, was a fleshy gross-looking man, red faced, with bulging eyes, a socialist sergeant-major. I could well imagine him in the part of a policeman suppressing the Liebknecht revolution at the end of the war, I could see him fighting with brute courage against a fascist enemy; but I could never see him building a society of freedom and fraternity. All the time I was on the Executive I never heard him contribute a constructive idea. There was one German, a rare attender, for whom one could not help feeling affection and respect despite political disagreement—Karl Kautsky. He was a shrivelled little man with a large head buried in shaggy grey hair, from which kindly eyes looked out through glasses under a broad forehead.

The first Congress of the International which I attended was at Marseilles in 1925. We met in a vast pavilion, with a platform and rostrum raised on a scaffold. Fifteen hundred delegates sat at long trestle tables, each with the name of one country above it. I remember only a speech by Turati, leader of the Italian Socialists. He looked like a square granite slab, a statuesque embodiment of the might of Labour.

Our I.L.P. delegation returned from the Marseilles Congress disappointed. The attitude of the majority of the delegates on two issues—Russia and Reparations—shocked us. The attitude towards Russia was largely influenced by the refugee Mensheviks and the Social Democratic parties in the border States, and both allowed their particular grievances to destroy a real perspective of the significance of the Soviet regime. The attitude of the Congress towards German reparations outraged us even more. We succeeded in getting a modification of the resolution, but even so it insisted that Germany should pay for the "material damage of the war in all countries"! The Marseilles experience led to a decision by the I.L.P. to act with more challenging independence in the International. This agreed with my own views and I readily became its instrument on the Executive.

There were three issues which we decided to press. The first was the need to form an all-inclusive International. The second was the extension of the activities of the International to the colonial countries. The third was the necessity to agitate for total disarmament and to mobilise international working-class resistance to war.

The I.L.P. resolution for the unification of the Internationals aroused interest throughout the world. "In view of the urgent need of working-class solidarity against capitalist and imperialist reaction and the menace of Fascism in Europe" (it is interesting that these words should have been used as far back as 1926), it proposed that the Executive should suggest to the Executive of the Third International a joint conference "with the object of exploring the possibilites of the formation of an all-inclusive International." At first there were signs of considerable support, but the Third International killed the possibility of success by contemptuously rejecting unity in advance of the discussions.

Adler wrote to me assuming that after this rebuff the I.L.P. would not proceed with the resolution, but we decided to maintain it. As I travelled to Zürich, however, I realised that I was tilting at the moon. In such circumstances I was a little surprised that the Executive gave serious consideration to the resolution, but in fact it did. The debate was regarded as a big occasion. The Socialist Press of the world was represented, the members of the staff left their duties at typewriters and duplicators to crowd at the door and, when I was called on to speak, the delegates listened intently, straining to understand what I said in English before the translation was made—a very unusual occurrence, for the custom generally was to chatter or to read whilst speeches were delivered in other languages.

I was aware of the grounds on which unity would be opposed and therefore suggested that the Second International should raise in discussion such questions as "the inevitability of armed revolution," the "dictatorship of the proletariat," the "destruction of Parliaments from within" the imprisonments and the suppression of political liberty in Russia, and, finally, "the disintegrating effect of Communist policies within the political and industrial movements in practically every country." Rather ingenuously I added that no doubt the Third International would, on its side, also desire to raise a number of questions!

Every succeeding speaker complimented me on my effort, but except for my faithful friend Josef Kruk (and even he was inclined to withdraw the Resolution after the Third International's rejection of it in advance) I had not a single supporter. Otto Bauer endorsed unity in principle, but argued that the Comintern's attitude showed that much preliminary work had to be done before a Conference would be of any value. One advance only the discussion denoted: it was carried through in a calm political atmosphere, in great contrast to the unreasoned emotionalism which had marked every previous consideration of Russia or the Third International. Although I got the vote only of the Polish I.L.P., I was not dissatisfied. The discussion had taken the subject on to another plane.

One of the questions which I suggested for discussion between the Internationals was the imprisonment of non-Communist Party Socialists in Russia. I was personally distressed about this, and the I.L.P. made a big effort to settle the issue. The Mensheviks and Social Revolutionaries supplied us with enormous tomes detailing the persecution, and, through the Soviet Embassy in London, they were passed on to Moscow. The Russian Communists replied with an equally large tome and, though we spent many long hours in trying to get to the truth of the matter, we had to give it up with little achieved. I was a member of the Political Prisoners' Commission of the International, endeavouring with some success to get the members to realise that there were political prisoners in Italy,

Spain, the Balkans, India and other parts of the British Empire, as well as in Russia. Nevertheless in spite of all my sympathy with the Soviet Union, I was shocked by the stories I heard. When the Soviet Government invited me to visit Russia, I declined to go as its guest, giving as my reason the imprisonment of provenly sincere Socialists. My letter was published throughout the world, and I am told that it had some influence in improving conditions, because the Soviet Government was at that moment anxious to cultivate good relations with the British Labour Movement.

The I.L.P. plea for increased assistance to the workers in the Colonial countries received the support of the Austrian, French, and Swiss Parties and a Commission was appointed to work out details. I had proposed that the International should act in conjunction with the International Federation of Trades Unions, that deputations should be sent to India and other colonial territories, that selected persons from the colonies should be offered political and industrial training so that they might become organisers, and that technical and monetary assistance should be given to develop workers' organisations. The reception of these proposals by the Executive was encouraging, but months passed and little was done. Meanwhile there was another development which complicated the whole issue.

In February, 1927, a conference representing Nationalist organisations from colonial territories and working-class organisations from Europe was held at Brussels. There is no doubt that the initiative came from the Third International, but, under the clever leadership of Willi Münzenberg,* Communist publisher of Berlin, a genius at organisation and publicity, most of the Nationalist parties were roped in, together with Left groups and individuals in the European parties. I attended the conference as I.L.P. representative, and was caught up by its dramatic enthusiasm. British Imperialism was engaged in one of its periodical military adventures in China and the I.L.P. had been prominent in the "Hands off China" campaign. "End your speech by a declaration of unity with the Chinese workers and peasants," whispered Münzenberg as

---

*He was found strangled in a wood in France in 1941. He is believed to have committed suicide. He broke with the Communist International in his last years.

I stepped on the rostrum. I did so, and as the sentences were uttered a Chinese comrade stood at my side with outstretched hand. I took it—and the whole audience, black, brown, yellow, and white, rose and roared its applause. Münzenberg was a master of such strokes of drama.

The conference resulted in the formation of the League Against Imperialism, and I became its first international chairman. Then the Executive of the Second International met and I found myself in hot water. Otto Wels, the German Social Democratic leader, made a terrific attack on me. He stormed like a mad bull, with a roar of fierce declamation which enabled me to understand for the first time his power over German Social Democracy—such speech directed against political opponents would have great demagogic effect. Wels complained that the German Communists were using my official connection with the League Against Imperialism to attack the German Social Democratic leadership who were refusing to allow their members to join it and angrily denounced me for stabbing my Executive colleagues in the back. My defence was that the League had the support of the most powerful Nationalist Movements in the colonial territories, that it was the duty of Socialists to co-operate with them in the anti-imperialist struggle, and that we should deserve to be brushed aside by the peoples in the Empires if we left this duty to the Communists. Bauer and Adler met this by agreeing that the International must press forward with its colonial work, but joined in condemning me for associating with a "Communist" organisation. Not even Josef Kruk was present to support me. Except for the representative of one of the Balkan parties, I was condemned by all and a resolution was carried giving me the choice of resignation from the League or from the International Executive.

When I reported this to the National Council of the I.L.P. there was a tendency to defy the Second International Executive, but the final decision was that I should resign from the Chairmanship and that Maxton should replace me in the League. This manoeuvre did not end happily. Maxton attended the second conference of the League and was duly elected Chairman, but shortly afterwards the Communists decided against an I.L.P. chairmanship and a small excuse was invented to depose him.

The third issue on which the I.L.P. concentrated within the Second International was total disarmament and working-class resistance to war. It is difficult today to realise how fully the British Labour Movement was committed to this policy only thirteen years ago. The Labour Party conference in 1926 carried a resolution, which I moved on behalf of the I.L.P., calling on the workers to refuse to bear arms, produce armaments, or to render any material assistance for war, and urging that steps should be taken to convene a World Conference of the Socialist, Trade Union and Co-operative Internationals to prepare concerted resistance. Having got this resolution through the Labour Party Conference, the I.L.P. submitted it to the Executive of the International. The Executive agreed to refer it to all the affiliated parties with a request that they should report their attitude within six months. Most of the parties did not take the resolution seriously, but the I.L.P. did not let the matter rest; at the triennial International Conference held at Brussels in 1928 we raised the question prominently. We succeeded in getting the commission dealing with this subject to agree that in any country which refused arbitration the working-class should resist war by direct action, but we were not satisfied with this success and we raised the issue again before the full conference. I put the I.L.P. view, received considerable support, and we got a large minority vote. The Swiss, German-Czech, and American parties, together with minority sections in the German, French, and Polish delegations (including the Bund and the I.L.P.) supported us.

I was chairman of the I.L.P. delegation at this Conference. It was the first occasion in the International when organisational conflict arose between the Labour Party and the I.L.P. Each national delegation was entitled to two representatives on a commission; at Marseilles the Labour Party and the I.L.P. had filled these positions by mutual agreement. At Brussels, however, the Labour Party claimed the two representatives on all the commissions, and only after a fierce protest agreed to withdraw one of their representatives temporarily when the I.L.P. wished to raise special issues. This was an indication of how the more independent line of the I.L.P., both in the International and in domestic policies, was bringing about a conflict with the Labour Party.

So far as disarmament is concerned, my memory is of interminable executives and sub-committees devoted to the consideration of proposals for submission to the proposed League of Nations Disarmament Conference. The conference did not meet until 1932, but as early as 1926 the International Executive was considering memoranda for it. I have rarely spent hours more futile than these long discussions in the International Executive, debating whether reductions in armaments should be applied to material or men or budgets and whether Socialists should be encouraged to go to the Disarmament Conference if they could get appointed to delegations from capitalist governments. I became so impatient that I found it difficult to stop myself from bursting into protests. Guns so many inches shorter, ships so many tons lighter, bombs so many pounds less—what was the practical value of all this in preventing war? Meanwhile, Fascism was beginning to lift its head in Germany, the world economic crisis of Capitalism was developing. But the Second International Executive gave only incidental attention to such matters; all its mind was on the League Disarmament Conference.

There was another International issue in which the I.L.P. took a leading part. The problem of migration had become urgent. The attitude of the working-class movement varied in different countries, and the Trade Union and political Internationals decided to call in 1926 a World Labour conference to discuss the subject. It was in fact one of the most representative working-class conferences that has ever met. Not only were the industrial and political movements of Europe, the U.S.A., and South America represented, but the Labour organisations of Canada, Australia, New Zealand, and India, although unaffiliated to the I.F.T.U. and the L.S.I., also sent delegations. The resolution submitted by the I.F.T.U. executive argued that migration had become so extensive that it could no longer be treated on the Liberal principle of the inherent human right of freedom of movement, and that what was described as the socialist principle of control and direction must be applied.

F. W. Jowett and I were the I.L.P. delegates, and we submitted an amendment which, whilst recognising the right of control of immigration if it threatened to lower standards of social life, declared that there should be no exclusion on grounds of race or colour. This amendment became the chief subject of debate. The I.L.P. view was strongly opposed by the delegates from Australia and Canada, but was as strongly backed by the representatives from India and New Zealand, as well as by most of the European delegations. I had the new experience of winning the enthusiastic acclamation of the vast majority of the delegates who crowded the hall, but eventually it was decided to ask a joint committee of the I.F.T.U. and the L.S.I. to report on the question. So far as I know the report was never issued.

The last speech I delivered at a Second International Conference was at Zurich on the eve of the triumph of Hitler. I made a despairing appeal to the Social Democrats to find a basis of re-uniting the German Workers' Movement for a policy of class action before it was too late. Breitscheid, Foreign Secretary in one of Germany's last "democratic" Governments, replied that we could count on German Social Democracy when the crisis came; but as I listened I knew that hope was vain. Breitscheid himself, handsome, dignified, correct, the perfect politician of bourgeois democracy, typified the old order which was incapable of leading the workers in the new type of struggle which the threat of Nazism demanded. Our appeal rejected by the Social Democratic leaders, we went direct to the German workers. But of that I tell later.

Our visits abroad were not all a matter of stern political controversy. We took our relaxations. I remember how during the Brussels conference Pat Dollan, supreme as a Master of Ceremonies, took command of the Moulin Rouge, brushing aside its usual programme, and improvising a medley of song and fun which entertained the audience for an hour. Oswald Mosley was his chief prop.

Chapter Eighteen
RETURN VISIT TO INDIA

I have told of my special interest in India. I was born there, members of my family remained there, and I had been secretary of the British Committee of the Indian National Congress. When I received an invitation to attend the 1927 meetings of the Indian National and Trade Union Congresses as a fraternal delegate from the I.L.P. I was delighted.

This was my first long sea voyage since my forgotten journey from India as a child and I enjoyed every moment of it. I joined the boat at Marseilles, attending a conference of revolutionary socialist parties in Paris en route. The Mediterranean lived up to its reputation; although it was December, the sky was blue, the sea calm and the air warm. Port Said, gateway to the East, introduced me to a new world of colourful movement. Aden I found horrible, a place of the dead past in which even plants would not grow.

The dawn was just breaking over the hills of Bombay when we docked, but Mr. N. M. Joshi, secretary of the Indian T.U.C., boarded the boat to welcome me. He was a picturesque figure—tall and broad, with a red and gold turban crowning his head, and a loose muslin garment instead of trousers; on his feet were purple sandals curving up at the toes in a formidable way. With him was a young journalist in a neat white suit, and Mr. F. J. Ginwala, Treasurer of the T.U.C., wearing the round, flat-topped cap of the Parsees. At the foot of the gangway other Indians were waiting and they embarrassed me considerably by garlanding my neck with huge halters of flowers, while Press photographers "shot" at me.

I had hoped to stay with my Indian friends, but saying "our ways are not your ways" they took me to the Hotel Majestic. I found the drive in the open taxi entrancing. The streets were thronged with people, and no two people were alike. Everything was ablaze with sunlight, and through the fierce whiteness men and women passed ceaselessly, dressed in innumerable styles and colours. White—cool and clean—was most common, but even with the white suits there were turbans of all hues— red, gold, green and purple. Girls and women glided about in richly-coloured sarees, with baskets on their heads or children on their hips. Motor cars, horse carriages and bullock carts

were held up in a row by smart policemen in blue and yellow
uniforms. To Mr. Joshi I expressed my appreciation of this
variety compared with the drab sameness of London clothes
and streets. "Yes," he said, "the variety is picturesque, but it
is our curse. It represents our disunity in race, caste, religion."
I was pulled up sharply: so soon had I been brought up against
one of the problems of India!

The East is called leisurely, but I have never been so rushed
from engagement to engagement as I was during the three days
I stayed in Bombay. When later I visited America, I found
that the Yankees' hustle was an afternoon's nap compared with
it. I did the round of the newspaper offices, attended a
reception to King Amanullah (the "rebel" monarch of
Afghanistan), was received myself by the T.U.C. General
Council, met a deputation from the Indian Communist Party
("delighted to welcome a sincere Leftist"—I wondered what
their British colleagues would say to that!), attended the
Annual Congress of the Peoples from the Indian (Native) States,
spent an evening in discussion with the Moslem leaders, was a
guest at a tea-party given by Mrs. Sarojini Naidu (the distinguished poetess), visited Mr. M. A. Jinnah (the Moslem
leader) and other Moslem representatives, addressed a huge
demonstration under Congress auspices, spoke to trade union
meetings of textile workers and clerks and to an open-air meeting organised by Congress Socialists, had a meal, Indian-style,
in Mr. Joshi's home, visited an Indian-run settlement in a slum
district, and "investigated" the housing and prostitution
problems of the city.

I can pause only to pick out incidents in this crowded
programme. King Amanullah was on his way to visit Europe.
I am not surprised that he was not popular with the British
ruling class and that he was subsequently manœuvred from his
throne. Sir Leslie Wilson, British Governor of Bombay, was
at the reception, a typical English ruler, handsome, courteous,
distant, but he was not in the picture and was treated with
indifference by Amanullah who remarked that he cared nothing
for forms of respect showed by "the powerful and the
privileged."

I made a special effort to see the Moslem leaders and to
understand their point of view. Mr. M. A. Jinnah lives in a

mansion in the wealthy residential district of Bombay overlooking the bay from the Malabar Hills. He is the most anglicised Indian leader I have met. His complexion is light, he dresses in faultless English style, speaks faultless English. He has a keen, sharp face and a keen, sharp mind. I got the impression that the main motive of his nationalism was pride— he knew that he and his friends were abler than many of the British officials sent to "govern" them and resented their subservience, but I felt that in any social crisis Jinnah would stand with the ruling class rather than with the Indian masses, and would use the Moslem issue to divide the masses. I found Mr. Jinnah supporting the boycott of the Simon Commission (the "seven God's Englishmen" sent by Mr. Stanley Baldwin to decide the future of India), but this was largely because Indian politicians like himself were excluded. I should describe Mr. Jinnah, brilliant barrister and opportunist, as the Sir John Simon of India.

I had a memorable luncheon discussion with other representative Moslem leaders. The scene was the home of Dost Mahomed Peer Mahomed, founder and head of a Girls' College at Poona, to which parentless girls from all Moslem countries can go. It was an extraordinary house. The mixture of furnishings gave the impression of an old curiosity shop crowded with valuables from both East and West. There were beautiful Greek statues, large brilliantly-coloured vases, two grandfather clocks, a huge mechanical musical instrument, English paintings in heavy gilt frames and Indian sketches with narrow black edgings. From the ceiling a swing was suspended; two men sat on it and conversed quietly as they rocked to and fro. On a mat our host was praying. He bowed, raised hands to face, kneeled, touched the floor with his forehead, stood—and then repeated the performance. No one took any notice of him.

Round the luncheon table was the cream of the Moslem intelligentsia—Hakim Ajmal Khan*, philosopher and scholar, Lakir Hussain, Principal of Delhi University (he reminded me that we had met at a Peace meeting in Berlin), Maulana Abdul Kalam Azad†, ex-President of the National Congress, and

---

* "Hakimji," as he was reverentially called, died whilst I was in India.
† The Maulana was re-elected Congress President in March, 1940.

Sheriff Serji Canji, Secretary of the Moslem Educational Trust. "Hakimji," whose knowledge I found very wide, regarded another world war as inevitable owing to the clashes of western Capitalism and Imperialism; he foresaw the revolt of the subject peoples supported by Russia. They told me, what I had heard before, that there are more Moslems in the National Congress than in the special Moslem organisations, such as Mr. Jinnah's Moslem League, and showed no apprehension at all that the Hindus would oppress them when India threw off British rule.

I am glad I attended the Congress of the Peoples of the Indian States, because later I shall have to tell how I failed to attend the meetings of the National Congress and T.U.C. It was in a huge tent in the compound of a temple, the entrance to which was like a farmyard, with cows and goats wandering about amidst mud and swamps of refuse. There must have been a thousand people present. At one end of the tent was a slightly raised platform. To this the Chairman, Diwan Bahadur M. Ramachandra Rao, distinguished looking with silver hair, advanced under an arch of staves held by volunteers. The proceedings opened with weird "welcome music"—a little box harmonium was brought forward and six girls, aged perhaps from ten to sixteen, five of them in charming sarees and the sixth in a rather pathetic European dress, stood opposite each other with folded arms and chanted in loud shrill voices. The speech-making took place from a high square rostrum raised on scaffolding in the centre of the tent. The rostrum looked like the ring at a prize fight and this impression was increased by the seating, which faced it from all sides. The two opening speakers read their speeches over the rail at the four sides in turn, but as their utterances, each 10,000 words in length, had already been distributed in pamphlet form to all present, no one took any notice.

I don't think social conditions have ever shocked me more than the housing in Bombay. I give two examples. We entered a tenement by a dark, tunnel-like passage and to left and right were the mill-workers' single-room houses, darker and smaller than prison cells. We entered a rough wooden building where the rooms were no larger than cupboards. I measured one—it was seven feet by five, with the roof cutting off half

the space because it sloped directly from floor to wall. Two
families lived in this box—four adults and three children! A
large part of the population of Bombay sleeps out except
during the monsoons. At night thousands of Indians just put
down a mat on the pavement, in a corner, against a wall or in
a doorway and sleep.

Mr. Joshi was leading a campaign to rid Bombay of some
of the worst features of prostitution. In no other city have I
seen the traffic conducted so openly. In Falkland Road—an
important thoroughfare and a main tram route—the girls'
bedrooms are set out like shop fronts, except that iron bars are
substituted for glass. Behind the bars the girls beckon and
bargain, screening their rooms from the road by curtains when
they have customers. The girls are exploited disgracefully.
They pay 3s. a night for accommodation and, in addition to
rent, have to pay for bedding, sarees and washing. Often they
cannot afford to buy bedclothes and dresses and hire them instead; most of them get into debt on which they pay 50 per cent.
interest. They charge the men from 3s. to 5s., and to exist at
all they must have several each night.

When my crowded programme in Bombay was over, I
travelled by train, two nights and a day, across the desert of
Deccan to Madras, the venue of the two Congresses I had come
to India to attend. My sister, Nora, who is Principal of a
Teachers' Training College in Madras, was the first person I
saw on the station platform, but we had scarcely exchanged
words when I was overwhelmed by the official Congress
welcome. A crowd swayed forward, but Congress "volunteers"
—dressed in white and wearing red and green badges—kept it
back by clasping hands in a semi-circle whilst Muthuranga
Mudalier, Chairman of the Reception Committee, and S.
Satyamurti, leader of the Congress Party in the Legislative
Council (I had met him in England), "received" me. I was
again garlanded.

I was to have two days with my sister before beginning my
official duties. On the way to her college we passed the
Congress camp. Its vastness astonished me; it was like some
great exhibition in England erected specially for the occasion.
In the centre was the Congress hall, a huge thatched pavilion
capable of holding 7,000 people. Around it were streets of

wooden huts and tents and a number of fair-sized buildings used for offices, committee rooms, ambulance stations, canteens, etc. A special railway station had been built to serve the needs of visitors. Ten thousand were expected.

My sister had planned a visit to a small Indian village ninety miles away. We travelled in a car borrowed from Mr. Joseph, one of the few Christians among Congress leaders: his son and a young Indian chauffeur accompanied us. For hours we travelled across the rice-fields, deep-green, well-irrigated, our road a yellow ribbon raised five or six feet above them. We had our evening meal at an Ashram (community centre) at Tirupa Hur, run by two doctors, Dr. S. Jesudason, an Indian, and Dr. Forrester Paton, a Scotsman, and then walked three miles under the stars by a rough path to Perum, the village where we were to pass the night. Dr. Paton and I slept in the courtyard of a small Indian bungalow.

Before I was up the next morning the village schoolmaster was waiting; he begged me to allow the village to present me with an address. I consented, largely because I wanted to see a gathering of the villagers. The schoolroom, where the presentation took place, was a long hut of mud walls and thatched roof, with a blackboard on one wall. The villagers squatted in crowded discomfort on the floor.

Proceedings began by the chanting of three boys, after which the schoolmaster proudly read the "address," the most amazing concoction of compliments on past achievements and of confidence in future eminence imagination could conceive. Then without any warning he called on me to deliver a lecture on "The Future of the Indian Village." I got up, uttered a few platitudes, which Dr. Paton translated, and sat down. Immediately there was a dramatic intervention. Among the "platform party" was a huge Indian of fierce aspect; he was wearing little more than a loin-cloth but was obviously someone of authority. He leapt to his feet, stood mountainously over me, pointed his finger menacingly, and shouted angrily in Tamil. I wondered what fearful charge was being brought against me. Dr. Paton turned to me, "This is the Chairman of the village Punchayat (Council)," he said. "He wants to know what you will do to get a road built from the village to the main highway." I indicated that I had no power to secure the building of the road. That would not satisfy him. I had come from England—a "great one" from England, as the words of the "address" had made clear. What was the use of my talk about the distant future if I could not get them a road so that they could take their produce to the market? The villagers muttered their approval, the children clapped their hands. When the meeting had dispersed, the gigantic figure, still shouting and gesticulating, accompanied us a considerable way, pointing out the deficiency of the footpath, and demanding the immediate construction of a road. Since this experience I have not doubted the capacity of the spokesman of a Punchayat to represent the requirements of an Indian village!

We left the Ashram on our return journey to Madras and the Congress. There is a unique fascination about the Indian road. It stretches before one for miles, a yellow strip through the green, narrowing to a point on the horizon. On either side are the great banyan trees, spreading their branches widely so that the road is mostly in dark shade, with dazzling, dancing pools of light. Monkeys scamper from side to side, swing from branch to branch, run up the trunks of the trees. Bullock carts slowly move along. They are to the Indian road what the gondolas are to the canals of Venice: there is a peculiar beauty about them; the clean white bullock, so dignified; the brown-skinned driver, often with long flowing hair, naked except for a red loin-cloth; the arched outline of the reed plaited roofs. There are Indians tramping from one village to another. There are the rich green rice-fields, stretching as far as eye can see to either side, with lonely men and women at work, looking, in their red loin-cloths and sarees, like poppies in a young cornfield. There are the wells with the bullocks on the sky-line.

Through these scenes we passed, mile after mile, the orange road always unfolding before us, between the banyan trees . . . A great content came over me: I was at peace with the world. The motor darted past a string of bullock carts, the drivers asleep, the animals trudging along as though they had eternity in which to reach their destination. "Motor-cars are an outrage here," I said to my sister. "They are a crime against the leisure of the East." I put my head back, closed my eyes and dozed.

I was awakened by a dull thump on the side of the car

and then a sudden swerve. I sat up and saw the driver pulling frantically at the steering wheel as we swung from side to side. The car headed for the edge of the road and I knew that nothing could stop us going over the embankment . . . . My thigh was broken and my shoulder and neck dislocated. Nora, thrown into a prickly pear-bush, was unhurt except for the prickles. Mr. Joseph's son was stunned, but no limbs were broken. The chauffeur's face was badly cut. Later we heard that an Indian pedestrian had been killed: the thump that awakened me was caused by contact with his body.

I spent the night at a small hospital at Vellore, eight miles away, and the next day travelled by train to the General Hospital at Madras. Once again there was a crowd at the station: the press had carried the story of my accident and it had caused consternation in Indian circles. Two doctors belonging to the Congress Medical Corps met me instead of the heads of the Reception Committee. Congress stretcher bearers carried me to the Hospital ambulance, the "volunteers" lined the length of the platform, again keeping back the people with linked hands.

I was three months in the General Hospital and found it of fascinating interest. I was placed in the "European Officers' Quarters"; cynically I noted the racial and class distinction. My room, containing only two beds, was so big and airy that one had the impression of being in the open. Sparrows built their nests in the rafters of the high ceiling, lizards climbed the walls chirping loudly and grey squirrels with yellow-streaked backs ran along the verandah blinds. I was on the fourth floor, and could watch the whole life of the hospital across the compound. There were separate wards for Europeans, Anglo-Indians (the new name for Eurasians) and Indians. The staff was of the same mixture of races. The superintendent and two of the principal doctors were English; otherwise the doctors were Indian. The matron and most of the sisters were English, but all the nurses were either Indian or Anglo-Indian, a few of the latter so fair that one could not tell them from English girls. The working conditions were disgraceful and, as soon as I was well enough, I began a campaign to improve them. The bearers and sweepers were paid eightpence for a twelve hour day or night; the ward boys ninepence. They lived out and somehow housed and fed their families on this miserable sum. The wages of the nurses were higher than is usual for women in India—rising over three years from 42s. a month to 72s., but they were on duty twelve hours. My letters to the press resulted in a full-dress debate in the Legislative Council, where the Indian Minister for Health explained that he had asked for money to make improvements but the English Finance Minister had refused it: a good example of the farce of "self-government" so long as the purse strings are in other hands.

I was, of course, bitterly disappointed to miss the meetings of the National Congress and the Trade Union Congress, but I had the advantage of visits from most of the best known Indian leaders. Mr. Gandhi visited me on each of the four days he was in Madras. He came in a white loin cloth with a loose white garment over his shoulders. His personality was much more vital and genial than I had expected; his eyes twinkled as he smiled, his walk and movements were vigorous. This was not the other-worldly mystic I had expected, but a surprisingly lively old man with a suggestion even of whimsical mischief. I was both fortunate and unfortunate in being very weak when he came: fortunate, because I found the influence of his personality soothed feverishness and helped to conquer pain; unfortunate, because I was unable to discuss Indian problems as fully as I should have liked.

On the occasion of one visit he was observing his "silence" day; he did not speak, but his vow not to allow a word to pass his lips did not prevent him from communicating by written questions and answers. I had been having a rather bad time and was restless. His left hand took mine and with the other he wrote: "How are you sleeping?" He had perceived the difficulty which troubled me most: for three weeks I had had no natural sleep. When I told him this his pressure on my hand increased, he closed his eyes in concentration and an influence which was almost physical seemed to pass into my body and at the same time a growing calmness came over my mind and nerves. I don't attempt to explain this, but that night I slept for the first time without a drug.

The political issue at the National Congress was "swaraj" or independence. Before the Madras Congress, its aim had always been defined as "swaraj" — a term meaning self-government through self-reliance but without a clear political form. Jawaharlal Nehru, the leader of the younger socialist elements, was demanding that the objective of national independence should be avowed openly and I was interested to learn Mr. Gandhi's view. He was not much concerned about the political form or definition. He wanted a change that would be basically spiritual—if the Indian people developed the sense of freedom and equality in their own minds and acted in accordance with this sense in their relations with the British authorities, refusing co-operation with all institutions and forms of administration which denied it, they would inevitably achieve a political form to reflect the spirit which animated them. Whether this political structure would be within the British "Commonwealth of Nations" or not would depend on the response of the British Government and people. If the British understood and met the mood of India, and if this attitude of racial equality were expressed by the British "Commonwealth" in all its relations, India would be glad to maintain association with Britain. If, however, the British "Commonwealth" proved an imprisonment of India's free spirit, India's "swaraj" could be expressed only through a break with Britain.

Jawaharlal Nehru also came to see me, but I did not need to discuss the principles of this matter with him; we had discussed it many times during our friendy association in England before he returned to India—indeed, he had spent his last week-end in my home and, after we had succeeded in packing the children off to bed (he was a great favourite with them), we had spent a large part of the night hours talking about the line of development in India and the tactics required to carry it forward to freedom, economic as well as political. In London, Nehru had been a well-dressed Englishman : here in Madras he wore the white Gandhi costume and hat, and very attractive he looked in them. He is one of the finest personalities I have known. He has a peculiar gentleness and charm, kindly eyes, a soft caressing voice, but there is also tremendous strength of character, a philosophic spirit, a good brain, a mind stored with knowledge both of the past and the present, and an imagination with a broad, constructive sweep. In his white suit his slim athletic body looked very young and his tenderness with me in my illness was such that it was difficult to think of him as the extremist in Congress or as the potential leader of the Indian revolution. It may be that Jawaharlal is too tolerant for that task; he has a deep respect for Mr. Gandhi, always finding it difficult to differ from him, and at a decisive moment a break with the veteran leader may prove necessary. Nor has he the demagogic characteristics of a popular leader: on the platform he eschews rhetoric or loudness of voice and manner, depending only on persuasive statement and sincerity. Nevertheless, I found in India that he was loved second only to Mr. Gandhi and that among the younger generation he was enthusiastically extolled as leader.

At the Madras Congress Nehru was the triumphant figure, carrying his resolution for independence (in a form of words accepted by Mr. Gandhi) and being elected leader. I was particularly pleased because Jawaharlal publicly avowed his Socialism and emphasised the necessity of giving the peasants and industrial workers a greater place in Congress to balance the bourgeois elements. Even in these days Nehru recognised the danger of war. "India will not support Britain in any war until India is free and able to make its own decision," he remarked.

Mrs. Annie Besant came to see me. She came dressed as a priestess in long cream coloured robes and the golden insignia of the Order of the Star hung on a heavy chain round her neck. She was accompanied by an impressive host of attendants. I was very ill the day she came, and we did little more than exchange friendly greetings. Major Clem Attlee, Labour representative on the hated Simon Commission, came (perhaps it was as well that his visit did not clash with that of any of the Congress leaders), and Sir John Simon, chairman of the Commission, sent me a kindly note of sympathy. I appreciated these courtesies from members of a Commission which I had denounced on every possible occasion. The two members of the British T.U.C. deputation to India—Alfred Purcell and Joseph Hallsworth—also looked in: I was to appreciate Purcell's jovial comradeship and Hallsworth's kindly companionship later.

Day after day the visitors came. Dr. Ansari, the retiring Chairman of the Congress, paid me an official visit accompanied by twelve Congress volunteers; he is a Moslem, a wise and kindly man. Mr. Sreenivasa Iyengar, the leader of the Congress Party in the Legislative Assembly, a man of fine presence and mind; Miss Creighton, daughter of the late Bishop of London, engaged in educational work in Madras; Mr. K. S. Venkataramani, the author, whose novel of Indian village life I had much enjoyed reading in England—these and many others came. In addition, I was visited by a string of members of the Indian Civil Service, Indian and English journalists, and English business men in Madras. Indeed, the visitors were so many that a large notice had to be displayed prohibiting them without the permission of the Resident Medical Officer. He limited them to two a day, but many others got through despite the vigilance of the staff.

During my last fortnight in hospital I was allowed to take motor drives, and this enabled me to see much of Madras. It is a scattered and varied city, with large open spaces (crowded in the evening with bare-footed hockey and football players) and even quite primitive forest lands. Its great pride is the Marina, a magnificent five mile promenade on the sea front, with imposing Government buildings on one side and wide sands on the other. There are many residential streets of large houses and vast gardens, wooded and ablaze with flowers, occupied by Europeans and rich Indians. I visited one of these houses, occupied by an Indian lawyer. It had every modern luxury: bathroom, electric light, telephone, wireless, gas-cooker, water-closet and modern furniture. At the gate stood a group of primitive mud and thatched huts, with mats on the earth to serve as seating and sleeping accommodation, with the cooking done outside on a fire of twigs. Never have I seen the contrast of two civilisations and ages in closer proximity. Imagine the huts of primitive Britons in Hyde Park under the shadow of Park Lane—that is the contrast which one sees in the suburbs of Madras; a contrast not merely between the Europeans and the Indian masses, but between the wealthy Indians and the Indian masses. India requires a social revolution to supplement any political revolution.

I spent an evening in the working-class Indian quarters with Mr. Venkataramani. We drove down alleys so narrow that a motor had never been there before. Men, women and children poured out of the huts and bungalows and gathered round the open car: naked babies, children with bits of string round their loins, men in red loin-cloths, women in sarees, old and bent men, cripples with ill-formed limbs. Soon they were pouring out their stories of hunger and overcrowding, of low wages and long working hours. They knew me through the newspaper reports and welcomed me as a friend. I found that the average wage was 8d. a day. Frequently the wife worked two or three hours a day in the home of richer Indians for 1s. a week, receiving also scraps of food and bits of old clothing which she took home eagerly. Existence was only possible because the rents were low; 2s. 3d. a month for huts with mud walls and thatched roofs, 4s. 6d. for masonry houses of one room (10ft. by 12ft.). I was shocked to hear that the rickshaw "boys" made only 6d. a day. The rickshaw is the European's taxi in Madras: a light seat on two wheels pulled through the streets by the fleet-footed boy.

I journeyed back to England under the care of Alfred Purcell and Joseph Hallsworth. Generous Congress had insisted on my returning first class and we shared a luxurious cabin. Alfred and Joe proved grand comrades—Alfred blunt and gay; Joe thoughtful and kind. Later, Alfred was to become Chairman of the International Federation of Trades Unions (in which capacity he delivered a sensationally revolutionary address) and Joe to become Chairman of the T.U.C. during the fatal year 1938-39.*

So ended my visit to India. I had not attended the National Congress nor the Trades Union Congress, but I had learned much. I had seen the miserable poverty of India under British rule, but I had also met the men who are the leaders of the movement which will make the new India, and I had no doubt that they are equal to the task. Indeed, so far as I had met British political leaders. I came to the conclusion that the Indian leaders were men of greater stature, bigger minds, more creative personality, than the rulers who regarded them as unfit to govern. Most of all I rejoiced in the evidence I had of the growth of socialist ideas particularly among the younger people, and of the self-reliant organisation developing among the workers and peasants in opposition not only to political subjection, but to economic subjection. Despite the vastness of its problems, India will win through.

*Alfred Purcell died in 1938.

Chapter Nineteen
INCLUDING THE GENERAL STRIKE

Under Maxton's chairmanship the I.L.P. became aggressively socialist and proletarian. The middle-class experts and careerists disappeared from Head Office overnight and those who were satisfied with Labour Party policy either resigned or retained a nominal membership only. Among those who resigned was Philip Snowden. Ramsay MacDonald remained with us on the principle that one should never resign; his view was that the other fellow should be manœuvred into the unpopular step of expelling you. We didn't expel MacDonald, but we refused to send him as a delegate to Labour Party conference.

I was in the centre of the fierce controversy which arose about this. MacDonald's friends burst into fury when they learned of the recommendation of the National Council of the Party. They were organised by faithful Ernest Hunter, still secretary of our Information Department. A protest was signed by a formidable list of members, including M.P.s and leading officials throughout the country and branches began to object in numbers which appeared disturbing. The day before we were to leave for the 1927 Conference which was to decide the issue, Hunter came into my office rubbing his hands and boasting that he and his friends would win. I smiled back with confidence because I knew I held a trump card: I had a letter from MacDonald himself saying that it would be better for him not to be an I.L.P. delegate in view of his differences with the Party. I think MacDonald must have forgotten he had written that letter. He was certainly aware of the agitation on his behalf; indeed, he expressed opinions in press interviews which added to the bitterness of the controversy.

Emanuel Shinwell moved the rejection of the recommendation. He was at his sarcastic and bitter best. I listened unperturbed, my fingers caressing the folder which held MacDonald's letter. A young dark girl took the rostrum, a puckish figure with a mop of thick black hair thrown impatiently aside, brown eyes flashing, body and arms moving in rapid gestures, words pouring from her mouth in Scottish accent and vigorous phrases, sometimes with a sarcasm which equalled Shinwell's. It was Jennie Lee, making her first speech at an I.L.P. conference. And what a speech it was! Shinwell was regarded as a Goliath in debate, but he met his match in this girl David. From the point of view of argument the case was won, but the delegates were mandated heavily against the recommendation and my trump card was still necessary. I suggested to the conference that it would be unfair to MacDonald to ask him to represent an organisation whose policy the Labour Party Executive would expect him to oppose. This semblance of consideration for MacDonald provoked the scoffing which I anticipated and provided the introduction I wanted for the reading of the letter. Never have I seen an opposition so flattened out; its vote melted away. Announcing the overwhelming victory, Maxton used a phrase which I have often recalled: "Comrades, our Movement knows and needs no giants."

A casualty of the change in the Party was H. N. Brailsford's editorship of the "New Leader." His "highbrow" paper did not reflect the increasingly proletarian temper of the Party; there was also strong criticism of the salaries paid to the Editor and Manager.

The issue was discussed by the National Council during the Labour Party Conference at Margate in 1926. David Kirkwood led the attack in forthright and not too kindly language, concentrating on the salary point. Brailsford is a sensitive man and, although I was convinced that we must depart from high salaries, all my sympathies were with him. He listened without any sign of hurt and when he spoke he did so with a philosophic calm which removed all personal feeling: he might have been discussing something quite unrelated to himself. I have rarely heard anything done better. He faced the issue squarely. Socialists aimed at equality; how, then, could we consistently pay a salary of £750 to an official when many members of the Party had only £75 a year? The logical alternative was to pool the resources of the members, as did the Servants of India Society, and to take out of the pool only what was necessary for life and work. Brailsford said there was much that attracted him in this proposal: it might give the Socialist movement a spiritual content which it lacked. If the Party adopted this communal way of life he would accept it; but if the Party had not the courage to do so, he did not understand why economic equality should be applied to him and not to others. He did not know what Mr. Kirkwood's income was, but with his Parliamentary salary, Trade Union associations and speaking fees it could not be much less than his own. Was Mr. Kirkwood prepared to apply to himself the principle of equality which he had urged so eloquently?

I don't think Brailsford's argument was sound—in a Party maintained by the coppers of workers on low wages there is a case for limiting salaries without going to the logical extreme of equality—but temporarily the critics were defeated. When criticism was renewed it turned to the character of the paper. The "New Leader" was a distinguished achievement, bringing credit to the Party among all who valued good writing, beauty and learning, but I had no doubt that the membership wanted a paper of another type—a paper not so much for the armchair as for the factory and the street. I stated this view with reluctance, first because of my admiration for Brailsford and secondly because if he gave up the editorship I knew I was likely to be asked to succeed him and I foresaw that my motive would be questioned. A large majority of the Council agreed with this view. Brailsford resigned. I was appointed editor (continuing to act as Political Secretary) and John Paton became General Secretary. This was in October, 1926.

The great event of this period was the "general strike" in support of the miners in 1926. On May Day the miners were locked out. This was surely the most momentous May Day in the history of British Labour. The Hyde Park demonstration was the largest in the memory even of the oldest. On the two following days—Sunday and Monday—the T.U.C. continued negotiations with the Government, but these broke down on the Monday night on the side-issue of the refusal of the "Daily Mail" compositors to set up an article attacking the miners. I was told by a member of the T.U.C. General Council that an agreed formula had been found by representatives of the Government and the T.U.C., but that the Cabinet, largely under the influence of Churchill, rejected it off-hand on hearing of the "Daily Mail" hold-up. Stanley Baldwin, the Premier, went to bed leaving the Trade Union representatives to be shown out of No. 10 by the doorkeeper. I stood in Parliament Square

G

with thousands of others that night. Except for a chain of students *en route* to volunteer in the strike-breaking O.M.S., everything was strangely quiet. As Big Ben boomed out the beginning of the "general strike" at midnight, a few voices started to sing the National Anthem. Then only did the crowd become vocal: the "Red Flag" swept the square. That over, the crowd dispersed at the bidding of the police, neither singing nor cheering. It was the mood of the eve of the Great War.

At the very beginning the T.U.C. made a big tactical mistake. Not only were the capitalist newspapers stopped, but the "Daily Herald" with them! The B.B.C. became the one source of news and the Government used it to the full. I was so impressed by this folly that I telephoned a protest through to the T.U.C.—to be told that the compositors employed on the capitalist papers were not prepared to allow the men on the "Daily Herald" to continue working! As I put down the receiver I despaired. How could a general strike be won with such little-mindedness in the ranks? The following day, however, the T.U.C. was compelled to reconsider the decision by the appearance of an official Government paper, the "British Gazette," edited by Churchill. It decided to meet this challenge by the "British Worker." Good—but with the lack of transport it would need to be printed in half-a-dozen places. I telephoned, putting our Party printing works in the Midlands at the disposal of the T.U.C. "Thank you—but the Typographical Association is raising difficulties." Was this a general strike or a general-do-as-you-please?

The staff of the I.L.P. were on duty for twenty-four hours, sleeping at Head Office. We had offered our services to the T.U.C. on the first day, but three days passed with no one called on. Then the office boy was summoned: I remember how proudly he left for duty. Meanwhile, we duplicated thousands of copies of the "British Worker" (the printed edition was painfully inadequate) and distributed them in the outlying parts of London through Party members. At last our pressure on the T.U.C. seemed to have some effect. Tracey, the Secretary of their Publicity Committee, asked us to work out a scheme for the distribution of the "British Worker." John Paton, Ernest Hunter, Francis Johnson and I got into a huddle and the same night I took a detailed plan to the T.U.C.

headquarters (ironically they were occupying Churchill's old home in Eccleston Square). My visit resulted in a strike job, but not the one I expected.

As I went into the Committee room the telephone rang. It was a message from Manchester that the Typographical Association had given permission for a northern edition of the "British Worker" to be printed there. Who was to be Editor? The Committee hadn't an idea. Tracey broke the silence. "I think the man you want is here," he said. Within five minutes it was arranged that I should leave for Manchester that night. I hurried away to pack my bag and to ask my secretary, Marguerite Louis, to accompany me. I was so excited that temporarily I forgot the original object of my visit, but at the door I remembered; I was promised that the distribution plan would be discussed with Paton next day. At midnight Marguerite and I were at the T.U.C. headquarters awaiting the car which was to take us to Manchester. We were driven by a young playwright, Hubert Griffiths, and his sister. They talked "county"—hunting and dances—and I wondered why they had volunteered for the T.U.C. transport service rather than for the O.M.S. "Don't know much about it," acknowledged Griffiths, "but I think the miners have had a raw deal and can't feel comfortable when I think about them." Since then Griffiths has become an avowed Socialist.

The T.U.C. had instructed me to produce an evening edition of the "British Worker" the day of my arrival in Manchester. I was handed the "copy" and told that the Co-operative Printing Society had agreed to print it. Everything else connected with the production and distribution of the paper was left to me to arrange when I arrived. They appointed Mr. H. Skinner, secretary of the Typographical Association and a member of the T.U.C. General Council, to be responsible with me jointly, but I found him ill in bed and had to take over the whole job myself. When I called at Skinner's house, his wife thought I was a detective bent on arresting him! My next blow was the discovery that the printers were not expecting to do the job—the last word they had had from London was to that effect, but the Manager immediately set about rounding up the necessary workers. Then I concentrated on getting the co-operation of the Trade Union organisations. I met the

Executive of the Typographical Association at their head-quarters in Fallowfield, a fine house in delightful gardens, and representatives of all the other unions connected with newspaper production and distribution. They were grand, both cordial and efficient. We were selecting reliable Trade Unionists to supervise the various sides of the work, clerical, despatching and transport, when the third and hardest blow fell. The Manager of the Co-operative Printing Society telephoned that his directors had decided against printing. The T.U.C. had stopped their ordinary printing: they weren't going to oblige the T.U.C. This from a Co-op. organisation!

I turned to the disappointed Trade Unionists and asked for the name of any other printer who might be ready to take on the job. There was another Co-operative firm, the Co-operative Publishing Society, but the Manager lived at Southport, fifty miles away. This made an edition of the paper the same day impossible, but I told the T.U. representatives to make all arrangements for the following day and set off by taxi for Southport. The Manager agreed to print.

It was a complicated job we had in hand—not only to edit the paper, but to transport and sell it without trains or trade. Before leaving London we had arranged for despatch riders to deliver copy from the T.U.C. headquarters every night. I got journalistic help from socialist members of the N.U.J., though the organisation wouldn't officially co-operate. The N.U.C. provided typists and telephonists and N.A.T.S.O.P.A. took over responsibility for the accounts and for despatching. The Transport Workers organised the distribution by road as far south as Derby, west to Holyhead, east to Hull, and north to Carlisle. As we completed this organisation, I realised its significance: for the first time a British newspaper was being produced under workers' control. I have never worked more happily. The enthusiasm of everyone was wonderful and the efficiency with which our selected heads organised their departments showed that workers' representatives could manage as skilfully as any boss's representative. Marguerite Louis and I worked an eighteen hour day—from 9 a.m. to 3 a.m., leaving pickets on duty during our six hours' sleep to receive any despatch riders who might arrive from London. Telephonists had to be on duty all round the clock to take down press messages from London. Night and day the transport workers were driving their cars with supplies of the paper to distant places.

When the end of the strike came on May 12th none of us in Manchester could believe the news. The workers in Lancashire were absolutely solid: the difficulty was not to keep men out but to keep men in. I was warned by telephone early in the morning to be ready to get out a "special," and just after midday news came through. It was meagre: the T.U.C. was assured that a satisfactory basis of negotiation had been reached, the miners had expressed gratitude for the support of other workers, the executives were arranging for their men to return. That was all. I took the news to the Strike Committee. They had heard over the wireless that the strike was to be called off, but they thought it was a fake and were proceeding with their business unmoved. I handed the chairman the official message from London and he pushed on one side a deputation (seeking permission to call out further men!) to read it to the committee. Still they refused to believe. Was I sure I had not been hoaxed? One delegate even suggested that I had been "got at" by the other side! Finally, they adjourned for a midday meal whilst their secretary telephoned London, sending out messages that meanwhile the men were to stay out. Everyone was confident, if the news proved true, that the Government must have climbed down.

The next news to come through to me was a summary of "terms." They were wired as though they had been accepted by the Government; there was no indication that they were an unofficial memorandum prepared by Sir Herbert Samuel and not binding on anyone. The "terms" represented a considerable advance, though a clause providing for a temporary reduction in miners' wages was not pleasant. There was no suggestion that the lock-out of the miners was to go on. Then fuller reports came over the wire. When they revealed the truth we could not believe our ears. My first reaction was that the T.U.C. General Council had become either demoralised or corrupted. With a heavy heart I sent the "special" of the "British Worker" on to the streets.

The next day was chaos. The "Gazette," the Government sheet, chortled over the great surrender, but the temper of the workers was more militant than ever and in Manchester there was no thought of going back to work. Telephone enquiries came to me from all over Lancashire as to whether it was true that the General Strike had been declared "on" again. For the first time feeling was bitter—bitter against the employers who were everywhere victimising the local strike stalwarts, and bitter against the T.U.C. General Council. It looked as though the end of the strike might be the beginning of the revolution. Even the T.U.C. responded to the general anger against the victimisation, particularly by the railway companies. The issue of the "British Worker" was the most outspoken yet authorised. But next day came utter humiliation. The railwaymen's representatives, led by J. H. Thomas, signed an incredible agreement, acknowledging "wrongful action" and promising, like naughty schoolboys, never to do it again. A spirit of fatalism came over the workers. The T.U.C. had ordered them back; their own Executives had ordered them back; there was no hope of concerted resistance—so back they went. But mingled with their bitter disillusionment there was a feeling of exultation in the memory of the solidarity of those ten days.

What was the explanation of the collapse of the General Strike? Was the General Council afraid of the cracking of the strike? There was little evidence of it. Tramwaymen at Birmingham and Bristol had gone back; newsmen belonging to the T.A. were shaky; it was reported that there were weaknesses at Reading and at one or two other places. But these were insignificant compared with the mass solidarity throughout the country, and thousands more men were straining to come out. Was the General Council misled into thinking that the Samuel "terms" would be implemented by the Government? I think it was. That the Government would accept the terms was implied strongly in one of the earlier wires sent from T.U.C. headquarters to me at Manchester and afterwards cancelled. If this is part of the explanation, who was responsible for misleading his colleagues? Was the General Council afraid of the extreme measures which it was rumoured the Government intended to take on the ground, authoritatively voiced by Sir John Simon, that the strike was "unconstitutional?" Were they afraid of arrests and confiscation of funds, and that the struggle would become a genuinely revolutionary one? Why did the T.U.C. ever begin a General Strike if it was not prepared to face such possibilities?

The explanation probably lay in the fact that the General Strike was led by people who did not believe in it. They, rather than the workers, cracked. Of course a General Strike must be revolutionary; it is of necessity a conflict between the workers and the capitalist State. The strike of 1926 was led by a General Council who did not realise this when they reluctantly authorised the struggle, and they drew back from it as soon as they understood its full implications.

For nine months the miners maintained their resistance with a courage perhaps more characteristic of them than of any other section of British workers. The I.L.P. took a foremost part in supporting them, not only by collecting money, food and clothing for their relief and providing hospitality for miners' children (a Welsh boy named Raymond joined my home, now at Loudwater, near Rickmansworth, for six months), but by the production of the miners' weekly lock-out paper, "The Miner," edited by John Strachey, and by a very active part in the miners' propaganda campaign. To avoid any suggestion that "The Miner" was being used for partisan purposes, we transferred its ownership to the Miners' Federation. Every issue contained a flaming lead from A. J. Cook, the miners' secretary. It appeared as an article, but as a matter of fact, Cook just talked for an hour to Strachey and it was his duty to reduce the torrent of words into coherent form.

I came into frequent contact with A. J. Cook during this period and fell for him with a mingling of affection and admiration. He was a refreshing contrast to most Trade Union officials, whose jobs so often become well-paid vested interests far removed from the existence of the workers whom they represent. Arthur Cook never left the rank and file. He had their thoughts, their language, their habits, their simple trusting comradeship and good fellowship. During this nine months' lock-out Arthur insisted on forgoing his salary and taking lock-out pay and nothing else. He lived in trains, travelling from one coalfield to another, addressing four or five demonstrations, thousands strong, day after day, wearing out his voice to rough hoarseness and sometimes to absolute speechlessness. He was loved by his men, who sensed his utter sincerity and who heard in his words their own thoughts expressed with a conviction and confidence which sent them back to their struggle with new determination. Someone once said that A. J. Cook never knew what he was going to say before he got on a platform, what he was saying whilst on a platform, and what he had said when he got down from a platform. There was some truth in this, but it did not matter greatly because Arthur Cook had the right stuff in him and nothing but the right stuff could come out of him.

The collapse of the General Strike and the defeat of the miners in their lock-out led to a serious demoralisation in the working-class movement. Despair replaced hope: the spirit went out of all activities. From the leadership, both on the political and industrial sides, came no encouraging word. Indeed, it appeared only too ready to take advantage of the apathy which grew among the rank and file to encourage new surrenders. The T.U.C. began conversations with the British Federation of Industries with the object of facilitating collaboration: they were known as the Mond-Turner talks, named after Sir Alfred Mond and Mr. Ben Turner (I think I am right in my memory that it was *after* this, and not before, that Ben Turner was knighted for his national services!). Throughout the whole movement the mood of co-operation with the possessing class in the reconstruction of Capitalism, rather than of independent struggle for the ending of Capitalism, began to grow.

It was in this atmosphere that the Cook-Maxton manifesto and campaign were launched. My impression is that John Wheatley was the real initiator of this effort to revitalise the workers. Wheatley was a unique figure in the Socialist Movement. He was a shrewd business man and a Catholic: I had first heard his name before the war as author of a pamphlet which sold in tens of thousands, "Socialism for Catholics." He was quiet and remote—a distant personality until one pierced his reserve; then he became a kindly, beaming, almost Pickwickian figure. He was an able organiser, ruthlessly logical in mind, and combined big imaginative conceptions with constructive qualities in a way that is rare. I know Maxton always regarded him as the biggest man in the Movement; indeed, Wheatley is the only man to whom I ever heard Maxton refer as his leader.

The Cook-Maxton campaign was planned in a good deal of secrecy and announced to the world without any consultation with the National Council of the I.L.P. or with its Head Office officials, despite the fact that Maxton was chairman of the Party. John Paton, who was general secretary, was very upset by this, as on organisational grounds he had every right to be, but I was in such complete sympathy with its purpose that I did not concern myself overmuch about Party prestige or niceties of procedure. The manifesto was in effect a popular statement of the "Socialism in our Time" programme. It denounced collaboration with the capitalist class and called challengingly for a frontal attack on Capitalism. Huge meetings were held and great enthusiasm created; but, as with similar campaigns, it had little enduring effect. My impression is that in Wheatley's mind the campaign was a try-out. If it had had concrete results, I believe he might have come out for a new political organisation of the working-class, incorporating the I.L.P., but taking in other elements as well.

The workers were not in the mood, however, to establish new political organisations. We were approaching the General Election and hopes were arising of a Labour Party victory and of a second Labour Government. The failure of industrial action in 1926 and 1927 had turned the expectations of the rank and file towards political action. In the spring of 1929 the Conservative Government dissolved Parliament, and with the return of the Labour Government in the subsequent election a new chapter in the history of the British working-class began.

Chapter Twenty
ELECTED TO PARLIAMENT

I was elected M.P. for East Leyton, a suburban London constituency, one-third middle class, two-thirds working-class, in
the General Election of May, 1929. I had been adopted by the
Divisional Labour Party on the nomination of the local I.L.P.
with a clear understanding that I stood for the programme of
"Socialism in Our Time" and opposition to all armaments and
war. My poll was 11,111. I could probably have made the
figure higher if I had contested the validity of a handful of
"doubtful votes"; but I liked its symbolism: it enabled me to
say that I had "won, won, won, won, won" or, in variation, that
I had four victories still to come.

My Conservative opponent was a Mr. Alexander, a local
business man without political ability. The Liberal candidate,
Mr. Wynne Davies, a young Welsh solicitor, told me at
the count that I had converted him to Socialism and that he
proposed to join the I.L.P. He kept his word and later became
the voluntary manager of the "New Leader." When, three
years afterwards, we disaffiliated from the Labour Party, he
did not see his way to following us, and became a Labour
candidate. Later, he became disillusioned with politics, but he
continues to give me willing help of a legal kind from time to
time.

The opening day of the new Parliament was like the first
day of term at school: it was a re-union rather than an initiation. The Members' Lobby was crowded with comrades with
whom I had been associated in all parts of the country. We
slapped each other on the back, linked arms, laughed excitedly,
whilst Jack Hayes, the large, suave policemen's M.P., distributed
buttonholes of red carnations among us in order to make a brave
show when the time came to mass on the Government benches.*

The Tory and Liberal M.P.s found themselves aliens in their
own House. They looked askance at this invading host, so
boisterous, a big family rather than a political party. They
slunk away to the smoking rooms to discuss whether this really
meant the "revolution" and to drown their gloom in drinks.
Had they possessed prophetic eyes, they would not have been
frightened.

* Jack Hayes died in April, 1941.

If my memory serves me correctly, the first gathering I attended in the House as M.P. was not the meeting of Parliament but of the Parliamentary Labour Party. We met, nearly two-hundred of us, in a big square Committee Room reached by broad stone stairs leading to the first floor: one of a series of rooms lining a long corridor, used not only for the Committee stage of Bills but, when available, for Party and even private meetings so long as an M.P. is present. On this occasion we gathered in a spirit of election-victory elation. A roll of cheering swept the benches as Ramsay MacDonald, Philip Snowden, Arthur Henderson, Sidney Webb ("promoted" to Lord Passfield), Margaret Bondfield and the other members of the Government filed on to a narrow, slightly raised platform, Margaret receiving a special cheer because she was the first woman Cabinet Minister. (How soon those cheers turned to criticism!)

I forget whether it was at this or an early second meeting that the voice of criticism was raised: the spokesman was John Wheatley, on behalf of the I.L.P. Group. Wheatley's speech challenged the whole policy of Labour's acceptance of office whilst the Party was in a minority. There were some who whispered that he was animated by a sense of disappointment because he had been left out of the Government, but any suspicion of this was forgotten after a sentence or two. There are few men who can speak as impersonally as Wheatley used to do. His thick-set body did not move, one could not see his eyes behind the thick pebble glasses. Nevertheless he gripped: there was a quality of strength and certainty in his voice, and his reasoning was masterly and remorseless. Two minutes after he had risen on this occasion, the members forgot their impatience with criticism at the moment of triumph: they listened and temporarily they were convinced in spite of themselves.

Wheatley pointed out that the country was passing through one of its periodical cycles of depression. Within the capitalist system, reduction in the standard of life would be inevitable. Wages would fall and the social services would be restricted. Did a Labour Government wish to be responsible for such things? It would necessarily become so *if it administered Capitalism*. Much better that it should throw the responsibility for the evils of Capitalism on the Conservative and Liberal parties which believed in the system. The Labour Party should have the strength to wait until it had obtained an absolute majority and then proceed to make the fundamental change from Capitalism to Socialism.

One of the Government "yes-men," I think it was Emanuel Shinwell (he usually filled this office), replied that Wheatley's speech had academic interest only: the Government had been formed. This encouraged me to speak. During Wheatley's speech I felt I ought to do so, because he had not put fully the I.L.P. case: the Party was not opposed to minority Government *if a Socialist programme were introduced.* But I was nervous of addressing this imposing gathering of Cabinet Ministers and M.P.s at my first appearance: it required Shinwell's speech to provoke me. I argued that the Government should introduce its socialist programme and stand or fall by it. The Party should concentrate at first on the more urgent needs of the workers and win their support: such legislation would be popular and the Liberal Party would hesitate to vote against us during the early months of enthusiasm for the Government. The point would be reached when the Liberals would no longer acquiesce: it would probably come when the cost of social legislation would have to be met by the heavy taxation of the rich. The bankers would also begin the game of sabotage. Good: then would come the moment for challenging Capitalism itself by a measure to nationalise banking and finance: a better opportunity for raising the slogan "The People versus the Bankers" could not be desired than the issue of financing popular social legislation. This would involve defeat in Parliament, but the Party would face the election which would follow con- fident in its achievements and backed by an enthusiastic membership. As I developed this argument I saw sceptical faces about me among the older types of Labour members. I asked what was the alternative? It was to do only those things which the Tories and Liberals would allow us to do, to go from compromise to compromise, and finally to face humiliation in a defeat which would thrust the Party into the political wilderness for a decade, while the membership recovered from disappoint- ment and disillusionment.

When MacDonald was called on to reply, most of the Labour M.P.s rose to greet him, clapping their hands rapturously and also cheering in the Parliamentary manner—a deep roar of "hear-hear-hear-hear-hear-hear" continued as long as breath will last. MacDonald was basking in the honour of his office and, with the radiant support of the men before him, he could afford to be condescendingly tolerant of his critics. The Labour Government, he said, would realistically serve the working-class in the large field of beneficial reform which was practicable even with minority support. Wheatley's policy of refusing government responsibility he dismissed as cowardly: Brockway's policy of throwing away government responsibility was romanticism. The Labour Government would show the country, notwithstanding Mr. Winston Churchill, that it knew how to govern. (Loud cheers).

Then MacDonald became stern. He turned towards the I.L.P. Group and warned the Party that the one thing which might destroy the Government was "sniping" from within. A roar of cheers resounded through the room. There was no misunderstanding the threat in MacDonald's voice or in the cheers: so early as this in the life of the second Labour Government the battle between MacDonaldism and the I.L.P. was joined.

I was disturbed by this meeting and wandered through the corridors towards the terrace on the Embankment. I opened the door of a small room and found four well-known Trade Union M.P.s there, large contented men. They greeted me with friendliness and asked me to join them for a smoke. "What's your idea, Fenner, suggesting the Government should go to the country before we've had time to settle down?" asked one. "You'll learn better. You'll find it darned comfortable here." There was some jocularity in this remark, but as I looked at those smiling figures, comfortably filling four large leather-bound arm-chairs, I realised that there was also seriousness. Later I was to learn what a big factor contentedness with Parliamentary life is in dissuading M.P.s from adventurous courses.

My first speech in the House was on a Bill which the Government introduced to encourage employment by Colonial Development. Mr. J. H. Thomas, Mr. George Lansbury, Mr. Tom Johnston and Sir Oswald Mosley had been appointed as a sub-committee to prepare work schemes and Mosley asked the House to accept this Bill on the ground that the credits which it provided would mean the purchase of steel and other articles from this country. I was nominated to watch this Bill for the I.L.P. Group, and, reading it carefully, found that it permitted the use of forced labour, and even of forced child labour, on jobs it financed. There was no requirement of standard rates of pay, nor any provision to prevent the increased value of property resulting from State-financed schemes passing into private hands. I decided to concentrate on these points.

I was nervous before I spoke. The thing which worried me was the habit which M.P.s have of passing in and out of the House during a speech, conversing quietly, handing in amendments or notices of questions to the clerks at the table in front of the Speaker's chair, or even of standing at the elbow of the Speaker and chatting with him on some official matter. It had been my experience at public meetings that the least inattention in the audience, such as people coming in late with others looking round at them, a bored man in the back row reading a newspaper, a couple more interested in each other than in the platform, always put me off my stride. As I waited to be called, I wondered how I would speak through the numberless interruptions of an indifferent House. Each time a speaker concluded, I rose in my place hoping to "catch the Speaker's eye," but from four o'clock to eight o'clock in vain. At six a long-winded speaker was called and I hurried out for a snack at the bar off the Members' Lobby, wondering as I ate if I had missed my turn. By eight o'clock I was almost indifferent whether I was called or not and rose in my place only half-heartedly. It was a shock when my name was uttered by those expressionless lips from the dim, robed, bewigged figure in the throne-like Speaker's Chair. I had repeated my intended opening sentences fifty times, but now I stumbled over them.

My I.L.P. colleagues in the library and smoking room, seeing my name on the scrolls which announce who is "up," came crowding in and gave me an encouraging cheer. I recovered confidence, looked only at the Speaker, addressed him regardless of what Members were doing in other parts of the Chamber, and proceeded quietly from point to point. As I concluded there was a resounding cheer from other parts of the

House as well as from our own Group, and I found that the House had filled considerably. I listened as courtesy demanded to the first sentences of the succeeding speaker, which included the customary compliment on a Maiden Speech, and hurried away to a meal. In the passage leading to the dining room I met Lady Astor.

"Oh, Mr. Brockway, I agreed so much with your speech," she exclaimed. "It would be too dreadful if African children were forced to work. To-night I'm having a party. Won't you come and tell us all about it?" I concluded that she regarded my speech as a success, but I declined the invitation: I did not want to become involved in the social world of the other side. Lady Astor's features, always reflecting her mood, became stern. "Mr. Brockway, I didn't think you were narrow-minded," she commented. "I can never get Mr. Maxton or Mr. Buchanan to my parties, but lots of the other Labour members often come. After all, we are all trying to improve the world." I asked to be excused, and passed on. More than two years later there was an amusing sequel to this incident. I was speaking at a luncheon at a working girls' club in Lady Astor's home town in Virginia when she was there. The organisers of the meeting sent Lady Astor an invitation to be present. Back came a telegram: "Fenner Brockway is such a good Socialist that he won't even speak to me. Under the circumstances it wouldn't be much fun lunching with him. Please excuse."

I hope Lady Astor didn't get the impression that my refusal was due to an inverted snobbishness. It was due to a realisation of the way in which social life associated with Parliament blunts the sense of identity with the working-class in their struggle.

When the Colonial Development Bill reached Committee stage I came into fierce conflict with Sir Oswald Mosley. He attempted to belittle the danger of child labour employed under its provisions. "Unless a provision is inserted definitely excluding child labour, I and my friends will vote against the Bill," I said. This was the first time the threat of revolt in the Division lobbies had been made and the House was startled. Mosley turned and looked at me speechless for a moment or two, but he could not ignore the volume of cheers from the Labour benches which greeted my remark. I remember specially the shrill "Hear, hear" of Ellen Wilkinson. Mosley consulted with Mr. J. H. Thomas, sitting at his side, and offered to postpone consideration of the Bill so that consultation could take place. I thanked him, and felt the thrill of achievement. Later I was summoned to meet Mosley and Colonial Office officials. The Minister compromised handsomely and accepted in principle not merely the amendment to prohibit child labour on Government schemes of work, but the other points which I had cited in my Second Reading speech. I was greatly pleased about this and felt that Parliamentary work might prove more worth while than I had come to think. Soon I came to regard this success as my one ewe lamb!

It was Charles Trevelyan, Minister of Education, who advised me to concentrate on one subject in Parliament. "You will soon find you cannot keep up with everything," he said. "Parliamentary life would be unbearable punishment if one attempted to listen to all the debates. Choose your subject and master it. Work on it in the library, keeping your eye on the indicator so that you can go into the House if any special speaker interests you. Don't take up too many things; if you do, you won't make your mark on anything." I never took Trevelyan's advice literally, because my interests were wide, but the I.L.P. Group asked me, in collaboration with Frank Horrabin, to pay special attention to Empire questions and it was on the subject of political prisoners in India that I made my second speech.

Within a day or two of his appointment as Secretary of State, Mr. Wedgwood Benn asked Maxton and me to go to see him at the India Office. We took with us Tarini Sinha, an able young Indian who was acting as secretary to our Party Committee on Indian affairs. Benn acknowledged that he knew little about India ("on the principle, I suppose, that Cabinet Ministers should be appointed to the posts about which they know least," he added mischievously) and asked for advice. With the concurrence of my colleagues I acted as spokesman and outlined a three point programme: (1) a new psychology should be created by the release of all political prisoners, (2) the Government should make a clear declaration of Labour's intentions to recognise India's right to full self-government, and (3) Indian organisations should be asked to appoint representatives to a round-table conference with British representatives to arrange for the transition from British to Indian rule. Benn was interested and asked me to prepare him a memo. about the political prisoners. With Sinha's help I drew up a detailed statement covering several foolscap sheets, including particulars of young men who had been kept in prison for twelve years for wartime offences committed as students. Benn promised to cable the memo. to the Viceroy for his opinion and he also indicated that my other suggestions would be considered by the Government both here and in India.

Three weeks later Benn sent for me and reported that the Viceroy had submitted the proposal for the release of political prisoners to the Governors of the Provinces, with the result that the majority of them had indicated that they could not acquiesce. "What can I do?" asked Benn, helplessly. "If I announced their resignations in the House, the Liberals would defeat us at once—and we can't face an election on the Indian issue." "No, not on that issue alone," I replied. "It's part of the whole problem. If you had introduced a socialist programme all round, improving the conditions of the unemployed and the aged, raising wages, then you could have applied your principles to India. The Liberals wouldn't have dared to defeat a Government which was doing the things the workers wanted." I warned Benn as seriously as I could that he would have to face the strongest resistance India had ever made to British rule unless he did what I suggested. He shrugged his shoulders fatalistically. I was sorry for him, because he had a genuine love of liberty and was trying to do his utmost for India under impossible political conditions.

A little later I was lucky enough to win the ballot for a Private Members' Motion. I put down a motion for the liberation of political prisoners in India. Again Benn sent for me. "Do you want to help me, Fenner?" he asked. "Yes, if it also means helping India." "It does," he said earnestly. "Like you, I want to bring the utmost pressure of Parliament on our people in India to secure the release of the politicals. But that influence will only be exerted if we show that opinion here is united. You can't expect the Tories and Liberals to vote outright for your motion." He showed me a new form of words: it urged on the Viceroy and the Government of India consideration of the question and requested the release of political prisoners not suspected of violence. I hesitated. I was friendly to Benn and knew he was desirous of doing all he could. I recognised the strength of the argument that a motion carried with the support of all parties would make an impression on the British officials in India. At the same time I did not want to compromise in a way which would disappoint my Indian friends. I promised Benn I would consider his suggestion and report back.

I consulted Maxton and he agreed that I should accept Benn's proposition, though when Campbell Stephen, W. J. Brown and others heard, they disapproved. Benn conducted his preliminary conversations with the Tories and Liberals successfully and, after I had introduced the motion, Sir Samuel Hoare blessed it for the Tories and Mr. Graham White (I think it was) for the Liberals. It remained only for Benn to endorse the motion and the House adopted it without a division. The Press congratulated me on another success, but I could not help feeling that a motion supported by the Tory and Liberal Imperialists could be of little value. In fact, a considerable number of Indian political prisoners were released (strictly on individual merits, it was emphasised, and not on principle), but would not the same, and perhaps even a better, result have been secured by putting up a fight for the whole case?

There was a similarly half-hearted adaptation of the two other proposals which I made to Benn. The Government made a declaration of policy through the Viceroy, but it merely announced Dominion Status as an ultimate goal and I could imagine the criticism with which it would be greeted by those good comrades whom I had learned to respect so highly in India. After this futility, the proposal for a round-table conference had lost its significance, but again the Government resorted to it in a manner which alienated rather than attracted freedom-loving India. Instead of inviting the Indian organisations to appoint their own representatives, the Viceroy himself nominated India's spokesmen.

My warning to Wedgwood Benn was fulfilled to the letter. Gandhi initiated the civil disobedience campaign by defying the salt-tax—and within six months sixty thousand Indians were imprisoned. I was shocked that a Labour Government should besmirch the record of the British working-class in this way and took all Parliamentary opportunities to protest, opportunities limited to question time unless the Government would permit time for a discussion. The session was nearing its end. Mr. Baldwin asked the Prime Minister what would be the business for the remaining period. Mr. MacDonald read out a string of Bills and Orders. I rose and asked quietly whether an opportunity would be allowed to discuss the imprisonments in India. "No, Sir," came the reply. I rose in my place again. "Is the right honourable gentleman aware that sixty-thousand Indians are in prison for demanding the freedom which he himself has claimed for them?" The Prime Minister did not answer. I addressed the Speaker. "I wish to protest, Sir, against the adjournment of this House whilst this injustice is being done in India." The Speaker rose. I remained standing. "I mean no disrespect to you, Sir, but I cannot be silent whilst this injustice persists," I said. The Tories began to shout "Order, Order." I remained standing. The Speaker rose again. "I must name the honourable Member if he continues to disobey the Chair," he said. I remained standing.

My further words were drowned by the angry cries from the Tories. The Speaker warned me a third time. I continued my protest. The Speaker rose and "named" me. The Prime Minister moved my suspension from the House. I sat down. I had deliberately challenged this. I wanted India to know that she had friends in the British Parliament.

The I.L.P. Group demanded a division on the motion for my suspension. I sat quietly whilst it proceeded. John Beckett was one of the tellers. With his three colleagues he advanced up the House, bowing three times as required and standing in front of the Mace on the Clerks' Table before reporting the figures. Suddenly his hands plunged forward, he gripped the Mace and lifted it to his shoulder; then he turned and strode as rapidly as its heavy weight would allow towards the door of the House.

The Members were scandalised. First, there was a gasp of astonishment, then a storm of angry cries of "shame," "scandalous," and even "you swine." The Labour M.P.s were as shocked as any, a revelation of how deeply they had fallen in idolatry to the institutions of the capitalist State. They regarded Beckett's action as sacrilege. I was surprised, then amused. I was also a little irritated that Beckett's sensational coup would get the Press and that my protest about the Indian prisoners would be smothered. Before Beckett reached the door, the Sergeant of Arms, a weedy little man in a black-beetle suit, with a sword dangling at his side, stepped out of his pew-like box and barred John's way, and two of the magnificent messengers clutched him and, after a brief struggle, regained the Mace. The Speaker solemnly named Beckett, the Prime Minister moved his suspension in a tone of disgust, and the M.P.s angrily shouted "Aye." Some of our group courageously challenged a division, but the vote for Beckett was small compared with mine. The Speaker requested us to withdraw. I bowed to him as I crossed the bar of the House. Beckett went out with head held defiantly. We were accompanied across Old Palace Yard by a Police Superintendent and Inspector and then given our freedom.

"What in the world was the idea, John?" I asked Beckett. He laughed. "It came to me suddenly—the House is in session only when the Mace is on the table. If I could get away with it, they couldn't suspend you."

John Beckett later became Sir Oswald Mosley's right-hand man in the British Union of Fascists and, after a row with his chief, joined William Joyce,* another of Mosley's henchmen, in forming the "National Socialist Party" (choosing the name the Nazis adopted in Germany), finally becoming secretary of an organisation which called itself the British People's Party, with a programme reminiscent of Hitler's early demagogy.†

I first met Beckett in the years immediately after the war; he was organising the National Union of Ex-Servicemen on a socialist and anti-war basis in opposition to the British Legion and I was able to help him by introducing a number of subscribers who contributed generously. Despite his subsequent political development, I have a friendly memory of earlier association with Beckett and particularly of the motive which led him to run away with the Mace.

* Lord Haw Haw of German radio fame.

† Beckett was interned in 1940.

Chapter Twenty-One

A "REBEL" UNDER THE LABOUR GOVERNMENT

The "not genuinely seeking work" grievance of the unemployed became a critical issue for the Government. Thousands of unemployed workers were refused benefits; unless they could give the Labour Exchanges detailed reports of how they had gone from place to place applying for jobs, they were struck off the register. This injustice was encouraged by the Tory and Liberal politicians, who, alarmed by the cost of unemployment pay, were sneering about "shirkers living on the dole," and it was facilitated by the "moral" attitude of Margaret Bondfield, Minister of Labour, who was far too ready to believe the stories circulated by the capitalist Press.

From the first days of the Labour Government our Group drew vigorous attention to this and other bitter wrongs from which the unemployed were suffering. We tabled "Minimum Demands," including the scales of benefit which the Labour representatives had put forward on the Blanesburgh Commission (appointed by the preceding Conservative Government), and the unchallengable right of the unemployed to benefit unless they refused a job to which standard rates of wages and conditions were attached. The Group decided to vote for these demands whether the Government accepted them or not.

This caused a crisis in the I.L.P. The number of M.P.s elected to the House of Commons with the financial responsibility of the Party was only 37, but all Labour members belonging to the I.L.P. were entitled to belong to our Group and in fact 140 did so. When the decision to vote against the Government became known, there was consternation among the MacDonald loyalists. They asked for an emergency meeting and there demanded the rescinding of the decision. The loyalists were in a majority and, led by Shinwell, they were aggressive, but from the chair Maxton declined to go back upon the decision already taken. He drew attention to an I.L.P. Conference resolution requiring M.P.s to implement its decisions and insisted that membership of the Group must be limited to those who accepted I.L.P. authority. Shinwell and the others bitterly contested this view, but Maxton held his ground. A few days later we insisted on pressing our amendments, receiving from 21 to 39 votes. This was the first step in the course which led to the disaffiliation of the I.L.P. from the Labour Party.

By an overwhelming majority the succeeding Annual Conference endorsed the action of Maxton and those of us who acted with him and authorised the reconstruction of the Parliamentary Group. The resolution was circulated to the 140 M.P.s—and only seventeen accepted it! We reorganised ourselves as a compact body, with regular meetings, a small executive committee, and two secretaries who acted when necessary as "unofficial whips." When in later years Maxton was sometimes criticised for unwillingness to impose discipline, he would retort that he had been responsible for the severest "purge" any Party had ever undergone—the exclusion of 123 members from its Parliamentary Group!

The indignation aroused by the Government's attitude to the unemployed was by no means limited to the I.L.P. The reference back of the appropriate paragraph in the Executive Committee's Report was defeated at the Labour Party Conference by the narrow margin of 1,027,000 votes to 1,000,000. Within the Parliamentary Party we had heated discussions on the subject, the Committee of the Trade Union Group, led by Arthur Hayday, M.P., taking as strong a view about the "not genuinely seeking work" clause as the I.L.P. On this issue we were clearly fighting a winning battle. Margaret Bondfield promised to introduce an amending clause, but when she did so it was still unsatisfactory, and the I.L.P. initiative of criticism was followed by so many Labour speakers that she had to withdraw it. Finally we got an acceptable form of words. It was a great victory.

Meanwhile the unemployment question was causing a crisis on another front. I have told how J. H. Thomas was given the task of preparing schemes of work with Lansbury, Johnston and Mosley as a sub-committee. Thomas failed completely. In the House he made grandiose promises which staved off criticism for a time, but the day came when he was remorselessly shown up by John Wheatley. I was sitting at Wheatley's side that afternoon and can still see the scene and recapture its atmosphere. Thomas had bragged of his plans with the customary show of confidence, but by now Members were becoming sceptical. Wheatley rose and quietly put a question to elicit the actual number of workers put into jobs for each thousand pounds expended. Thomas dodged it. Wheatley rose again and put his point so directly that the Minister could not evade it. After some hesitation, Thomas admitted that the work provided was insignificant compared with the money spent. By now it was clear that Wheatley was bursting Thomas's balloon. He rose a third time and in his dry, matter-of-fact way gave the final piercing stab. There was nothing for Thomas to do but to gather the deflated wreckage.

The I.L.P. had published a very thorough pamphlet on useful schemes of work and I was one of a deputation who took it to Lansbury and Mosley. Both were utterly disillusioned with the Government. They thanked us, but gave no hope that Thomas would do anything about it. They revealed confidentially that with Johnston they had decided to prepare a full plan of their own and to present it to the Cabinet over the head of their chief. It was the rejection of this plan which led Mosley to resign from the Government and started him on the path towards the formation of the New Party and, afterwards, of the British Union of Fascists. A word or two about Mosley.

We have an I.L.P. rule that no one can stand as a Parliamentary candidate for the Party unless he has been a member for twelve months: this rule is sometimes set aside, and on the proposal of P. J. Dollan, later Provost of Glasgow,* it was so in the case of Mosley. Soon his drive and brilliance as a speaker brought him to the National Council and responsible Party committees. He came with detailed schemes, particularly on the subject of financial policy, though under discussion his mastery of detail proved less exact than his elaborate memoranda led one to expect: this indicated that they were principally the work of his secretaries, who included one of our ablest young members, Alan Young. Mosley always gave the impression that he was more concerned with his personal career than with the Party. Despite his wealth, his contributions to the I.L.P. were meagre, though we found he was making large

---

* Dollan, conscientious objector in 1914-1918, was knighted for his services to the war effort in 1941.

donations to the Labour Party whilst negotiating with it for a Parliamentary constituency. He also made a bad impression by the manner in which he wooed the friendship of MacDonald when it became clear that the Premiership was soon to be his again. Lady Cynthia Mosley, though she always struck one as a more sincere Socialist than her husband, fitted into this rôle perfectly. She flattered MacDonald with attentions, on train journeys and in hotels she saw that his every need was met, she fussed about him in a way which pleased his pride. Just before the election of 1929, MacDonald travelled over a large part of Europe as the Mosleys' guest, and it was freely whispered that Sir Oswald was to be the Labour Foreign Secretary. It was a bitter disappointment to him when he received only a minor appointment in the Government.

The Labour Party conference at Llandudno in 1930 was the occasion chosen by Mosley to come out openly as a critic of MacDonald and the Government. That conference was also memorable in another way. We had intended to make it a battle-ground between the I.L.P. and the Government. MacDonald was to speak and we had arranged that Maxton should follow him with a broad, thorough-going attack and with an appeal that even at this late hour the Government should stand up to the capitalist parties by the introduction of a bold socialist programme.

When I went down to my hotel breakfast that morning I found that the newspapers carried headlines of the disaster to the airship R101 and of the loss of many lives including that of Lord Thomson, the Minister for Air. Everyone at the tables was talking of the disaster. Some suggested that the debate would be postponed. But that was not MacDonald's idea. He announced that he must return immediately to London and devoted most of his speech to a panegyric on Lord Thomson. MacDonald could do this kind of thing supremely well, and in a few sentences had the whole conference hushed in solemn sympathy. I cannot judge how far his speech was guided by political strategy, but he carried it to a point which made it practically impossible for Maxton to follow with criticism. "Ah, my friends," said MacDonald, "at moments like this the eternal principles which unite us, not the temporary differences which divide, are remembered. My good comrade Maxton has known, as I have known, what it is to stand at the marble gates of death and see one who is dearest pass through."

Maxton was sitting beside me. Tears were on his cheek; I knew how deeply the death of his wife, so soon after his release from war-time imprisonment, had affected him. My immediate thought was to offer to take his place on the platform, but that was checked by a startling exclamation from his lips, which made clear to me that, despite his emotion, Maxton had kept his critical faculty very much alive. I had little fear as Jimmy squeezed past me to make his way to the platform. He had a great reception and began, as was inevitable, with a personal tribute to Thomson and an expression of sympathy to all the bereaved. But he was allowed only five minutes and lingered too long on the theme, every sentence deepening the uniting emotion and making his task of criticism more difficult. A few sentences more, and I knew that the attack and the constructive case we wanted could not be made. Maxton concluded with little more than a hint of criticism and of socialist evangelism.

It may be that no speaker could have made the contribution we desired in such circumstances. With wise precaution Mosley waited his time and did not intervene till two days later. MacDonald had left and the memory of his speech was dim; the underlying anxiety of the delegates about the Labour Government's policy, not reassured by the series of speeches we had heard from Ministers (except a bold declaration by Trevelyan on education), was rising to the surface of their minds. At the psychological moment Mosley came in with a challenging utterance, calling on the Government to inaugurate a bold unemployment programme, urging it to withstand the financiers, assuring MacDonald that he could count on the support of the common people. The speech was exactly what the delegates wanted and was magnificently delivered; confidence, strength, fire were all there. As Mosley ended the delegates rose *en masse*, cheering for minutes on end. I have never seen or heard such an ovation at a Labour Party conference.

That ovation went to Mosley's head. When he resigned from the Government I have no doubt his intention was to make a bid for the leadership of the Party. He transferred the struggle for his unemployment programme from the Government to the Parliamentary Party, but here his conceit defeated him. He had the bad taste to remind the Labour M.P.s of the reception accorded him at Llandudno and to say that if they rejected his proposals he could appeal with confidence to the Movement outside. His arrogance lost him the sympathy which his case on its merits might so easily have won. The I.L.P. Group voted with him, but without any personal enthusiasm.

Mosley might have staked out a claim for the leadership of the I.L.P. at this moment, for Maxton's chairmanship was nearing an end and there was a readiness for the type of precise, direct, constructive policy which Mosley advocated. But he was after bigger things than the leadership of the I.L.P.; if he couldn't become leader of the Labour Party, he was determined to become leader of a new Party which would gather together all the discontented and disillusioned elements in the old parties and challenge their prestige and place. So long as he thought there was a chance to win the leadership of the Labour Party, Mosley stepped warily. He was outspoken in criticism in the House, but he never joined the I.L.P. in the division lobby against the Government. He and his two immediate associates —Cynthia, his wife, and John Strachey, who had been his Parliamentary secretary—sat on the bench beneath the I.L.P. Mosley remained aloof from us, but Cynthia and Strachey began to make friends with some of the group, and particularly with W. J. Brown and Dr. Forgan, who were attracted by the definiteness of Mosley's criticisms and of his positive case.

One evening W. J. Brown asked to see me privately. I was attracted by Brown. He had a great reputation as a negotiator for the Civil Service Clerical Association, of which he is secretary, and as I listened to him in the House I was not surprised: without exception he is the clearest, most persuasive speaker I have heard. He is a man of personal charm and courage, of wide interests and imagination, and with a touch of mysticism which surprises. His two faults, as I saw him in Parliament, were an over-confidence in his own capacity and an adventurousness which led him into serious mistakes as well as into brilliant successes. The proposals which he brought to me in the little Conference Room at the head of the narrow, circling stone staircase rising from the Central Lobby, were one of his mistakes. He came with a manifesto outlining a new policy under the leadership of Mosley, and asked me to sign it. I refused for three reasons: first, I held that the matter should be discussed by the I.L.P. Group before any of us signed; second, I disagreed with some of the contents of the manifesto (particularly a section endorsing tariffs); and, third, it was clear to me that the object of the manifesto was to initiate a new Party. Brown tried with all his skill to alter my decision, but failed.

The Mosley Group had planned their signature-collecting cleverly. They had listed those they hoped would sign in the order of anticipated willingness. I was sixth on the list and was the first to refuse. The five names above mine were: Cynthia Mosley, John Strachey, W. J. Brown, Robert Forgan, John McGovern—McGovern signed owing to a misunderstanding and immediately withdrew. One other M.P. signed—W. E. D. Allen, Unionist member for a Belfast division. Within a few weeks the New Party was announced and in time it gave way for the British Union of Fascists. Both Brown and Strachey broke with Mosley before the fascist stage was reached.

Meanwhile, events were moving to a crisis in Parliament. Trade was in steep decline and the capitalist parties were demanding economy on the social services, just as their friends the employers were demanding reductions in wages. The Liberal Party was foremost in making this demand and, dependent on their votes, the Government was making concession after concession. We were seeing day by day a literal fulfilment of the course of "from moderation to compromise and from compromise to humiliation" which our Group had forecast at the beginning of the life of the Government.

The wage rates of State workers were the first to go. The I.L.P. protested. Then came the supreme test. The Liberal Party proposed an Economy Commission to report to the House on how national expenditure could be cut down. We had no doubt how the Commission would report: it would propose cuts in unemployment relief, education, housing, and the other social services. With despair we heard the Government announce that it would accept the proposal. With still greater despair we heard the announcement of the names of those serving on the commission. Its chairman was the director of a powerful insurance company and other members were equally reactionary. Our group challenged a division, but we were overwhelmingly defeated by a combination of Conservatives, Liberal and Labour votes. It was this "May Commission" which recommended the Means Test and the savage cuts in unemployment pay and the social services introduced by the National Government in 1933. No votes ever given by working-class representatives in Parliament were more justified than those given on this occasion by the I.L.P. against a united House.

The Liberals were not satisfied with the appointment of the Economy Commission; they demanded immediate economy and, as a result of their joint pressure with the Tories, the Government introduced a Bill to remove what it called the "anomalies" of Unemployment Insurance. Seasonal workers, casual workers, week-end workers and large numbers of married women were to be denied benefits. Our Group fought this Bill tooth and nail, arguing that it did not remove the manifold anomalies from which the unemployed suffered, but only those from which they were alleged to benefit and that it would create more anomalies than it would remove. The seventeen of us carried on the struggle continuously from 3.45 p.m. in the afternoon to 10.30 a.m. the next morning, one of the longest sittings of Parliament on record. Sometimes we obtained the help of other Labour members, but generally we were left to maintain the fight alone. The loyalist Labour members had instructions to keep silent in order to facilitate the passage of the Bill; the Tories and Liberals practically deserted the House, quite content that Government supporters should be left to the unpopular task of voting us down. One young Liberal supported us, as he did on many occasions: Frank Owen, now one of Lord Beaverbrook's star journalists, shining alternately in the "Daily Express," the "Sunday Express," and the "Evening Standard." Frank Owen was the youngest M.P. in those days, ousting our Jennie Lee from that honour, and was also one of the best.

As I went to bed at 11 o'clock the next morning, I was proud of our night's work. Most all-night sittings are silly occasions: mere obstruction, giving rise to pantomimic scenes. But this night had been serious fighting for the workers, carried out with ability, a fine team spirit, and without a word spoken of which we had reason to be ashamed. Minor concessions were won, but the Bill went through without serious alteration. Few working-class representatives would say now that we were wrong in opposing it: three hundred thousand unemployed were docked of their benefits when the Act came into operation.

By this time the I.L.P. Group was frankly in opposition. The deterioration of the Labour Government had gone so far that it had become merely an instrument for doing disagreeable work for the capitalist parties. I have not told how we fought to secure the scale of benefits for the unemployed to which Labour was pledged: 20s. for a man, 10s. for his wife, and 5s. for each child. Nor how, when a Bill was introduced for the capitalist reconstruction of the mining industry, we moved that the miners thrown out of work by the closing down of obsolete pits should have compensation on the same principle that the mineowners were to have compensation; nor how we voted for "token" reductions of the credits for the armed forces, which we recognised as potential instruments for the defence of British Capitalist-Imperialism and for the slaughter of our fellow-workers in other countries. I record these points to indicate that the front on which we resisted was broad and that the failure of the Government was by no means limited to isolated issues. On all these occasions we voted on the principle for which F. W. Jowett had always contended: not for or against the Government, but on the merits of the question before the House.

The mistake which the I.L.P. made at this period was to refrain from challenging the Government in the country. The logic of our position made a break with the Labour Party inevitable; we should have done much better to break with it at once, while the political issues on which we differed were hot, rather than delay eighteen months while events occurred which threw up entirely new issues. Will Brown and I proposed that we should all resign our seats and fight by-elections on the issues between us and the Government. This would have meant a miniature general election with seventeen contests proceeding simultaneously and with the full blaze of publicity thrown on the I.L.P. and the policy for which we stood. The proposal was rejected but, looking back, I am certain that the bold course at this time would have been the best course. As things turned out, when the general election came the I.L.P. candidates were identified in the public mind with the failure of the Government and we suffered in the general debâcle scarcely less than our colleagues. If we had had our preliminary "general election," the I.L.P. would have stood distinct both from the Labour Party and the new National Government, and on this we could have begun to build the Party with much better prospects than we had when the decision to disaffiliate from the Labour Party was finally taken.

It was in June, 1931, that I heard that MacDonald was entering into secret conversations with representatives of the Conservative and Liberal Parties to scuttle the Labour Government and to form a National Government. I will not even now reveal how I heard, but the source was authoritative and I published a front page article in the "New Leader" sounding the warning: this was the first public anticipation of coming events. The charge was denied by Arthur Henderson, the Foreign Secretary, but not by MacDonald and Snowden; later we learned that MacDonald and Snowden had been conferring without the knowledge of their Cabinet colleagues.

The session ended with the Government and the Labour Party completely demoralised. I forget whether the May Commission had issued its report before we dispersed for our summer holidays, but every Labour M.P. knew that the inevitable sequence to the long series of compromises which the Government had made must be a calamitous surrender to the demands of the capitalist class. A heavy cloud of despair hung over the Members as they said farewell in the lobbies.

I had arranged with Left associates in the International to address a series of meetings in Poland and Germany during the recess. Marguerite Louis accompanied me, and we were sitting in a cafe in the Unter den Linden, Berlin, when newsboys came down the street displaying their papers. I saw the heavy top line on a front page: "MacDonald Forms a National Government": . . . It had come so soon! We bought a paper and painfully made our way through the German text, piecing the story together. It was evident that the bankers had given an ultimatum to MacDonald and that he and Snowden had caved in.

I got back to London in time for the re-assembly of Parliament under the new Government. I was taken aback by the viciousness of the Labour M.P.s who had not gone over with MacDonald. Men who would have been ready to lick his boots a few weeks back, and who described the I.L.P. members as "dirty traitors" for attacking MacDonald, were incoherent with fury against their idol. What was said publicly in speeches was severe enough, but what was hissed in whispers on the benches was savage beyond description. The situation had become reversed. Those of us who had consistently attacked MacDonald were unaffected by this hysterical storm: we had long ago accustomed ourselves to the inevitable. On the other hand, the Labour M.P.s who had stood so blindly by MacDonald were shocked to their inmost beings and were indignant with us because we remained cool amidst their heated denunciations.

Thousands of words have been written and spoken in criticism of MacDonald. By thousands of rank and file Socialists he and Snowden, who had been so much admired and loved, were reviled as traitors. Were they in fact so? Snowden's conduct was a far greater disappointment to me than MacDonald's. He had been so uncompromising all through his political career: in the years before the war, during the war, and in the years immediately after the war. Often it was said that he was led away from militant Socialism by the influence of his wife. I do not know.

All of us who were ever associated with Philip know how he revered the woman who over so many years of a stormy and often unpopular political career had nourished his frail strength with unfailing loyalty, but it is difficult to believe that his wife's influence can have been the only explanation of Snowden's change of front. Added to that were perhaps the elements of comfort, position and age, and a noticeable reversion to the Liberalism from which as a young man he had been converted to Socialism. I am also convinced that he was genuinely influenced by contact with City financiers, particularly by Mr. Montagu Norman, who believed that the country was rushing towards a financial crisis. The most charitable view of Snowden's final surrender is to assume that he conscientiously believed that it was necessary for even the poorest of the poor to "tighten their belts" temporarily in order to avoid a worse calamity of financial crash and the more bitter poverty of precipitous inflation.

MacDonald's surrender was not nearly so surprising. I think it can be explained both by his character and by his political views. The truth is that MacDonald always loved social status and power: even in the days of the war it was pathetic to see how he would ignore old comrades for the sake of notice by anyone with status or a title. Indeed, this was so much an obsession with him that an analyst would have called it a "complex"; I believe it arose from the psychology of his early years—a social "inferiority" which this proud lad felt on account of his illegitimate birth, and his determination to win recognition by the highest of the land at all costs. It was still more pathetic to meet MacDonald in the years of his political black-out after the war; he literally made himself physically ill through his sense of eclipse and frustration. But as soon as recognition and popularity returned he became a whole man, vitality shining in his eyes, tireless in his energy, standing with an uprightness which showed unbounded strength. The Premiership was a great thing for him, qualified only by the criticism his policy evoked. When the criticism threatened to overwhelm him, the thought of becoming head of a National Government, a government representing the leaders of all parties, must have appealed to his pride as a dazzling prize. The son of the servant girl of Lossiemouth to prove his worth by becoming the greatest personal power in the world!

But a political explanation can also be given. MacDonald was by philosophy an evolutionary Socialist. In his work "Socialism and Society" his thesis had been that the transition from Capitalism to Socialism must be biological, by slow growth, by the gradual change of one form of life into another. He had always opposed catastrophic change; he never believed that the collapse of Capitalism would provide the opportunity for Socialism.

In 1931 the financiers convinced him that the British capitalist structure was collapsing. To him the alternatives were retreat, the surrender of conditions gained in order to stabilise the economic system before another advance—or chaos, inflation such as had brought Germany down to collapse, and then hopeless revolutionary struggle.   That was the intellectual explanation of MacDonald's destruction of the Labour Government and the formation of the National Government.   How far it was a rationalisation of the deeper instinctive impulse which I have suggested, no one can judge.

The end we had prophesied came: in the general election which followed, the Labour Party was overwhelmingly crushed. My vote at East Leyton fell only by 678, but I was defeated. J. Maxton, J. McGovern, G. Buchanan, David Kirkwood, and R. C. Wallhead were alone returned to carry on the I.L.P. Group.

Chapter Twenty-Two
THE PERSONAL SIDE OF PARLIAMENT

Sometimes I remark that I have spent three years in prison and three years in Parliament and that I saw character deteriorate in Parliament more than in prison. It is true. The conditions of Parliamentary existence are fatal to the average man unless he has compelling interests or activities.

The theory of Parliament is that there is a Government side and an Opposition side. It is the duty of the Opposition supporters to obstruct the completion of business; it is the duty of the Government supporters to facilitate it. If you are on the Opposition side, the more often you speak the better, because it holds up business; if you are on the Government side, the less part you take in debates the better, because that enables business to get through. The ideal Government supporter is the man who leaves speaking to the Front Bench, who is always on the premises so that he is available to vote, and who does so obediently according to the instructions of the Whip. The ideal Opposition supporter is the man who is skilled at making long speeches, on any subject in the world, sufficiently relevant and original to avoid the censorship of the Speaker.

The Opposition supporter has the better time. If he is politically ambitious, he has plenty of opportunity to develop the art of Parliamentary oratory and to impress his leaders and the Press Gallery. He can get his fun by sniping at some less competent Minister at question time or indulging in a rag during an all-night sitting. If he keeps within certain limits, he can engage in every kind of political warfare to harass the Government and to upset its legislation and administration, knowing that he will have the approval of his Front Bench. But for the Government supporter, unless he is a Minister or a Parliamentary secretary to a Minister, there is little to do in the House except vote. A Member may be appointed to one of the Committees which consider the less important Bills on one or two mornings a week, but there he will find the same rule applies—if he is on the Government side his duty is to vote always and to speak rarely. Ordinarily a Member must be in the House from 2.45 p.m. to 11 p.m. The first hour is devoted to questions to Ministers, and that is always interesting, but then the debates begin and, except on important occasions, they are boring. A new Member may begin by conscientiously listening to speeches, but soon he will slip away to the library, the smoke-room or the bar.

Some private members have plenty to do during these long hours. I certainly had. My mail was heavy, and it included correspondence from India and all parts of the Empire, arising from my activity on colonial issues. I visited East Leyton every Friday evening and invited my constituents to come to me about their grievances, with the result that I had numberless cases relating to unemployment insurance, pensions, rents, soldiers' allowances, etc., which required interminable correspondence with Government departments. I had journalistic work and I was engaged on a book on India. Besides, I was a member of the I.L.P. Group (which never accepted the rôle of silent support for the Government) and this meant preparation of speeches, the drafting of amendments, and daily consultations with my colleagues. And I became involved in many unofficial committees dealing with the case of Inspector Syme, with an Indian deputation from Canada, with the abolition of capital punishment, and so on. No, time certainly did not lag with me.

But there were many members who did not experience such pressure. Some of them were little known outside their constituency and their correspondence was limited. They did not have to handle constituency "cases," because these were dealt with by their agents or through powerful Trade Union organisations. They did not do journalistic work, nor have the driving interest attached to a "rebel" group. More and more of such members settled down to an existence of inertia. They descended after question time to one of the lounges and smoked, gossiped, drank, according to their tastes, or slept until the division bell rang. Then they would make their way upstairs, enquire of the Whip at the entrance to the division lobbies which was the Government side, and often enquire whilst voting what the division was about. Automatic machines would have filled the part just as efficiently.

The inevitable deterioration of their existence was hastened by the ease with which drink could be obtained. The Houses of Parliament are classed as a Royal Palace and accordingly there are no licensed hours; drink can be had all day and night. I do not wish to exaggerate the drunkenness which occurred at the House, but it was rare during my period in Parliament for one or more members not to be intoxicated after nine o'clock at night; the temper of the debates always rose after this hour and unseemly interruptions were common. One Member had the habit when he drank too much of maintaining an unceasing "hear, hear" like a small machine gun. There was one occasion when the Cabinet Minister responsible for winding up a debate on Unemployment could stand only with difficulty. By this I was utterly shocked and left the Chamber, remarking to Dr. Marion Phillips, beside whom I was sitting, that a workman would be sacked if he were found drunk at his bench.

I know it is the habit of Members of Parliament, and even of ex-Members of Parliament, to be silent on this matter. I am writing of it, not because I am unconscious of human frailty in myself, but because the drunkenness which occurs at the House of Commons is only a reflection of the futile, wasted existence which large numbers of M.P.s are encouraged to live by the procedure of Parliament. It causes many personal tragedies known to everyone who has been in the House. I have told already of Victor Grayson. There was a similar case whilst I was in the House: a young idealist I had known in the anti-war struggle, who entered Parliament eager to work for the ending of war, but who became demoralised in body and mind by drink. In his day Keir Hardie laid down the rule that no M.P. should touch drink during Parliamentary hours, and most of the Members of our Group carried out this practice.

There were other ways in which Parliament tended to blunt a keen sense of the class struggle. The House of Commons is more than a scene of political conflict; it is a club, and if one is human at all one cannot live in it for years as an "enemy" of the other side. There is a tendency for different parties to appropriate particular smoking-rooms: in my day the Labour loyalists crowded the Map Room of the Library, the Conservatives occupied the smoking-room on the ground floor, and the Liberals monopolised the Chess Room.* But even so, social contact was inevitable, and very often one saw Labour M.P.s falling to the glamour of the social life of the

* These latter rooms later became the Members' restaurant.

other side, steadily leaving their own class behind them and becoming conditioned by the amenities and atmosphere of the class which exploited the very men and women whom they had been sent to the House of Commons to represent.

Maxton seemed to me to have got nearest to the solution of this problem. He always lived his own life, he was never to be seen at social functions of the other side, yet he retained an attitude of equality and geniality with everyone. Every Member spoke to him and he spoke to every Member, usually parting from them with an anecdote which left them chuckling. Yet he never compromised himself politically, never separated himself in thought from the workers of Bridgeton, whose spokesman he was. I think the secret of Maxton's conduct was an inherent sense of human equality. He never felt that other individuals or other classes were above him, he could meet them as equals without desiring in any way either to emulate their habits or to enter their social circle. Some rigid Labour Members criticised Maxton's personal popularity with the other side. In truth it was Maxton's strength that he could be friendly to all without being subservient to any. It was an inferiority complex, together with a hankering after the flesh-pots of life, which undermined the fighting quality of certain Labour M.P.s. To them parliamentary life and its associations became a vested interest.

When I attended meetings of the Parliamentary Labour Party, I often asked myself why it was that this great body of men, most of whom, at one time or another, had been leading figures in their localities in the struggle of the working-class, were so docile and servile in the acceptance of the policy imposed on them by the Government. I decided that they could be divided roughly into four sections. Fifty of them had posts of one kind or another associated with the Government: their loyalty could be counted on. Fifty more wanted posts: they were even more loyal than the loyalists. A third fifty, largely composed of elderly Trade Union officials, rewarded for long service by safe seats in Parliament, had no understanding of Socialism and little knowledge of politics; they, like those four men I met on the opening day of Parliament, were content with their existence and shrank from any policy which was likely to upset it. A fourth fifty were politically minded, keen, self-reliant, rooted in socialist principles, and eager, despite all the deadweight of the Parliamentary institution and of the mentality of the Government and of their colleagues, to get things done. They did not all vote with the I.L.P.—many of them often thought the I.L.P. was pursuing wrong tactics and were even deterred from criticism of the Government because they did not wish to be identified with us. But, defying the influence against them, they remained Socialists, sincerely desirous without thought of self to serve the cause. Many of these remain in the Labour Party and are men of real worth.

I think the occasions when I felt Parliamentary procedure to be most futile were when we had to stay up night after night voting the separate items of the estimates. In the early hours of one morning I found the frail figure of Sir Norman Angell beside me in the division lobby; his expression, never robust, was weary and drawn. How stupid, I thought, requiring a man of his weak physique but brilliant mind to spend the night tramping the division lobbies so that the revenue of the country should be assured! I thought back to an early speech which I had heard Angell deliver in the House: I did not agree with it, but he gave an illuminating analysis of the economic situation in Europe and made important constructive proposals. Angell had not the Parliamentary manner: he spoke too much like a professor. The consequence was that he had a small House and his speech went unnoticed by the Government, the Press and the public. I never heard Angell speak again: he contented himself with doing literary work in the library. What a misuse of valuable talent!

F. W. Jowett, away back in the days of Blatchford's "Clarion," first exposed the stupidities of Parliamentary practice. His alternative was to divide up the whole membership into committees, which should have the duty of handling the legislation and administration of the various Departments of State. I think Parliament will require a bigger revolution than that before it is competent to deal with the affairs of the people in the interests of the people, but Jowett's scheme would at least have prevented the waste of capacity which now occurs. It would give every Member a job and an opportunity to prove his worth.

The best side of Parliamentary life was the friendships it developed. One such was my own friendship with Charles Trevelyan, Minister of Education. Every Thursday I used to have a meal with him in his delightful house in Great College Street, within a stone's throw of Parliament, so near that Charles had a division bell in his hall: on many occasions we scrambled across, via subterranean passages under the House of Lords, and voted in divisions on the summons of the bell. Trevelyan was very conscientious about not passing on Cabinet secrets to me, but he sympathised with the I.L.P. desire for a more courageous policy, and we co-operated a good deal within the limits of our respective positions. Another friend I made was Oliver Baldwin, son of the Conservative Leader. Oliver had a great respect for his father, despite the difference of political views, and one often saw them chatting together in the smoking rooms. Oliver was a curious mixture in character: half mystic, half man of the world. He soon became disillusioned with Parliament, and one met him wandering the passages with eyes on distant things or found him sitting on the edge of the most distant bench of the House, as though to emphasise his apartness. Then he would give way to the mood of devil-may-care. He would turn to young Conservative friends in the House and forget the serious side of life, until some issue pulled him up sharply. He generally voted with the I.L.P. Group but spoke little, though on one occasion he delivered a startlingly frank speech against war preparations, illustrating it with graphic stories of his own experiences in the Services.

We had one woman member, Jennie Lee. I liked her, admired her speeches, and generally regarded her political judgment as sound. Her speeches in the House combined natural persuasiveness and human passion in just the correct degree. Jennie is in my opinion far and away the ablest woman who has been in the House of Commons.

Chapter Twenty-Three
VISITS TO AMERICA

I visited America three times, twice while I was still a Member of Parliament and once in the following year. I went on lecture tours. Bertrand Russell warned me that I must not attempt to deliver serious lectures: my audiences would desire only personal stuff and amusing anecdotes. My actual experience was the exact opposite. I found that the American people to whom I spoke wanted facts, analysis and political philosophy.

I travelled to America the first time on a boat which included Alistair MacDonald among its passengers. I had already met him several times and liked him, though I knew his brother Malcolm, now High Commissioner in Canada, better. Malcolm was a serious socialist student: Alistair a gay Bohemian with, nevertheless, fundamentally a sound socialist outlook. For several years Malcolm had been a speaker on I.L.P. platforms, quiet and thorough, though never brilliant. It was Alistair who had his father's magnetic personality and his flair for occupying the centre of the stage.

As the Prime Minister's son, Alistair was given a marvellous State cabin by the Cunard Line. I was travelling Tourist, but as Alistair's friend, I was allowed the run of the First Class and, indeed, of the boat; a young man and woman in the tourist class joined us, and we became an inseparable four. Alistair became a kind of Pirate Prime Minister, with the three of us as his secretariat. He planned the maddest adventures and raids and was permitted a freedom in doing so which would have been denied to anyone else. One night I became tired of a round of excitement, and retired to my cabin at three a.m. Alistair and his two colleagues arrived and solemnly presented me with "an illuminated and perforated address." Having delivered a pleasant little speech, Alistair proceeded to unravel a toilet roll and festoon my cabin with it, from floor to ceiling and bunk to port-hole, until nothing was visible except the criss-cross of endless paper. I was too sleepy to remove the mad chaos about me. When the cabin boy called me in the morning, he was not sure whether he was still drunk or had merely been so last night.

America was passing through three distinct phases on each of my visits. In 1929 the States were still enjoying a trade boom. On the hoardings were large posters with the slogan: "Forward America—the Land of Prosperity!" On my second visit, two years later, America was moving down to depression. The confident posters were replaced by pathetic pictures of the destitute, accompanied by moving appeals for contributions. The third time, in 1933, America was concentrated upon a tremendous campaign for recovery. The posters of destitution were replaced by designs of a Blue Eagle, the symbol of the "New Deal," above the slogan: "We Do Our Part." On each occasion I discussed the position with members of the Government.

I was fortunate on my first visit to Washington to meet Dorothy Detzer, and she appeared to be able to unlock the doors of all the Government Departments. Someone in England had given me an introduction to Dorothy as the Secretary of the Women's International League; I expected to find a well-meaning, bourgeois pacifist of the Geneva type. In fact, I found one of the most vital personalities I have met, the cleverest "lobbyist" in Washington, intimately informed about all America's political affairs and remarkably well-informed about world affairs, a Socialist and anti-Imperialist. One of the biggest things she pulled off was the public enquiry into the Arms Traffic, which exposed not only the American armament concerns but almost equally the British; she prepared for this Commission for months and beat the lobbyists representing the arms interests to a frazzle. It was through Dorothy's influence that I saw the leading political figures.

The American Congress has the curious custom of admitting members of other Parliaments to the floor of its debating Chamber while discussions are in process. I was met the first time by members of the "rebel" group, led by Bob la Follette, and taken on to the floor. The atmosphere and arrangements were very different from the House of Commons: the Chamber was like a British Town Hall, with the representatives sitting at desks arranged in horse-shoe form, the public looking down at them from a curved gallery. The discussion proceeded between one standing member and another in conversational style. I was conducted past them to the Chairman and introduced: the

Chairman signalled to a deputy to take his place and we adjourned to his private room where two members of the Government joined us. It was all delightfully informal and chummy: I cannot imagine the Speaker of the House of Commons and two members of the British Cabinet receiving a private member of the American Congress in such a way.

Sometimes in America I found a tendency to look up to Britain and British institutions. There was not the least trace of this in the attitude of these Ministers. Indeed, they were inclined to be a little condescending about the situation in Europe and in contrast to have a very full confidence about the situation in America. The economic depression which had overcome Europe and Britain was in their view an indication of obsolete business methods and industrial decadence. There was no fear of America suffering similarly: America was young, vigorous and modern. When I suggested that fundamental faults in an economic system common to Europe and America had caused the crisis, and that America would not escape it, they pooh-poohed the idea. America's system of high wages would prevent a gulf between production and consumption. There was no need to drop the American belief in "rugged individualism" and adopt Socialism.

On my second visit I met two members of the Cabinet at a small tea party given to me at the home of one of America's leading financiers. One of Lady Astor's sisters was present: there are three sisters famous for their beauty (including, of course, Lady Astor), and certainly this lady was both lovely and gracious. I felt a little ill at ease in such company, but soon we were discussing social problems with complete freedom. Although America was now plunging into depression, these Government representatives were still cocksure. Europe was responsible, they argued, and America had been dragged down because she had been too closely associated with Europe! America was self-sufficient: except for rubber (and her chemists would soon produce that synthetically) and tea (and American women could be weaned from the bad habits of their English sisters), the United States could provide every need of her population. Very well: that meant that she could save herself economically behind her tariff walls, whatever happened in

Europe. The depression was temporary, superficial, almost accidental. Nothing was radically wrong.

On my third visit, the political atmosphere was completely changed. The financial collapse had shaken politicians and people alike out of their confidence in "rugged individualism." Few of us in Britain realised the extent of the crash. One morning United States citizens awoke to find that between eighteen and nineteen thousand banks had closed: six thousand of them never opened their doors again and the savings of thousands of people were lost. Unemployment leaped to the figure of fifteen millions. How rude must have been the shock to those Cabinet Ministers at Washington who would not listen to any suggestion that America might suffer as Europe had done!

But, once the crisis came, American politicians faced it with a resolution which put to shame the European reaction to the same situation. In a book, "Will Roosevelt Succeed?", I have analysed in some detail the Recovery Plan which was launched from Washington. The Plan did not deal with the fundamental causes of capitalist crisis and in many respects was grotesque, as, for example, its wholesale destruction of crops, fruit, cattle, and cotton, while millions of American people went hungry and ill-clad; but at least it was carried through with a boldness which was refreshing after my experience of the incompetent futility of the Labour Government in Britain and of the cowardly economy of the National Government's programme which followed it.

I was in Washington at the height of enthusiasm for the Recovery Plan. I spent a week seeing the heads of the various departments of the New Deal and I was amazed by the spirit in which they were undertaking their task. They believed they were engaged in a revolution and were glorying in the fact. I met men who two years previously had been regarded as dangerous "Reds" working enthusiastically for the Government. I had the impression that the New Deal was being run by men and women who had voted in the Presidential election, not for Franklin Roosevelt, the Democrat, but for Norman Thomas, the Socialist, and Foster the Communist.

In one office I found a social student whom I had met four years before at an I.L.P. Summer School: he was then enthusiastic about the constructive planning which he had investigated in Soviet Russia. "This is the same," he said, as I reminded him of that conversation. "*We* are planning, too." In another office I met a man who had been introduced to me on my last visit to America as the most hard-boiled cynic among Washington newspapermen. Now the light of enthusiasm was in his eyes. "We're on a mighty big thing," he exclaimed. "We're rebuilding a continent." In a third office I recognised a young man whom I first met at the London School of Economics and who had told me in New York a year before that he intended to join the Communist Party. "This is better than agitating for the revolution," he now declared. "I'm working in the revolution." Later I met Harold Ickes, one of President Roosevelt's right hand men in the Cabinet. I found him less dogmatic about the ultimate success of the Recovery Plan than his lieutenants, but he had no doubts about the clean break with past American psychology which the New Deal represented. This interview is worth describing, not only for what Secretary Ickes said, but for the characteristically American circumstances under which he said it.

Shortly before leaving for America I had been on a deputation to the British Foreign Office with James Maxton and Dr. C. A. Smith to urge that British influence should be used to modify, if possible, the manner in which the newly-triumphant Hitler was persecuting our Socialist comrades. We were received on the Foreign Office steps by two uniformed officials. On the first floor we were met by more uniformed officials, who showed us to a large and impressive waiting room. Another uniformed official conducted us to Sir John Simon's room, where we were received by the Foreign Secretary, immaculately dressed, Sir Robert Vansittart, a lofty, distant, figure, and the Foreign Secretary's Private Parliamentary Secretary, silent and cold. Such is the official and frigid atmosphere of a British State Department.

An American State Department might belong to a different period of history. As one passes through the swing-doors the lobby is like a public place: the moving crowd might be drawn from the street. There is a stall on one side, at which refreshments and newspapers are sold. The lift is thronged with a cross-section of the population—civil servants, out-of-work clerks applying for jobs, a Negro workman with tools obtruding from his baggy blue trousers, women cleaners. On asking a Negro porter for the Assistant Secretary to the Department, I was directed to a door labelled with his name and told to knock: anyone might do the same. Inside, there were no clerks or stenographers to pass. The Assistant Secretary sat at his table, divided from the public outside only by the name-bearing and inviting door. He took me to the room of Secretary Ickes. "We call this Child's Restaurant," he said as he showed me in. The Child's restaurants are the Lyons of America: the popular eating places where one sits not only for a meal, but for a smoke and a chat over a cup of coffeee.

Secretary Ickes was sitting at a table at the end of a long dark room. Near him sat three men—a self-opinionated Congressman, showing off before his companions, a countrified-looking farmer, and a spruce young man who looked like a lawyer. Secretary Ickes was without coat or waistcoat, in a blue shirt with a broad belt round his waist. He looked like a Western Sheriff on the Movies. He puffed at a cigarette, sitting back and watching his visitors: one got the impression that he was sizing them up as much as listening. He is a middle-aged man, hair thinning, clean shaven, heavy-jawed with a pugilist thrust.

I took a seat at the other end of the room, among twenty or so people waiting their turn. They were lounging in chairs, smoking and chatting. I understood the description: Child's Restaurant—we lacked only the cups of coffee. Above the conversation loomed the voice of the Congressman at the Minister's table. One could overhear his words: it is Secretary Icke's idea to have his interviews in semi-public, so that it may be clear that he treats everyone with equality and above-board. At last a neatly uniformed Negro porter—his green suit looked well against his dark features—signed to me that my turn had come. I walked the long room and took a seat at the side of the table where the Minister was seated. He welcomed me cordially, but without the exaggerated heartiness which one so often finds in America.

I took up at once the point which differentiated American and British policy in handling the depression. The Labour Government had been sabotaged by British financial circles because it was spending too much; the National Government was practising "economy" at the expense even of the unemployed in order to reduce expenditure; yet here was the American Government facing the depression by expending millions! I put to Secretary Ickes the argument used by British capitalist politicians: expenditure on State work reduces the capital which would be used otherwise in private industry and does not therefore add to the total volume of employment. Secretary Ickes was diplomatic enough not to comment on the British experience, but he insisted that, so far as America was concerned, private industry as well as public welfare benefited by the Public Works schemes. If private capital were doing the job, something might be said for applying the British principle; but private capital was not doing it. I was thunderstruck as I heard this complete repudiation of the confidence in individualism which had been impressed on me by Cabinet Ministers on my earlier visits. Whatever the limitations of the New Deal, it evidently meant a revolution in the whole approach of American statesmen to the economic problem.

The best thing about the New Deal was the stimulus which it gave to Trade Union organisation and action. I took part in strikes of textile workers in Paterson, New Jersey, and of engineers in Detroit. At Paterson all the thirty thousand silk workers were on strike against the New Deal code which, whilst reducing working hours, also reduced wages by nine dollars a week. I spoke to a vast meeting of 2,000 workers, mostly of Italian origin, and afterwards had tea with a striker in his home. He told me that three months previously the silk workers of Paterson were practically unorganised; now eighty per cent belonged either to the A.F. of L. or the Communist Union. At Detroit I found an ex-Scottish I.L.P.'er leading the strike. He took me to a huge theatre demonstration, but was a little fearful of prejudicing the strike by a speech from a non-American and particularly from a socialist non-American, but he agreed that I should say a few words of greeting. To his surprise I received a tremendous welcome, and when I ended within five minutes the men cheered continuously until the chairman called on me to speak again. This is one of the few occasions when I have been encored for a speech and showed how the class solidarity engendered by a strike leaps over all prejudices whether national or political.

I met Norman Thomas, the Socialist Party leader, on many occasions. He was originally a minister of religion and still has the appearance of one. He is tall, silver-haired, clean-shaven, large featured with a domed forehead: a distinguished scholarly figure. My criticism of him personally would be that he always speaks as though he is addressing a public meeting, but he has some excuse for that habit because he usually is! He is respected throughout America by members of all parties: again and again one heard the phrase during the presidential election, "Thomas is the best of the three, but he stands no chance, so I am voting Roosevelt." On the alternative voting system I believe Thomas would have received twenty per cent of the Roosevelt vote as a first preference. He has an open and continually developing mind. On my first visit to America he was a typical Social Democrat of the Centre, except that he was uncompromisingly against war from the pacifist point of view. By my third visit he had moved far to the Left, and in recent years he has shown courage in defending Revolutionary Socialists (for example, the POUM in Spain) against both social democratic and communist attacks.

The most politically-educated Socialists I met belonged to the Communist Opposition. Their leader was Jay Lovestone; he was once America's Communist leader and a popular figure in Moscow, but at one stage he opposed the Moscow line and, although he had the majority of the American Party behind him, he was deposed. The headquarters of his organisation were in a long, low room at the top of a narrow stairway in Fourteenth Street, New York. The whole of one side was covered by some remarkable mural paintings by Diego Riviera. illustrating the working-class struggle; on my first visit the famous artist was at work on the final picture depicting the 1914-18 war. In a scene representing the Treaty of Versailles he had still to paint one head, and paused to ask me whether he should portray Montagu Norman or Lloyd George. With some hesitation I said Lloyd George, and Riviera at once began to sketch the familiar features.

My lecture engagements were very varied. At towns scattered all over America I was one of a series of lecturers at open forums held in large halls and well-attended by a cross-section of the local Socialists, Liberals and Radicals. I visited most of the important universities and was impressed by the keenness of the students, particularly at the women's colleges. I addressed a number of Rotary Clubs and Luncheon Forums (these were thrown in by the organisers of the tour to make up fees), and I spoke frequently over the radio. Perhaps my most impressive gatherings were three-cornered debates on the subject of Palestine before the New York Foreign Policy Association and on Capitalism, Socialism and Communism before a crowd of several thousands which thronged the Mecca Temple.

The Mecca Temple debate was run by a speculative show-man who paid good fees and threw vast publicity into it to make big profits. The defender of Capitalism was Dr. Seligman, a professor at Columbia University, famous for books on economics defending American individualism. The communist spokesman was Scott Nearing, an able, sacrificing and respected devotee, but his Party put him into a difficult position by expelling him three days before the debate. We had three rounds of speaking: the professor was knocked out in the first. Then Nearing and I concentrated on each other, the audience excitedly cheering our points. Few debates are satisfactory, but this was a real combat of convictions and was a success. The New York Press carried descriptive reports which were as dramatic as football write-ups. One celebrated writer was both candid and kind about me. My suit he described as having been bought at Horne Bros. three years ago and as having never been pressed since (he was about right). He described my neck as stretching out of a collar three sizes too large, like the extended neck of a hen through the bars of a chicken-coop. Nevertheless, he said I was a gentleman; my voice told him that—Jesus College, Cambridge, he guessed—and behind my English pince-nez shone the eyes of Savonarola!

The debate on Palestine at the Foreign Policy Association, the most authoritative society discussing international affairs in America, was a surprise to me. I arrived in America to find it announced three days ahead. "But I know nothing about Palestine," I protested to Mary Fox, the secretary of the League for Industrial Democracy, which had arranged my tour. "Oh, you do!" she exclaimed. "Our papers have often carried reports of your questions in the House of Commons." My questions had been efforts to save both Arabs and Jews from execution: I realised that hanging, whether on one side or the other, would only make any solution more difficult, but what the solution was I had no idea! I spent the three intervening days studying the subject, and when the moment came faced the large audience with every appearance of confidence.

The chairman was Mr. J. G. McDonald, afterwards head of the international committee at Geneva handling the refugee problem arising from Hitler's racial and political persecution. My line was that Palestine must become an Arab-Jewish State freed from British Imperialism, and the Foreign Policy Association afterwards published the speech among its series of "expert" pronouncements! I could not help feeling a little ashamed of this performance and I am not sure that I should have gone through with it had I foreseen the sequel. The debate was broadcast throughout America by a network of radios, with the result that I received invitations to repeat it from a dozen different cities. Fortunately, my schedule was too full to allow these requests to be fulfilled.

I travelled long distances in America, including one journey on which I left Chicago in icy winter to reach Galveston in Texas to find everyone sun-bathing on the beach. But no journey was comparable to my flight by 'plane from Chicago over the Rockies to Seattle, on the Western coast, and back. The 'plane rose at night with Chicago a million lights. For hours we flew over a dark earth and in my comfortable reclining chair I fell asleep. When I awoke it was dawn and we were flying through a valley in the Rockies, with rugged mountains on either side. Then we rose into clouds, an eerie grey world; streaks of sunshine began to break them—and then suddenly, we were in a world of utter enchantment, the purest beauty I have ever seen. Above, nothing but eternal blue: below, nothing but eternal white. The blue had no form or shape or varying shade; its depth was infinite and it went on to the horizon where it met the white. The white was of every rounded form and shape, curved and curled in rolling waves, and there, there and there, five times, coned peaks rose, mountain tops covered with snow. These two colours—blue and white—there were no others in the universe, and they went on forever. I have never had, before or since, such a sense of ecstasy in beauty. I felt at that moment that I should not mind if we crashed.

My return journey to England across the Atlantic was enlivened by the presence in the tourist class of a troupe of Paramount dancing girls, who were planning to give shows in Paris, Berlin, Vienna and London. Among them I was surprised to find university students whose careers at College had been interrupted by the depression; two of the girls, as I learned subsequently when I met them in Paris, actually took courses at the Sorbonne by day whilst they danced at night. One experience on this journey gave me the idea for the only novel I have written. The girls were asked to stage a show in the first class: tourist and third passengers were invited on condition that they wore evening dress. At the suggestion of a few of us who wanted to see the show, the girls told the captain that they would not dance if the dress qualification were maintained. The captain gave way, and that night the tourist and third class invaded the first class quarters *en masse*.

I had always felt that a liner mirrored class divisions exactly. I made friends with sailors and stewards and learned of their intolerable conditions; they even smuggled me down to see their crowded quarters. Then the idea grew of a social revolution on a boat and the dancing girls gave it the popular touch. The idea was good; but I knew without my friends telling me that the novel which grew out of it was bad!

BOOK FOUR

Chapter Twenty-Four
LEAVING THE LABOUR PARTY

I was elected chairman of the I.L.P. at Easter, 1931, and remained chairman until the end of 1933. During this period the I.L.P. disaffiliated from the Labour Party and began its inner struggle towards a revolutionary socialist position. In the course of this inner struggle the I.L.P. experimented in many directions, at one time approaching the Communist International and at another moving towards the Trotskyist position, at one stage attaching its hope to united fronts and at another reverting to purism, at one period going all out to prepare for Soviets and at another recognising again the value of Parliament. This striving of the I.L.P. towards a true revolutionary position, during years of world events which have compelled a reconsideration of fundamentals, is a chapter of working class history of importance to all interested in the development of Socialism.

The establishment of a revolutionary socialist party can be attempted in one of two ways. A few theoreticians can lay down a watertight programme and invite those who agree with it to join: this is the method of the Trotskyists, and the Fourth International has remained in a vacuum. Or a party which already has its roots in the working-class movement can evolve, *grow,* to the revolutionary position by thought applied to experience, by learning its lessons from mistakes, by discussion, by the study of the history of the movement in other countries, and by a sincere and constant effort to find the right way. This second has been the method of the I.L.P. Since 1932 the Party has been a crucible of the change from reformism to revolutionism. Into that crucible every idea, every tactic, has been thrown and has worked itself out; it has been a microcosm of all the conflicts of theory and practice which have stirred so deeply the world movement.

To those of us who have been in the centre of this ferment the effect has been exciting, vitalising, and enlarging. If I can reproduce it faithfully, it will be of value far beyond the one party to which it relates.

We did not hurry the decision to disaffiliate from the Labour Party. Even during the life of the Labour Government discussions of the relationship of the two parties had begun. After a joint meeting between representatives it was mutually agreed that "the matters in dispute appeared to be capable of amicable discussion," and Arthur Henderson and James Maxton were appointed to "formulate a basis of agreement." But no formula emerged. I have the impression that Maxton deliberately permitted things to take their course.

At the general election of the autumn of 1931 the nineteen candidates of the I.L.P. were refused endorsement by the Labour Party Executive: this was, in effect, an act of expulsion. Our crime was a refusal to sign a pledge, presented to candidates for the first time, that we would obey the Standing Orders of the Parliamentary Labour Party which required among other things that Members would not vote against its decisions. Immediately after the election I went down to George Lansbury's Bow home to discuss the matter with him. He was the chairman of the Labour Party. I was disappointed. Lansbury was kind, as always, but he put the view that the departure of MacDonald and Snowden from the Labour Party did not alter the situation. There was no place for a Party within a Party. The I.L.P. must either be wholly in the Labour Party, subordinating its own policy to vote according to majority decisions, or it must stay outside. He rejected altogether the federal conception of the Labour Party which the I.L.P. urged and which, indeed, had been the earlier basis of the Party; there could be no room for group freedom within it. This interview was not encouraging, but I followed it up by a talk with Arthur Henderson, the Labour Party secretary, at Geneva. I had been attending an international conference at Berne and went on to see Henderson, who, despite the National Government, was still acting as the chairman of the World Disarmament Conference. I was surprised by Henderson's attitude. I knew what a stickler he was for recognition of the Labour Party Constitution and had expected a discussion about the letter of the Standing Orders. Instead, he argued much more fundamentally. Organisational difficulties could be overcome if there were agreement about political method; but was there? He challengingly raised the issue as to whether we had any real faith in Parliament. He had gathered that we believed that ultimately the transition from Capitalism to Socialism would be made not through Parliament but by a direct struggle for power between the working-class and the possessing class. Did this mean that we stood for Socialism by revolution? As a matter of fact, Henderson was pressing the I.L.P. further towards its logical end than it was prepared to go at this moment, but he was quite unsatisfied by my reply that the I.L.P. would use Parliament so long and as fully as it could be used.

I reported both these conversations to the I.L.P. National Council, to find it acutely divided. James Maxton, F. W. Jowett, and Campbell Stephen were for disaffiliation and, after a time, John Paton joined them. Frank Wise, Pat Dollan and David Kirkwood were against—and they were a difficult "Opposition." Kirkwood used to irritate some of my colleagues by the length, irrelevance, egotism and emotion of his speeches, but I could never become angry with Davie: he was sincere and simple. Dollan was by no means simple. I once told him that he was the most honest comrade on earth in his social relations and the most dishonest in politics. That shocked him, and it may have been cleverness rather than dishonesty which led him to adopt every debating trick, hiding his real purpose behind an air of reasonable innocence, twisting the argument of the other side with an impudence which took away one's breath. It was Frank Wise, however, who troubled me most, despite my admiration for his knowledge and long-view constructive mind. He lectured us at length from Olympian heights, showing his contempt for the contributions of less educated and more emotionally elementary colleagues and forgetting that the working-class experience of comrades around him might be as valuable as his civil service experience and his mastery of economic facts.

The National Council of the Party was so divided that it made no recommendations to the Annual Conference whicn met at Blackpool over the Easter week-end, 1932. The decision was left to the delegates without any lead. Personally, I was not greatly excited over the disaffiliation issue. I placed first emphasis on the development of a revolutionary policy and regarded the issue of the Standing Orders as important only in so far as they prevented the expression of such a policy. If I could have got reasonable liberty within the Labour Party I would have stayed inside.

There has been only incidental indication in this book so far of my developing revolutionary views. It was the growing Nazi challenge to democratic institutions in Germany, and the retreat of the powerful Social Democratic and Communist Parties before it, which compelled reconsideration. During 1931 I had been in Germany and I was profoundly impressed by what I saw and heard. I realised that the Parliamentary Revolutionism of Clifford Allen was not enough, because in a decisive crisis Reaction would suppress Parliament. I began to see that in the last resort the workers would have to depend on their strength in a direct struggle with the capitalist class.

I expressed this view in the chairman's speech to the Blackpool Conference. No one would say that it was a clear outline of the policy to which the Party has since advanced, but it reflected a turning-point in I.L.P. thought. I urged that it was not only the gradualism of the Labour Party which was inadequate but the *method* of the "Socialism in Our Time" programme. "In a sentence, our policy must become revolutionary instead of reformist." Socialists were living in a fool's paradise if they thought that a majority in Parliament was enough. Socialist legislation would meet with resistance from the "aristocratic, plutocratic, financial and capitalist classes generally." The duty of the I.L.P. was to prepare the workers for the struggle for power and for maintenance of that power during the introduction of Socialism. This fundamental conception of policy was the important thing. Compared with it the issue of disaffiliation was a small matter of strategy.

The conference had to decide between affiliation, disaffiliation and continued negotiations. The case for immediate disaffiliation was led by Dr. C. K. Cullen, a young East London Medical Officer of Health, and Jack Gaster, a young Jewish solicitor, son of the famous Rabbi: they had formed a Revolutionary Policy Committee within the Party to advocate disaffiliation at all costs, supplemented by association with the Communist International. Support on different grounds was given by such influential figures as Maxton, Paton, McGovern and Buchanan. (Wise and Dollan were their leading opponents), but the discussion indicated that a majority of the delegates wished to remain in the Labour Party if liberty to express I.L.P. policy could be secured, and the vote went in favour of resuming negotiations.

As chairman of the Party I was mainly responsible for the negotiations with the Labour Party which followed. I did my utmost to meet the Labour Party view so long as the necessary minimum of freedom could be obtained. A deputation consisting of F. W. Jowett, James Maxton, R. C. Wallhead, Campbell Stephen and P. J. Dollan met Labour Party representatives with myself as spokesman. I recognised that constitutionally only the Parliamentary Labour Party could amend its Standing Orders, and proposed a procedure which would not infringe this: a preliminary discussion between four representatives of the two Parties and, if agreement were reached, a recommendation from the Executive of the Labour Party to the Parliamentary Party, which should retain unimpaired its power to decide. The I.L.P. had tabled amendments as a basis for discussion. They were drafted in a spirit of reasonableness and it was made clear that we would consider alternative suggestions. The main points of difference between our proposals and the Standing Orders were that we demanded (I) the policy of a Labour Government should be controlled by the Party, and (II) a member should not be *prohibited* from voting contrary to Party decisions, though, if he did so, he would be liable to be reported to his Constituency Party and to his nominating organisation. The Labour Party was adamant, however. It demanded the acceptance of the present Standing Orders before any consideration could be given to the I.L.P. amendments. Looking back on this dispute I can come to no conclusion other than that it was the obstinacy of the Labour Party Executive which closed the door to agreement. If there had been a real desire for a settlement it could have been reached. As it was, there was no alternative for the majority of the National Council of the I.L.P. but to recommend disaffiliation.

A special conference was summoned for Bradford during the last week-end in July. We met appropriately in the Jowett Hall, the splendid headquarters of the Bradford branch, named affectionately and proudly after its veteran leader. It was a tense conference from beginning to end. The hall was crowded, the floor with delegates, the gallery with visitors, many of them from other countries. The debate was worthy of a great occasion. I had to come down heavily once on Pat Dollan and to suppress Davie Kirkwood when he strode forward from the back of the hall, shouting and gesticulating melo-dramatically, but apart from these incidents the case was argued out reasonably and with a quiet sincerity in speeches directed alternatively for and against disaffiliation. There was one noteworthy contrast with the discussion at the Blackpool Conference four months earlier: the greater part of the debate turned on fundamental issues of policy rather than on the Standing Orders. The motion for disaffiliation was carried by 241 votes to 142, showing a considerable majority but neverthe-less indicating a serious split in the Party. I announced the figures confidently but without bragging. I knew that the high hopes which had found expression in some of the speeches, prophesying that the I.L.P. would sweep the workers behind it, would not be realised until a long and hard road had been travelled.

When the conference turned to consider the organisational consequences of disaffiliation, it made a mistake which seriously crippled the work of the Party for many years. Behind the point at issue was a principle which was fundamental. Was the I.L.P. to go all out as a rival of the Labour Party, seeking to destroy it as the Labour Party had destroyed the Liberal Party; or was it to serve as an advance guard, independent of the main force because the Labour Party prohibited freedom of move-ment, but understanding nevertheless that victory could not be won until the heavy machine lumbering behind was stirred to speed by leadership and example? The logic of the situation demanded the former, because an advance guard must be a section of the army and we had deliberately severed ourselves from it; but there were long-sighted comrades in our ranks who held that logic must give way to reality and who foresaw futile isolation if all organisational contact were destroyed.

The decision between these opposing principles was made on the question of whether members of the I.L.P. should continue to pay the political levy in their Trades Unions and remain individual members of the Labour Party. When the matter was discussed by the National Council, John Paton and R. C. Wallhead had strongly urged that members should stay in the Labour Party as long as they were allowed to and that they should maintain their Trade Union political levies in order to retain their right to participate in political activities. Others insisted that the logic of disaffiliation must be accepted: Party members must sever all connection with the Labour Party. Finally, there was a compromise decision: instead of "must" the word "should" was adopted. When we faced the conference, however, the delegates would not listen to compromise. Led by the members of the Revolutionary Policy Committee, the majority shouted in unison *"must"* as each of a long list of clauses allowing permissive action was reached. The platform gave way, but many minds were uneasy. Dick Wallhead, who subsequently reverted to the Labour Party, voiced this view courageously by saying that he regarded the decision of the conference as a "regrettable necessity," and that he hoped we should proceed in a temper which would allow the breach to be healed. The conference, however, was not in this mood: it was all out to replace the Labour Party by the I.L.P.

The decision to refrain from paying the Trade Union political levy proved particularly disastrous. It meant that the influence of Party members in the industrial movement—our main contact with the organised working-class now that we were no longer affiliated to the Labour Party—was seriously impaired: they were frequently not permitted to take part in any political discussion in a Trade Union branch, they were removed from official positions which they held, and they had to resign their delegations to Trades and Labour Councils. At the Annual Conference of 1934 the decision was reversed, but by then much damage had been done. The mistake of 1932 was recognised even by the R.P.C. Its reversal was seconded by Dr. C. K. Cullen.

Another controversy which loomed large in the Party in the post-disaffiliation years was initiated at this Bradford conference: the place of Parliamentary activity in the revolutionary movement. The R.P.C. tried to get an amendment accepted reorganising the Party on an industrial basis. This was rejected, but the issue persisted. To the succeeding Annual

Conference the National Council submitted a report on this subject which went very far in modifying the traditional Parliamentary view of the Party. It laid down that the power to overthrow Capitalism will depend finally on the industrial and class organisations of the workers and that the belief must be discarded that Socialism can be achieved simply through Parliament, "the instrument of the Capitalist State." Nevertheless, Parliament should be used while the instrument of working-class government is being developed: it can serve for propaganda and occasionally for wringing concessions. This far-reaching report was moved by one of the most skilled of Parliamentarians, James Maxton.

The R.P.C. pressed strongly that the Party should go all out to form British counterparts of Russian Soviets, namely Workers' Councils, in preparation for the revolution. They wanted the Party membership to get busy at once in forming workshop committees and street committees, which (with the local Trade Union, Co-operative and political organisations) should form the new instruments of socialist struggle and the prospective instruments of workers' power. The idea that such Workers' Councils could either be formed or function in normal periods was scouted by our practical Trade Union members, particularly in Lancashire, who recognised the existing Trades Councils as the authentic representation of the working-class in the localities. Despite this, the R.P.C., led by Jack Gaster, who had been elected London representative on the National Council, succeeded in getting their view to a considerable extent accepted temporarily by the Party.

I accept my share of responsibility for the adoption of these impractical schemes. This swing to "ultra-leftism," as a consequence of the failure of Labour Party Parliamentarianism, stands as a permanent warning against theoretical elaboration of revolutionary structure unrelated to the actual conditions of the class struggle.

Before ending this chapter I must include a relevant contribution from Mr. Bernard Shaw. I sent him a copy of the new I.L.P. Constitution for his comment. He dismissed it contemptuously and re-wrote it entirely. He marked his communication "private," but I now have his permission to publish it with the explanation that he was not so much expressing his own views as endeavouring to help us to express ours. This was the document I received:

Dear Fenner,—I wish you would send your manifestoes to the Orthological Institute in Frith Street and have them translated into Basic English. The horrible jargon that resulted from the early attempts to translate Marx into the inhuman English of the nineteenth-century-political essayists still haunts Socialist literature, though it is dead everywhere else.

I have read the statement of policy, which has left me without the faintest notion of what that policy is. All I know is that you feel bound to use the old Marxian catchword "revolutionary" as often as possible. When you have frightened off enough people with it, you will have to explain that it means just nothing. I should have said something like this:

The I.L.P. was founded to establish a Labour Party in the House of Commons, and to bring about Socialism by parliamentary procedure.

It succeeded completely in the first part of its programme. It established the Party at Westminster in sufficient strength to enable it to form two Governments, with its most prominent members as Prime Minister and Chancellor of the Exchequer.

The unforeseen result of this success was to prove that the introduction of Socialism by the existing parliamentary procedure is impossible, and that the attempt disables and wastes its leaders. The climax was reached when the Socialist Prime Minister became leader of the Conservatives.

The Labour Party then divided into those who were capable of learning from experience, and those who persisted in the futile work of sending more Labour members to Parliament to be wasted and corrupted in the same manner. The I.L.P. represents the first section.

Meanwhile there had come into being the so-called Communist Party. There is no difference in principle between Socialism and Communism; in fact a Socialist who is not a Communist is not a Socialist; the only possible difference is one of tactics.

The Communist Party made the grave tactical mistake of affirming the international character of the Socialist principle by accepting money from a foreign Government and placing itself under its direction. The I.L.P. could not and cannot associate itself with a body capable of such suicidal stupidity. It has every sympathy with the Government in question, and can be depended upon to support it uncompromisingly in every permissible manner; but its sympathy and support cannot be purchased; its policy must be its own; and its funds must be British funds contributed to give effect to British opinion.

Sane Internationalism means, not centralisation, but the

co-operation of Socialist communities which have worked out their own salvation in their own way within their own limits.

Beside the Communist Party there has grown up the Fascist Party. The I.L.P. agrees with the Fascists that our existing parliamentary procedure is not only useless as an instrument of positive regulative and organising government, but an effective means of defeating it. It agrees that the Fascist ideal of the Corporate State, with its Corporations acting as public Trusts in command of the nation's industrial and cultural institutions, is also a Socialist ideal. But it insists that unless and until the Corporations own the land and the industries they control they will be forced to control them in the interest of the private owners and not of the nation, in which case they will make no more difference to the workers than our City Companies do. Therefore, until the Fascists become Socialists as well, the I.L.P. has no use for them.

A Party calling itself the Distributist League has gained some attention through its chief member, a very eminent writer. Its denunciations of Capitalism exceed in vehemence and in literary picturesqueness those of any other Party; and its title is an excellent one. Unfortunately it proposes the distribution, not of income, but of property, which is possible only in a peasant State, and in that only by a refusal of civilisation. Further, the Distributist League's express repudiation of Socialism, and its complicity in the conspiracy of vulgar abuse and misrepresentation against Communist Russia, class it, from the point of view of the I.L.P., as a reactionary organisation.

The Fabian Society has been stifled by the Labour Party which it helped to create, and is now, for all militant purposes, dead. Its helpless silence during the crises of the last few years, contrasted with the brilliant activities which made its reputation forty years ago, testifies to its superannuation.

With the exception of the Labour Party all of these sections share the common European disillusion as to the old Liberal parliamentary methods. This one exception is more nominal than real. The Party is led in the House of Commons by Mr. George Lansbury and Sir Stafford Cripps. It is quite clear from the speeches of Sir Stafford that he has no faith in the routine of Parliament, and foresees either a complete rupture, or a period of prorogued parliaments, with the Cabinet governing as a virtual "dictatorship of the Proletariat" by means of Orders in Council, with special tribunals and commissions to supersede recalcitrant courts and departments of the Civil Service.

Whether this Polish device for saving the face of Constitutionalism is feasible, and if so how far, remains to be seen; but what is certain is that unless the workers are fully and frankly instructed as to its nature and objects, they will be played upon by the Capitalist Press and the pseudo-patriotic bunk of hired orators at expensive pageants to such purpose that the camou-

flaged dictatorship will be seized by the proprietary and financial interests, and become Fascist.

Meanwhile, events in Italy, Germany, Turkey, Persia and Jugoslavia are demonstrating the ease with which any Napoleonic adventurer can raise a force of young men with machine guns and tear gas, and effect a coup d'état. For an overwhelming majority of citizens nowadays have no intelligent interest in politics nor knowledge of social conditions outside their own social circles, and can be roused to intolerant fury or gushing idolatry by any appeal that plays skilfully on their ignorance and their cinema nourished enthusiasms. Thus dictatorships, as all the plebiscites have proved, are democratic as far as majority votes go. The dictator has only to excite the delusions and passions of patriotism and nationalism, and raise a hue and cry against Jews, or foreigners, or Communists, or any other convenient scapegoats, to be entrusted with and confirmed for years in powers which nobody in normal times in England dare propose to entrust to the King.

It is useless and silly to face this peril with no better equipment than a handful of worn-out negative Liberal platitudes about liberty. Nothing can fortify us against such facile bulldosing and political cocaining but a positive faith stronger and more resolute in resistance than the drunken crazes excited by mob oratory and sensational journalism. The I.L.P. consists of men and women who have found such a faith in Socialism; and its business is to propagate that faith and organise the people both for its positive application and for resistance to the attempts of Capitalism to suppress it. It preaches neither Pacifist sufferance nor the sort of law and order established by its opponents for their own purposes. It is subject neither to Marxian dogma nor anti-Marxian dogma. Its end is the transformation of the existing Capitalist régime into a Socialist régime; and its methods are those of Trial and Error.

There you are, Fenner. That is the stuff I should give them. What do you think of it?   Faithfully,

G. BERNARD SHAW.

P.S.—I mark this letter private, as it is not for publication but for the private edification of you and your friends. But if the I.L.P., in an interval of common sense, wished to issue my draft as its own statement, it would be quite welcome to do so provided the identity of the draftsman were not disclosed.

If I were a young man I should *not* join the I.L.P. on the strength of the existing statement. My object has been to produce a statement that *would* attract young Fenners and Shaws.

I did my best to get Mr. Shaw to allow me to publish this document, but he would agree only on the conditions he laid down, and those we could not accept. The consequence was that it has remained in my drawer unpublished until now.

Chapter Twenty-Five
NEGOTIATING WITH MOSCOW

The decision to disaffiliate from the Labour Party was followed by a strong move within the I.L.P. towards unification with the Communist Party and affiliation to the Communist International. Once more it was the Revolutionary Policy Committee which pressed this course and once more there was considerable logic on its side. It argued that there could not be two revolutionary parties: having adopted the revolutionary position, the I.L.P. should find a basis for association with the Communists and prepare for unification.

We slipped into a united front with the Communist Party, however, without considered intention. After the triumph of Hitler the National Council of the Party approached all working-class organisations for a united campaign to assist the victims of Fascism in Germany and to resist the advance of Fascism in this country. We wrote to the Labour Party and the Co-operative Party as well as to the Communist Party, but only the Communist Party agreed. From this beginning the scope of united activity steadily grew so as to include all issues on which there was agreement. Maxton, Harry Pollitt, J. R. Campbell (or Willie Gallacher) and I had frequent consultations. Pollitt was a skilled and persuasive negotiator. A short time before I had debated with him and he had declared war to the knife with the I.L.P.; it was I who had argued that as a revolutionary situation developed we should draw together. But in these consultations he was reasonableness itself. He went out of his way to give the I.L.P. even greater prominence than the C.P. He suggested an ultimate amalgamation which would mean not the I.L.P. joining the C.P., but the coming together of the two Parties on an equal basis. He was full of an infectious confidence, sure that if we recognised the opportunity we could build a mighty movement which would sweep the workers in support. I remember one discussion when he became quite personal in his approach.

"Look here, Jimmy," he said, "I'm not prepared to spend all my days pursuing a line which doesn't bring results. It's all very well to have principles, but the test of any course is its success. The C.P. has failed to build a mass revolutionary party. So has the I.L.P. Together we can do it. You can't be any happier than I am at the thought of all our work ending in nothing. Well, here's our opportunity. Unite our forces, the I.L.P. and the C.P., and we can make a movement in this country which will change history." Maxton was more cautious, not committing himself to Pollitt's plan, but admitting that he would not be content if his days ended in an isolation which, however much it satisfied his socialist conscience, did not assist the emancipation of the working-class. We soon found ourselves co-operating not only in an anti-Fascist campaign, but in the Anti-War Movement, Hunger Marches, agitations against U.A.B. cuts, rent disputes, and unofficial strikes. Finally, our scope of co-operation had extended so far that we signed an agreement for co-operation in "day-to-day" activities in practically every sphere.

Meanwhile, at the 1933 conference, a resolution was carried by 83 to 79, in face of the opposition of the National Council of the Party, instructing it "to ascertain in what way the I.L.P. may assist in the work of the Communist International." The correspondence with the Secretariat of the Communist International which followed is of historic interest. On our side the letters were prepared by a small committee. From Moscow the replies came back, signed on behalf of the Secretariat by O. W. Kuusinen. At that time Kuusinen was unknown outside intimate Communist circles; since I began to write this chapter, he has become known to the whole world as the head of the ill-fated puppet government set up by Russia in Finland.

Our first letter quoted the terms of our conference decision and asked how it could be given practical effect. We received a two-thousand word reply, proposing that the I.L.P. should assist the work of the C.I. by (1) extending co-operation with the Communist Party in Britain; (2) ruthlessly attacking the reformists; (3) developing a united front with the Labour Party rank and file from below (that is, despite the leadership); (4) studying the programme of the C.I. with a view to adopting it, and forming "a single, strong, mass Communist Party" in Britain. "We on our side," said the letter, "declare our complete readiness for such collaboration, but of course retaining the right of comradely criticism when necessary."

The I.L.P. reply did not accept the rôle of tutelage which the C.I. sought to impose. It endorsed the view that co-operation was desirable and agreed that comradely criticism was essential *on both sides*. It argued that the disastrous position of the international working-class movement was due to the failure of the policies of both the Second and Third Internationals, and acknowledged that the Independent Socialist Parties had failed to rally mass support. "We realise that all sections of the working-class have to learn the lessons of the present situation and to re-examine their policies with these lessons in view." Then the I.L.P. put forward its concrete proposals: (1) continued co-operation with the C.P. of Great Britain, with the object of united action by *the whole of the working-class* and the retention of the right of inter-party criticism; (2) the extension of co-operation to the international field on the understanding that there should be responsible collaboration by the participating parties; (3) a World Congress to secure united action by all revolutionary sections of the working-class.

This letter displeased the Communist International. Two months later came a three-thousand word reply which was obviously aimed at splitting our Party. It denounced the proposal for a World Congress of revolutionary socialist parties as a manœuvre to lead the workers back into the Second International and then proceeded to attack the I.L.P. leadership, and particularly myself, for criticising Russian foreign policy and Communist Party tactics in Germany. "In short, many members of your Party are revolutionaries, but many leaders are reformists." The C.I. therefore proposed *discussion* in the I.L.P. on (1) mass action on the basis of the C.P.—I.L.P. united front, and (2) the desirability of the I.L.P. joining the C.I. "as a Party sympathising with Communism, with the right to a consultative vote."

In reply, we despatched a considered document dealing in a comprehensive way with the whole question of international tactics and organisation. It is worth summarising in some detail because it was widely recognised as being of permanent importance. Three primary duties were laid down: (1) the defence of the U.S.S.R.; (2) the creation of the broadest United Front to resist Capitalist Reaction, Fascism and War; (3) the national and international union of revolutionary Socialists. Then a series of questions were put regarding the precise obligations of association with the C.I. as a sympathetic party. What limitations would such association impose upon the self-governing powers of a national body? Would the I.L.P. be free to state its policy publicly on any issue which involved criticisms of the C.I. or the C.P. of Britain? Would the I.L.P. be free to make proposals relating to the structure and tactics of the C.I. to its Executive or Congress? Was association regarded as necessarily the first step to complete affiliation? The letter proceeded to list the functions of a revolutionary International, as follows: (1) To ensure that in every capitalist country there shall be a section which (a) accepts the class struggle and the "dictatorship of the proletariat" *expressed through working-class democracy,* and (b) combines internal party democracy with strict discipline; (2) to pool experience, to organise joint international action (including action against war) and to give assistance to parties in need; and (3) to prepare for the federation of Workers' Republics in a World Socialist Commonwealth.

An analysis of how the C.I. differed from this basis followed. Instead of applying democracy within the International, the Executive took detailed control over the national sections, over-riding their desires, reversing their policies, removing and expelling the leaders against the wishes of the membership, and forcing whole parties out of the International. The Executive itself was under the effective control of only one section, the Russian. This resulted in repeated misdirections being given to national sections. Finally, we proposed a practicable form of organisation: (1) the extension of the right of criticism, at present enjoyed only by the leadership; (2) the preparation of important C.I. decisions through international discussion; (3) the replacement of the actual monopoly of the Russian leader-ship by a real collective international leadership.

It was six weeks before the reply came. When it did, the purpose of splitting the Party was clearer than ever; indeed, the letter was implicitly directed to the members against the leaders. I was selected specially for attack because I had begun to criticise the changed line of Russia's foreign policy and was dismissed as a "left reformist" and a "slanderer of the Soviet

Union." The C.I. did not attempt to respond to the analytical and constructive contribution which we had made.

Despite its abortive results, this correspondence was of the highest value. It educated not only the membership of the I.L.P. but thousands of Socialists in other countries who followed it with interest. I had letters from all over the world, many of them from prominent figures in the international movement, thanking the I.L.P. for having raised so clearly the fundamental issues regarding the Communist International. When the 1934 Annual Conference of the I.L.P. met, it rejected by 98 votes to 51 a resolution in favour of "sympathetic affiliation."

Whilst this correspondence proceeded, important developments took place in connection with the united front of the I.L.P. and the Communist Party in Britain. Nationally, co-operation became more difficult because of the criticism which I, the chairman of the Party, was voicing of Soviet Russia's foreign policy. Harry Pollitt complained bitterly of this at one of our consultations, but when the I.L.P. representatives, including Maxton, backed me he realised that his hope of dividing the leadership and of absorbing the greater part of the I.L.P. in the C.P. was dead. It was locally, however, that the united front broke down most seriously. In the Lancashire I.L.P. there was open revolt; in South Wales the minimum effort was made; from all over the country letters of criticism began to reach Head Office. We decided to take a detailed census of Branch opinion, and the result was startling; it was clearly revealed that two-thirds of the Party were participating in the united front uneasily if not unwillingly. The criticism was on two grounds—first, that co-operation with the Communist Party was prejudicing the hopes of a wider working-class front, because the Labour Party, Trade Union and Co-operative representatives would not touch the C.P.; second, that the Communist Party was proving untrustworthy by exploiting the united activities for its own sectarian advantage.

The National Council of the Party recommended the 1934 conference to drop "day-to-day" co-operation with the C.P. on general issues. Instead, it proposed that united front activities should be limited to specific issues. With a feeling of relief the majority of delegates accepted the recommendation. But even this recommendation did not go far enough to keep the Lancashire leadership and a large section of its membership in the Party. They resigned and with a few scattered members outside Lancashire, including Mr. Middleton Murry* and his followers, formed the Independent Socialist Party. I was particularly sorry to lose Tom Abbott, the Lancashire Organiser. I had known him ever since my first visit to Blackburn in 1911 and there was no grander working-class fighter in our ranks.

Nor did the modification of policy come early enough to prevent the resignation from the Party of John Paton, our general secretary, in December, 1933. Paton's reasons for resignation were partly personal and partly political. Disaffiliation from the Labour Party had caused a considerable drop in membership and a withdrawal of support from sympathetic subscribers; the result was a serious fall in income and a decision to cut down the salaries of Party officials to a maximum of £5 a week, a figure which Paton was not in a position to accept. But there were also political reasons. John found himself increasingly isolated. He was antipathetic to the Parliamentary Group, taking the view that they were failing to use their opportunity to make a national position for the Party, and he was opposed to the tendency of the Party to accept the policies of the R.P.C. It is possible that if the decision of the 1934 conference to modify co-operation with the Communist Party had been reached six months earlier Paton might have remained with the Party.

The resignation of Paton as secretary placed the National Council in a serious position. During the larger portion of a morning session we could not reach agreement about his successor; it was Jack Gaster, during the luncheon adjournment, walking arm in arm with Maxton and me across the lawn of Digswell Park (we were meeting during the Summer School of the Party) who made the proposal which was eventually adopted. It was that I should resign the chairmanship to become secretary again and that Maxton should resume the chairmanship.

---

* Mr. Murry had been an enthusiastic recruit to the Party two years previously and had tried to convert it to a spiritual interpretation of Marxism.

Chapter Twenty-Six
THE BEGINNING OF DISILLUSIONMENT

During the period of united activity with the Communist Party the Soviet Embassy was very friendly to the I.L.P. Indeed, this friendliness had begun before, because the I.L.P., despite its differences with the C.P., had always defended Soviet Russia. At the time of the Arcos Raid, when the Russians anticipated that the directors of all their trading organisations would be asked to leave the country, provisional arrangements were made for half a dozen of us to become directors of the Soviet companies registered in London. I was astonished that the Soviet authorities should be ready to place these large commercial undertakings in our inexperienced hands, but they insisted that business knowledge was of no account. All they desired was to be certain of political trustworthiness and personal honesty. We were ready to step into the breach, but in keeping with I.L.P. practice, we insisted that the duties should be fulfilled as a socialist service in an honorary capacity without fees or salaries. Perhaps the fullest sign of confidence was the Ambassador's habit of approaching me when he wished to appoint English members to the staff.

Out of the past comes the memory of another proof of official Soviet friendliness: when M. Krassin died I was selected as one of the three speakers at the funeral service at Golders Green Crematorium. I spoke with considerable reluctance. In the front pew was the family of the dead Ambassador; standing within a yard of them I felt it was an affront that a mere political acquaintance should speak on such an occasion. In addition to M. Krassin, I learned to know both M. Rakovsky and M. Sokolnikoff when they served as Ambassadors; as for M. Maisky, as I have already recorded, we were colleagues in the anti-war struggle of 1915 and when he returned to London he greeted me as an old comrade. The best friend I made at the Embassy was M. Bogomoloff, the first Counsellor. On the night before he left to take up his appointment as Ambassador in China we sat in the Embassy car for two hours, talking about the future of the Socialist Movement in Britain and Europe, whilst the chauffeur drove us about the country to the north of London. It is a sad memory that Rakovsky, Sokolnikoff,

Bogomoloff were all victims of the subsequent purge: Rakovsky was shot, Sokolnikoff was imprisoned, the fate of Bogomoloff, the best of comrades, I do not know.

There was one feature of Soviet Embassy life which disappointed me keenly. I was proud of Russia as a Workers' State; I had read how Lenin and other leaders had led lives of simplicity, yet here at Embassy receptions there was a riot of luxury such as I had never seen elsewhere. Bluntly, these were revolting shows; a large proportion of those present came for the drinks and food which could be obtained *ad lib.* I have memories of fat women guzzling at heaped tables and of men jostling each other before the bars in order to snatch the last opportunities of vodka, champagne and wine, lifting coffee cups greedily for their portions when all the glasses had been exhausted. It was not a pleasant picture of Russo-British working-class solidarity. The one note of democracy was the option allowed for dress.

Now I come to think of it, I remember a contrast. In the earliest days of Russian representation in Britain I went to a reception which was really proletarian; leaders were there, the Ambassador and his wife received us, but the refreshments were moderate and we danced as we should have done at a social run by any socialist organisation. It was boasted, I remember, that the office boys and junior typists on the Embassy staff were present and on every side one saw rank and file members of the Movement. Even in this matter Soviet Russia seems to have gone back upon its earlier proletarian practice.

Our negotiations with the Communist International were still proceeding when the "Daily Worker" one morning splashed across a page the streamer "Brockway Goes Over to the Counter-Revolutionaries"; in another Communist journal I was described as "a hound of War and Fascism." I had committed the unforgiveable sin of criticising Russia. My criticism was caused by the first steps of Russia's change in foreign policy, reflected in its attitude to the new Hitler Government. When Hitler triumphed in the Reichstag Fire election, the I.L.P. urged international working-class action to bring down the new Fascist régime; we proposed that the Trade Union, Co-operative and Political Internationals, in conjunction with the Russian working-class, should organise a world-wide refusal to make or handle goods destined for Germany. This proposal was not merely theoretical. Within the international Trade Union Movement there were strong elements which advocated it and the International Transport Workers' Federation explored the possibility of giving a lead. But all hope of the realisation of such a plan was destroyed by the announcement that the Russian Government had extended the Trade Agreement with Germany which had been in operation before Hitler's coming to power. In Germany, Thaelmann and Torgler, the Communist leaders, were in prison, and if reports were to be believed, were the victims of torture. Thousands of Communist Party members were being shot, beaten up, imprisoned, thrust into concentration camps. The whole Party organisation was outlawed, its premises occupied by the Nazis, its papers suppressed. Yet, while this repression was going on, representatives of the Soviet and Hitler Governments were meeting in conference and concluding an agreement for economic co-operation. The announcement of this agreement was not merely a moral shock; it showed that Russia would not co-operate in any direct action by the international working-class against the Hitler régime. It implied that the Communist Parties of the different countries, obedient to Moscow, would fall into line. Indeed, in Holland, where transport workers began to refuse to handle goods on boats carrying the Swastika flag, the Communist Party came out against their action. When Soviet workers were busily loading German ships in Russian ports, it was impossible for Communist Parties to urge workers to refuse to do so in other countries.

My articles on this issue created a fierce controversy, but I was confident of my ground and, when the Communist Party called a discussion meeting, announcing in the "Daily Worker" that "Brockway had been invited to attend" (although, in fact, no invitation was received until three days later), I immediately offered to debate the issue with Pollitt. The debate took place in Conway Hall, which was crowded. I was at a considerable disadvantage. I suppose that three-quarters of the audience were Communist Party supporters and I was conscious that a large part of the I.L.P. members present were critical of my attitude, because London was the stronghold of the R.P.C. Many probably had a vivid memory of a previous encounter between Harry Pollitt and myself, when the debating honours certainly went to Pollitt (though within a year the C.P. had to withdraw a verbatim report because developments had vindicated my case rather than his), and no doubt their expectation was that I would again be trounced. But this time I held my own. A descriptive writer in one of the daily papers said that I had the better of the argument and Pollitt the better of the oratory, and that judgment I am prepared to accept. Pollitt argued that the boycott is not a working-class weapon, but I countered this by showing that ten years previously the Communist International had declared for the very policy against fascist Italy which I now urged against fascist Germany. The Enlarged Executive Committee of the Communist International in June, 1923, decided "to prepare for an international boycott of all workers against Italy, to stop coal supplies to Italy, to urge all transport workers not to carry goods from and into Italy, and so forth. To this end we set up international committees of miners, seamen, railway workers, etc." If this was a working-class weapon in 1923, why not in 1933? I asked.

The following year the Soviet Union took two steps in foreign policy which marked a still sharper turn: Russia joined the League of Nations and began negotiations for a political and military alliance with the reactionary Government of France. I believe I was the first person in Britain to criticise these developments from a socialist standpoint. I pointed out that Lenin had described the League as the "thieves' kitchen," and that the Sixth World Congress of the Communist International, 1928, had denounced alliances with capitalist governments "because they would represent an alliance for the suppression of the proletarian revolution and of the national liberation movements of colonial peoples."

My articles brought down on my head terrific abuse from the Communists and criticism almost as severe from many sections of I.L.P. I took the matter to the National Council of the Party and received its backing. Maxton was remarkably far-seeing in his reaction. I had laid emphasis on the inevitability of a Communist retreat from the struggle against British and French Imperialism. "Not only that," said Maxton, "the Russian Government cannot become allied with the French Government without subduing the class struggle previously carried on by the French Communists. It cannot seek an alliance with the British Government without moderating the class struggle carried on by the Communist Party here."

The next development which disturbed my confidence in those who controlled Soviet Russia was the series of Moscow Trials. My "New Leader" article on the first trial was headed with a question mark, but I wrote: "Stalin may make a purge of his critics; but this trial has been a bad day's work for Soviet Russia. Putting the most favourable impression upon it, it leaves in the mind a picture of antagonisms and repressions which are far from the free, happy and united society which Socialists everywhere hoped was being built in Russia." My doubts were deepened by the subsequent trials. Those arrested included Rakovsky and Bogomoloff. My personal knowledge of the prisoners undoubtedly influenced my judgment, and the effect of this was strengthened when in Paris I met revolutionaries who had escaped from Russia after imprisonment, as well as Soviet officials like M. Barmene, the First Counsellor at Athens, who had refused to return to Moscow. It was impossible to come in contact with these men without recognising them as genuine Socialists or paying heed to their descriptions of the growing bureaucratic dictatorship of Stalin and his colleagues.

But the greatest impression was made on my mind not so much by the fact that the leading prisoners were the trusted colleagues of Lenin and proven revolutionaries (impressive though that fact was) as by the huge proportions of the purge. We shall never know how many men and women were done to death in this "terror," but reports from Russia said that at least sixty thousand officials of the Russian Communist Party, local and national, were imprisoned or done to death. Individual leaders may always become traitors, but it is not possible to indict thousands of the most active members of a Party in this way.

The one possibility of checking the allegations at the trials seemed to be an investigation of the indictment made of Trotsky; he was an exile in Norway and an impartial enquiry could take the specific charges made against him and give him an opportunity to disprove them. He asked for such an enquiry, and both the I.L.P. and the International Bureau of Revolutionary Socialist Parties supported the demand. For some weeks I was active trying to get together a Commission composed of French, Scandinavian and American comrades. Meanwhile, however, the Norwegian Government found Trotsky an inconvenient guest and he took refuge in Mexico, making a European enquiry impossible. Finally, the Trotsky Defence Committee in America started a Commission of Enquiry. The chairman of this Commission, Professor Dewey, whom I had learned to know well on my visits to America, had my complete confidence, but I did not feel that an enquiry initiated by a *Defence* Committee could be accepted as impartial. When I expressed this view in a letter to the Committee, Trotsky denounced me as "Mr. Pritt Number Two," a reference to Mr. D. N. Pritt, the K.C. and Labour M.P.* who had attended the first Moscow Trial and whitewashed it entirely. Perhaps the "old man" (as his followers call him) was suffering from nerves. Certainly he had reason to do so.†

I was still anxious to get at the truth of the matter, however, and decided myself to make a thorough study of the evidence both of the Moscow Trials and of the Dewey Enquiry. I secured verbatim reports and checked the charges and repudiations in detail. I put on one side matters which could not be proved, as for example the Moscow allegation that Trotsky had been communicating with the "plotters" and Trotsky's denial that he had done so: no original letter was produced by Moscow, but the absence of any copies in Trotsky's files certainly could not be regarded as conclusive. There were three concrete matters which could be tested: they concerned places and dates relating to individuals who were still free. The first was an allegation that three of the prisoners had visited Trotsky in Copenhagen in November, 1932; the second was an assertion by a witness that he met Trotsky on behalf of Radek, in Paris in July, 1933; the third was a statement by a prisoner that he met Trotsky in Norway in December, 1935. I cannot here give the evidence in detail, but my conclusions were definite that the first and third of these alleged events never took place and that it was very improbable that the second event took place.

I was more concerned, however, to find the explanation of the underlying conflict which the widespread purge reflected than to vindicate this or that leader. I read every Russian book

---

* D. N. Pritt was subsequently expelled from the Labour Party for activities associated with the Communist Party.

† Trotsky was assassinated in Mexico in 1940.

on which I could lay my hands; histories of the Revolution and what had followed, as well as books, laudatory and critical, about existing conditions. I questioned everyone I could find who had been in Russia, both Communists and critics. The final conclusion to which I came was that, putting more superficial issues aside, the conflict expressed a contradiction between the economic and political structures in Russia. Basically the economic structure was potentially socialist; private capitalism had been abolished; a new generation had grown up taught to be conscious that they belonged to a Workers' State; the Communist Party officials at least had been trained in Marxism, with its emphasis on equality and workers' freedom. But politically the State had never been an expression of workers' democracy and was becoming less so. The power originally placed with the Soviets, representing workers on a wide basis, had been transferred to the Communist Party, and control by the Party had become more and more control by a bureaucratic leadership. Inevitably a clash developed between the potentially socialist economic system and the dictatorial political system. This study led me to the view that the root cause of the disappointing development in Soviet Russia was the absence of workers' democracy.

We restrained our disappointment about what was happening in Russia for many months, speaking of it only among ourselves because we did not want to encourage capitalist attacks on Russia; but at last we could be silent no longer. The imperative urge to speak out came to me whilst at an international conference in Paris in March, 1938; as I listened to speaker after speaker telling of the disastrous moral effect which the events in Russia were having on the Movement in the different countries I became convinced that the only way to overcome this evil was to face it openly. I discussed the matter with Jay Lovestone, leader of the Communist Opposition in America, and he urged that the duty of issuing a supreme appeal to Stalin to save the honour of Socialism by stopping the "terror" rested with the I.L.P. Jay was coming to London and we agreed that he should put the proposal with me to the members of the I.L.P. Parliamentary Group. Lovestone and I met Maxton, Stephen, and McGovern over a table in the Tea Room in the House of Commons. The result was the letter which the four I.L.P. M.P.s and I addressed to Stalin.

on March 9th, 1938, calling on him to end the persecution. It made a world-wide impression. From far distant countries we had messages from socialist comrades, leaders and rank-and-file, thanking us for having said what was in their hearts. We were, of course, bitterly denounced by the official Communists for daring to make this appeal, but I believe it helped to re-establish for the Socialist Movement a standard of honour and truth that was being lost by the effect of the tragic happenings in Russia.

Meanwhile Communist Party policy outside Russia was justifying up to the hilt the forebodings which I had expressed when the U.S.S.R. directed its policy towards alliances with the French and British Governments. The first effect was upon the anti-imperialist struggle; the Russian Government recognised that there would be no hope of an alliance with the two greatest Imperialist Powers in the world if the Communist International continued to stir the colonial peoples to revolt. I have told about the formation of the League Against Imperialism under Communist inspiration. It became an organisation of real significance, uniting the Left in the European working-class movement with all the more important Nationalist movements in the Empires; but when the Russian Government changed its foreign policy it was allowed to sink into futility, becoming nothing more than an information bureau, issuing a monthly bulletin which was careful not to clash with Russian interests. I have often wondered what was the honest view which Reginald Bridgeman, its secretary, held of this liquidation. Bridgeman was a sincere anti-Imperialist who sacrificed a diplomatic career to take on the work of the League.

A still deeper impression was made on me later by the story told by George Padmore. Padmore represented the Negro workers on the Executive of the Communist International He was held in high esteem in Moscow for his intellectual abilities, energy of ideas and strong personality, and he was allotted the special task of organising the libertarian movement in North Africa, encouraging the growth of the demand for political independence and stimulating among the native conscripts the idea that when a suitable opportunity came they should fight for their own national freedom. But as soon as the move towards a Russian-French alliance was made this plan of activity was cancelled.

Later Maxton's forecast of the depressing effect of the Russian-French alliance upon the class struggle in France also proved true. When during a critical stage of the development of the Popular Front, strikes broke out at Brest and Toulouse and the Liberals became nervous, not only did the reformist Labour leaders play their normal rôle of urging moderation and a return to work, but the strange news came through that the Communists were also exerting their influence in the same direction; at no cost must the alliance with the Liberals be jeopardised! When under the stimulation of working-class and Trade Union unity and of electoral victories the remarkable stay-in strike movement broke out in June, 1936, the Popular Front Government not only got the strikers to return to work on terms which proved almost a complete swindle within twelve months, but proceeded to issue regulations making stay-in strikes illegal. Because of its Liberal elements and its alliance in foreign affairs with the reactionary National Government of Britain, the French Popular Front Government could not lift a hand to help its brother Popular Front Government in Spain when Franco and his fascist colleagues rebelled against it. That the main purpose of the Communists was to make France at any cost a strong ally of Russia was revealed when they came out for a Government of "National Unity," including many of the most reactionary and anti-working-class elements in French politics. It became obvious to everyone except the amazingly blind membership of the Communist Party and its satellite concerns, like the Left Book Club,* that the turn in Russian and Communist International policy was leading progressively to the repudiation of every principle of the struggle against Imperialism and Capitalism, and that it had as its goal the very "social patriotism" which the C.I. had been formed to challenge.

In this country these tendencies did not develop so rapidly or openly because the desired alliance between Russia and Britain was not consummated, but parallel moves occurred. When Mr. Eden visited Moscow in March, 1935, he was told by Stalin that the British Empire was "the greatest factor in the world for peace and stability." How was it possible, under such circumstances, for British Communists logically to

* At the end of 1939 the Left Book Club began to see light, mainly as a consequence of the Russo-German Pact.

denounce the National Government and British Imperialism as dangers to peace?   When the Popular Front Movement was initiated in this country, the platform included a "democratic" Tory M.P., a Liberal, and a Communist.   The Liberal told the blunt truth: "The basis of our unity as democrats against the menace of Fascism in Germany and Italy must be a truce in the class war between workers and employers in this country."   Even in Britain, despite the absence of an alliance with Russia, the Communists finally came out for a government of national unity in which Winston Churchill, Sir Archibald Sinclair and Mr. C. R. Attlee were to be leading figures.*

I have often been called a "Trotskyist."   Much of my criticism of Russia's policy was similar to Trotsky's, but my conclusions were reached quite independently.   On other issues I found myself in disagreement with Trotsky.   His view that it was possible to form a "Fourth International" by a thesis thrown into vacuum I regarded as nonsense: I held that a revolutionary International could come only from an upsurge of the workers arising from some historical development and that without this accompanying mass movement the most perfect thesis had little significance.   Trotsky's dealings with his followers convinced me that, despite his advocacy of "proletarian democracy," he had the same instinct for personal power as Stalin and that were he head of the Russian State he would treat dissentients from his policy with a ruthlessness similar to Stalin's.   The personal authority which Trotsky imposed on the little groupings of the "Fourth International" was that of an absolute dictator; unless his word were obeyed in every respect, expulsions followed on the pattern of the Communist International, irrespective of majorities and minorities.   The effect was ludicrous.   Never large outside the United States of America, the Trotskyist groups splintered until they became mere fractions engaged in internecine war about the pure revolutionary word and the correct interpretation of instructions received from Mexico.   I frequently concurred with Trotsky's analysis of events, but I saw little difference in spirit between Mexico and Moscow.

---

* In May, 1940, this very Government was formed, but the Communist Party did not seem to like it—until the invasion of Russia by Germany in June, 1941, when it became commendable again.

Chapter Twenty-Seven
PROBLEMS OF WORKING-CLASS UNITY

Despite our deep divergence from the Communist Party, we again became involved in a united front campaign with it during 1936-37. The initiative was taken by the Socialist League, and particularly by Sir Stafford Cripps. Before the campaign was opened publicly we had a series of long and difficult discussions between representatives of the three Parties in his chambers in the Middle Temple. Stafford Cripps and Will Mellor represented the Socialist League, Harry Pollitt and Palme Dutt the Communist Party, and Maxton and myself the I.L.P.

This was the first time I had come into close contact with Cripps. About his burning sincerity there could be no doubt; he was convinced that the official leadership of the Labour Party had not the inspiration or policy to lead the workers to Socialism and (his son had obviously influenced him) that the younger generation particularly were looking to a movement resurrected through a new leadership. He had faith that a combination of the Socialist League, the I.L.P. and C.P. would bring about this resurrection, and with skill and patience he devoted himself to the task of overcoming the differences which stood in the way. I learned to respect Cripps greatly as he presided over our discussions; he had the earnestness of a crusader, and, when deadlocks between the I.L.P. and the C.P. threatened to bring all his efforts to nought, he refused to give up until his purpose was achieved.

But I realised also that Cripps suffers from two limitations which make his future a matter of doubt; he has no experience of the working-class and he has no real knowledge of socialist theory. Although he cares little about material things—he is ascetic in his habits (I once heard a miner say that his fruitarian meals would not satisfy a sparrow) and is generous with his gifts to causes in which he believes—he is not at home among the working-class and workers do not feel at their ease with him. When his voice is raised on their behalf it is as a humanitarian from outside their circle and not as one identified with them. As for socialist theory I doubt whether he has ever read Marx or any book of fundamental socialist economics. In these talks which preceded the Unity Campaign he was obviously lost when William Mellor put the Marxist case against the Popular Front; he acknowledged that he had not thought out the subject. He was equally at sea when we discussed the policy differences between P.O.U.M. and the Communist Party in Spain; he was impatient with controversy about such issues as social revolution versus capitalist democracy. Similarly, when we approached the question of the Moscow Trials, he argued that it was an internal matter for Russia and did not see that principles of importance for the international socialist movement were involved. It is this absence of a basic socialist philosophy which is responsible, I think, for the rapidly-occurring turns and inconsistencies which have marked Cripps' career.

Nevertheless, Cripps' simple enthusiasm, his spirit of a human mission, were of great worth at the head of the Unity Campaign. His friends sometimes say that his mysticism will take him eventually into the Church rather than into a Soviet, but his appeal to elementary values and liberties contributes something essential which those of us who are submerged in the clashes of political theory and sectional action are apt to miss. There was no doubt that Harry Pollitt understood Cripps' value. He wooed him assiduously, playing up to him in committees, staying on for chats with him after committees. I was fully aware, of course, of Pollitt's moves in the struggle going on underneath the superficial unity of our committee, the struggle as to whether the Popular Front view of the C.P. or the Workers' Front view of the I.L.P. should win the allegiance of the Left in the Labour Movement. Harry's methods succeeded temporarily in the case of Sir Stafford Cripps; his paper "The Tribune" became shortly afterwards virtually a Communist Pary organ, and Will Mellor, the editor, had to leave. But I doubt whether even Pollitt's romantic optimism could lead him to believe that he had won Cripps permanently.*

Palme Dutt was an interesting study. He gave the impression of a Buddhist monk, a withdrawn and mostly silent personality, secretive, suspicious, waiting and watching. When he did speak it was in a curious impersonal tone, reciting the far-distant creed of Moscow, putting it well, every thread

*Early in 1940 "The Tribune" swung violently again to an anti-C.P. line.

building up the pattern, but as a chapter read from a book rather than as a spontaneous, living contribution. Mellor was the most decisive personality to set against Pollitt. He had a basic philosophy and expressed it in strong, direct terms. Mellor ought to have gone much further in the Labour Movement than he has done. He has the brain and the force of leadership; he speaks and writes well. He appears only to lack the ability to fit in with others.*

It will be clear even from these sketches of some of the members that our Unity Committee was not all unity. The preliminary negotiations nearly broke down half-a-dozen times and even when the campaign was launched serious differences emerged. The first problem was the form of organisational unity at which we should aim. There was no suggestion that the three sections should amalgamate; the idea was that the I.L.P. and the Communist Party should, like the Socialist League, become affiliated to the Labour Party. The Communist Party wanted such affiliation without conditions, but the I.L.P. was not prepared to enter the Labour Party unless either its policy were changed or freedom were granted to advocate and carry out a revolutionary socialist programme. This problem was settled by a far-reaching concession which Maxton made. He said that if the Unity Campaign succeeded in convincing the Labour Party that it should open its doors to the C.P. and the I.L.P., he would regard this as evidence that its attitude had changed sufficiently to justify re-affiliation. I heard this statement with some surprise, because Jimmy had always been the most "isolationist" among I.L.P. leaders.

The second problem was the programme of the campaign. The Communist Party submitted a full "Popular Front" document which was impossible for the I.L.P. Pollitt insisted on its main features; I rejected them as decisively. To rescue us from this impasse, the document was handed over to the Socialist League for revision in consultation with the C.P. It came back with most of the offending clauses removed, but two remained: a pledge to defend the Soviet Union's "fight for peace," and endorsement of a Pact between Russia, Britain, France and other countries. To neither of these would we agree. Cripps and Mellor proposed that the "Peace Front"

*Will Mellor died in 1942.

should be limited to democratic countries, and the clause was amended to read "States in which the working class have political freedom", but this did not satisfy us—we were in favour of a pact only between *working-class* governments. On the subject of Russia's "fight for peace" we were adamant; we did not regard its foreign policy as either socialist or peace-making. A deadlock threatened; the C.P. said it would not sign the manifesto unless this pledge were included. Cripps found the way out; he proposed that the I.L.P. should make reservations on these two points in a letter addressed to him, and that this dissent should be accepted by the Committee. At first the C.P. resisted, but after an adjournment it concurred. Thus an uneasy agreement was reached.

When the proposed manifesto came before the I.L.P. Executive Committee, two reservations were made. The first accepted the principle of Maxton's declaration regarding affiliation to the Labour Party, but defined it more closely, saying that the I.L.P. looked to the Unity Campaign to create a spirit within the Labour Party which would give reasonable hope of its democratisation and of freedom to express socialist policy, thus enabling the I.L.P. to re-affiliate. The second reservation maintained disagreement with the Soviet Government's policy in respect of the League of Nations, collective security and military pacts with capitalist governments, but recognised the need to subordinate criticism in order to mobilise support for Russia's action in sending arms to Spain. Pollitt and Dutt were furious when they arrived at the next Committee; they regarded the publication of the I.L.P. reservations as a betrayal of the secrecy of the negotiations between the three bodies. I was flabbergasted; the negotiations had been secret, but no suggestion had been made that the conclusions should be secret. Did the C.P. leaders really believe that the I.L.P. would sign a document contravening its policy in important respects without making clear its position? Did they think we had written to Sir Stafford Cripps merely to salve our political consciences?

Differences arose during the campaign itself which threatened our continued co-operation. The first referred to Spain. The Communist International was beginning to spread

its slanders about our brother-party in Spain, the P.O.U.M.*
I knew these charges contained not a shred of truth and in a
factual speech I put our case to the Committee, ending with the
suggestion that Cripps, Pollitt and I should go to Spain and
seek to re-establish unity in the anti-fascist ranks. I think
Cripps would have agreed, but Pollitt rejected the proposal out
of hand. All he would say was that time would prove the
truth of the allegations. We had to leave the matter with my
declaration that, despite the Unity Campaign, the I.L.P. considered it its duty to vindicate its Spanish comrades. The Campaign went on; Pollitt and I spoke together from the same
platform and were both scrupulously careful not to reflect our
Party differences, but the inner spirit of unity was dead.

The Socialist League also had its difficulties. The Labour
Party Executive threatened to expel the League if it maintained
a common platform with the C.P. and the I.L.P. When we
considered this ultimatum Harry Pollitt proposed that it
should be met by the dissolution of the League—and to our
surprise Cripps supported him. They argued that by this
tactic the Labour Party Executive would have to deal with
individuals and that this would widen the resistance by bringing
in a considerable number of influential Labour M.P.s and
Trade Union officials who were not members of the League.
The strategic moment for resistance, urged Pollitt, was when the
fight developed on the widest possible front.

Mellor disagreed. He emphasised the importance of the
League as an organised Left unit in the Labour Party; if the
League were dissolved, we should play into the hands of the
Right Wing of the Labour Party, who wished to rid it of all
separately organised Left organisations. But a divided Socialist
League and a united Communist Party gave Pollitt and Cripps
a majority, and the Council of the League subsequently agreed
to dissolution. Did the Communist Party deliberately destroy
the Socialist League? I do not know, but I learned later that
the opponents within the League of any campaign associated
with the Communist Party had forecast that it would lead to
this very result.

The Unity Campaign proceeded as a partnership of Labour
Party *individuals* with the I.L.P. and C.P., but the Labour Party

*See Chapters XXX and XXXI.

Executive was quick to strike the next blow. It announced that
if G. R. Strauss, M.P., fulfilled an engagement to speak with
Pollitt and Maxton he would be expelled. The challenge on
the wider front had come; this was the occasion which Pollitt
had pointed to as the strategic moment for resistance. Strauss
stated that he was willing to carry on if the Committee
supported him . . . . and then once more Pollitt sounded the
retreat and once more Cripps backed him. It was agreed by
a majority that the I.L.P. and C.P. should withdraw from the
campaign and that it should be transformed into an agitation
conducted solely by Labour Party members with the object of
winning their Party to support the unity proposals. Pollitt and
Cripps spoke enthusiastically of the possibilities; but I think we
all realised that the campaign was killed.

It is fair to Cripps to say that he was probably influenced
by the fact that the spirit of unity had gone already. The
conflicts about Spain and the Moscow Trials had grown more
intense. Whilst the leadership of the I.L.P. and the C.P. kept
the letter of their agreement when speaking together, the
second rank of speakers in both Parties were not so disciplined,
and the memberships were flaming with the fierce controversy
which had broken out in the columns of the "Daily Worker"
and the "New Leader." Cripps remarked on the irony of unity
meetings when at the door members of the two parties were
selling literature bitterly attacking each other. I had always
defended the right of inter-Party criticism, but I realised it had
reached a stage which was making co-operation a farce.

The campaign had begun with a great flare. The largest
halls in the country were crowded; tens of thousands of the
rank and file signed the "pledge cards" in favour of unity. But
as the Labour Party Conference approached, the cause of unity
was killed by something additional to internal controversy; it
was killed by the effect of the Moscow Trials, which caused a
deep revulsion in the minds of the ordinary British workers.
When the Conference met the proposals for unity were
defeated by a bigger majority than at the preceding Conference.

Thus ended ingloriously the Unity Campaign. Its result
was the destruction of the Socialist League, the loss of influence
of Cripps, Bevan, Strauss and other "Lefts," the strengthening
of the reactionary leaders, and the disillusionment of the rank

and file. And yet, if I am asked whether the I.L.P. made a mistake in entering the campaign, my answer is "No." The effect would have been disastrous if we had refused the invitation of the Socialist League to participate in an effort to realise what was in the heart of every class-conscious worker—the need for the unity of the working-class.

The real lesson of the Unity Campaign was the need to limit united action to specific issues. In fact, such united action was carried on by the I.L.P. and the C.P. before and after the Unity Campaign. It took place locally in industrial disputes and nationally in unemployment agitations and in opposition to the Mosley Fascist Movement. We co-operated in Hunger Marches, though with considerable inner conflict about control and leadership, and in the huge agitation, extending far beyond our Parties, which compelled the withdrawal of the cruel U.A.B. regulations in the early months of 1934. John McGovern, M.P., led the Hunger Marchers from Glasgow to Edinburgh and London with a spirit and adventure which put the Communists in the shade. When the marchers were refused accommodation at Edinburgh he set them the example of sleeping on the pavement of Princes Street, making a tremendous propaganda impression. On the march to London, John's irresistible fun found expression in one of his richest jokes. At Carlisle the marchers put up at the Public Assistance institution and, in accordance with the rules, the Master asked for their names. McGovern pulled out of his pocket a copy of Hansard and wrote down in the register the required number from the Government side of a division list! Some historian of the future, studying the books of the institution, will be perplexed to find that on this particular night Mr. Stanley Baldwin, Mr. Neville Chamberlain, Mr. Winston Churchill, Mr. L. S. Amery, Sir John Simon, Mr. Anthony Eden and other distinguished statesmen partook of the hospitality of the Carlisle Public Assistance authorities.

The most impressive co-operation between the I.L.P. and the Communist Party was in opposition to the offensive conducted by Sir Oswald Mosley and his British Union of Fascists in East London.* Playing on the prejudice against Jews,

* This had been preceded by remarkable demonstrations against Mosley at his rallies at Olympia and Hyde Park.

Mosley had succeeded in securing the support of a considerable number of Irish and British workers and planned a march through the East End on October 4, 1936. I regarded this as deliberate racial provocation and co-operated readily in resistance. Both the I.L.P. and the C.P. held meetings calling on the workers to mass on the streets to bar the way of the fascist procession; the idea was that if the streets were crammed the march would have to be abandoned. The C.P. was stronger in East London than the I.L.P., but by a chance our propaganda had the bigger effect. On the day before the procession I issued to the press a call to the workers to fill the streets in their hundreds of thousands. The "Star," the most widely read paper among the workers, ran a heading, "I.L.P. Call to the Workers," right across the front page and set out our appeal in full, with all the arts of bold type and capital letters to give it emphasis. Every newsagent's shop in the East End had the poster: "I.L.P. Calls on Workers to Stop Mosley." The main responsibility had fallen on our shoulders.

I went down to the East End early and joined the crowd at Gardiner's Corner beyond Aldgate. Every moment more people came. From a balcony the cinema and press photographers took their shots of the surging masses through whom mounted police tried in vain to force an avenue for the procession. Glass windows crashed as the weight of the crowd was thrust against shop fronts; the temper of the police began to rise and they used their batons freely. I sought a telephone box. There was a man using the 'phone and three men and a woman were waiting. I did not want to delay and pulled open the door urgently. "I want to get through to the Home Secretary to tell him to stop Mosley coming further," I said. The man put down the receiver immediately and the waiting group crowded into the open door. It was Sunday afternoon and Sir John Simon was not at the Home Office, but I appeared to impress the First Secretary who was left in charge and he promised to telephone my message both to Sir John in the country and to the Commissioner of Police accompanying the procession. I insisted that if the procession were allowed to approach Aldgate there would be bloodshed and that, after this warning, the responsibility would rest with the Home Secretary. Having spoken to the Home Office, I rang up the Press Association and told the news editor what I had done.

I returned to the crowd and in one police rush was knocked over and trampled on a little. By now some among both the police and the people were losing their heads. The crowd was jeering provocatively; sometimes the police used their batons fiercely and with anger in their faces. But this was not the temper of all. I was amused to find myself pressed against a big policeman who remained genial, telling us with smiling face to "pass on now," though neither he nor we could move three inches by our own volition. I heard word passing from mouth to mouth that "Brockway had 'phoned Simon to stop Mosley"—my companions at the telephone box had been busy with their tongues,—and after about an hour rumours began to spread that he had been stopped. When I got the chance I squeezed my way to the telephone box again and got through to the Press Association. "Yes, half-an-hour after your message instructions were given; it's a feather in your cap," said the voice at the other end. I've always doubted whether my message had anything to do with the decision to call off the procession, but round the world the press stories went reporting the two news items in succession and even from America I had messages of congratulation.

Despite these clashes on the streets, the I.L.P. and the British Union of Fascists had not passed the stage of debating their respective policies on the platform. I debated with Mosley's first lieutenant, William Joyce,* before the students of Aberdeen University. I am humiliated to say that on the vote I lost the debate; I hope this was due to the confirmed reactionary attitude of the Aberdeen students rather than to the merits of our respective cases, though Joyce's indictment of the inequalities of Capitalism might have been uttered by any Socialist. British Fascism was in the stage of social demagogy which characterised the early days of Nazism. After the debate we both accompanied our supporters to a students' ball, but Joyce didn't dance. The only moment when he rose to his feet was when "the King" was played at the end. Then he sprang to the salute dramatically and stood rigid, hand to head, looking like

---

* Early in 1940 Joyce was identified as "Lord Haw Haw." He left London for Berlin just before the outbreak of war.

an executioner in his black uniform, until the last note had died away.

Working-class unity remained a desired end despite all our disappointments in seeking it. Among the general body of workers the urge for unity was wide and deep. There seemed no hope of removing the National Government so long as division continued. But the difficulty was that our divergences of policy with both the Labour and Communist Parties were increasing rather than decreasing. They spoke of "peace" but, according to our analysis, they were making directly for war. At a May Day demonstration in Hyde Park I spoke from the same platform as Harry Pollitt. His speech horrified me; it was a repetition of the anti-Germanism of the war of 1914-18. In domestic policy the breach between the Labour Party and the I.L.P. was growing. Whilst we had reached the view that the change to Socialism involved a decisive struggle for the overthrow of capitalist domination, replacing it by workers' control of industry and a refashioned Workers' State, the Labour Party was declaring with growing emphasis that the progress to Socialism must take place through the extension of public corporations, which would guarantee the dividends of the investing class and maintain the subordinate status of the workers as mere wage earners. We regarded these corporations as potentially fascist rather than socialist.

Nevertheless, the tendency grew in the I.L.P. to reconsider its relationship with the Labour Party. I expressed the view that no issue of principle was involved in the question of re-affiliation; it was a matter of tactics. We left the Labour Party because we had not freedom within it to defend the interests of the workers and to express our socialist policy; once we were confident that the necessary freedom could be secured, our place would be inside the Labour Party, however much we differed from its policy. My mind began to go further than this; I reached the view that some sacrifice of freedom was justified in order to function within the mass political movement of the workers. After all, we held our principles not to satisfy ourselves by self-righteous purism, but to gain their acceptance by the working-class, and it was important to be operating where such acceptance could be gained.

A further consideration influenced me. When the I.L.P. was in the Labour Party it had no fundamental philosophy or policy and could not act with united purpose; but during its period outside it had developed a revolutionary socialist basis and its personnel, although smaller in numbers, had become vastly improved in dependable quality; the I.L.P. of 1938 was very different from the mixture of reformism, sentiment, utopianism and awakening revolutionism which characterised the I.L.P. of 1932. This being so, was there not a great deal to be said for entering the Labour Party as a disciplined unit, regarding it not as a socialist party with a policy which commanded our consent, but as the class party of the workers and therefore the right and most fruitful field of activity?

These issues were strongly debated in our Party during 1938 and 1939. Though this is not generally known, the initiative in seeking negotiations was actually taken from the Labour Party side; Stafford Cripps approached Maxton and told him that he had the authority of Attlee, the leader of the Parliamentary Party, and George Dallas, Chairman of the Labour Party Executive, for the encouragement of discussions. Following this, the 1938 I.L.P. Conference gave the National Council of the Party instructions to commence exploratory talks, and a deputation consisting of James Maxton, John McGovern, Campbell Stephen, John Aplin (our London representative) and myself were appointed to conduct the conversations. The Labour Party took our approach seriously and asked us to meet the whole Executive. We did so in one of the Committee Rooms of the House of Commons.

It was interesting to find that the majority of the Labour Party Executive were clearly desirous, despite differences of policy, for the I.L.P. to re-affiliate. Only once was the issue of policy raised and only one member, J. Walker, expressed opposition in principle to I.L.P. affiliation. This discussion was only preliminary, but it had a considerable effect. Many members of our Party had held that the Labour Party "would not have the I.L.P. back at any price"; this had been proved a wrong judgment.

The 1939 Conference of the I.L.P. authorised the National Council to continue negotiations on the basis of *conditional affiliation*, but except for a conversation between James

Middleton, the Labour Party Secretary, and myself, no more meetings took place. Middleton gave me the interesting information that only four members of the Labour Party Executive had voted against I.L.P. affiliation in principle; sixteen had voted in favour. Letters were exchanged which did little more than confirm the position that we could re-affiliate on the 1931 conditions, that is, the I.L.P. could continue as an organisational unit, with its own branches, conferences, press and propaganda, and its M.P.s would be allowed to express I.L.P. policy by speech in the House of Commons. The one limitation was that our M.P.s would not be permitted to vote against the Labour Party.*

By a narrow majority the National Council of the I.L.P. decided to recommend affiliation on this basis. Two of the three I.L.P. M.P.s—McGovern and Stephen—held this view, and Maxton became reconciled to it for the Party, though he did not accept it personally. It also had the backing of younger members of the Council, like Will Ballantine (a member of the N.U.R. Executive), who had become converted to it, and Bob Edwards, of Lancashire, who had ably advocated it over a long period. The opposition was, however, formidable, including Dr. C. A. Smith, the new chairman of the Party, and F. W. Jowett, the treasurer. We called a special Conference for September to discuss the matter.

The September Conference was never held. War broke out, and with the Labour Party supporting the war and entering an electoral truce with the National Government, affiliation was—temporarily, at least—out of the question.

*The Standing Orders of the Parliamentary Labour Party which imposed this restriction were in 1946 suspended for two years.

Chapter Twenty-Eight
TOURS ABROAD: A CAMPAIGN AGAINST HITLER

It is time I went back to international activities, which remained prominent in my life despite the break from the Second International in 1932. Even before this break, the I.L.P. took the initiative in drawing together the Left Socialist sections of Europe, whether they belonged to the "Second" or not. I remember as though it were yesterday the journey I made with James Maxton and Campbell Stephen to Holland in the summer of 1930 with the object of establishing close relations with the Norwegian Labour Party, the Bund (Poland), the Left in the Dutch Social Democratic Party, and the Polish I.L.P.* It is typical of the changes which have taken place in the working-class movement that the two former, which were unaffiliated to the Second International in 1930, now belong to it, whilst the two latter, affiliated in 1930, broke from it two or three years later.

Our meeting was at a summer school of the Dutch Left, held in a castle-like mansion with large grounds surrounding it. Under the leadership of Peter Schmidt (he had been politically trained in the I.L.P. whilst serving as London correspondent of a Dutch paper during the War) the opponents of the official Social Democratic policy had formed themselves into an organised group with their own paper and their own discussion meetings. Peter was a young hatchet-faced man of forceful personality and popular as a speaker. He had won the allegiance of considerable sections of the Party, particularly of the youth.

The Norwegian Labour Party was represented at this meeting by Finn Moe, its International Secretary, a quiet, kindly but not dynamic personality. The Norwegian Party had been an early member of the Communist International, breaking from it as early as 1923 after flatly refusing to obey orders from Moscow. Radek once remarked that the Norwegian Party had entered the Communist International on a false passport, and

---

* I have another reason for remembering this journey. I returned alone, after taking meetings in Germany, via Ostend. At the pier there were three telegrams addressed to Maxton, which I opened as I knew he was returning by another route. They reported the illness and then the death of John Wheatley.

it is probably true that the Party never accepted Communist
fundamentals. The Bund of Poland was represented by its
Chairman, Ehrlich, whom I have already described. Like the
Norwegian Labour Party, it was big and influential, and in
addition it had a good revolutionary record. I don't think
Josef Kruk, of the Polish I.L.P., was at this meeting, but his
little party identified itself with the new international grouping
immediately.

For tactical reasons we did not set up a formal committee
(it would have led to disciplinary action by the Second International against the I.L.P. and by the Dutch Social Democrats
against their Left), but we signed a joint manifesto. Reading
it now, after many years, I am surprised to find what a good
document it was; it did not state the full revolutionary position
but the essentials were there. Among other things it declared
against coalitions with capitalist parties, denounced the League
of Nations as a capitalist-imperialist institution fostering
illusions, urged opposition to armaments expenditure by
capitalist governments, and advocated revolutionary action
against Fascism and War. Its international economic policy
was an adaptation of the "Socialism in Our Time" programme
of the I.L.P., about which the Norwegian Labour Party was
specially enthusiastic. This statement was circulated throughout the world and we got responses which enabled us to call a
much more representative meeting at the time of the Second
International conference at Vienna in 1931. Among those
present on this occasion were delegates from the Left of the
German Social Democratic Party, who already recognised that
a break with their party was inevitable. A few months later
they were expelled for opposition to the Brüning Coalition and
established the German Socialist Workers' Party.

By the following year the I.L.P., the German Socialist
Workers' Party and the Left in the Dutch S.D.P. were all outside the Second International. The way was therefore open for
a formal organisation, which became known as the International
Committee of Independent Revolutionary Socialist Parties.
The Norwegian Labour Party, the Bund and the Polish I.L.P.
continued their association with us, and we had a valuable
recruit in the Maximalist section of the Italian Socialist Party,
the majority within the party when it split on the question of

entering the Second International. A small addition was the French Party of Proletarian Unity, which, owing to the fortunes of proportional representation, had a group of ten members in the Chamber of Deputies. John Paton became secretary of the International Committee and I its chairman.

There was no thought of forming a new International. In the early days of the Committee the hope was still retained by most of us that it would be possible to unite the Second and Third Internationals and to bring in the workers' and peasants' movements of the colonies, giving the all-inclusive International a revolutionary content; but with the increasing tendencies in both Internationals to become less revolutionary this hope disappeared though we favoured united action on specific issues. The organisational aim of the Committee then became the co-ordination of the activities of all revolutionary sections in preparation for the historic moment when it would be practical to form a united Revolutionary International.

My duties as chairman took me on interesting visits to various parts of Europe. In 1931, accompanied by Marguerite Louis, I went to both Poland and Germany. I had a tumultuous reception at the headquarters of the Polish I.L.P. in Warsaw and addressed a huge joint demonstration of the Bund and the I.L.P. It was fiercely interrupted by Communists and there were wild scenes of fighting. I had not before seen such political ferocity. A surprising incident, which led to our being placed temporarily under arrest, followed this meeting. The Bund had arranged a reception at a large restaurant; several hundreds came, and after tea Ehrlich made a little speech and I rose to reply. I had hardly begun, however, when the military entered and an officer announced that everyone present was under arrest and must not leave the restaurant until permission was given. Ehrlich took me to await events in a small side room. We found military police on guard in the passage and the building was surrounded. Our comrades warned us that we might be prisoners for an hour or so, but need not fear more inconvenience than that. They turned out to be right. The trouble had arisen because there is a law in Poland that the authorities must be informed of all meetings. Regarding the occasion as private, the Bund had not given notice of the reception, but our voices when speaking had been heard through the windows, information had been 'phoned to the authorities, and within a few minutes a force had been despatched.

My Warsaw programme included a lecture at the University, where my audience, I was told, included "the cream of the bourgeois intellectuals of Warsaw." On Josef Kruk's advice I paid a formal visit to the British Ambassador, who warned me to refrain from touching on the "minorities" question; some Labour M.P. had recently offended. Thinking of the masses of the poor, I told him that I intended to speak only on the "majority" question, which left him puzzled. Josef also took me to see the Soviet Ambassador, Antonov Ovseenko, afterwards the Russian representative in Spain, where my friends and I came severely under his displeasure.* But on this afternoon in Warsaw he was very friendly, welcoming us as comrades without any formality, in great contrast to the severely official attitude of the British Ambassador.

I had to hurry back to Germany for an important tour of meetings, and visited only one other town in Poland, Czenstochowo. Here I had a big surprise—across the I.L.P. headquarters, which served both as a political centre and a workers' school, there was bold lettering and I was told it read "Fenner Brockway Institute." Among the local members I found a knowledge of British politics and an enthusiasm for our I.L.P. which astonished me.† The military police here made some trouble at a large public meeting. During the afternoon two officers visited us, examining our passports and cross-examining me closely about my politics; I doubt whether they would have allowed me to speak had I not been an M.P. The presence of military at the meeting did not disturb me; they had been present at all the meetings; but when Josef interpreted my speech, a reference to Soviet Russia immediately brought the officer to his feet and in a loud peremptory voice he ordered Josef not to refer to the subject again. "That is the only reference the speaker made," smiled Josef, and continued the interpretation, the audience listening excitedly. He

* Unless I am mistaken, he was, despite his service to Stalin in Barcelona, a subsequent victim of the "purge."

† I wonder what has happened to those good comrades and their Institute now, for Czenstochowo was one of the cities to suffer most severely from the German invasion in September, 1939.

began to translate a passage advocating strike action against war. The officer rose again and ordered the meeting to be stopped. The audience began to shout in angry protest and the military police sprang into line; it looked as though an ugly situation would arise. But Josef was accustomed to such difficulties. His hand went up and, having secured silence, he called for cheers for the British I.L.P. and me. They were given passionately and, their feelings relieved, Josef asked the people to disperse.

The propaganda tour which followed in Germany had been arranged with our comrades of the Left who were then still in the Social Democratic Party. It was during the period when the struggle with Hitler was speeding to a crisis. I was held up in Weimar, where Hitler was to review his forces and address a demonstration. The larger houses and shops were decorated with vast swastika banners covering their entire frontages, waggon load after waggon load of uniformed Storm Troopers arrived, shouting "Heil Hitler" and giving the Nazi salute, huge crowds cheered them excitedly, on the square the Storm Troopers fell into military formation and marched and turned under orders with army precision. This experience filled me with foreboding. I realised then that Hitler would make a bid for power at all costs, not excluding civil war.

But I also saw the other side of the picture. My first engagement was at Breslau, near the Polish frontier; here the Left was in entire control of the Social Democratic Party and one got the impression of its mass strength. My visit coincided with the commemoration of the anniversary of the death of Ferdinand Lassalle; it was a wonderful demonstration. A long procession marched from the centre of the town to the cemetery, red flags flying, bands playing the music of Beethoven. At the cemetery itself two flags were dipped over the grave, whilst the huge crowd stood with bared heads and lowered flags between the white tombstones as far as the eye could see. I was asked to deliver the funeral oration; it was the first time in the sixty-seven years of the ceremony that a non-German had spoken. I felt the situation a little incongruous because, with all that there was to admire in Lassalle, he was a nationalist; but his romantic spirit of adventure (it brought his life to an end in a duel at thirty-nine), his insistence on liberty, and his refusal to bow to the dictates and conventions of authority had always attracted me and it was to these qualities I referred—they were not inappropriate to the struggle against Fascism. The translation finished, the scarlet flags over the grave were lifted, a forest of red banners rose between the tombstones, the band struck the opening notes of "the Internationale" and thousands of voices took it up to the distance of the cemetery gates.

In the evening I spoke to a huge demonstration of thousands more in the People's Hall. Eckstein, the loved leader of the Socialists of Breslau, presided. At his request I delivered a frank policy speech, criticising the Social Democrats for their compromising coalition with the undependable Liberals, criticising the Communists for their splitting "social-fascist" tactics, and appealing for workers' unity behind a challenging socialist offensive as the only method by which the Nazis could be defeated. When the speech was translated its concluding appeal received an ovation. It was clear that the Breslau Socialists were waiting for a lead against the Nazis on a united and militant working-class basis.

A little more than a year later Eckstein was dead, one of the first victims of the Nazi terror. He was put on an open lorry and conveyed through the same streets where our socialist procession had marched, an object of vicious hatred, both as a Socialist and a Jew, to the Nazi crowds who lined the pavements jeering and reviling. Within a week a report was issued that Eckstein had committed suicide in a concentration camp. I did not believe it. Eckstein was not the man to take his own life while breath gave hope that some day, somehow, an opportunity might come to renew the struggle. We remembered his name by attaching it to the Fund which the I.L.P. and other revolutionary socialist parties raised to assist the underground work in Germany.

From Breslau I went to Thuringia, another stronghold of the Left. Here the meetings had a different atmosphere, though they were crowded and determined. Like their brothers in Lancashire, the textile operatives of Thuringia were more stolid. I remember being disappointed by one meeting and, until my actual parting from him, I was perplexed by the mask-like reserve which remained on the face even of the comrade at whose cottage we had tea afterwards. As we left he held my hand in a grip and looked straight into my eyes. "Thank you, comrade," he said. "We shall all remember this meeting when the struggle comes. It has put new heart into us." There was a depth of emotion under his words which I knew reflected unbreakable resolution. I do not know where that comrade is, but I would be prepared to swear that, with all the terror of Hitler, he never gave in.

At most of these meetings elaborate precautions were taken to guard against attacks by Hitler's drilled thugs. Socialist Youth, in bright blue shirts and spreading red ties, were massed at the doors, stood every few yards down the gangways, and acted as a bodyguard on the platform. At a demonstration in the suburbs of Leipzig the Brownshirts attacked us in force, but the Socialist Youth beat them off after a fierce fight. At the end of the meeting we left the hall in tight groups, because the Brownshirts were given to assaulting isolated "Reds" in the dark.

My final meeting was in Berlin, announced under the auspices of the Youth Section of the S.D.P. About this a crisis arose. Although I was still a member of the Executive of the Second International to which the S.D.P. was affiliated, the leadership prohibited the Youth Section from holding the meeting and the League for Human Rights took it over. Ernst Toller presided, but the translation was still made by Dora Fabian, secretary of the Youth Section; for this she was expelled from the Social Democratic Party. I had met Dora on an earlier visit to Berlin, and she had translated my book on India into German. I remained friendly with her until her tragic death as a refugee in London. To that I refer later.

In 1933 I visited Scandinavia, with the object of coming to an understanding with the Norwegian Labour Party, whose association with us was weakening, and of securing the affiliation of the Swedish Socialist Party. I travelled from Brussels through Germany, the one time I have been in Germany since Hitler's triumph. I wondered whether I should be detected, but I got through all right, leaving the train only at Hamburg, where I crossed the road from the station and sat for an hour in a café, trying to realise the change under a surface which appeared much the same, thinking of my many comrades in concentration camps, thinking of brave comrades in this very city who were carrying on with the underground work.

I liked both Oslo and Stockholm. With Tranmael, the Norwegian Labour leader, I sat on the front, overlooking the bay with its delightful islands, and talked about international working-class politics for two hours. Then we went by the funicular railway up the mountainside and in a restaurant overlooking the town, the wooded valleys and the sea, we discussed international relations in detail. Most of the men who took part in that discussion are now in the Norwegian Government; they had departed far from the revolutionary position then and have departed still further now, but I found they were honestly trying to work out realistically what was best for the cause of Socialism in Norway.* Two questions were dominant in their minds: the need to win the peasants and the need to act in common with the Labour Movements in Sweden and Denmark, both of which were Social Democratic and in the Second International. This discussion made it clear that the Norwegian Party was lost to our Centre, but nevertheless I was invited to address a great demonstration and was encouraged freely to express my view.

At Stockholm my task was easier. The Socialist Party had also been in the Communist International, but on leaving it had not joined the Social Democrats. It remained a Party of considerable strength, with its own printing press and daily paper and with eight members in the Lower chamber and even one in the Upper House. I met its executive in a Committee Room of the Houses of Parliament and the decision to affiliate with our International Centre was taken. An amusing incident occurred on this occasion. I missed my way in the passages and found myself lost among the private rooms of the Cabinet Ministers. A door opened and the Prime Minister, Mr. Hannsen, came out. We had been members of the Second International Executive together and he recognised me at once and greeted me cordially. "Are you ready for a reformist to show you the way?" he laughed, as he directed me down the correct corridor.

*I am correcting this MS. in April, 1940, the month of the temporary Nazi destruction of Norway's Socialist hopes.

K

Chapter Twenty-Nine
EUROPE'S REVOLUTIONARY LEADERS

Except for one year, the secretariat of our International Committee remained with the I.L.P. for eight years. The Committee had various changes of name but was known generally as the London Bureau. It influence extended steadily. We developed contacts in twenty countries, including India and the colonies, and made affiliations in Sweden, Holland, France, Spain, Italy, Germany, Austria, Czecho-slovakia, Greece, the U.S.A., and Palestine. The name finally selected was the International Revolutionary Marxist Centre. Its adoption marked the transference of the headquarters to Paris in 1939 and the affiliation of two new and important sections: the French Socialist Party of Workers and Peasants (a breakaway under Marceau Pivert from the Socialist Party) and the Independent Labour League of America (previously the majority in the Communist Party, expelled with Jay Lovestone for resisting the formation of the so-called "Red Unions"). We chose Paris as the headquarters because, in addition to the French P.S.O.P., five of the refugee parties had their central committees there. Julian Gorkin, of the Spanish P.O.U.M., became secretary, but I remained chairman.

When I compare the personalities of our International Centre with those of the Second International, there can be no doubt where the more heroic characters are. These revolutionary leaders are of a stuff different from the politicians of the Social Democratic Parties; they are revolutionaries not as a matter of theory but in their lives, their thoughts, habits, interests, the things they like and dislike. Many of them have gone through revolutionary experiences, the fierce struggles which followed the last war, repressions, imprisonments, escapes, exile, desperate poverty. They have sacrificed everything. With many Socialists one feels that while they desire a better society, they belong to the present society. But these men and women are strangers in the capitalist order; their whole loyalty is to the new order and to the struggle to establish it.

I think of Angelica Balabanoff, of the Italian Party. She was born an aristocratic Russian, but, a convert to Socialism, turned her back on all her past. She has directed her whole life by the question: "Where and how can I serve Socialism best?" Exiled from Russia, she went to Italy. If there is one thing which she regrets, it is probably her part in bringing Mussolini into the Party, but it was characteristic of her. She was speaking to a group of Italian socialist exiles across the Swiss frontier; in the audience was a hungry, ill-clad, distraught lad. Angelica picked him out, saw that he was clothed and fed, taught him Socialism, trained him to speak and write. Proudly she saw him progress, until he became a skilled orator, an editor of the Party paper, secretary of the Party. That lad was Benito Mussolini. Since Mussolini's triumph she has been an exile, but I've never felt that Angelica had the sense of frustration from which many refugees suffer. She has a knowledge of six languages and still she went wherever the struggle was in its most urgent stages; to Vienna, Prague, Berlin, Barcelona, or New York. Her comrades collected the fare and she travelled "hard"; once she had made contact with the comrades, she lived "hard" until the struggle was over. She must have been in her sixties when she acted as interpreter at some of our conferences, but she went on until the early hours of the morning, translating into French, German, Italian, or English, as required.

Angelica had a personality all her own, but this trait of living entirely for the social revolution was characteristic of nearly all my international comrades. Four of the most interesting were famous for their part in the Communist struggles in Germany after the war: Brandler, Thalheimer, Froelich and Walscher. Heinrich Brandler always reminded me of Lon Chaney's impersonation of the dwarf of Notre Dame. An accident when an infant has left him hunch-backed and hugely broad of shoulder, but from his stunted body rises a head of extraordinary strength in shape and feature, while the muscles of his arms and hands are like cords of steel. During most discussions he sits quiet and brooding, often cynical and contemptuous, because his judgments are rigid and harsh; but suddenly he speaks and then his passion is volcanic. He shouts fierce phrases; his face grows red and his veins swell; his giant arms bring his closed fists crashing on the table. One understands the dynamic force with which Brandler led the revolutionary struggle at Chemnitz after the war.*

Thalheimer was Brandler's constant companion in the German struggle; he is the theoretician, whilst Brandler is the man of action. The two provide a complete contrast. Thalheimer looks like a university professor or doctor; tall, distinguished, silver-haired, well-dressed, cultured, courteous. He was one of the authors of the first thesis of the Communist International, and his utterances are still theses—clear analyses and statements of principle, but often unrelated to the facts and forces of reality. Paul Froelich is again a different man. I should rank him above Thalheimer as thinker and scholar, and he has a generosity and tolerance of mind and a sincerity of comradeship which win affection as well as respect. He was one of the first editors of the Communist daily paper in Germany.

These three men had all been prominent figures in the German Communist Party. Lenin selected Brandler as Party leader after his masterly handling of the Chemnitz revolution in 1920, when, having won power for the Soviet, he had the wisdom to retreat rather than invite suppression in isolation. Later, Brandler was not so wise: with Thalheimer and Froelich he was one of the leaders of the ill-fated rising of 1921. When they reacted from this disaster to a policy of caution and moderation, they were joined in the leadership by Jacob Walscher. Jacob is a workman and looks and speaks like one. He has none of the refinements of Thalheimer or Froelich, but commonsense is added to his tempestuous personality, and, if at our international committees he shouted at us sometimes at great length, his policy generally tended towards compromise.

When the German Communist Party took the "ultra-Left" turn of splitting the Trade Union Movement by forming Red Unions and of denouncing the Social Democrats as "Social-Fascists," all these four leaders opposed the policy and were thrown out of the Party. Brandler and Thalheimer formed the Communist Opposition (known generally as the "Right Opposition"). Froelich and Walscher joined the German Socialist

* Brandler was interned by the French Government when war broke out. When the Germans entered Paris he was ill in hospital and could not escape. Later he got to Cuba with Thalheimer. Froelich and Walscher reached America.

Workers' Party, formed by the split of the Left from the Social Democrats which I have described. I was present in Berlin at one of the first conferences of the German S.A.P. (the Socialist Workers' Party was known by its German initials) and was struck by its similarity to the I.L.P. when we left the Labour Party. Some were pacifists, some Utopian Socialists, some revolutionaries,—and it took some time for revolutionaries of the Froelich-Walscher school to gain the leadership. Meanwhile, however, the S.A.P. did good work in attempting to form Workers' Councils to unite all working-class forces despite the bitter conflict between the Social Democrat and Communist leaderships. Had this policy been generally accepted, Hitler might never have won. The S.A.P. joined our international committee from the beginning; the Right Communist Opposition never in fact did so—Brandler and Thalheimer participated in our enlarged committee and in our international conferences, but they were too rigid ever to consent to affiliation. There was intense bitterness between the S.A.P. and the Communist Opposition and in turn I came into political conflict with both.

The conflict with the S.A.P. was on the Popular Front. Our International Committee took from the first an uncompromising line against it. We regarded a long-term and limiting alliance with the Liberal capitalist organisations as requiring inevitably the surrender of the class struggle. The S.A.P. differed; it entered a German Popular Front Committee with the Social Democrats and Liberals, it supported the French Popular Front in its early stages, and it gave considerable backing to the Spanish Popular Front. Its theory was not identical with that of the Communist Party; it held that the Popular Front tactic should be used up to the point where it would intensify rather than modify the class struggle. After long committee and conference discussions, the S.A.P. finally broke from us on this issue.

Our conflict with the Right Communist Opposition arose on the issue of Party relationships. Although Brandler and Thalheimer had left the Communist Party, they still believed in C.P. methods, they still had the C.P. psychology. In fact, until 1937 or 1938 they still placed all their hope in the Communist International: they regarded themselves as only temporary exiles from it. When they began to associate with our international committee they schemed to form groups inside the other parties to secure support for their policies. They sat at the table with I.L.P. representatives in Paris, but in London and Manchester they had their representatives intriguing to split the Party. This issue reached a crisis at a meeting when we were developing the old commitee into the larger International Revolutionary Marxist Centre. I was in the chair and intended to speak judiciously, but Thalheimer's attitude angered me beyond restraint. He claimed that the Communist Opposition was a fully developed revolutionary organisation; the others were not: the C.O. had the right, therefore, to conduct group activity within the other parties until they were as fully developed as itself. The arrogance of this utterance led me to deliver the most savagely ironic speech I have made. I acknowledged that the I.L.P. was not a fully developed revolutionary party, but, nevertheless, on the big isssues of recent years it had proved right and the C.O. wrong. I reminded Thalheimer of a discussion I had had with him in Paris five years previously, when he had defended the turn in the foreign policy of Soviet Russia and the I.L.P. had opposed it. Which of us had proved right? I reminded him of the attitude of the two Parties to the first Moscow trials. The C.O. had defended them: the I.L.P. had criticised. Which of us had been right? I reminded him of C.O. faith in the Communist International and of the I.L.P. realisation that a new revolutionary instrument must be developed. Which had proved correct? On all these issues the C.O. had come round to the I.L.P. view. Where then lay its claim of revolutionary perfection entitling it to interfere in the inner life of other parties?

The extended Centre was established without either the S.A.P. or the C.O., but this did not mean that we were without German affiliations. The Neue Weg (the Opposition in the S.A.P.) and other sections with groups in many towns in Germany and Austria joined us. As a matter of fact, our contact with the underground activities against Nazism increased rather than diminished.

I should like to dwell on the personalities of the other members of our Committee; they are all so well worth knowing as socialist comrades. Mariani, the Italian, black-haired and black-eyed, passionate in nature and speech, but the most loyal, dependable comrade one could ever wish to have; Witte, previously one of the leaders of the Greek Communist Party, quiet and thoughtful; Marceau Pivert, leader of the French P.S.O.P., the school-master type, growing towards the revolutionary position, a man of character and friendly sincerity—these are typical in their devotion to the cause of the social revolution. But I cannot do more than mention them; they would be the first to expect me to devote space to another—Joaquim Maurin, leader of the Spanish P.O.U.M.

Maurin attended only one meeting of our Committee, in May, 1936, but he made a deep impression on me. You would not have picked him out at first as a leader: he looked a quiet, thoughtful young man, overshadowed by the more irrepressible personalities about him. But whenever Maurin spoke his power was evident: he was clear, decisive and convincing. His description of the situation in Spain was one of the most masterly analyses I have ever heard.* Less than six weeks later the storm which he saw coming broke. As it developed I was again and again surprised by the accuracy of Maurin's estimate of forces and personalities; this speech gave me an insight into men and movements which continually clarified what otherwise would have seemed a hopelessly confused situation.

Maurin was M.P. for Barcelona—the one member of the P.O.U.M. in the Cortes — and was known as "The Lenin of Catalonia." He had been a leader of the C.N.T., the huge syndicalist organisation, and had gone to Moscow to negotiate on its behalf. He had become a Marxist, had joined the Communist Party, had broken with Moscow and formed the Spanish Workers' and Peasants' Party. Later he joined forces with Andres Nin, the Trotskyist leader, in establishing the Workers' Party of Marxist Unity. It had considerable mass support in Barcelona and Catalonia, opposing both the non-political tendencies of the Anarchists and the compromising reformism of the Social Democrats. It was far stronger than the Communist Party. When in July the Franco revolt took place, my fear for Maurin was great because I knew he was on a temporary visit to a reactionary part of Spain. News came of

* Maurin's best-known book is "Revolution and Counter-Revolution in Spain."

his arrest, and then in September the "Times" reported that the Fascists had shot him: I never regretted the loss of a political comrade more. The I.L.P. equipped a motor ambulance in his memory: I named it the "Joaquim Maurin Ambulance" before it started its long drive from Clapham across France to Barcelona. Then rumours began to reach us that Maurin was alive; in Barcelona the people refused to believe their leader was dead. I dismissed this as a myth based on the hero-worship which Maurin's character and leadership aroused.

At the I.L.P. Summer School in August, 1937, Maurin's wife, Jeanne, was one of the lecturers. I had got to know her well; she represented the P.O.U.M. on our international committee and I used to stay with her on my visits to Paris. She had a good political mind and her Summer School lecture reminded me of Joaquim's gift for analysis. After the lecture she called me to her room and put a letter in my hand. *It was from Joaquim!* Only John McNair and I were let into the secret. Joaquim was a prisoner in Franco's hands, but he had disguised himself, had given another name, and was unrecognised. To Jeanne he sent his monthly prison letter, addressed to her by her maiden name, but she did not dare tell a soul: if information spread that Joaquim was alive, Franco would certainly make a search of his prisons until he was found. McNair and I locked the good news in our minds.

But later it came out. Maurin escaped from the prison, was caught as he tried to cross the fascist line on the Aragon Front, was recognised and handed over to the military. When we heard this we gave up hope, but Joaquim was not shot; he has been in a Franco prison ever since. As I write this chapter, news comes that he is to be put on trial for his political activities *before* the Franco rising. The sentence may be long imprisonment; it may be death. We are trying to move heaven and earth to secure his liberation, but I cannot be optimistic. Nevertheless, one hopes.*

So far I have described some of the European and American associations of our Centre. Unlike the Second International its scope went beyond these; it laid emphasis on the importance of

---

* In February, 1941, the Press reported that Maurin had been sentenced to loss of civil rights for 15 years, the confiscation of his property (that would not worry him) and deportation. I cabled him immediately, but no reply came and the latest news, April, 1942, was that he is still in prison.

activity in the colonial territories. It had close relations with the British and French Centres against Imperialism, and both at its enlarged committees and conferences representatives of the colonial workers were with us and planned common action. One of the most difficult questions was Palestine.* To most problems one can apply general principles, but to Palestine—no. By no other question have I been so puzzled; on no other question have I so allowed facts and influences to surround me, examining them quietly, weighing and estimating them before reaching a conclusion. I found nearly everyone divided into opposite camps. The Second International, for example, identified itself completely with the Jewish Labour Movement and its Zionist aims; the British and French Centres against Imperialism identified themselves with the Nationalist movement of the Arabs. Two Jewish workers' organisations were associated with our Centre: the Palestine Workers' Party, which was affiliated, and the Hashomair Hatzair, which sent representatives to our Enlarged Committee. On the invitation of the former, the I.L.P. sent John McGovern, M.P., and Campbell Stephen, M.P., as a deputation to Palestine. McGovern had an open mind when they left; Stephen was anti-Zionist. They came back pro-Zionists. One fact which influenced them was the high development of Labour organisation among the Jewish workers compared with the absence of any real organisation among the Arab workers and peasants. The Jewish workers have their Trade Unions, their Co-operative Societies, their Agricultural Communes; the Arab masses are almost entirely dependent upon their feudal lords. Our delegation came back with the view that the Jewish working-class were the only hope of developing Socialism in the Near East.

I could not accept the McGovern-Stephen view without qualification because I realised that Zionism had been a British imperialist instrument and that behind it were powerful Jewish financial interests. It seemed to me we had to find a policy which recognised the contribution of the Jewish workers towards

---

* I have told how I became involved in this issue during my visit to America; when I returned I began to study it more thoroughly. Among the people I saw was Dr. Weizmann, the Zionist leader, who had a meal with me at the House of Commons. I was rather terrified by him; never have I met a man with sharper brain or more directness of purpose. In appearance he was startlingly like Lenin—broad forehead, axe-like jaws, pointed beard.

the socialisation of the Near East, but which also encouraged Arab resistance to British Imperialism and which aimed at the establishment of an Arab-Jewish Workers' State, independent of Britain and the forerunner of a federation of Workers' States in the Arab territories. I prepared a policy statement on these lines which was endorsed by the I.L.P. by a majority of our International Centre, by the Palestine Workers' Party and, with certain reservations, by the Hashomair Hatzair; but for a long time it remained a paper policy. I was told again and again by representatives from Palestine that our hopes were unrealisable. Then in 1939 came encouragement.

The physical conflict between Arabs and Jews died down; both peoples felt they had been betrayed by the Government's proposals; there was a new opportunity to direct the agitation of both against British Imperialism rather than against each other. Coincident with this turn of events the Workers' Party sent its secretary, Itz'haki, to London to plan a big drive towards unity. I spent long hours with him working at this scheme in detail; indeed, he became such a familiar figure in my rooms that one particular chair, low enough to allow his plump legs to reach the ground, seems incomplete without him now, with his smiling face and curly-crowned head.*

Of all the men who came from the Near East, Itz'haki had the greatest sweep of constructive imagination. Beginning with a movement for Arab-Jewish unity in Palestine, he wished to go on to build a Socialist Federation for all the Near Eastern countries and to extend it later to India. His conceptions were expressed in practical terms; he wanted first to form a strong committee in Britain to stimulate unity; second, to initiate an organised movement in Palestine; third, to win the help of the British Trade Union movement in developing interracial Unions in Palestine, Turkey, Persia, Iraq and Syria; and then, when this series of steps had been taken, to call a conference of the workers' organisations in the Near East with a fraternal delegation present from India. Systematically we set about realising this plan.

---

* Itz'haki returned to Palestine in December, 1939, and after his third speech was arrested for anti-imperialist and anti-militarist utterances. He was not tried but was informed that he would be detained for six months. He was liberated in April, 1940, after much pressure on Mr. Malcolm MacDonald, the then Colonial Secretary, by the I.L.P. Group.

We set up a strong British Committee for Jewish-Arab Socialist Unity, including Sir P. Chalmers Mitchell, Mr. H. W. Nevinson, Mr. D. N. Pritt, M.P., and Lord Faringdon, besides our M.P.s and Dr. C. A. Smith, the successor to Maxton as chairman of the I.L.P. Its manifesto secured wide publicity, not only in Palestine, but throughout the world.* Our Party in Palestine succeeded in forming similar Unity Committees there, with the participation of Jewish and Arab intellectuals in addition to workers' representatives. To further the scheme for inter-racial Trade Unions Itz'haki saw the leading Trade Union figures in this country, including representatives of the T.U.C. General Council and the Trade Union Parliamentary Committee. He had an encouraging response and the foundations were laid for the desired development.

And then came the war.

* Mr. Bernard Shaw signed our manifesto, but when I invited him to join our Committee replied "No. Too old. And I won't be a deadhead."

A NOTE ON INITIALS

Before the reader turns to the next two chapters, it may be useful to list the confusing initials of organisations and indicate what they mean:—

P.O.U.M.—Workers' Party of Marxist Unity.   Spanish equivalent of the I.L.P.

C.N.T.—Strongest Trade Union organisation in Catalonia, Spain.   Anarchist ideology.

U.G.T.—Social Democratic Trade Unions in Spain.   Strong outside Catalonia.

F.A.I.—Spanish Anarchists.

P.S.O.P.—Socialist Party of Workers and Peasants.   Equivalent of I.L.P. in France.

O.G.P.U.—Russian Political Intelligence Service.

Chapter Thirty
WAR AND REVOLUTION IN SPAIN

On a Thursday afternoon in June, 1936, my telephone rang just as I was going to lunch. John McNair's voice surprised me. I asked him to join me at the meal.

McNair's history was extraordinary. I had heard of him in the years before the Great War as an active socialist propagandist, but it was not until 1923 that I met him; then he walked into our I.L.P. offices, temporarily housed with the Agricultural Workers' Union headquarters in Gray's Inn Road, and offered his services in any capacity we desired. He had had twelve years as a merchant in Paris, was fed up with it, and the call to return to the Movement was compelling. He had made enough money to be able to offer his services without payment. We gave John a trial. He had a personality which made him a friend of everyone and he proved efficient in the office; within a few weeks we made him Organising Secretary. John worked with us for two years and then a breakdown in health necessitated his return to France. Since then I had seen him several times, either when he was on business trips to London or when I was on political trips to Paris.

Over lunch, this Thursday in June, John told me his one desire was to renew his part in the Movement. The upshot was that within a fortnight he was back at our Head Office. He offered to work at little more than his expenses, and all of us who had known his earlier value jumped at the opportunity. This was a quick-change development for John, but it was only the preliminary to a still more startling change. On July 19th, the Franco revolt broke out in Spain. Our Party—the P.O.U.M.—was in the thick of the struggle and, when we heard from Barcelona how the workers had not only defeated the fascist-led army, but had carried through a social revolution, our members thrilled in response. Early in August McNair left for Barcelona with an instalment of our Spanish Fund; he was the first workers' representative to go with aid from British workers.* Once in Spain, the P.O.U.M. found him so useful that it asked that he should stay. We agreed, because it was also of value to have him there as a representative of our Inter-

---

* It is worth recording that one of the first contributions to our Spanish fund came from engineers in Berlin. They had collected it secretly at their factory.

national Centre. Except for one month, when he returned to Paris and London to organise an international conference, John remained in Spain for nearly a year.

The International Conference was held in Brussels in October. There was a strong Spanish delegation, led by Julian Gorkin. It is pathetic now to look back on the confidence of our Spanish comrades, most of whom were on leave from the Aragon Front. They had won over the army in Barcelona, taken the fascist officers prisoners, driven the enemy a hundred miles from the city. The workers were running everything— industry, transport, agriculture, the army, the police. Two central Workers' Councils had been formed, representing every section—the anarchist C.N.T. (most powerful Trade Union organisation in Catalonia), the U.G.T. (the reformist Trade Unions), the Social Democrats, the P.O.U.M., and the Communists (then weak). The first of these Councils co-ordinated the Workers' Militias of the separate organisations, the second the economic processes; they were the real government controlling the army, industry and agriculture. But the workers' organisations had also entered the Catalan Government on the understanding that they should have a majority, and that the social revolution should be maintained.

Reporting these developments with pride, Gorkin denounced (as we all did) the refusal of Britain and France to allow the Spanish Government to buy arms, and recognised appreciatively the aid from Russia; but he insisted that the Spanish workers would not allow this help to influence their revolution in a Stalinist direction. He acclaimed Barcelona as the new, but different, Moscow. The delegates, representing twelve countries, gave Gorkin and the Spanish comrades an ovation; but already some of us had our doubts. We were apprehensive both about the entry of the workers' representatives into the Coalition Government and about the effect of the Russian aid. On the first point, Gorkin assured us that participation in the Government was a tactic only—it would facilitate continued relations with the Madrid and foreign Governments, and real power would remain with the Workers' Councils. I was not convinced: I foresaw the administrative departments of the State, still bourgeois in outlook and personnel, steadily regaining control.

I was equally certain that Russia would not sell arms to Spain without demanding control of the use of the arms. Russia was already an ally of France and wanted to become an ally of Britain; but the last thing France and Britain wanted in Spain was a social revolution; any sympathy their Governments had for the Spanish Popular Front (and this was very uncertain in the case of Britain) would disappear if Spain went "red." For this reason I was sure that Russia despite its earlier revolutionary tradition, would use its influence to sabotage the revolution in Spain. Already Harry Pollitt had written in the "Daily Worker" that those who said the object was social revolution were enemies of the Republican cause: it was merely the retention of bourgeois democracy. But I recognised the dilemma of our Spanish comrades: they could not afford to reject Russian help—the planes and guns and ammunition were absolutely necessary to defeat Franco, who was being assisted by modern arms from Mussolini and Hitler, and British and French workers had certainly no right to criticise whilst they were unable to compel their Governments to allow arms to be sent. The one hope I saw was in direct action.

We were told at Brussels by Marceau Pivert, leader of the Left in the French Socialist Party (it had not then broken away to form the P.S.O.P.) that considerable direct help was being given by the French workers. From Perpignan, a socialist town on the frontier, large supplies of arms were being smuggled through, and even 'planes had been flown over. In the armament factories the workers had struck for twelve hours behind a demand that the arms they made should go to Spain, and there was a move among the transport workers to take ammunition across the frontier whatever the obstacles. In Britain the problem was more difficult—we had no common frontier with Spain,—but I was attracted by H. N. Brailsford's proposal that the Labour Party and Trade Union representatives should lead a procession of loaded lorries to one of the ports to stimulate a mass agitation for "arms for Spain" throughout the country. At the time of our Brussels Conference, however, this proposal seemed particularly romantic. The British Labour and Trade Union leaders were supporting the National Government's policy of non-intervention.

The mood of confidence among our Spanish comrades was so great that we decided to hold a Congress at Barcelona in the following January, and many of the delegates hoped that the Spanish Revolution would provide the inspiration for a new Revolutionary International just as the Russian Revolution had been the background for the formation of the Communist International. Eager to be in the centre of the struggle, representatives of a number of our Parties had gone to Barcelona. They were constituted into a committee, with Gorkin and McNair as secretaries, to prepare for the World Congress; but it was never held. Soon after we got back from Brussels news came that the Russian diplomatic representative had stated publicly that the price of the Russian sale of arms to Catalonia must be the expulsion of the P.O.U.M. from the administration. The Government reprimanded him for his intervention in internal affairs, but in the end it had to bow to his ultimatum. Andres Nin, Minister of Justice, was asked to resign. I never met Nin, but from John McNair and others I got an intimate impression of his character. He had been leader of the Spanish Trotskyists, but like others he had become disillusioned with Trotsky. Later in Paris I saw a letter from him in which he said "the old man" was proving an "inverted Stalin," adopting Moscow methods in opposition to Moscow. In habits, Nin was the complete revolutionary of the Angelica Balabanoff type, living entirely for the revolution, never thinking of comfort or rest; during my visit to Barcelona his comrades told me how he was so careless about money that when he set out on a tour by car a purse was always handed secretly to the driver to meet his needs. On becoming Minister of Justice he cancelled the old code of law and set up People's Courts of Justice. His new legal code protected life and liberty rather than property and a panel of workmen's representatives acted as judges. John McGovern visited Spain at this time and has described the fairness and democratic atmosphere of these courts, even when trying prisoners suspected of being Fascists.

In Britain, the I.L.P. was conducting a vigorous campaign on behalf of Spain, joining with other organisations in demanding arms and mobilising relief, and, on the initiative of Bob Edwards, sending a contingent to assist in the military struggle.

Our contingent left a few hours before the law making the sending of men illegal came into operation, and we had an exciting rush to get them away, acting all the time under the close surveillance of the police. The Yard even took up quarters on the opposite side of the road to keep us under observation. I rang up the firm and asked to speak to the Inspector. "Our staff is flattered by the attention you're paying us," I said, "and invite you and your men to come and join us for tea this afternoon." The inspector was embarrassed, but fell back on the disciplinary regulations of the force. "We couldn't do that without the permission of the superintendent," he said. So I rang up Whitehall 1212, and asked for the head of the Political Department. He was more taken aback than the inspector, saying at first that he saw no reason why the men shouldn't accept the invitation, and then remembering suddenly that it was time for them to finish duty. I was satisfied—I had got my story. A call to the Press Association brought a reporter and the next morning the whole country was laughing at his account of the incident. We never saw the Yard men again. Whether this was due to Maxton's angry protest to the Home Secretary or to our publicity I do not know.

An effort for Spain with which I was particularly associated was the Spanish Exhibition; I was the chairman of the Committee. Two colleagues in this work were Emma Goldman,* the veteran anarchist leader, and Roland Penrose, the surrealist artist. Penrose went to Spain to collect material for us and did a great deal of designing and preparation of the screens. I liked him immensely: a gentle, friendly person who was sincerely seeking to work out the relationship of art to the revolution. Emma Goldman was very different—a stocky figure like a peasant woman, a face of fierce strength like a female pugilist, a harsh voice, a dominating mind, a ruthless will. But I liked Emma too—she would make tea for me in her rooms with a housewifely care which no hostess could exceed; she was simple and sincere in her comradeship, and like my Paris friends, she was the absolute revolutionary, living for nothing else, entirely fearless and uncompromising. She contributed some beautiful pictures of anarchist schools to our Exhibition. I was associated with Emma, also, in getting

* Emma Goldman died in Toronto in May, 1940.

Spanish C.N.T. films shown in Britain. Of this Film Committee, Ethel Mannin, the novelist, was a member. I had known Ethel for several years and was friendly with her. Maxton first told me of her interest in the I.L.P.—she had been to see him at the House of Commons,—and she was always a Maxton worshipper. I forget where I first met her, but I know I was surprised. I had read her "Confessions and Impressions" and seen her photographs, but she was neither the adolescent Bohemian suggested by the former nor the mystical Madonna suggested by the latter. She was an earnest Socialist, coming from a working-class home, who had been taught Socialism by her father and inspired by the I.L.P. attitude in the war of 1914. She joined the party with active interest when the decision to leave the Labour Party was reached. Despite their differing temperaments, a warm friendship sprang up between Emma Goldman and Ethel Mannin, and Ethel's views came to approximate closely to the anarchist position.

Whilst participating in all the general activities for Spain, we defended the P.O.U.M. against the attacks which were being made on it from Communist, Labour and Liberal quarters. We invited Gorkin to come to England to take part in this campaign and arranged large meetings for him in London and Glasgow. I stayed at the office one Saturday afternoon awaiting a message to indicate where he would arrive. The message came. Julian Gorkin and two Spanish comrades were at Croydon airport—but they were prisoners in the police station and were to be sent back to France by the next 'plane. I got through to Croydon on the 'phone, obtained permission to visit the prisoners, arranged for an interpreter (a teacher of Spanish at one of the Universities) to meet me at Victoria Station and dashed off. We had an hour with Gorkin and his two comrades in the detention room of the police station. One of Gorkin's colleagues was the head of the transport system in Catalonia, a C.N.T. member, placed in charge as a specialist when workers' control had been introduced; his purpose in coming to London was purely technical—nevertheless, he was refused admission. The other comrade was a younger brother of Maurin—so like Joacquim that for a moment I thought it was he. This boy returned to Spain to fight for months at the front; then he was arrested by the Communist secret police and died in prison. It reflected the tragedy of Spain: Joacquim a prisoner in Franco's hands, his brother dying a prisoner in Communist hands. I used the hour to take down from Gorkin's dictation what he had intended to say at our meetings so that his message could be read and published in pamphlet form. The police entered; the returning plane was about to leave. As it moved, our comrades saluted us with the clenched fist from the windows.

My fears of the effects of Russian influence on the revolution in Spain were being fulfilled. The exclusion of the P.O.U.M. from the Catalan Government was followed by a campaign of slander such as I don't think has ever been equalled. The Party was denounced as Franco's "Fifth Column," as fascist agents and spies, as guilty of betrayal at the front by retreating at critical moments of battle. Finally they were charged with a plot to assassinate Largo Caballero, the social democratic Prime Minister, Azana, the President of the Republic, and La Passionaria, the popular woman Communist leader. Six months earlier this campaign would have had no effect, but Russia's aid to Spain had naturally made the U.S.S.R. and the Communist Party tremendously popular among the Spanish masses. In a few weeks the Party sprang from insignificance to powerful strength, particularly among the middle class which was reassured by its insistence that Parliamentary democracy and not social revolution was its aim. Among the masses of workers who loved Maurin, who had known Nin in a hundred struggles, with whom the P.O.U.M. members were comrades in arms, the Communist Party propaganda had little effect, but among those not versed in politics, the daily repetition of calumnies made an impression. As for the Liberal, Social Democratic and Communist journalists in Barcelona, they swallowed the charges eagerly and the pro-Republican press in all parts of the world spread the defamation of the P.O.U.M.

I saw that the scales were weighted too heavily against the P.O.U.M. and in letters to John McNair and talks with Gorkin, whom I met occasionally in Paris, urged that our Spanish comrades must readjust themselves realistically to the situation. John did his utmost to stop the disastrous consequences which we foresaw, though it was with considerable misgiving that the

Executive of the P.O.U.M. gave him permission to approach Communist representatives. On five occasions he met influential Communists, urging that everything must be done to overcome the threatening division of the workers' forces; on each occasion he was promised that his proposals would be taken to the Communist leadership for consideration; on each occasion nothing came of it. In Paris I urged on Gorkin the need to reconsider P.O.U.M. tactics. I had no doubt that the attitude of our Spanish Party was fundamentally correct; I regarded the policy of the Communist Party as a betrayal of the social conquests of the workers; but I saw that all the cards were in its hands. It was urging the disbanding of the Workers' Militias, the formation of a Popular Army on a professional basis, and unity of command. The case for unity of command was overwhelming. This could have been done through the united Workers' Military Council, but the authority of this Council had become less and less and that of the War Department had increased proportionately.

Under these circumstances I took the view that the P.O.U.M. should accept *force majeure* for the moment, not resisting the transference of control to the Popular Front State, but striving to maintain as far as possible workers' control of the factories and transport, peasants' control of the land, and keeping alive in its propaganda the idea of the social revolution as the object accompanying Franco's defeat. Gorkin argued, on the other hand, that the forces opposing the "liquidation" of workers' control were still of potentially decisive strength. In Catalonia the C.N.T. remained the mass organisation of the workers, and, whatever the compromises of their leaders, the rank and file would resist to the death all withdrawals of workers' authority. The duty of the P.O.U.M. was not to compromise or retreat.

Whatever the rights and wrongs of this issue, I doubt whether any modification of policy by the P.O.U.M. would have made any difference; the "Communists" were determined to destroy its organisation and to ruin the reputation of its leaders at all costs. As they became stronger the "liquidation" of the social revolution was speeded up. The equality of the Workers' Militia, in which officers and men had the same pay, was replaced by the class differentations of all State armies; privates had their pay reduced from ten to eight pesetas a day, whilst officers received from 25 to 100 pesetas. This was followed by decrees abolishing the Workers' Police and re-establishing the State Police Force (composed largely of middle-class elements), the destruction of the peasants' collectives, and, finally, the transference to the bourgeois State and local authorities of all public services such as the telephone system and transport. It was this final measure which led to the "May Days" rising in Barcelona.

On May 3, 1937, the Government decided to occupy the telephone building and to disarm the workers; the C.N.T. staff resisted, and within an hour the workers of Barcelona, from one end of the city to the other, were on strike and were throwing up barricades in the streets. Although the City, except for its "Whitehall" area, was practically all in the hands of the workers, the struggle was called off by the C.N.T. leaders after four days. The rank and file responded to their advice to end the struggle not because of any sense of immediate weakness, but because of fear of divided forces in the face of Franco and knowledge that large Government forces were marching on the city from Valencia. Responsibility for this Barcelona "rising" was immediately ascribed by the Communists to the P.O.U.M., and so the Liberal, Social Democratic and Communist journalists in Barcelona told the world. In truth, the P.O.U.M. only participated when the resistance began, and then ordered its members not to fire a shot unless attacked. When the spirit of the struggle died down the "Communist" representatives in the Madrid Government got their Social Democratic and Liberal colleagues to outlaw the P.O.U.M. and to authorise the imprisonment of its leaders. They even forced the resignation of Largo Caballero, the Prime Minister, and broke the Madrid Government to achieve this.

I heard of these developments with concern not only for our P.O.U.M. comrades but for John McNair and the members of the I.L.P. contingent in Spain. The members of the Contingent were in Barcelona; they were enjoying a normal fortnight's leave after three months' service at the front and had been in the city a week when the attack on the Telephone Building took place. I was nervous about their fate because reports came from Barcelona that all foreign sympathisers with the P.O.U.M. were being arrested by the Communist secret police as Franco spies. Then we heard that young Bob Smillie, grandson of the famous miners' leader and son of Alex. Smillie, one of our Scottish I.L.P. leaders, had been arrested on the frontier. The reports were ludicrous; they charged him with having anti-Republican messages on his person and carrying a bomb!* Bob was taken to Valencia and he died in prison. His death was stated to be due to appendicitis; but there is good reason to think that he was criminally neglected while ill. The death of young Smillie affected me deeply. Without exception, he was the finest lad I knew in our Movement. Socialism was his life and his own character reflected all that is best in socialist spirit. He had his grandfather's personality and perhaps in an even robuster way. Among his fellows he was a natural leader, not by self-aggression but an inevitable recognition of the quality of his spirit. He was chairman of our Guild of Youth; indeed, we had called on him to return to Britain to conduct a campaign for the Guild. His death in the Valencia prison—a prisoner held by the very side he went to help—was a tragedy the memory of which still hurts.

Meanwhile McNair's presence in Spain had become untenable. After narrowly escaping arrest he crossed the frontier with Eric Blair (George Orwell, the author) and Stafford Cottman (a boy of eighteen with the heart of a giant). As McNair was contriving to leave Spain I was contriving to enter it. Disturbing reports reached us in London of the fate of the P.O.U.M. leaders. They had been transferred by the secret police from Barcelona to Madrid and it was reported that Andres Nin had "disappeared." It was alleged that they had been engaged in a vast conspiracy to assist the Fascists including both military and economic sabotage within the Republican ranks. A hairraising story was published by the "Communists" about Nin. A communication from a fascist spy in Madrid to General Franco was said to have been found including a miniature map of Madrid marked with military information and with a coded message in invisible ink referring to "the directing member of P.O.U.M.—N." It was alleged that "N" used the P.O.U.M. radio to communicate military information to Franco and that he received instructions from the Spanish Fascists for his "Fifth Column" activities among the Spanish workers. I may

---

* In fact, he carried only his diary and a "dud" bomb as a souvenir.

anticipate events by saying that when finally the P.O.U.M. leaders were tried not one of these charges was proved; examination showed that they were sheer inventions by the "Communists." As for the story of the "N" letter, when I got to Spain I found no one believed it except credulous members of the Communist Party. The British, American and European journalists had refused to circulate the charge because it was so obviously a fabrication. But the position was nevertheless serious. The police administration was entirely in the hands of the Communist Party, including a special secret force organised under Russian direction on the lines of O.G.P.U. The columns of the Communist Press were splashed with daily stories of the fascist infamies which had been committed by the P.O.U.M., and even in Britain the allegations were coming to be accepted by members of the Labour and Liberal Parties.

My departure was hurried by two reports. The Press Association 'phoned me that John McNair had been arrested in Barcelona and a telegram came from Paris stating that the P.O.U.M. leaders were in immediate danger and begging me to join a delegation of Deputies, which was ready to start. I took the next 'plane from Croydon. My last visit to the airport had been to bid farewell to Gorkin on his deportation; now I was leaving the same airport in an effort to save his life. In Paris I had an impressive reception from three German comrades, two Italians, one Spanish and four French,—but I found that there was no delegation ready. "Tomorrow it will be ready to go" I was assured, so I spent the day getting the necessary papers to cross into Spain. In the evening when I met the French Committee I despaired: there was not only no deputation waiting, its personnel was undecided. But one reassuring thing happened: McNair telephoned from the frontier village of Cerebère that he and his companions had reached France safely.

I decided to travel the next night to Perpignan to meet them and to wait there for the French deputation which, I was promised, would follow two nights later.

I met McNair, young Cottman, and Eric and Eileen Blair. Eric had missed death at the front by the fraction of an inch, a bullet just scraping his windpipe, and his voice was thin and husky. He was staying at a nearby village on the coast for a few days' holiday. I only saw him for a few hours, but I liked and respected him at once. He was transparently sincere, concerned only about getting at the truth of things. His "Homage to Catalonia" expresses his character as I sensed it: the beauty of its writing and the careful striving to be exactly accurate— artist and scientist together. John and Stafford were travelling on to Paris and I had to make the most of the opportunity to get a detailed report and to collect tips about my best procedure in Spain. He was a little nervous about my visit; the Communist secret police were powerful and remorseless in hunting down friends of the P.O.U.M. His worst news was support for the rumour that Nin had been assassinated; he said everyone in Spain accepted it as truth.

I was held up in Perpignan four days waiting for the French delegation; finally, I decided to go on to Barcelona alone and to let it catch me up. Had it not been for my impatience to get on I should have enjoyed Perpignan. It is a picturesque little town in the shadow of the Pyrenees and its rôle in the Spanish struggle deserves a large place in working-class history. In its cafes was planned the smuggling across the frontier of a continual flow of material and men for the anti-fascist struggle. The innocent-looking headquarters of this assistance was the Continental Bar.

I felt very much alone when I got into that 4 a.m. train for Spain; what I had heard from others in Perpignan had strengthened the impression received from John McNair of the ruthless suppression of P.O.U.M. and its friends. I reached Cerbère, the last French village at 5 a.m. I was somewhat apprehensive as to whether the French frontier officials would let me through, but there was no difficulty. The little train which took us beneath the frontier mountain was crowded; as we came into the light I found that we were running along the platform of Port Bou, the first village in Spain.

Chapter Thirty-One
AIDING THE REVOLUTIONARY LEADERS

Passports and customs were a much more formidable matter than on the French side. First we had to produce what money we had and it was counted and noted. Then we were "searched": our pockets as well as baggages were carefully examined and every paper scrutinised. Then we went before a higher official, who questioned us closely about the object of our visit.

I had no difficulty about the first two stages, but at the third I was put on one side for further examination. In the earlier days of the civil war it had been easy for P.O.U.M. sympathisers to get across the Catalonian frontier because the workers' officials in charge were mostly C.N.T. or P.O.U.M. members: one of McNair's most treasured possessions is the workers' passport given to him at the frontier, bearing the stamps of all the Spanish working-class organisations, and calling on everyone to afford him comradely facilities. But now a uniformed State staff of the old type was in command and I knew that the official with whom I was dealing might well be a "Communist" who would regard me as a fascist agent. Finally, however, I convinced him that I was a Socialist and anti-Fascist. He did not know, as I passed into the dazzling whiteness of sun-bathed Port Bou, how weak I felt from my fear that at this last moment I might be turned back. Even in my anxiety I had been thrilled by one feature of the station: every railway engine had painted on its front in huge white lettering "C.N.T.—U.G.T." So the "revolution" still remained thus far: the Unions ran the railways! I transferred the scene to Britain. We shall feel we are making progress when "N.U.R.," "A.S.L.E. & F." and "R.C.A.," or, better still, one Union combining them, have replaced "L.M.S.," "L.N.E.R.," and "G.W.R."

I was delighted by Port Bou. It is a beautiful seaside village, but I took it to my heart for a deeper reason—on its walls, on its house fronts, on the exposed concrete banks of the river, *everywhere,* were P.O.U.M. posters. The Party was outlawed, but here in the first village of Spain was evidence of its strength. I wished as I walked that I knew where to find the

Continental Bar of Port Bou; I desired intensely to greet our comrades with encouragement at this moment of suppression. I caught the train to Barcelona at three. It was a memorable journey of seven hours. We stopped at every station and at every station peasants got in and out, carrying with them much of their stock, both from their houses and fields, so that the long wooden-seated compartment became a mixture of a furniture depository, a cloak-room and a farm-yard. A peasant woman would climb in, her back buried under a huge bundle of newly-cut grass, or clasping in her arms a gobbling turkey. A peasant man would struggle through the crowd, trying to control two dogs pulling at their straps excitedly in opposite directions, eager to get at a rabbit held on a girl's lap or a goat clutched round the neck by a boy.

Gerona was the only large town we touched before Barcelona. It is a mass of jumbled houses dominated by huge rugged grey buildings like fortresses, one a church. At the station the Barcelona papers were bought eagerly, and I noticed that nearly everyone in our carriage asked for "Solidaridad Obrera," the C.N.T. organ. At first silence, men, women, children eagerly crowding round each sheet, followed by a fierce clamour of excited talk, accompanied by rapid gestures. I regretted my ignorance of the language, listening keenly to catch any recognisable words. Then came—"Nin," "P.O.U.M.," "C.N.T.-F.A.I.," "Stalinists"! Even though I did not know Catalan, there was no mistaking the emphatic trend of what was being uttered on all sides—anger with the Stalinists, concern about Nin and the P.O.U.M. prisoners, approval of something which the C.N.T–F.A.I. had done. When my neighbour had finished reading and gave himself to the verbal storm, I borrowed his paper and word by word puzzled out the significance of the news. The C.N.T.-F.A.I. had published a manifesto criticising the suppression of the P.O.U.M., demanding to know where the imprisoned leaders (and particularly Nin) were, claiming a public trial for them, declaring that the workers and peasants of Catalonia were not fighting to set up a Stalinist dictatorship as a substitute for a Franco dictatorship. As I spelled out the words I became as excited as the others and, throwing discretion to the winds, took the hands of the peasant beside me and shook them warmly. He called me "camarado" and shook me by the hand all over again when he understood that I came from the British "P.O.U.M."

I was anxious to get an impression of Barcelona but could see little from the window of the taxi which took me from the station because of the black-out. Dimly one sensed broad streets, large buildings, avenues of trees. The Continental Hotel at which I had been told to stop by McNair was "collectivised" by the C.N.T., but it remained bourgeois in atmosphere for the satisfaction of foreign visitors: the waiters wore starched shirts and the guests were reserved and didn't mix. The bedroom with private bathroom was delightful, and supper was the best meal I had had since leaving Paris: soup, fish, salad, fruit. I had breakfast with David Crook, McNair's journalist friend. Crook had belonged to the Fabian Nursery in London and had joined the International Brigade. He had been wounded, but, disillusioned by the counter-revolutionary activities of the "Communists," had not joined up again. Instead, he had begun to do journalism from Barcelona.

After breakfast I went to the C.N.T. headquarters to see my friend, Antoine Souchy, its international secretary. I had met him several times in London and Paris, the fairest of Germans, blue-eyed, a real comrade. The Barcelona C.N.T. had taken over what had been the headquarters of the Catalan Federation of Industries, the most powerful capitalist organisation in Spain. The building was vast, a monumental seven-storey mass of stone which reminded me of Broadway House in London. Instead of white-collared clerks and spruce captains of industry, men with shirts wide open at the neck or in rough khaki uniforms thronged the corridors, greeting the girls as they passed from office to office as comrades. I found the international floor and Souchy's office: in a little ante-room a charming girl, whom later I came to know as Elsa, recognised me at once; the "New Leader" was on her table, she was an I.L.P. enthusiast. Souchy's greeting was equally warm and he immediately got down to practical details; there was no time to waste, he feared Nin was dead, and the fate of the other prisoners, whisked away to the Communist stronghold of Madrid, was uncertain—I must go to Valencia at once and see the Ministers. But that was not easy: I was alone, could not speak Spanish, and for foreigners travelling had its dangers. Souchy took me to the Secretary of the Regional Committee of the C.N.T., who placed all the facilities of his organisation at my disposal. A C.N.T. car would take me to Valencia that night, it would carry permits which would be accepted at once by the military and police, and, best of all, he released Souchy to accompany me as interpreter. I felt that I was really on the job at last.

Souchy had a surprise in store for me. He led me to a room at the very end of the corridor. We entered—and I found myself among half-a-dozen of the foreign sympathisers of the P.O.U.M., men and women, German, French and American, who nearly embraced me in their excitement. They included Kurt Landau, a young Austrian, who was afterwards done to death by the "Communists." They were in hiding here. This was a surprise, but even as they crowded round me I had a greater surprise. A fat, smiling man entered and immediately I ceased to be the centre of interest. The comrades gasped with astonishment, burst into laughter, and then poured questions upon the new arrival. At last they turned to me to explain: this was Comrade Moullins, the one member of the P.O.U.M. Executive who had not been arrested! All the police at Barcelona were hunting for him, but he came from another part of Spain and was not known: he showed us identity cards in another name and told us how he had been visiting the P.O.U.M. members in different towns and villages of Catalonia, arranging with them to continue the struggle, putting through plans for the secret printing of "La Batalla," the P.O.U.M. daily, and other literature.

Whilst I had been talking with the comrades in hiding, Souchy had been trying to fix appointments with members of the Catalan Government, but he had failed: the influential Ministers were out of town. He had learned, however, the important news that all the non-Communist Ministers had protested to the Central Government at Valencia against the suppression of P.O.U.M. and the imprisonment of its leaders, particularly of Nin, who, in addition to his reputation for political honour, was revered as a Catalan author. Those who had protested included Companys, the President of Catalonia. Souchy suggested that I should use the time before my night journey in seeing two examples of workers' control in practice—a visit to the film-making institute and to the printing works of "Solidaridad Obrera."

I was deeply moved by what I saw at the film institute. If I had gone to one of the textile mills and seen the rows of machines with the workers tending to them, I should have been thrilled by the realisation that they owned these machines, that they were not wage slaves. At this institute I had that thrill and something more. Here one had a sense of the freedom not only of physical labour, but of the creative spirit. The building was beautiful, the apparatus delicate and clean, the testing theatre lovely in its colouring and outline—and all who worked here had the air of belonging to the place as well as of the place belonging to them. The printing press was no less an inspiration in another way. The premises had been a convent: modern rotary machines occupied its hall, messengers with "copy" and proofs hurried through its cloisters, the editorial staff occupied the cell-like rooms which had been the spiritual retreats of the nuns. Sacrilege? No! These busy men had one thought—to establish a society of happiness, liberty, equality and friendliness, and to what better purpose could that building be put? I was interviewed* in the Mother Superior's room, all the members of the Editorial Board sitting in a circle round me, whilst a reporter took a note of my replies to Souchy's interpretation. I enquired what had happened to the nuns—were they outraged and shot, as the fascist supporters declared? The editor brought me a letter. It was addressed from France and, whilst praying that God would show them the errors of their ways, the writer expressed to the anarchists the gratitude of the Mother Superior for safely conducting her and the nuns to the frontier.

Just before I was due to leave for Valencia the French delegation arrived—yes, really! It consisted of M. Wolfe, a socialist journalist from the League of Human Rights, and a tall, bearded anarchist whose name I do not recollect. I was disappointed that a more representative deputation had not come, but it was good to have colleagues, and Wolfe immediately showed practicability and initiative. He proposed that

*Little of this interview appeared in "Solidaridad Obrera." Instead there were great white spaces where the censor's hand had been at work.

whilst I proceeded to Valencia, he and his colleagues should visit the Catalan Mininsters whom I had not been able to see.

Valencia is not comparable with Barcelona as a city, and I found its psychology very different. In Barcelona one felt the currents of two conflicts—the war against Franco and the struggle for the social revolution; in Valencia everything was given over to the military conflict. Nevertheless, here too, the social revolution had gone far and much of it had remained. I was interested to find that the paper serviettes at every café were decorated with the monograms of the U.G.T. and C.N.T., and the factories and cinemas had similar inscriptions announcing Trade Union control. In Barcelona the C.N.T. was dominant, here the U.G.T. was equally as strong. Our first task was to get accommodation; it was not easy because Valencia was crowded with refugees from besieged Madrid and the Franco territories. Souchy went to the C.N.T. Committee and after some difficulty got a room in one of their hotels; it was a proletarian hotel, and I enjoyed its atmosphere much more than that of the Continental at Barcelona. The workers had taken it over in July, 1936, deposing the proprietor, who had Franco sympathies, but keeping his son on as manager and his daughter as a clerk: I talked to them both and they were happily accepting the new régime. The waiters and chambermaids behaved as comrades, the waiters serving at meals in open blue shirts, chatting and joking with the guests as equals, and smoking cigarettes as they went about their duties.

Our room booked, Souchy took me to see Vasquez, the General Secretary of the C.N.T. Here was another sign of the revolution: the C.N.T. had taken over the magnificent premises of a Spanish marquis. We passed through a marble hall and mounted a marble staircase bordered by glittering mirrors to a waiting room still furnished with richly upholstered chairs, pink and gold. Vasquez was in an inner room, sitting at a beautifully carved table. He impressed me at once as an unusual man. He looked like a bear: a mop of tousled black hair, massive shoulders, long hanging arms. He had the deepest voice I have heard; rich and powerful and vibrating. His eyes, speech and gestures showed tremendous dynamic force: I could imagine that as an orator he would be terrific. He was only 29, a building trade worker, but I have met few men who showed more of the natural qualities of a leader. Put this man among British statesmen or the leading figures of the British Labour movement, and his personality would stand out among them all.*

I found Vasquez completely sympathetic with the object of my visit. He showed me a finely worded protest which the C.N.T. had sent to the Government against the arrest of the P.O.U.M. leaders and told me that the C.N.T. had organised a great protest demonstration which 3,000 workers had attended. He was angry because the censorship had not permitted the C.N.T. protest to be published, although the Communist Party papers were allowed to continue the wildest attacks on the P.O.U.M. as a "fascist organisation" and to work up hysterical demands for the death penalty. The practical help of the C.N.T. was expressed by its offer of the services of its lawyer, Dr. S. Pabon, member of the Cortes for Saragossa, as Defence Counsel for the prisoners. Needless to say we accepted this offer gratefully.† When I asked Vasquez for advice as to how I should proceed, I was a little surprised to find him recommending that I should go first to the British Chargé d'Affaires. Despite his anarchism, Vasquez was practical and shrewd. "You want two things," he said, "access to the Ministers and protection from the Communist terrorists. Well, use the cloak of respectability of the British Government. What you wear does not determine how your heart beats."

So I made my next visit to Mr. Leche, the British Chargé d'Affaires. I've visited Embassies of one Government or another in London, Paris, Berlin, Warsaw: they have all been palatial. The British Government's quarters in Valencia were the most cock-eyed, ramshackle hole I've ever seen decorated by Government emblems: they might have been the offices of a disreputable stockbroker. I went up dark stairs to a scruffy little room, partitioned from the light of the windows. Behind the partition were two boxes, one for Mr. Leche, the other for his assistant and secretary. This was the total British representation at the seat of the Spanish Government. No doubt

*In 1939 Vasquez tragically met his death when bathing in the Marne near Paris, to which city he had escaped at the last moment when the Franco forces swept over Valencia and Catalonia.

† Pabon was driven out of Spain by threats of assassination for daring to take on the defence of the P.O.U.M. leaders.

the crowded conditions of Valencia made it difficult to secure adequate accommodation, but the attitude of Mr. Leche, a typical diplomat of the aristocratic school, suggested a casual-ness which reflected his surroundings. The Embassy did not appear to take Spain or the civil war or the Government seriously. Mr. Leche's personal solution of the whole problem was to get General Franco and Mr. Prieto together—"good fellows, both of them"—and patch up a compromise. When I spoke of the P.O.U.M. prisoners he was disturbed by my inten-tion to intervene in the internal affairs of Spain, but was sympathetic because he was also very anxious about some prisoners—a blue-blooded family confined in a mansion some little distance from Valencia, "charming ladies who could be a danger to no one." When I mentioned Bob Smillie, he shook his head: very sad, but Bob shouldn't have meddled in the affairs of another country. Nevertheless, Mr. Leche was ready to arrange for me to interview available Ministers. Indeed, he embarrassed me by saying he would act as interpreter. I fore-saw a difficulty. The British representative would be ready to assist me in getting information about Bob because he was a British subject; but I felt that he would stone-wall my enquiries and demands about P.O.U.M. prisoners. I settled the matter by accepting his offer to accompany me to the Spanish Foreign Secretary, Signor Giral, but got him to give me written intro-ductions to other Ministers so that I could have Souchy's services as interpreter.

The next morning I and my French colleagues, who arrived during the night, had an important interview with Largo Caballero, secretary of the U.G.T. The atmosphere of the U.G.T. headquarters was very different from what I had found at the C.N.T. Caballero was no longer Prime Minister, but he was surrounded with protecting officials as though he were. We were shown into a chamber with a long green-baize covered table, four chairs one side of it, an empty chair the other side. Swing doors opened, Caballero entered bowing, and took the empty chair. Frankly, I got the impression that he was an old man unconscious that his days of greatness were past. His record undoubtedly has greatness about it, but as he talked, complaining about the "Communist" conspiracy against him but without any indication of plans to meet it or any vigour of spirit or decision, I realised that there may well have been some ground for the criticism that he was unequal to the task of combining the Premiership with the Ministry of War or of giving the leadership in action which the Government and the Republican forces required. He declared that the "Communists" adopted any and every means to destroy their political opponents, not refraining from manipulating "justice" and using their complete power over the police, but when we asked him to take action on behalf of the P.O.U.M. leaders, he excused himself because of the influence which the "Communists" had gained in the U.G.T. I left Caballero feeling rather sad. It was quite evident that we could not expect him to become the driving centre of the united Left forces in Spain, as I had hoped. Compared with the dynamic energy of Vasquez, he was a corpse.

The next day was Sunday and there was no opportunity to see anyone influential. I jumped at the opportunity to visit a Peasants' Collective at Segorbe, a little town thirty miles away in the mountains. It was like a Russian film. The peasants had taken over the mansion of a fascist Colonel as their headquarters; the heavy upholstered furniture remained, and on the walls were pictures of battles with kings triumphant, bullfights, court ball-rooms. The chairman of the Collective was the Mayor of Segorbe—a young man of 25 or so, dark, stocky, able, charming. He had an excitable assistant, who recited how he was learning French so that he could examine the fascist literature which the Colonel had left behind. He brought us an armful of these books—they were cheap French novels! From a group of workers we heard all about the economics of the Collective. More than eighty of the ninety peasants in the district had joined, all voluntarily. They had taken over the large estate of a local Marquis who had fled and had pooled their land and stock and drew out from the proceeds equally. The Collective was in its early stages, but already the peasants were doing better co-operatively than they did individually. Most surprising news was that even the half-dozen "Kulaks" who had stayed outside—those with larger holdings—had asked to be allowed to market their goods through the Collective, and very generously the Collective had agreed.

We visited the central farm. The place was a chaos of
dirt and smells and flies and half-built sheds, but the peasants
were simple-minded enthusiasts whom it was an inspiration
to meet. In the stable were six horses—three fine animals
"expropriated" from the Marquis's estate and three ponies. The
peasants had contributed the ponies from their own little holdings and were far prouder of them than the magnificent steeds
which occupied the neighbouring stalls. In the "Communist"
Press in London I had read of the tyranny of these agricultural
Collectives, how they were being imposed compulsorily on
unwilling peasants. There was not a sign of any such thing.
These men were wholehearted and proud, caught up in the
fraternity of what they were doing and in their liberty. Their
friendliness and faith were almost those of children. Yet here,
as in other parts of Spain, the "Communists" were doing all
they could to destroy the Collectives. Meetings had been held
at which the well-to-do peasants and shopkeepers had been
invited to join the party in order to oppose collectivisation and
defend their right to private property. Shades of Lenin! I
had read H. N. Brailsford's statement that the Spanish Communist Party was building up a membership of the petit
bourgeoisie on such grounds, but it was nevertheless startling
actually to come across this example.

The following day I had the interview with the Foreign
Minister. I drove from the British "Embassy" with Mr. Leche,
who emphasised *en route* that I was only entitled to raise
questions relating to British prisoners. Signol Giral received us
in a friendly way in a room which had a domestic rather than
an office atmosphere. He looked the Liberal bourgeois statesman he was: a kindly, cautious, earnest grey-haired man.
Conscious of Mr. Leche's presence, I approached the subject
from the British angle—the service which the I.L.P. had
rendered the anti-fascist cause, our distress about the imprisonment and death of Bob Smillie, our indignation that the "Communists" should describe the I.L.P. as an agent of Fascism, our
concern that our brother party, the P.O.U.M., should be
suppressed and its leaders imprisoned. Mr. Leche jibbed a
little as I approached the last subject, but translated what I
said after dissociating himself from any idea of intervening
in Spanish domestic affairs. Signor Giral did not seek to limit

L

the discussion to British subjects. He paid his tribute to the help of the I.L.P., "which no one ought to suggest is fascist," regretted the circumstances of Smillie's death, and then went into the question of the P.O.U.M. trial in some detail. I won't repeat here what he promised, because we secured subsequently more definite promises from the Minister of Justice, but he made the important statement that there was no intention to charge the P.O.U.M. with being pro-fascist (though the censor allowed the "Communist" press to do this daily).

When, in company with my French colleagues, I went to the Home Office, we were met by Signor Pabon, the Defence lawyer, but the Home Secretary himself had gone to Madrid. "The news that you had arrived scared him into action," Signor Pabon said to me. "He flew to Madrid to get personal information about the P.O.U.M. prisoners. Before going he assured me that Nin is alive and that Gorkin, Andrade, Bonet and Esquador are with him in Madrid." We decided to ask certain assurances from the Minister. These were telegraphed to Madrid and the following day the Home Secretary replied that the five P.O.U.M. leaders, including Nin, were alive in Madrid, that they would be brought to Valencia within three days, that the trial would be held in public, and that it would be by the normal method of the Popular Tribunals and not by any special or military court.

So far so good, but doubts remained in our minds about Nin; the report that he had been assassinated was on everyone's lips. That afternoon I went to see Mrs. Bonet and Mrs. Nin, who were in hiding in a workman's home in Valencia. Mrs. Bonet was a bright-eyed little woman, cheerful and smiling. Mrs. Nin never smiled. She was a fair-haired, strong-featured woman (not, I should think, Spanish) and listened to my report without a flicker of an eye-lid or a movement of her mouth: I don't think she believed the assurances of the Minister that her husband was alive. Her only expression of emotion was as she said "Thank you" when I left, holding my hand with a tight grip; I realised that she had already faced the truth. We also met secretly the Executive of the Valencia P.O.U.M.; they were in great spirits and full of activity. Despite the presence of the Government in Valencia, the working-class of the city, as distinct from the petit bourgeoisie and the civil servants, refused to believe the charges against the P.O.U.M. Perhaps most significant was the fact that the City Council had declined to carry out an instruction to expel the P.O.U.M. representative. The C.N.T., U.G.T., and even Liberal members had all taken this stand: the "Communist" was the only representative who had voted for his exclusion.

Souchy and I left Barcelona in the early hours of the next morning and the following day I left Spain. I stayed a day in Paris to plan with John McNair an international campaign to follow up our work for the fair trial and release of the prisoners. Then I took a train for London. I had been away only a fortnight: it had seemed a year. Shortly after I got back news came through which left no doubt that Nin had been assassinated by the "Communists" despite the assurances which the Home Secretary gave us. I thought of his wife in Valencia. We were too late to save the life of Nin, but I record thankfully Gorkin's public declaration that our deputation saved the lives of the other prisoners. Had not our visit stirred the Ministers to action, and in particular induced the Home Secretary to make a personal investigation in Madrid, it is Gorkin's conviction that he and his comrades would have been assassinated even as Nin was assassinated.

I add a postscript to the story of my visit to Spain: two experiences which enabled me to understand as never before the Moscow technique of dealing with political prisoners. One day we read in the "Daily Worker" an amazing statement purporting to have been made by a member of the I.L.P. contingent in Spain. It described among other things how the writer had observed communication between the P.O.U.M. and Franco forces under the cover of night. A few days later the boy arrived in London and came at once to McNair at the I.L.P. Head Office. He broke down crying and begged forgiveness. He had been imprisoned in Barcelona and had been presented with the document to sign as a condition of freedom.

The second instance was still more illuminating. George Kopp, a Belgian engineer, had been smuggling war materials to Spain; he was discovered, but got across the French frontier and into Spain before he could be arrested. He was a man of military experience, and volunteered immediately for service. The next militia proceeding to the front was a P.O.U.M. contingent; he went with it and was in charge of the sector of which the I.L.P. contingent afterwards formed a part. When the foreign supporters of the P.O.U.M. were rounded up, Kopp was arrested and taken to the secret "Communist" prison, but he succeeded in maintaining contact with us, by the help of a boy who, in the early hours of the morning, took messages through a grating of the basement in which he was confined. When finally he got free he visited London and one afternoon, sitting in my room, he told John McNair and me the dramatic story of what had happened.

After some weeks he was summoned for examination by two Ogpu agents—one Russian and one Belgian. The examination began in a friendly and leisurely manner. First his record was taken—date and place of birth, his work in the Labour movement, how he became a Socialist. Then followed a long but comradely discussion of socialist policy; the Russian and Belgian "Communists" were at great pains to convince Kopp that their policy was correct. There were no threats; they argued patiently and listened patiently. There was no hurry; the discussion was again and again adjourned so that divergences of view could be thrashed out reasonably. But the point came when the Ogpu agents found that, despite all their skill, they could not convince; then their tactics and tone changed. "Comrade," they said, "you are a revolutionary and you under-stand that there can be no room for sentiment between revolutionaries. Your reputation is already ruined in the working-class movement. Our statement that you have been arrested as a fascist agent has been published in the press of every country. We know, of course, that it isn't true, and we should like to put the matter right. There is one way in which your reputation can be regained. We can issue a statement, to be published as widely as the former one, that your case has been investigated and that the charge of fascist espionage has been disproved, that there can be no doubt that you are a genuine anti-fascist. We are prepared to issue that statement. We ask of you only one thing—that you sign this document."

Kopp read the document. It was a catalogue of allegations against the P.O.U.M., including the assertion that the Party's military leaders had conspired with fascist military leaders for its forces at the front to retreat at critical stages of the battle so as to give the Franco forces a victory. It included the allegation that John McNair was a member of the British Intelligence Service. "And what if I refuse to sign this statement?" he asked. The Ogpu agents shrugged their shoulders. "There can be no place for sentiment between revolutionaries," they repeated. "You would be dangerous to us if you remained alive. We should be compelled to shoot you, comrade."

Kopp asked how long he could be given to decide. Twenty-four hours. During those twenty-four hours he carried out successfully a desperate plan which he had long had in mind—he stole certain documents relating to the fate of past prisoners and smuggled them out of the prison by the boy messenger. He gave instructions that the documents should be taken to a friendly journalist living at the Continental, who should be asked to place them immediately on a plane for Toulouse.

The loss of the documents was discovered and suspicion fell on Kopp. He acknowledged that he had stolen them. "There can be no doubt about our shooting you now," said the Ogpu agents. "I should say there is every doubt," Kopp replied quietly. "The documents are no longer in this country, *and I have instructed my friends abroad to publish them unless a letter is received from me within a week, and thereafter once a month.*" The Ogpu men were defeated; they did not dare to face the publication of the two dossiers which Kopp had stolen and got away. They kept him alive.

The story ends with tragic irony. The boy was instructed to deliver the dossiers to a socialist journalist named Georges Tioli, who lived at the Hotel Continental,* but the previous night Tioli had been kidnapped by the "Communists," in company with Landau, the Austrian Socialist, and nothing has been heard of him since. The dossiers never reached France at all; they were destroyed with Tioli's other papers by a P.O.U.M. sympathiser on the hotel staff, who had been given instructions for such an eventuality. But, so far as the "Communist" police knew, the documents had left Spain and they made sure that Kopp wrote once a month to France so that the publication which they feared might be avoided.

* Tioli was at the Continental whilst I was there. He was an Italian anti-fascist of proved record. He helped me considerably and there were few men in Spain of whom I have friendlier memories.

Despite our disappointment with the course of the Spanish struggle, we continued to assist the anti-Franco cause. The most dramatic effort was a plan in which Maxton and I were partners to break the blockade of Bilbao. The Basques held out, but the fascist armies were isolating their province by land, and Franco announced a blockade of their ports by sea; there was the danger that they would be compelled to submit from hunger. I went to the Basque Legation and put the proposition that the I.L.P. should purchase and fill a boat with foodstuffs, and that we should secure a crew of volunteers to run the blockade. The idea was welcomed enthusiastically, and with the financial representative of the Basque Government I worked out the details of a plan by which it could be realised. The cost would be £40,000. That seemed an impossible sum to raise within the ten days which we estimated to be the limit of time available, but this did not deter us. The Basques had boats held up in ports; they would raise a mortgage on one of them and loan us the money at interest; they would charter our boat for six months at the market rate, and pay us in advance at interest. That would leave a balance of £6,000 to raise, which I was confident we could get. We calculated that at the normal rate of profit which ships chartered for the Spanish trade were making we should pay back the loan within twelve months.

I got Maxton's consent to the scheme, and on a Saturday we launched it. The Sunday press made it the sensation of the week-end, carrying our appeal and personal interviews on their front pages, with great black headings from the first column to the last. Our Head Office staff, with the aid of volunteers, worked all Saturday afternoon and Sunday sending out thousands of letters. One of the volunteers was Wilfred Roberts, the Liberal M.P., who addressed envelopes as assiduously as any of them. Among our most enthusiastic supporters were Ethel Mannin and her husband, Reginald Reynolds. Ethel was heroically generous. She gave instructions to her brokers to sell out all her stocks and to hand over the total amount to us: it would have realised £1,000—all her available capital. Reg helped on the business side. Having started the negotiations for the purchase of a ship and the enrolment of volunteers to serve on it (it was amazing how they came in: we could have filled every position, from captain downwards, twice over), I handed over the conclusion of the details to him. Within a week we had raised the £6,000.

Reg went to the Basque Legation to report progress, and returned to report a set-back. The Basques no longer had the authority to act: all control of finance had been taken over by the central Spanish Government, and the Embassy in London could not act without consent from Paris. I got through to Paris on the 'phone and spoke to the External Minister of Transport. He arranged to come to London by 'plane and the next morning he was in my office. "Why worry about a loan and an advance on a charter and paying us interest?" he asked. "We want ships under the British flag. I'll hand over the £40,000 to you here and now. No-one need be any the wiser." I declined. We were ready to help the anti-fascist struggle in Spain in any way we could, but we were not ready to become the agents of the Spanish Government, or to pretend that we were raising money to assist Spain when in reality the money was being found from Spain itself. My visitor shrugged his shoulders and smiled. "Very well, if you insist," he remarked, "but British ships are worth their weight in gold to us. Why do you let your bourgeois morality stand in the way?" He agreed that we should secure the option for the purchase of the ship over the week-end, and that Reg should fly to Paris the following Tuesday to complete the deal. I announced in the press that the I.L.P. boat would start on its venture to break the Bilbao blockade the following week.

Reg went to Paris—only to learn that the Spanish Minister had changed his mind. The Government had decided to conclude an arrangement with a British shipowner, a Mr. Billmeir, to provide a service of transport to Spain. I was disappointed—a gesture of working-class solidarity had deteriorated into a profit-making contract; but I found some consolation in the fact that Spanish officials in London told me that it was the initiative of the I.L.P. which led to the negotiations providing the Spanish Government with the service of ships it needed so badly.

The problem remained of what we were to do with the money which we had raised for the Bilbao project. We spent a considerable part of it in buying foodstuffs to send to the

Basques, and then wrote the donors offering either to return the balance or to use it for the establishment of a refuge for Basque children. Many agreed to the latter course, and for two years we ran a delightful home at Street, in Somerset, where Mr. and Mrs. G. R. Clarke placed a building at our disposal. At the end of the civil war most of the children returned to Bilbao, but a number of them who had lost their parents were adopted by our members and remain in this country. They will grow up embodying an international solidarity which was defeated in Spain, but which we hope they may live to see triumph still.

Chapter Thirty-Two

OPPOSING THE UNITED FRONT FOR WAR

We saw the war in Spain as a national manifestation of a disaster threatening the world. The whole working-class movement, with the Communist Party particularly active, was carrying on a vigorous agitation "Against War and Fascism." We in the I.L.P. accepted the slogan, but opposed the policy by which it was expressed and sought also to extend it. The policy advocated by the Labour Party and the Communist Party was a military alliance between Britain, France and Russia against Germany and Italy. We took the view that this division of Europe into two antagonistic groups would provoke rather than prevent war. We sought to extend the slogan by including "against Imperialism." We held that the liquidation of British Imperialism was essential to peace.

This did not mean that we underestimated the evil of Fascism in Italy or of Nazism in Germany. How could we when our own associates were suffering so severely there, facing imprisonment and death? But we could not identify ourselves with our own ruling class in their imperialist rivalry with Italy and Germany. Such surrender of the class struggle would in our view be an invitation to Fascism to penetrate Britain, for we held that Fascism was at bottom the political and economic structure of national unity in a class State. We believed that our best service against War and Fascism was to intensify the struggle against Capitalism and Imperialism in Britain, whilst assisting our comrades in the fascist countries in every possible way. As Chairman of our International Centre I was associated with several adventurous efforts to assist our Italian and German comrades.

We helped the Italian Socialist Party to print their "Avanti" in Paris. It not only had a large circulation among Italians in France, but penetrated the frontiers to Milan and other centres in Italy. This was difficult and dangerous work; in the case of Germany it was even more so. The Socialist Workers' Party had been suppressed and many of its leaders, local and national, imprisoned, but in a dozen or so towns groups carried on illegally. They begged our Centre to supply them with literature; we hesitated because we knew that to be found with it meant the concentration camp, torture and perhaps execution; but they insisted. We then helped to print in Paris, "Das Banner," the microscopic-type organ of the Socialist Workers' Party and to smuggle it into Germany; we also co-operated in printing pamphlets, camouflaged as cheap novels. Many of our comrades in Germany were arrested for distributing this literature. We succeeded in sending a British lawyer to "observe" one trial in Berlin, when twelve leaders were sentenced to long terms of imprisonment.

Again and again I was amazed by the courage of the German Revolutionary Socialists. I think of one of them who hid his activities sufficiently to take his holiday in London in the summer of 1939 so that he could discuss common action in the event of war, and who returned to Berlin with cheerful fearlessness. I think of a Viennese girl who crossed the frontiers three times in 1938 and 1939, reporting to us the work her group was doing, securing our help in the emigration of comrades whose lives were in danger, arranging for our contacts to be maintained. I can now safely tell how we enabled a prominent Austrian Revolutionary Socialist to pay a visit to Vienna. He was a member of the Schutzbund, and had been sentenced to death for his part in the armed revolt against the beginnings of Fascism in 1934. He wanted to make a personal contact with key comrades in Vienna to prepare in advance for a social revolution against Hitler should war break out: I remember he sounded the warning that it would not happen at once, but was confident that it would come as war-weariness developed. But how get him to Vienna? I thought suddenly of a sympathetic young aristocrat who was remarkably like him, and with a borrowed passport he travelled across Europe by car with two English companions, and the German frontier police were so impressed by his distinguished name that they didn't require him even to leave the car! We used this period to make arrangements as complete as possible to maintain contacts should war come. I had never any doubt that these comrades in Germany, Austria and Italy, who had already gone through so much, would remain true in the event of war.*

* Up to the Nazi invasion of Holland we received eight war-time messages from our German comrades, smuggled across the frontier by railwaymen. Our International Centre received one message via China in January, 1941, and we received another via Sweden as late as July, 1942, telling of the re-establishment of the Spartacus Bund in Hamburg.

But we were not content with this contraband help to the comrades inside the Fascist and Nazi countries: we were always striving to find ways by which we could assist their struggle by our own direct action. The Italian attack on Abyssinia in 1935 promised to give the opportunity. The problem was to work out a policy which would obstruct Mussolini's imperialist aggression without identifying ourselves with the war-like preparations and imperialist aims of French and British Capitalism. When the crisis arose our International Centre met in Paris and we hammered out a policy which seemed to me to meet the need. It declared against support of the British and French Governments in their imperialist rivalries with Italy, but advocated an international working-class boycott of Italy and its allies, the prevention of the transport of armaments to Italy, and the stoppage of the transport of troops to Africa. In other words, it urged international class action by the workers instead of national unity behind imperialist Governments.

This policy was similar to what the I.L.P. had advocated when Hitler seized power in Germany, and I had no doubt that it would have the backing of the Party. Indeed, the resolution of the International Centre was accepted without opposition by the National Council of the Party. I elaborated the policy with confidence in the "New Leader." In view of the conflict which arose from this article I quote its essential passages:

"How can the workers act? They must demonstrate two things: *first,* that they will not go into an imperialist war behind the National Government; *second,* that they will, nevertheless stop Mussolini's attack upon Abyssinia . . . .

"Mussolini depends . . . on the co-operation of the workers of other countries. Unless the workers of other countries provide him with the war materials which he needs, he cannot maintain his attack upon Abyssinia . . . .

"The Italian Government has opened a Bureau at Cardiff to buy British coal. The Italian Government is ordering British boots for the Italian army from Northamptonshire.

"Coal is being sent to Italy through the ports of Antwerp and Danzig. During the last six months the supply of scrap iron, convertible into arms, from America to Italy has doubled.

"Supplies of wheat and oil are being sent from Soviet Russia to Italy. Oil is Italy's most urgent need. Her army cannot move without it.

"Surely in this crisis the workers of the Capitalist countries we have named, together with the workers of France, Holland and the Scandinavian countries (all of which are involved) and, above all, the workers of the Soviet Union—surely a united working-class movement can reach a clear and determined decision that they will not provide Mussolini with the means to carry out his fascist aims . . . ."

So far as I could judge, this article and succeeding articles on the same lines were received with enthusiasm by the Party. For the first time over many years all groups pulled together. The R.P.C. and the Marxist Group (Trotsky sent a congratulatory letter from Mexico) joined in acclaiming the lead given, and in London particularly the Party membership went on to the streets with leaflets and speech-making, confident that they had a working-class policy with which to meet the campaign of the Labour and Communist Parties, both of which were demanding Governmental action which in our view would lead to war.

Our agitation had been running for three weeks when the Inner Executive of the Party (composed of our three M.P.s, John Aplin and myself) met—and turned down this policy. Maxton carried his Parliamentary colleagues with him when he urged that "working-class sanctions" could not be distinguished publicly from League sactions and would help to create a psychology for war against Italy. As Secretary of the Party I had to accept this decision until Annual Conference, but within the membership a fierce controversy arose, leading the R.P.C. to resign and join the Communist Party. That they should choose this occasion surprised me a little because Jack Gaster, their leader, had been severely critical of the C.P. line of League sanctions against Italy.

The issue was debated at the Annual Conference in a tense atmosphere. The resolution dissociating the Party from the Inner Executive was moved by C. L. R. James, the Negro Socialist, in a typically torrential speech. He appealed as a black worker for help for the black population of Abyssinia; this had an emotional effect, but was used to support the argument that the case was nationalist rather than socialist. My main argument was directed against the view that international working-class action involved support of the capitalist Governments in their imperialist aims. I urged that direct action by the workers would be as distasteful to their Governments as it would be to Italy. The leaders on the other side were George Buchanan, M.P., and John McGovern, M.P. Buchanan spoke as a Trade Unionist, and his argument that the policy I advocated was impractical and that, if one really wanted to defeat Mussolini, the only course was to urge action through the Government and the League, carried weight. McGovern insisted that Haile Selassie was as much a dictator as Mussolini.

When the tellers announced that the resolution had been carried by 70 votes to 57, Maxton remarked calmly that the Parliamentary Group would have to reconsider its position, but I realised at once from his demeanour that a serious Party crisis would follow. At a special meeting of the National Council the same evening the crisis broke. Maxton tendered his resignation as Chairman of the Party and as a member of the Council and he reported that McGovern and Campbell Stephen would resign with him. He added that the Parliamentary Group was unable conscientiously to carry out the policy endorsed by Conference and would therefore act independently on this issue, whilst hoping to carry out I.L.P. policy in other respects. This announcement fell like a bombshell. I had to make a quick decision: should I stand out and split the Party or compromise temporarily in the confidence that fuller discussion would bring unity? I had no doubt that if Maxton's statement were repeated to the Conference a split would be inevitable. Nor had I any doubt about the dimensions of the split: faced by the prospect of losing Maxton and the Parliamentary Group, the majority would rally to them, leaving those who took my view a futile and isolated section. I saw the policy of the Party not as complete but as developing. I saw there was little hope of building a revolutionary socialist party in Britain except through the I.L.P. I decided on compromise and when James Carmichael proposed a ballot of the membership I agreed at once, though without any illusions about the result. I knew it was inevitable that the vote would be influenced more by the desire to retain Maxton and his colleagues than by the political issue. I myself drafted the compromise resolution and moved it at the conference next day. Although many of my supporters thought I had "ratted" (thirty-nine votes were given against the compromise), I had no doubt I had done the right thing from a long view. The plebiscite resulted in a three to two vote for the policy of the Parliamentary group.

Two years later, at the annual conference at Manchester, the principle of independent working-class action against imperialist aggression was endorsed unanimously in a resolution declaring that it was the duty of the working-class movement to organise a world-wide refusal to make, handle or transport supplies to the fascist territories of Spain, to Italy and Germany so long as military assistance to Franco and fascist suppression of the working-class continued, and to Japan so long as its imperialist attack on China was maintained.

Hitler's occupation of Austria was the next development of the war situation. I deplored the harsher repression which would accompany German Fascism (more efficient than Austrian), but I could not get excited about the issue of Austrian independence. The Labour and Communist Parties based their case against Hitler mainly on the ground of Austria's right to independence: the Austrian Communist refugees in this country formed Popular Front Committees with reactionary capitalist refugees to maintain this national demand.* In Austria itself, however, even the Second International Socialists did not take this view: they continued to oppose Fascism, but they did so on a class basis and were realistic enough to recognise that the social revolution against Hitler could not be limited by the frontier, that their duty was to make contact with the Socialist Opposition in Germany and to strive to assist it from their greater strength in Vienna.

Meanwhile, the war clouds had burst in the Far East with Japan's attack on China. At the League, Sir John Simon "explained" Japanese action so well that the Japanese delegate remarked that it was quite unnecessary for him to supplement the speech. The I.L.P. took part in the "Hands Off China" campaign, but refrained from supporting propaganda which would identify it with the British Government in an imperialist

---

* This unity was maintained at the outbreak of war in September, 1939, so long as the Communist Party supported the war, but when, three weeks later, the Communists discovered that the war was "imperialist," the capitalist refugees reported their recent "comrades" to the British authorities, who promptly interned them. When later the Communists decided to support the war again, the united front with the Austrian capitalist refugees was renewed.

war with Japan over the body of China. The Party made an appeal to the organised workers to refuse to make or handle materials which would assist Japan. This appeal failed, but not by much. Not only did the International . Transport Workers' Federation (always to the front under the influence of its secretary, Edo Fimmen*) announce its readiness to operate a world working-class boycott, but even in this country the Executive of the National Union of Railwaymen called on the T.U.C. General Council to consider measures to the same end. I was proud of the fact that one of our young members, Will Ballantine, Scottish locomotive-men's representative on the N.U.R. Executive, had taken the lead on this question. Ballantine is a man who will be of increasing significance in the working-class movement.

The growing danger of war led our International Centre to take the initiative in 1938 in forming an International Workers' Front against War. Its object was to secure united action with other sections which took the same view on the war issue. These included at that time the French Socialist Party of Workers and Peasants, the Revolutionary Socialist Workers' Party of Holland, and the colonial workers' organisations attached to the British and French anti-imperialist centres. The International Workers' Front took the full revolutionary socialist view. All of us recognised that German Capitalism must either expand or collapse and that the pressure to expand would bring it into inevitable clash with British and French Imperialism. We recognised that so long as Capitalism continued the alternatives were either a patched-up imperialist peace or an imperialist war. A patched-up peace would mean an extension of Hitler's tyranny over more peoples; a war would be fought by Britain and France for their own imperialist interests. We held it was the duty of revolutionary Socialists to denounce both imperialist peace and imperialist war as the inevitable consequences of Capitalism and, whichever came, to carry on the independent class struggle of the workers, directing it towards the conquest of Workers' Power and its use for Socialism.

Upon this general analysis we all agreed, but there was some difference of opinion regarding the policy to be pursued in the event of war. The Italian Socialists insisted on the policy of "revolutionary defeatism" as advocated by Lenin, Liebknecht

*Fimmen died in 1942.

and Luxemburg. I had always disliked the phrase. Why talk about defeatism? Revolutionary victory was what we sought to achieve. Of course the defeat was intended to apply to the capitalist government, but even here there was an ambiguity. Did it mean that Socialists should work for the military defeat of their own governments by the enemy capitalist governments, or did it mean the defeat of one's own government and all capitalist governments by the working-class? Liebknecht and Rosa Luxemburg interpreted it as the latter, but Lenin, whilst aiming at the same end, regarded the former as the necessary step towards it. This seemed to me both illogical and psychologically disastrous from an international socialist point of view. Were German Socialists to work for the defeat of Germany in the event of war and British Socialists for the defeat of Britain? If so, our propaganda would be mutually destructive. Moreover, with all my hatred of British Imperialism I was certainly not prepared to work for a Nazi victory involving the complete destruction of the working-class and socialist movement. As leader of the I.L.P. delegation I associated the Party at the Workers' Front conference in Paris with the attitude of the French P.S.O.P., which defined socialist duty in war-time as a continuation of the class struggle with a view to gaining working-class power and ending the war by stimulating a socialist revolution in all countries. This policy was subsequently endorsed by the National Council and Annual Conference of the I.L.P.

When the international crisis of 1938, which reached its climax at Munich in September, grew acute, we had a meeting of the Executive of the Workers' Front "somewhere in Europe." I will not say who attended because in their present circumstances this might involve them in danger, but I was present for the I.L.P. We issued a manifesto against the war, and planned in detail the continuance of common action should war occur. We arranged two war-time headquarters—one to serve as a political centre, the other as a centre for refugees. We conveyed instructions to selected persons where they were to proceed. A few weeks later, when Europe seemed within twenty-four hours of war, our plans were put to the test, and on the whole worked well. All those chosen for the political centre reached their destination except the representative of the

I.L.P.—and he had his bag packed and at hand, ready to leave at a moment's notice.*

I returned from "somewhere in Europe" satisfied that we had made the fullest possible arrangements to maintain contacts should war come. Each day the crisis grew. When Neville Chamberlain returned from Berchtesgarten without a settlement war seemed inevitable, though as I listened to the wireless accounts of Hitler's demands and of Chamberlain's concessions I could not see any dividing principle. It was evident, however, that we were faced by either an imperialist peace extending Nazi oppression or a war fought in the interests of the imperialist oppressors on the two sides. The analysis of the Workers' Front was proving tragically accurate.

The National Council of the I.L.P. met a few days before the crisis reached its height. It adopted a manifesto drafted by F. W. Jowett concentrating on the immediate need to stop the war. At the same time, general endorsement was given to a fuller draft which the London I.L.P. had prepared, and John Aplin and I were authorised to put it in a form suitable for "New Leader" and pamphlet publication. This document sounded a warning against both war and a Hitler-Chamberlain patched-up peace. So far there was no hint of any renewal of difference between myself and the Parliamentary Group. The Party was united and on its toes. The anti-war manifesto and the longer policy statement were received with enthusiasm; the former was not only quoted widely in the press, it was broadcast in the wireless news, and from all over the country I learned how thrilled our members were to hear the Party's clear, strong line recited by the B.B.C. announcer, whilst our correspondence showed how great had been the response from thousands outside the Party.

When Chamberlain set out for Munich, Maxton, together with the other Party leaders, wished him well in the House of Commons. Some of our members were disturbed, but I reassured them: Maxton's words did not commit the I.L.P. to endorse any peace which Chamberlain might bring back, and they clearly indicated the opposition of the Party to war.

*The International Workers' Front Against War had its centre during the war in Mexico, where Marceau Pivert and Julian Gorkin served as the Secretariat. They succeeded in maintaining contact with our sections on both sides of the war frontier until Mexico became involved in the war.

Chamberlain brought back a peace handing over thousands of working people to Hitler's oppression. I was relieved that war had not come, but I could think only with bitterness of the peace which had averted it. I knew of the heroic work of our comrades in the Sudetenland. I saw these men being hounded to concentration camps and death as a result of Munich and I was filled with anger against the Capitalism which offered as alternatives either the massacre of war or a peace with fiercer injustice.

The Parliamentary debate on the Munich agreement fell on Monday and Tuesday. On the Monday afternoon John Aplin and I, accompanied by John McNair, saw Maxton at the House and urged that he should not endorse the agreement. Maxton would not commit himself and I was apprehensive. When the B.B.C. summary of the debate came over the radio, I listened intently. Only one sentence of Maxton's speech was given: a sentence in which he congratulated the Prime Minister. I was quite certain, of course, that this isolated sentence did not represent the emphasis of Maxton's speech, but that he should have used the words at all dismayed me. I could not wait patiently until McNair, who had been in the Press gallery, arrived with the full report. "A great speech," he said. "One of the finest socialist utterances I've ever heard. It made a tremendous impression on the House." Eagerly I turned over the pages of the report. Whilst my breath caught at the congratulatory references to Chamberlain at the beginning and end, I saw that the utterance as a whole was even more moving, especially in its indictment of war-making Imperialism, German and British, than are Maxton's speeches as a rule.

But the press next morning only strengthened the impression given by the B.B.C.; great headlines told how Maxton had congratulated Chamberlain. I had slept on the incident and my conclusion was that, despite Maxton's powerful analysis of Imperialism and his warning that the war danger would recur if Capitalism persisted, the speech was regrettable from a revolutionary socialist point of view for two reasons: first, for the praise of Chamberlain and, second, for its omission of any denunciation of the terms of the Munich pact. It seemed to me clear that a revolutionary socialist analysis would have denounced the pact mercilessly as illustrating the inability of Capitalism to provide a just alternative to war: it would have aimed at showing the workers that Capitalism can offer only a war involving the slaughter of millions—or a peace involving the slavery of millions.

At my request an emergency meeting of the Inner Executive of the Party was called. Meanwhile, the situation had been made worse from my point of view by a Parliamentary speech from John McGovern which endorsed Maxton's utterance. The discussion at the Executive was political and friendly. I was pained to be in political conflict with Maxton in this acute way. Except over the Abyssinian question, we had had no political difference over many long years of comradeship; indeed, again and again on issues which divided our colleagues we had worked together in complete agreement. I admired him as I did no other public man; in the case of Jimmy the admiration had become, in me as in thousands of others, an affection which was intensely personal. I knew that on this issue he felt as deeply as I did: the Party wanted Peace; Chamberlain had secured Peace; it was his duty to thank him for having averted war. I sensed also that Maxton had put his whole being into this speech. I knew how I felt about such speeches; one makes them once in years, and then criticism becomes more than finding fault with one's reasoning, it hurts one's inner self.

When I asked for permission to dissociate myself publicly, Maxton, with his usual tolerance, raised no objection; he asked only that I should think it over for twenty-four hours. Campbell Stephen objected to the Committee "giving permission"; at his suggestion the decision was to "put no obstacle in my way." John Aplin alone associated himself with my attitude. Next morning I issued to the press a short reasoned statement of dissent and published it in the "New Leader." Afterwards I found that my failure to respond to Maxton's appeal to delay 24 hours distressed him more than anything else; if I had understood how he felt I think I should have agreed.

My hope was that the difference of view which had arisen in the leadership of the Party would be discussed politically by the membership and a decision reached democratically at the annual conference. I spoke in the debate at the conference, but I could not do so with the same confidence as when I had intervened in the not dissimilar debate on the Abyssinian issue. My mind was obsessed by the larger international crisis which was approaching and I did not want to emphasise any differences in the Party; I knew that the members, divided though they were about imperialist peace, would be united absolutely in opposition to imperialist war. The debate ended with the defeat of the London resolution condemning the M.P.s, but immediately afterwards the conference rejected a resolution congratulating the Parliamentary Group on its Munich speeches. "Well," said Maxton to me, as he rose from the chair at the end of the session, "that means the Party did not like what we did, but is not prepared to chastise us for it." I think Maxton's summing up was correct.

One effect of the victory of Fascism in Germany and the extension of Nazi rule to Austria and Czechoslovakia was to place on us the responsibility for aiding our comrades who were refugees. Among the German exiles was my friend, Dora Fabian, who, after being expelled from the Social Democratic Party for organising my meeting in Berlin, had joined our Socialist Workers' Party. In London she continued to co-operate with comrades in Germany, assisting them in their illegal activities and exposing the plots of the Gestapo outside Germany. She lived with Mathilde Wurm, who had been a Social Democratic member of the Reichstag, and together they were specially active in revealing the circumstances under which Berthold Jacob was kidnapped by a Nazi gang in Switzerland. I was in close touch with Dora at this time because she was translating a book of mine into German for publication in a refugee paper in Paris.

One afternoon my telephone rang: a German voice told me that Dora and Mathilde Wurm had been found dead in their beds and that the circumstances pointed to suicide from poisoning: I could not believe it. I had recently had tea with Dora and she was vitally alive in her plans to expose the kidnapping of Jacob. I co-operated with Scotland Yard in their investigation (learning from them, incidentally, that a "refugee" visitor to my office about whom I had been suspicious, and to whom I had refused the addresses of German comrades in

London, had proved to be a Gestapo man), but all the surface evidence pointed to suicide and the Coroner gave that verdict. It may have been so, for I am aware of the desperate psychology which develops among refugees, but I am still doubtful. Dora and Frau Wurm were not in unusual difficulties, either personal or financial, and they were living eagerly in the anti-Nazi work which they were doing.

A tragedy of another kind occurred in connection with the Czech refugees whom we helped to reach this country at the time of Hitler's occupation. Our comrades were in the Sudeten area, heroically working in dangerous circumstances for unity between the German and Czech workers on a class basis against both Nazism and Czech Capitalism. They had won considerable local success, gaining control of several Councils, when the Nazi invasion took place. During the period between the occupation of the Sudeten area and the occupation of Prague we had urgent appeals to get forty-eight of them to England; their lives would not be safe for a day if they fell into Nazi hands. John McNair put everything aside to secure the necessary visas and had the extraordinary success of getting forty-five to this country. Most of them arrived in December, 1938.

On the morning of Christmas Eve I was just preparing to leave London to spend the week-end with my family when the Kensington police 'phoned. There had been a fire at the small hotel where three of our Czech refugees had been placed for their first night in London; one of them had been burned to death and his two companions were being treated for injuries at Paddington Hospital. I went to the hospital and brought the two injured men, one slightly burned, the other suffering from the effects of smoke-filled lungs, back to my rooms. The dead comrade was Bruno Reichert, deputy mayor of his home town, where his wife and children remained. Although no possible blame could be attached to us for his death, I could not throw off a feeling of responsibility. It was not a happy Christmas.

There was one disturbing feature of our experience with the Czech refugees which reminded me of my experiences in Spain: it became clear that the Communist Party officials in Prague were sabotaging the efforts to enable our comrades to escape.

There was a Central Committee which was supposed to represent all the relief organisations (except the Catholics), but in fact it was officered by "Communists," including the German representative of the Comintern. We found later that they had drawn up a list of eighty Socialists opposed to the Comintern line in readiness for imprisonment should the Red Army come to the defence of Czechoslovakia, and when the Nazis advanced on Prague they decided to leave these men to the tender mercies of the Gestapo. We had overwhelming difficulties to overcome before we could get visas for those on this list. In some cases we found that our comrades had been denounced to the authorities as Nazi spies; this was particularly the case with those who had resigned from the Communist Party because of their disagreement with its later turns in policy.

During the summer of 1939 the clouds of war over Europe grew blacker and blacker. In all the campaigning of this period one gathering stands out in my memory—a debate on conscription at the Gray's Inn Union in June, 1939. It took place in the wonderful hall of the Inn. From the walls of panelled oak portraits of ancient monarchs and statesmen looked down on us; the openers of the debate sat at a long ebony table on a raised platform; barristers and legal students sat in order of seniority at still longer ebony tables the length of the hall; in the far distance the wall was a marvel of elaborate carving, said to have been built from the bow of one of the Spanish ships captured from the Armada.* As the debate proceeded waiters distributed claret and port.

On one side I was the opener; my principal opponent was Sir J. Hutchinson and his seconder Mr. Randolph Churchill. Randolph outdid his father in denunciation of the flabbiness of Mr. Neville Chamberlain and passionately called for the mobilisation of all the nation's forces for war. He prophesied that war would break out in September, and that half of those in the hall would be dead within six months. As I listened to the subsequent speeches I began to think I was back in 1914. There was even the old man of seventy who wished he were forty years younger so that he might fight himself and who would proudly give his sons. When I rose to reply I felt it

* Grays Inn Hall was destroyed by air bombing in May, 1941.

would be impossible to convey the beginning of our case to those who listened. I expressed my difficulty: I lived in another world of thought, my loyalties were not to a country, but to the dispossessed of all countries who were denied real life in peace and summoned to die in war for the very system of which they were the victims. I tried to depict the possibilities of the new socialist world where the potentialities of abundance would be realised to make both poverty and war unnecessary.

Most of the audience listened intently and I hoped that I had pierced the wall dividing our two worlds of habit and conviction, but when the senior barrister rose to move the vote of thanks I realised as never before how impenetrable the barrier is. He expressed himself as shocked to his inner being by my utterance; he expressed surprise that "Good King Charles" and "Good Queen Bess" had not descended in protest from the frames of their portraits on the walls.

As I walked back to my rooms that night I thought of Randolph Churchill's prophecy: war in three months. Yes, it might be so. We had not prepared too soon.

. . . .

Postscript: Correcting this chapter in proof, in September, 1942, it is possible to give one name of the continental comrades who helped us establish the International Workers' Front Against War—Heinrich Sneevliet, chairman of the Revolutionary Socialist Workers' Party of Holland. Heinrich was shot by the Nazis in July, 1942, for organising an underground workers' movement against Nazism and for social revolution.

Chapter Thirty-Three
AND AGAIN WAR

When I decided to write this autobiography an experienced friend suggested that I should begin by drafting the notes of my last chapter so that I should have in mind the conclusion towards which I was working. I did not begin in this way, but as the book approached the complicated period following the last war, I decided that it would be useful to define the conclusions to which my life had so far brought me. I spent the first fortnight of August, 1939, in the little French village, Etretat, on the Normandy coast. In this quiet retreat I tried to examine afresh my socialist philosophy and values.

My contact with the Spanish civil war compelled me to revise my thought about fundamental things. It made me face up squarely to the pacifist philosophy which I continued to cherish despite my rejection of reformism. When I became disillusioned with gradualism, I had endeavoured at first to elaborate a technique of non-violent revolution. I found inspiration in Mr. Gandhi's civil disobedience campaign in India and I worked on ideas of revolution by the method of a general stay-in strike and the penetration of the armed forces with propaganda so that they would not fire upon the workers. I never quite convinced myself about this, and Emrys Hughes, the editor of "Forward," was justified in asking me at the Blackpool I.L.P. Conference in 1932 to explain my belief in both Gandhi and Lenin. The Spanish Civil War challenged me to resolve this issue.

When I heard that in Barcelona and other places the workers and peasants had followed their defeat of the Fascists by taking over the factories, railways, hotels, offices, shops, mansions and land, there was a burning desire within me to see them maintain their social revolution. I turned eagerly to the papers each day to read how the conflict went, and I rejoiced whenever the Fascists were defeated. This reaction made me examine my thoughts. How could I regard myself as a pacifist when I desired so passionately that the workers should win the civil war? Feeling like this about Spain, was it not clear that if I were faced personally with the issue of defending a social revolution I would do so despite theoretical views about non-violence?

I was put inescapably to the test by the suggestion from Bob Edwards that he should take an I.L.P. contingent to Spain. I knew this would have the support of the great majority of the membership, but I saw that my encouragement of it meant a final break with pacifist traditions. Faced with the issue I did not hesitate: I wanted the Spanish workers to win and could not refrain from a venture which would help them to win; but it was some time before I adjusted my philosophy and thinking to the emotional instinct which had determined my action. Let me try to trace the process of this adjustment.

I had long put on one side the purist pacifist view that one should have nothing to do with a social revolution if any violence were involved. Whilst still chairman of the War Resisters' International I had urged that the duty of the Socialist-Pacifist was to identify himself with the cause of social revolution and to influence it towards non-violent courses. I realised that in any revolution violence was bound to occur, but I saw also that violence is a part of present existence, inextricably bound up with Capitalism and Imperialism, and that to dissociate oneself from a movement because violence may occur was to dissociate oneself from life altogether. Nevertheless, the conviction remained in my mind that any revolution would fail to establish freedom and fraternity *in proportion to its use of violence,* that the use of violence inevitably brought in its train domination, repression, cruelty. This is the core of pacifist philosophy and in the beginning I could not think myself out of it.

Strangely enough, despite all the viciousness which I found there, it was my visit to Spain which led me to see the incompleteness of pacifist philosophy. In Spain I met not only "Communists" with their scorn of human kindness and the ethics of brotherhood; I met also anarchists whose personality breathed fraternity, liberty, equality. I do not mean that all who called themselves anarchists had this nature: the press stories of those who "took the bourgeoisie for a ride and bumped them off" had some basis of truth. Nevertheless, the fact remains that among Catalonian anarchists, I met a type of liberty-loving and equalitarian human beings such as I had not met before. I met them particularly among the peasants and fishermen, many of whom had been living already in communities where they shared everything in common and enthroned freedom in all their social and personal relationships. In their attitude towards each other, in their attitude towards those engaged in the workers' struggle, these men and women more closely approached the ideal of both pacifist and socialist conduct than any I had known. Yet I saw these simple kindly fishermen and peasants, *armed*, prepared to kill and prepared to die to defend their freedom and equality.

Brought up against such facts, I asked myself whether it was true, as pacifist philosophy held, that violence used by these equality-living men and by tyranny-practising Fascists would necessarily result in similar oppression. I had to answer No. Even if these Anarchists used exactly the same degree of violence as the Fascists, I had no doubt that the society resulting from an anarchist victory would have far greater liberty and equality than the society resulting from a fascist victory. *Thus I came to see that it is not the amount of violence used which determines good or evil results, but the ideas, the sense of human values, and above all the social forces behind its use.* With this realisation, although my nature revolted against the killing of human beings just as did the nature of those Catalonian peasants, the fundamental basis of my old philosophy disappeared.*

Perhaps I should add that I did not become converted to the anarchist conception of social organisation. I believe anarchist philosophy has a great deal to contribute: its insistence upon personal liberty and direct local control as distinct from a centralised State bureaucracy is of supreme importance. On the other hand, the experience of Spain revealed the weakness resulting from indifference to the political institutions of the State. The Spanish anarchists compromised with their principles when they appointed representatives in governments, but these representatives were playthings in the hands of the Social Democratic. Liberal and "Communist" politicians. Their contempt for politics made them the victims of the politicians.

The revision of my fundamental philosophy only made more difficult the thinking out of the other problems which the Spanish war raised. If one held that violence *in itself* inevitably causes further strife, oppression, contempt for truth, cruelty and degradation of social ethics, it was possible to explain all the

* The absolute pacifist may retort that this same distinction would involve support for a war for "democracy" against Fascism. No, not whilst the dominant social forces on both sides are imperialist.

things which shocked me in Spain on this basis alone. But having rejected this simple view, the internecine strife within the Spanish working-class movement, the deliberate propaganda of lies and slander by one section against other sections, the imprisonments and assassinations, the extortion of "confessions" by threat of death, the abandonment of any moral code, demanded some other explanation. It was necessary to think through this problem, too.

My concern in this mental stocktaking was not so much the economics of Socialism as the moral code of the Socialist Movement. I had no doubts about the soundness of the economic basis of Socialism; though I rejected certain incidentals of the Marxist analysis, I accepted without hesitation its essential principles. My doubts were about the ethics of socialist conduct in the struggle for power—before the social revolution, during the revolution, and in the period of transition from Capitalism to Socialism.

I saw that conduct depends in the last resort on where one's inner loyalty lies. That loyalty can be given to an ideal or to a human group or to both. I considered first the effect of loyalty to the socialist ideal.

The socialist ideal expresses fraternity, service, mutual trust, truthfulness, liberty, respect for personality. The true Socialist strives to live according to this social code, and everything within the present system which prevents him doing so serves only to stimulate him to devote his energies to the cause of Socialism. One thought remains in my mind from all the thousands of forgotten words which I read during my twenty-eight months in prison. Plato wrote in his "Republic" that the man who really sees a vision of a better world becomes at that moment a citizen of that world. The inner loyalty of a man whose personality has been captured by the ideal of Socialism influences him to live honestly and fraternally towards others.

Of course, so long as we have the system of Capitalism, with its class divisions and antagonistic sectional interests, the ideal of conduct in a socialist society is not attainable. A Socialist may be philosophic enough to understand that the members of the possessing class are as much the creatures of their environment as are workers and feel no enmity towards them as persons; nevertheless, he will devote himself to the class struggle, participate with all his energy against capitalists in strikes and lockouts, and, if need be, defend the cause of the socialist revolution by arms against those who attempt to destroy it. He will do this because he sees that the overthrow of the class ownership of what is necessary for all must be carried through before a classless co-operative society can be established.

As they carry on this class struggle, however, Socialists who are true to their ideal, will be honest, disinterested, generous-spirited. Leaders worthy of the name will be so much citizens of the socialist world that they will feel alien to the values of the capitalist world. They will be indifferent to wealth, they will not be tempted by careerism. Few leaders have attained this standard, but the lives of those who have are among the inspirations of the movement. And everyone who has experience of the working-class struggle of this and other countries has met many men and women, generally simple workers, unknown outside a small circle, whose way of life is a continual inspiration. They have lived entirely for the Cause, undergoing victimisation, careless of material gain or social status, devoting their "leisure hours" to unrecognised routine tasks, striving to gain the knowledge which will help them to be more useful Socialists, and all the time breathing a spirit of comradeship and acting with an uprightness towards their fellows which command affection and respect. These men and women are the salt of the Movement. When one meets them the conviction is renewed that the ideal is attainable.

But it is not only an ideal which determines inner loyalty or inspires conduct. Most people give their loyalty more readily to human groups than to ideals: every war shows that. In the story of mankind this loyalty has extended from family to tribe and from tribe to nation. To whom is the group loyalty of a Socialist due? Not to the nation, but *to the dispossessed of the world,* to the millions of workers and peasants who are doomed by Capitalism to exist in poverty, who are denied the good things of human life, who are driven to slaughter each other in war. Identity with them is the fundamental group emotion of all who have any right to call themselves Socialists. This is the revolution in feeling which divides Socialists from others.

Group loyalties inevitably develop a moral code among their adherents. Where true loyalty to family, tribe or nation exists, it is impossible for the individual to act dishonestly, untruthfully or treacherously towards his group. Should war or other national crisis occur, the real patriot drops his lesser loyalty to family or Party in favour of loyalty to country. To intrigue for the advantage of one section, to lie about other sections of the national front, to use temporary power for sectional purposes—this would be impossible for any really patriotic man or group.

In exactly the same way the wider loyalty of Socialists requires a moral code which makes dishonesty, untruthfulness or treachery towards one's fellow workers unthinkable. If our Socialism is sincere, our sense of identity with the exploited victims of Capitalism of all lands must be as absolute as the identity of the true patriot with his nation, and demands as much from us in straightforwardness and service.

This loyalty will be expressed supremely to the workers in their organised capacity, because this is the instrument through which the change to Socialism will be made. To a Socialist the working-class movement will occupy the place which the State occupies to a patriot. To whatever section of the movement a class-conscious Socialist belongs, he will regard his section only as a part of the bigger movement, as a servant of the whole working-class; his loyalty to his section will be based on the conviction that through it he can best serve the whole. Dishonest dealing and physical outrage against other sections would be utterly impossible to the Socialist who is impelled by this sense of solidarity and loyalty.

Why did not this socialist moral code operate in Spain? The explanation is that Communist Parties do not owe their first loyalty to the working-class movement as a whole, either in the country where they operate or internationally, but to their own organisation, to the Communist International, and to Russia. They do not regard their organisation as an instrument to be used for the working-class; they regard the working-class as an instrument to be used for their organisation. And though among "Communists" there is often selfless devotion, their Party has no place for ethical considerations of fraternity, honour, truthfulness outside their own associates. Any section of workers which is critical of Russia in any respect becomes an enemy; no more quarter must be shown to it than is shown to an enemy by national patriots in war. Accordingly,

"Communists" will adopt any means against it; they will intrigue, sabotage, lie, assassinate, denounce old comrades to the capitalist authorities, and, if they have the power, extort false confessions, imprison, terrorise, execute. They will stop at nothing to achieve their purpose, even if their victims are fellow members of the working-class.

It is worth emphasising that this indifference to the socialist moral code does not characterise the *normal* conduct of other sections of the working-class movement. Social Democrats in Spain differed from the P.O.U.M. as much as the "Communists" did, but they refused to identify themselves with the Communist Party lies and terrorism. The I.L.P. is in sharp political conflict with the reformist sections of the working-class movement, but I cannot remember a single instance since the I.L.P. left the Second International and the Labour Party when we have had reason to complain that either of these organisations has acted in an underhand way towards us, and I think they would say the same of the I.L.P.

The "Communist" apologist may retort that in giving his entire loyalty to his own party and to Russia he is in fact serving the working-class movement as a whole. Apart from the political issue as to whether this is true or not, the fundamental question of working-class democracy is involved. Someone whose first loyalty is to the working-class movement may well take the view that the policy of the Communist Party and of Russia is best for the working-class at any particular moment; if so, he will urge it within the Movement, but he will do so feeling that he is *of* the Movement, he will never think of intriguing against it or of becoming an agent within it for an outside organisation whose loyalty is elsewhere. The Communist Party, however, hasn't the conception of the movement as a democracy into whose pool of thought it throws its ideas, influencing others and ready to be influenced by them, but rather as something to be captured for the Party and Russia. It approaches the working-class Movement, not as something to be served but as something to be seized, as an organisation which must be manipulated and manœuvred or even forced to accept dictated policies.

In this issue of working-class democracy one touches the heart of the whole problem. Working-class democracy is the organisational expression of working-class solidarity. Loyalty to the working-class means that one approaches it instinctively in the spirit of democracy, contributing one's thought and service to it, discussing and criticising, but always with the feeling uppermost that one belongs to the Movement, giving, receiving, never attempting to impose or force from outside the policy of the particular section to which one belongs.

At this point I became aware of another voice of criticism, coming now from the Labour Party. If the view here expressed is true, why is the I.L.P. outside the Labour Party, the political expression of the organised working class? I believe the solution of this difficulty also is to be found in working-class democracy. Everyone in the Labour Movement knows that, despite its enthusiasm for democracy, the organisational machinery of the Labour Party and its political control are grossly undemocratic. Its policy is determined not by the individual members who so largely carry on the work of the Party, not even by the Divisional Labour Parties, which include also the Trade Union branches, but by the block vote of a few large Unions. In an organisation without democracy minorities feel frustrated, cannot adjust themselves, and always tend to be driven out. If a spirit of democracy had animated those who control the Labour Party, the I.L.P. need never have left it. By this I do not want to imply that the whole fault has been on the Labour Party side. We in the I.L.P. have sometimes forgotten that our supreme loyalty is to the working-class, and that the Labour Party is the political expression of the working-class. One cannot prophesy now what the future political structure of the working-class will be, but the I.L.P. will not find its right place until it is a part of it.

I face the inevitability of a stern struggle before Capitalism is overthrown, before the possibility comes to build the new world of Socialism, but even in the midst of this struggle and the critical period of the transition following it, whilst, of course, large powers of direction must be given to the leaders, even then the final decision on issues of principle should remain with representatives of the workers. And all the time it must be the vision of a free, happy life which moves us. Socialism is a world in which not only physical poverty will be removed, but in which richness of mind and personality will develop. The removal of physical poverty will destroy the material prison, but there will remain other things to achieve—the recognition of the supremacy of truth, the freedom of the mind to grow. And of what avail is all our striving if oppression and cruelty remain? Where is the happiness, the fraternity, the equality, the liberty which are the essentials of the ideal which has inspired us?

Socialism is then, finally, the medium for the realisation of a full, free and fraternal human life. There cannot be full human life so long as there is material poverty, so long as opportunities of mental and spiritual fulfilment are denied. There cannot be a free human life so long as economic exploitation or political suppression continue. There cannot be a fraternal human life so long as class and national divisions are embedded in our social and political systems. But the end of Capitalism is not enough: private ownership may be abolished to be replaced by a State ownership, even in a nominally Workers' State, where there is neither full nor free nor fraternal life. These will come only with loyalty to the deeper and enduring values which Socialism represents and in the real democracy which reflects the spirit of equality and freedom. Social ownership will require to be accompanied by a living democracy and by cultural opportunity and personal liberty. It is a libertarian Socialism for which we must strive.

* * * *

My thought about these basic things was interrupted during my holiday at Etretat by urgent, immediate events. Hitler was threatening Poland—and Poland, with promises from the British and French Governments, was defying Hitler. This was the crisis of Czechoslovakia over again, but more formidable. I had no doubt on this occasion that if Hitler's troops crossed the Polish frontier Britain and France would declare war.

I had to be at the I.L.P. Summer School at Fort Mahon, between Dieppe and Boulogne, during the third week-end in August for a meeting of the Executive of our International Centre. German, French, Italian, Spanish and Greek comrades were there. When on the Wednesday I read of the German-Soviet Pact, I was convinced it meant war. With Russia neutral, Hitler would march. I 'phoned to London that I would journey through the next day.

I travelled back to England with Edith King. We had a difficult cross-country journey to Dieppe, with many trains already cancelled to facilitate troop movements. At all the stations mothers and wives were seeing off their sons and husbands. More often than not the mothers were dressed in black, widows of men killed in the last war. They said farewell with white, stern-lipped faces, eyes full of foreboding. At Abbeville we had a long wait and two incidents occurred which will always remain silhouetted in my memory against this background of departing soldiers.

We stood on the station platform watching the groups of women about their men. How many of those boys would live to return to mothers and wives? Then our attention became gripped by a more immediate issue of life or death. Across the rails stood a huge engine, steam puffing from a pipe to the ground. Within six inches of the bursts of steam a Red Admiral butterfly lay. As the steam touched its wings they shrivelled; the wind blew the steam in a different direction and the butterfly lifted itself a little, revealing the delicate pattern of red on black. Then the steam burst over it once more and the butterfly lay as dead. Again and again this happened while we watched, forgetful of the war and the women and men. I could watch no longer. I jumped down on the line, crossed the rails, returned with the butterfly to the platform and laid it on a ledge. Its wings moved: it was alive. Was it as an escape from the larger tragedy that we fastened our attention on this struggle for life? I saw it afterwards as a symbol of the life and beauty threatened by the war.

The second incident was of more enduring interest. Three hundred yards from the station by a canal bank stood a stone monument which I took to be a war memorial; I strolled towards it for lack of anything better to do. It was not a war memorial. Its inscription read:

"A Monument erected by the Proletariat to the Freedom of Human Thought. In commemoration of the martyrdom of Chevalier de la Barre, beheaded at Abbeville, July 1st, 1766, at the age of nineteen years, for having refused to salute a procession."

I looked at the name of the road; it was Rue Jean Jaurès.

* * * *

Back in London I worked night and day that week not only in the production of what I knew was likely to be the last issue of the "New Leader" before war broke out, but in the final preparations of the Party to meet a war situation. The printing of the "New Leader" on Wednesday morning was held up and I was summoned to meet the big chiefs of Odhams, who printed for us. The consultation included Sir Wyndham Childs, a member of the staff of "John Bull," who, as head of the legal department at the War Office during the last war, was regarded as an authority. I had not seen him since he gave evidence against me in the trial at the Guildhall in August, 1916, when the members of the National Committee of the No Conscription Fellowship were charged under D.O.R.A. "I got you two months last time," he said and added laughingly, "You deserve two years this time." But Odhams agreed to print on condition that all copies of the "New Leader" were off their premises before war was declared.

It was in Keir Hardie's old room in Nevill's Court that I listened in on Sunday morning, September 3rd, to the Prime Minister's statement announcing that war had been declared. Half an hour later the door-bell rang: an urgent communication was handed to me. It was a message from our comrades in Germany, smuggled across the frontier to a neutral country and written only four days previously. It contained these passages:

"In the moment before the cannons speak, before the world faces horror and manslaughter, we send our message to you. The German workers do not want this war; the German peasants do not want war. Hitler begins the war with Poland against the will of large masses of the population. . . .

"This war is not our war, this fight is not our fight, and we ask you, in the midst of death and destruction, do not forget the ideas for which we have died under torture, do not forget the ideals for which we have suffered in the concentration camps.

"Comrades, you like your country and we like our country, but our common fatherland is humanity."

My emotion as I read these words can be imagined. Governments may be at war, but in these brave comrades of Germany and in similar groups in all the warring countries lies the hope that still remains of the establishment of a world in which not only war, but all that maims human life and prevents its fulfilment will be ended.

THE END

INDEX OF NAMES

Preface to
Post-War Edition

When the Foreword to the first edition of this book was written we had just passed through the Munich crisis. When the last chapter was concluded war had just been declared. The final paragraph tells of a message received from German Socialists within a few minutes of the historic broadcast on that Sunday morning in September when Mr. Neville Chamberlain announced that hostilities between Britain and Germany had begun.

I am now writing twenty months after the defeat of Germany and sixteen months after the defeat of Japan. The "aggressor" nations have been utterly shattered. And yet as I write the fear of a Third World War is in the hearts of both statesmen and peoples.

Politicians and Press are now speaking and writing of Soviet Russia in almost exactly the same terms as they applied to Nazi Germany before the Second World War. In Parliament Mr. Winston Churchill arouses fears by reference to the size of Russia's forces just as he aroused fears in 1938 by reference to the size of Germany's armies.

I have been regarded for ten years as unsympathetic to Russia because, since its turn of policy in 1936, I have criticised the part it has played in international affairs and its repression of liberty at home. In fact, this reflected my attitude only partially, because I have never lost sight of the overriding consideration that private Capitalism has been ended there. My criticism of Russia's foreign policy and its denial of liberty are, if anything, stronger now than when this book was written, but nevertheless I feel that the supremely important duty of Socialists to-day, both as a matter of justice and for the sake of the peace of the world, is to retain an objective international attitude towards the power-politics struggle which threatens to bring war again and not to allow themselves to accept without unprejudiced examination the case against Russia which the politicians, the press and wireless broadcasts are piling up.

Let us start with Mr. Churchill's complaint of the size of Russia's armed forces in Europe. The armed forces of Britain and America also remain posted on a scale more suited to war than to peace, the difference being that our troops and those of the U.S. are more widely scattered. Britain has its forces not only in the ex-enemy countries, Germany, Austria and Italy, but in Greece, where we have bolstered up the reactionaries; in Egypt, where they inevitably prejudiced the freedom of the negotiations for a new treaty; in Transjordania and Iraq, which are supposed to be independent nations, as well as in Palestine; in India, Burma, Ceylon, Malaya, Sarawak, and, until November, 1946, in Indonesia; in West, East, Central and South-West Africa; in the West Indies and British Guiana. *In none of these countries is the population British.* America has its forces not only in ex-enemy Japan, but on a chain of Pacific Islands and in China, where they have served as a bulwark for reaction just as our troops have in Greece and Indonesia.

We have the right to condemn the maintenance of large Russian armies in Europe only if we condemn with the same forthrightness the maintenance of equally large British and American armies in other parts of the world.

Take another illustration. Britain and America have objected to the Russian claim for a share in the control of the Dardanelles. But what of British domination of the Suez Canal and the Straits of Gibraltar and Singapore, what of American domination of the Panama Canal? These waterways are more important international highways than the Dardanelles, which lead only to the closed-in Black Sea.

The Socialist cannot just line up with Britain and America on this issue; he should demand the internationalisation (under U.N.O. until something better is evolved) of all international waterways.

Behind the conflict between Russia and Britain in the Near East is OIL. Britain owns rich wells in Iraq with pipelines carrying the precious liquid through Palestine to its warships in the Mediterranean. America has obtained oil concessions. Russia wants them also. Socialists have the right to condemn Russian intervention in Persia, *but only if they also condemn the Oil Imperialism of Britain and America and demand the pooling of all the oil resources of the world according to the needs of peoples.*

Russia's chief count against America and Britain is the dollar Imperialism of the former and the political Imperialism of the latter. Both charges are true. It is no answer for America to say that it desires opportunities for the trade and capital of all nations in every part of the world. The truth is that the financial power of America is so great that under these conditions it would inevitably dominate the life of the world. It is no answer for Britain to say that it has granted the claim of India to independence—though Russia and America ought to realise that this has been the greatest act of political liberation in the history of mankind. It is no answer because Britain has not yet faced the implications of what it has done in India: that the same independence must be granted to the other Asiatic peoples who are under British rule, and to the African peoples. Because Britain is still thinking in terms of political Imperialism it continues to desire to dominate the sea route *via* the Mediterranean, the air route *via* Iraq, and the waters to the south of Malay. It clings to political influence in Greece, to military power in the Near East, to naval power at Singapore. Because it has not yet repudiated the system of Imperialism, it held the fort for the Dutch in Indonesia until they were strong enough to take over.

As Socialists we have the right to regret that Russia has adopted some of the methods of Imperialism, but we have this right only if we demand persistently that Britain's Labour Government shall repudiate Imperialism entirely and follow its action in India by speeding the independence of other peoples and transforming its entire policy on lines of Internationalism.

Finally, there is America's monopoly (with Britain as junior partner) of the use of atomic energy. Whilst the potentialities of this power, both destructive and constructive, are withheld from Russia she must inevitably feel that the hands of the Western Powers are raised against her and that her security demands that she take every available step, including pressing ahead with her own scientific research, to perfect her preparations for the event of war. Two things are necessary here. The first is the prohibition of the use and preparation of atomic bombs. The second is the internationalisation of the process of applying atomic energy for constructive purposes.

To prove the reality of the former, America should immediately destroy its reserve stock of atomic bombs. To facilitate the latter, the secrets of the harnessing of atomic energy should be made known to the world and U.N.O. should take over the production and distribution of the newly-discovered power. Its world-planning for construction might well prove the beginning of the World State.

If our Labour Government were to come out boldly for an international policy on these lines, it would change the whole face of world politics. A Britain which proved by its *deeds* in every sphere of foreign affairs that it had utterly repudiated Imperialism could no longer be denounced by Russia, to its own people and to the world, as the *arch-imperialist*. A Britain which proved, beyond a peradventure, that it was acting in an international attitude of mind could not be denounced as a fomenter of the Third World War. Russia would have to change her own tactics when confronted by this new Britain; she would have to do so, if for no other reason, because the common peoples of all the world would acclaim such a Britain.

I have put this issue of Peace first because it is the most important. It is no use concerning ourselves with the economic and social basis of future civilisation if atomic warfare is to shatter us all to bits before we begin building it. But, given the hope of peace, another fundamental issue is being decided to-day. It is the issue whether we are to move towards a totalitarian collective society or a democratic socialist society.

Outside America the fight against private Capitalism has been won. All over Europe the principle of the public ownership of the main structure of the economic system is accepted, and in the developing countries, such as India, it is generally agreed that the new industrialisation must be on this basis. But the question of democracy and freedom within the communally-owned structure is not yet decided; over a large part of the earth where private Capitalism has lost its battle there is little respect for liberty.

During this first year after the war I have been in Germany, and I have met Socialists from the Russian sector of Berlin. They were men who had come through the Nazi Terror unbroken in spirit, despite long terms in concentration camps and prison; but some of them acknowledged to me that they had been broken under the Russian régime. Because they opposed the Russian proposal for the forced unification of the Communist and Social Democratic Parties they had been "interrogated" for days by Russian officials and had been deposed from their posts in the political and Trade Union movements. They had seen comrades thrown out of jobs and homes, deported long distances, and even returned to the same concentration camps where they were interned by the Nazis. Under threats of like treatment they had given way: they were morally destroyed, and they knew that they were.

This issue is difficult to define, but to me the compulsion of a man to do what he believes to be wrong is the last tyranny. A society may solve the economic problem, but so long as it is contemptuous of human personality and of the freedom to know and to think and to speak and to act (the last within the limits of the similar rights of others), there can be no human emancipation. This is why it is so supremely important to-day to strive not only for the economic basis of Socialism, but for democracy within its structure, for respect for the individual, and for liberty of the mind. Without them mankind must become stultified and there will be no advance towards the good and the true.

One regrets that here, too, the conflict is between the Russian and the Western conceptions of Socialism, but the urge towards democracy and freedom is so fundamental to human progress that it is difficult to believe that, if the other divisions between Russia and the West were overcome, the Communist régime itself would not become democratic and liberal.

And we are driven back to our own duty in the matter. Britain has a unique opportunity to give a lead in the world for democratic Socialism, not only by the example of its own reconstructed society at home, but by its encouragement of Socialism *plus* liberty in all parts of the world.

Too often in world affairs it is assumed that there are only two alternative policies: the American policy of Capitalism *with* democracy and the Russian policy of Socialism *without* democracy. It is the great task of Britain now to stand out for the third policy—Socialism *with* democracy. Sometimes Britain's representatives speak as though this were their purpose, but so far their policy has fallen far short of it. The responsibility rests upon us to see that the Labour Government lives up to the conception of Socialism which has been the historic contribution of Britain since the pioneer days of William Morris and Keir Hardie.

January, 1947.   FENNER BROCKWAY.